Intersected Identities

Remapping Cultural History
General Editor: Jo Labanyi, University of Southampton

Published in association with the Institute of Germanic & Romance Studies, School of Advanced Study, University of London

The theoretical paradigms dominant in much of cultural history published in English tend to be derived from northern European or North American models. This series will propose alternative mappings by focusing partly or wholly on those parts of the world that speak, or have spoken, French, Italian, Spanish or Portuguese. Both monographs and collective volumes will be published. Preference will be given to volumes that cross national boundaries, that explore areas of culture that have previously received little attention, or that make a significant contribution to rethinking the ways in which cultural history is theorised and narrated.

Intersected Identities

Strategies of Visualisation in Nineteenth- and Twentieth-Century Mexican Culture

Erica Segre

Berghahn Books
New York • Oxford

First published in 2007 by

Berghahn Books

www.berghahnbooks.com

© 2007 Erica Segre

Library of Congress Cataloging-in-Publication Data

Segre, Erica.

Intersected identities : strategies of visualisation in nineteenth- and twentieth-century Mexican culture / Erica Segre.
    p. cm. -- (Remapping cultural history)
Includes bibliographical references and index.
ISBN 978-1-84545-291-9 (hardback : alk. paper)
1. Arts, Mexican--19th century. 2. Arts, Mexican--20th century. 3. Arts and society--Mexico. 4. Visual communication. 5. National characteristics, Mexican. I. Title.

NX514.A1S44 2007
700.972--dc22

2007008595

British Library Cataloguing in Publication Data
A catalogue record for this book is available from the British Library.

Printed in the United States on acid-free paper

ISBN: 978-1-84545-291-9 hardback

Contents

List of Illustrations

Acknowledgements

This book has had a long gestation period during which I enjoyed the support of family and friends, my students in Cambridge and colleagues in Britain and Mexico. I am particularly indebted to Doris Heyden for providing an inspirational space for writing and reading in Mexico City during many, memorable sojourns. Mariana Yampolsky and Arjen van der Sluis were illuminating and encouraging interlocutors. Jorge Foulkes initiated me into surprising bibliophilic itineraries through the libraries, archives, book shops and book markets of Mexico City. Clive Griffin in Oxford helped to nurture my interest in nineteenth-century Mexican literary and visual culture and guided me through the intricacies of archival research in Mexico, Britain and the United States. Simon Carnell offered steadfast and insightful criticism at every stage of the research without which the present book would not have been possible. In addition over the years Debbie Nagao, Laura Salinas, John Wainwright, Geoffrey Kantaris and Jo Labanyi have all contributed to the development of my work. I am grateful to Trinity College and Newnham College Cambridge for facilitating my research through regular travel grants. The generosity of contemporary Mexican photographers enabled the project to delve more deeply into the connections between form, technique and visual strategy: special thanks are owed to Mariana Yampolsky, Pedro Meyer, Gerardo Suter and Francisco Mata Rosas. I would also like to thank Laura Cordy for her careful preparation of the typescript.

During the course of my research the following libraries, collections and archives have been consulted: The British Library, The Taylorian in Oxford, the Nettie Lee Benson at the University of Texas in Austin, the Cambridge University Library; in Mexico the Hemeroteca Nacional, the Biblioteca Nacional, the Archivo General de la Nación, the Museo Nacional de Antropología, the Centro de Estudios de Historia de México CONDUMEX, the Instituto Mora, the Fototeca Nacional in Pachuca (Hgo.), the Centro de la Imagen, the Museo de Arte Carrillo Gil, the Museo Soumaya, the Museo Nacional de Historia, the Museo Nacional de Arte, the Museo de Arte Moderno, the Museo Casa Estudio Diego Rivera, the Museo Nacional de Culturas Populares. In addition I was given generous access to the private archives of Doris Heyden and Mariana Yampolsky in Mexico.

Earlier versions of some chapters appeared in the *Bulletin of Hispanic Studies*, the *Hispanic Research Journal*, the *Forum for Modern Language Studies*, the *Journal of Latin American Cultural Studies* and the *Journal of Romance Studies*.

Abbreviations

AFA	Agrasánchez Film Archive
AGN	Archivo General de la Nación
BNM	Biblioteca Nacional de México
CEHM-CONDUMEX	Centro de Estudios de Historia de México CONDUMEX
CIESAS	Centro de Investigaciones y Estudios Superiores en Antropología Social del Sureste
CNCA	Consejo Nacional para la Cultura y las Artes
CONACULTA	Comisión Nacional para la Cultura y las Artes
FCE	Fondo de Cultura Económica
FCMY	Fundación Cultural Mariana Yampolsky
FINAH	Fototeca del Instituto Nacional de Antropología e Historia
FONCA	Fondo Nacional para la Cultura y las Artes
HN	Hemeroteca Nacional
IIE	Instituto de Investigaciones Estéticas
IMCINE	Instituto Mexicano de Cinematografía
INAH	Instituto Nacional de Antropología e Historia
INBA	Instituto Nacional de Bellas Artes
INE	Instituto Nacional de Ecología
INI	Instituto Nacional Indigenista
MACG	Museo de Arte Contemporáneo Carillo Gil
MAM	Museo de Arte Moderno
MNA	Museo Nacional de Arte
NLB	New Left Books
SEMARNAT	Secretaría de Medio Ambiente y Recursos Naturales
SEP	Secretaría de Educación Pública
SINAFO	Sistema Nacional de Fototecas
TGP	Taller de Gráfica Popular
TURMEX	Secretaría de Turismo de México
UAM	Universidad Autónoma Metropolitana
UNAM	Universidad Nacional Autónoma de México

Introduction

A Tradition of Intersections?

Interdisciplinary Slippages, Borrowings and
Collaborations in Mexican Visual Culture

This book seeks to configure the ways in which the interdisciplinary, the eclectic and the combinatory have served a strategic purpose in the development of a self-aware and identity-conscious visual discourse in Mexico, from the formative nineteenth century to the post-national 1990s. It ranges over observational writing, illustrated periodicals, graphic art, painting, photography and film, through a series of linked studies which focus on specific interrelations in context. The construction and interrogation of visual identities in reproductive media provides the unifying analytical interest. The book incidentally exposes the crucial ocularcentric vein in the discourse of identity in post-independence Mexico.

It sets out to explore areas of visual culture that have tended to be seen as subordinate or mere adjuncts to the triumphalist pictorial canon founded on the modern Mexican Mural movement (usually represented by Diego Rivera, José Clemente Orozco and David Alfaro Siqueiros) and, while acknowledging the centrality accorded to this figurative tradition, points to forms of resistance as well as complementarity mounted by the graphic arts, cinema and photography. It consciously places the emphasis on transformative receptions of well-known and extensively covered art and artists (including the now obligatory Frida Kahlo), rather than on these all too familiar subjects, in order to highlight the formal complexity, independence and critical pungency of those 'modern' art forms that rely on mechanical means of reproduction (magazines, film, photography). It prefers to evidence selectively and in detail the richly schismatic and multiform character of contemporary strategies of visualisation and in the process suggest some revisions to seductive generalisations about the monolithic nature and persistence of a fundamentalist 'mexicanicity' in the visual arts. By analysing the refractions and fracturing of pictorial paradigms in alternative visual media it provides a meaningful context for the insertion of the questioning of analogue visuality at the end of the twentieth century by artists and critics embracing digital image-making.

The aim of the individual chapters is to explore the character of interdisciplinary mediations in particular practices and to point to paradigmatic affinities across periods without sacrificing important distinctions and oppositions. What emerges is a kind of 'discordia concors' which yokes together the apparently unlike in order to convert heterogeneity into an enabling, shifting ground for the discussion of the formation of cultural identities in Mexico – a formation which has historically been predicated on a crisis of legitimacy and a pursuit of singularity. In other words, the book turns the notion of a problematic heterogeneity, an ontological as well as semantic anxiety which has traditionally stoked nation-conscious reflection in the arts, into the missing place of origin conceived as a practice rather than a place or destiny. The trope of 'intersection' (which acquires its specific cultural resonance in some chapters) provides a visual marker for this siteless encounter between discourses, disciplines and practices, a temporary form for an exercise which is dynamic rather than systemic and the definability of which is often inflected rather than fixed.

The book is based on a process of quite conventional 'archival' research and intellectual serendipity. It is heteroclite in style and content in pursuit of something akin to a reflective spiral which moves seamlessly between high and low, circling on itself as well as its subjects, moving freely backwards and forwards in time with connective intent. Each chapter can be read as a discrete essay, but read in sequence each is also designed to resonate with cumulative interconnections and contrasts, and to reflect the conceptual richness, acute self-referentiality and formal reflexivity of visual practices in Mexico in the modern and post-modern period. The inclusion of nineteenth-century topics is intended to provide a more complex and nuanced perspective on the strategies adopted by cultural nationalism in the twentieth century, while the studies of modern visual traditions on autochthony introduces the material for the manipulations of deconstructive and post-essentialist conceptual and multimedia art and photography at the end of the century. The multimedia eclecticism employed by those seeking to construct a visual nation in the mid-nineteenth century (Chapter 1) sources the interdisciplinary splicings and convergences which shape nationalist visualisations in the post-Revolutionary period in the twentieth century

(Chapter 3). The problematisation of Indian ethnicity and memory by the champion of cultural nationalism in the latter part of the nineteenth century (Chapter 2), echoes revealingly in the study of contemporary women photographers and their Indian subjects in the 1980s and 1990s (Chapter 5). The interplay of graphic arts and film in the fractious *Mexicanismo* of the 1930s and 1940s (Chapter 3) offers a counterpoint to the disabused perspectives on modernisation and urbanism in visual media in the subsequent decade (Chapter 4). A critique of the history of photographic discourse and its social complicities that matured in the 1950s (Chapters 4 and 5) illuminates the questioning of objective identities in photographic practices in the 1990s (Chapter 6). The final section (Chapters 7 and 8) considers the conceptualisation of identity as absence in photography and multimedia art and revisits the foundational tropes of cultural nationalism through post-nationalist aesthetic practices.

This study is unusual in the centrality it accords to photography in the analysis of visual strategies. It could be argued that it is the photographic double rather than the pictorial or filmic imaginaries that provides the infrastructure for the definition of identity in Mexico, and it is through photography's own disenchantment with such a history of circumscription and subordination that the exercise of producing identity itself is most fittingly interrogated.

The book borrows an illusionistic scenario conjured in the seventeenth century by Sor Juana Inés de la Cruz in a poem about the projections of the magic lantern to envisage its own questioning of identities which shapes and unmakes what it finds in a play of disclosure and apposition inviting intellectual transit rather than settlement:

Así linterna mágica, pintadas
representa fingidas
en la blanca pared varias figuras,
de las sombras no menos ayudadas
que de la luz: que en trémulos reflejos
los componentes lejos
guardando de la docta perspectiva,
en sus ciertas mesuras
de varias experiencias aprobadas,
la sombra fugitiva,
que en el mismo esplendor se desvanece.
[And so a magic lantern, painted
represents various illusory figures
on the white wall,
aided no less by shadows than by light;

in moving reflections
the distant elements
preserving through scholarly perspective,
in their faithful proportions
by wide experience approved,
the fleeting shadow,
which in its very radiance fades.][1]

Notes

1. *Sor Juana Inés de la Cruz: Antología poética*, ed. F.J. Cevallos (Salamanca, 1989),
    98–9, translated by the author. For a complete English translation see A.S.
    Trueblood, *A Sor Juana Anthology* (Cambridge, MA, 1988), 171–95.

Chapter 1

The Development of *Costumbrista:*

Iconography and Nation-building Strategies in Literary Periodicals of the Mid-Nineteenth Century

The Role of the Cultural Press

The tumultous years between 1830 and 1857 witnessed the rise of a diverse and vibrant political and cultural press in Mexico which was concerned with constituting and entitling an autochthonous identity, and visualising a national order. The zeal with which these objectives were pursued and the foundational strategies adopted by broadly literary magazines and miscellanies were informed by the circumstances in which the press as a whole operated. This was a period marked by seemingly endemic 'grotesca provisionalidad' as regards national governments and territorial sovereignty – a period of ideological revisionism generated by political instability.[1] A vocal press emerged as a refracting medium of a civic polity subject to corrosive disorder – acutely conscious of the questionable permanence of post-colonial Mexico's integrity, and even of its definability.

The cultural press in particular eschewed the overt polemics of feuding newspapers in an attempt to foster civic and intellectual homogeneity. The editors professed to subscribe to an integrative and consensual model of cultural transmission which was intended to inculcate similar values in its readers. The notion of a cultural press as providing a contemplative sanctuary from protracted civil strife for non-aligned patriots was one of the sustaining myths of these sophisticated publications.[2] Most journalism was propagandistic or denunciatory, and most prominent writers were polymaths who appeared in the guise of poets, historians, philologists, storytellers, educationists, naturalists in the pages of compendious publications, but were principally engaged as ministers, generals, legislators and administrators involved in a turbulent public life.[3] The educational and museological impulse which drove these would-be popular publications aimed to foster the conditions in which its constitutive project could prosper. As the editorial of the *Revista Mexicana* of 1835 explained, the aim was to 'difundir hasta los confines más remotos de la república acentos de paz, de orden y de unión, pues sin estos tres dones no puede haber artes, ni ciencias, ni repúblicas' ['to disseminate to the most remote corners of the republic notes of peace, order and unity, for without these three gifts there can be no arts, sciences nor republics'].[4]

During a period of crisis and partition, the semblance of a broadly based cultural sphere was maintained by these illustrated publications, the inclusivity of which aimed to complement the more ceremonious and discriminatory 'high' culture of newly established scholarly institutions.[5] The activities of the Academia de la Lengua and the Academia de la Historia were in theory meant to consecrate and systematise disciplines which were regarded as both engines of change and repositories of tradition. Whilst the eclectic magazines had to contend with the conditions of the time (including paper shortages, censorship and imprisonment of staff) to provide a coherent although discontinuous source of instruction, patriotic conscience and amusement, the academies never fulfilled their proper roles.[6] Founded to provide an official canon of learning and discernment at a time when the traditional provision of education and the established promoters of culture had been suspended, these bodies proved rhetorically useful but frequently inconsequential emblems of a hypothetical restoration of cultural values in the new republic. Shaped and sundered by society's pervasive instability, cultural dissemination was concentrated informally in café *tertulias* [cultural gatherings] (Café del Progreso), bookshops situated in printing establishments (la Librería del Siglo XIX and La Librería Mexicana), literary fraternities (Academia de San Juan de Letrán, el Liceo Hidalgo), and synthesised in the comparatively urbane magazines which fostered the emergence of a more explicitly nation-conscious cultural practice. In the absence of public collections or circulating libraries, and given the inflated cost of books and a dislocated education system, these magazines assumed the role of popularisers of useful as well as edifying information.[7] They subsumed pamphlets, samplers and elements of the civic *catecismos* [catechisms/manuals] originally pioneered and distributed by Ackermann throughout the Spanish-American republics.[8] Before the emergence of a professional identity for literati, these *portmanteau* periodicals were genuinely collective enterprises, where anonymity – albeit often strategic or feigned – rather than authorship was the norm. They were not commercially driven, and regularly foundered because of lack of official patronage, skeletal subscriptions and poor circulation.[9] The studied congeniality and moderate pluralism which they espoused attempted to nurture a readership whose character and very existence remained nebulous.[10] It is a tribute to the sense of mission of the period's journalists and publishers, to the generative input of figures such as Ignacio Cumplido and Vicente García Torres, that their steadfast advocacy of culture as a facilitator of nationhood became formulaic, whilst the production values and graphic invention of the magazines which they devised were to remain unequalled for most of the rest of the century.

The Printed Museum

The titles of these publications alluded strikingly to eighteenth-century European institutions which symbolised encyclopaedic education for all and the reappropriation of collective heritage: *El Museo Mexicano, El Gabinete de Lectura, La Ilustración Mexicana, El Liceo Mexicano, El Mosaico Mexicano*. A central institution of the nineteenth century, a place where the products of nature, science and the arts were preserved and exhibited, the museum provided a key metaphor deployed by the popular press. The proliferation of French publications which sported the word in their titles was characteristic of a wider trend in Europe, and found a fertile reception amongst publishers and editors in Mexico, who drew a good deal of their miscellaneous material from French, Spanish and English journals.[11] Ignacio Cumplido's *El Museo Mexicano: o miscelánea pintoresca de amenidades curiosas e instructivas* [*The Mexican Museum: or Picturesque Miscellany of Curious and Instructive Pleasantries*], clearly indicates how the metaphor of the 'printed museum' which subsumed the earlier 'cabinet of curiosities' was adapted to a Mexican context (figure 1.1). In Mexico it became associated with the empowerment of the citizen, who through the prismatic magazine had access to a representation of the world and the nation in microcosm. The introductory editorial in the first issue of 1843 explains the degree to which its table of contents was conceptually analogous to that of a museum gallery.[12] The contiguity of image and text, which became a distinguishing feature of these publications and of the brand of Mexican *costumbrismo* (a literary and pictorial genre dealing with customs and types) which they showcased, further stressed the analogy with an instructive gallery. The reproductions of universal and indigenous artistic or archaeological objects and scenic views would encourage each reader

Figure 1.1 Frontispiece of *El Museo Mexicano* (1845). CEHM-CONDUMEX.

to compile a private collection – to appropriate cognitively as well as materially a kind of multifarious birthright (figure 1.2).[13] The prominence given in the multifaceted *El Mosaico Mexicano*, for instance, to syncretic or Indian toponyms, in articles and illustrations, formed part of this descriptive appropriation of the national terrain. The notion of the *magasin* publication (or general store), rendered as *Almacen* in Mexico, became a virtual synonym for the museum, although with rather more prosaic associations to the trade in curious articles and commodities exhibited and exchanged in town shops and marketplaces.[14] The title of *El Almacen Universal: Artículos de Historia, Geografía, Viajes, Literatura y Variedades* [*The Universal Store: Articles on History, Geography, Travel, Literature and Diverse Subjects*] of 1840, for instance, stresses the acquisitive impulse as regards national production – whether it be in the arts and sciences, or manufacturing industries, agriculture and natural resources – which most publications in Mexico sought to stimulate in their readership.

The Emergence of *Costumbrismo* as a Nation-Building Strategy

Editors and contributors in Mexico expressed the questing sensibility fomented by the instability of the period. Many found that if the quotidian was ephemeral and hard to capture, it was due to the

PIRAMIDES DE SAN JUAN TEOTIHUACAN.   Litog. de Cumplido.

Figure 1.2 Anon., *Piramides de San Juan Teotihuacan, El Álbum Mexicano* (1849). CEHM-CONDUMEX.

revolutionary age in which nothing was held sacred but, rather, was subject to scrutiny and change. The external manifestations of flux are internalised to express the predicament of the writer's social vocation: the vagaries of local politics blur personal identity and agency even as the principle of authority and the organicity of a national body are destabilised: 'Nosotros los del tiempo presente, aparecemos como sombras, y desaparecemos del mismo modo' ['We who dwell in the present appear like mere shadows and vanish in the same way'].[15] The perceived disjunction between enunciation and essence is posited as a predicament typical of a society in a transitional state. The liberal journalist and reformer Francisco Zarco concluded that, 'En México lo cierto es que no hay carácter nacional. La faz de nuestra sociedad es desigual y tornasol, es un mosaico en que aparecen desvanecidos todos los colores' ['The truth is that in Mexico there is no national character. The countenance of our society is irregular and changeable, it is a mosaic in which all the colours appear faded'].[16] It is to counter both in Mexico and internationally the invisibility of a collectivity to which legitimate nationality and territory could be ascribed – tribal memory, geographical parameters, homogenous ethnicity, autochthonous traditions – that the outpouring of iconic graphic images and exhaustive descriptive typologies occurred in the pages of a cultural press whose impulse was foundational as much as divulgatory. Periodicals mounted a resourceful campaign to make the disparate cohere in the inspiring representations of a Mexicanized 'República de las letras' [Republic of Letters].

The desire to rationalise the problematic heterogeneity of Mexican society informed the literary manifestos in miscellaneous magazines which called for cultural regeneration as an inaugural stage to full autochthony. The authors borrowed the legalistic terminology of judicial and constitutional process in their discussion of the prerogatives and obligations of a socially conscious literature at a time when most published writers were – when not personally involved – certainly aware of the legislative debates.[17] Periodicals which carried such manifestos endeavoured to amend the paradigm of prescriptive but ineffectual constitutions in their own rather more empirically grounded designs for a cohesive cultural order.[18] In their wide-ranging scrutiny of local phenomena these illustrated publications essayed a foundational diagram of an integrated nation based on observed specificities – the little-studied idiosyncrasies of the prosaic, and grassroots phenomena. The exalted spirit of civic mission was tempered by a strain of pragmatic realism. Celebratory of the local in their taxonomic compass, these magazines did not preclude an exhibition of indigenous malformations. Patriotic but wary of complacency, these pedagogic enterprises welcomed alongside lyrical eulogies a more robust reflexive vein, inviting native-born writers to adopt the anatomist's scalpel as well as the moralist's satire in their explorations of contemporary society.[19]

One such agitator for civic-minded scepticism was the liberal writer, *cronista* [chronicler/journalist], populist balladeer and sometime government functionary, Guillermo Prieto. He called for 'menos constituciones y mejores veredas' ['fewer constitutions and better highways'] from the pages of the *Revista Científica y Literaria de México*.[20] Acutely conscious of the need to foster a collective sense of identity which was at least in part based on observable fact rather than on the lexicon of official oratory, he was the most determined advocate of the pungent literary *costumbrismo* which he admired in France, Spain and Britain. Revelatory and instructive, this genre would help to invest literature in Mexico with the social relevance and accessibility appropriate to the gravity of the times.

The need to bind together a divided country, lacking any sense of overarching communality, was widely recognised in the turbulent 1840s. The difficulty for writers such as Prieto, whose multiple vocation included that of legislator, telluric poet and visionary of independence (the period's characteristic 'hombre-crisálida' [human chrysalis] in Francisco Zarco's comic physiology),[21] was how descriptively to encompass a heterogenous population – a population whose ethnic diversity and cultural polarities questioned the verisimilitude of the term *pueblo* [the people/community] in political and historical discourse. In his illuminating memoirs Prieto revisited the struggle that all attempts at a totalising *costumbrista* perspective had entailed: 'Lo que lucho por caracterizar y no acierto como es la fisonomía de aquella sociedad heterógenea, formada de secciones completas, pero sin relaciones con las demás que formaba conjunto a lo lejos y de cerca se componía de lo más disímbolo' ['What I am struggling to characterise, and do not know how, is the physiognomy of that heterogeneous society made up of discrete parts with no ties to each other, which formed a whole from a distance, but seen up close was composed of the most dissimilar elements'].[22] The problem in this representative passage is the difficulty of visualising faithfully the apparently disparate and discontinuous. Prieto's *artículos de costumbres* [verbal sketches of customs] played repeatedly on a number of pictorial analogies related to the use of perspective, in order to envisage a complete yet faceted reproduction of Mexican culture and society. The aim shared by Prieto and his associates in the press was partly to achieve compellingly finished simulacra – hence the ubiquitous sobriquet of *cuadros* [pictures] for such writings – rather than a passing reflection/impression. As in Prieto's recollections, a distant/distanced point of view lends a semblance of coherent identity, a panoramic lucidity akin to landscape painting and topography, which immersion into the foreground, or microscopic scrutiny, quickly belies. Such shifts of vision and focus, and the phenomenological differences which they seemed to illustrate, were interpreted by the writer as pointing to a number of related problems: firstly, the conceptual inadequacy of language as a mimetic instrument; and still more disturbing, the unstable identity of a sociocultural order seemingly determined by the application of a changing point of view. Contemporary optical technology, both as regards practice and as a source of metaphors for interpretative lucidity, accounts for many of the articles concerned with the dissemination of useful knowledge in Mexican cultural periodicals of the period. The analogies to scientific technologies prefaced and to a certain extent authenticated the writers' figurative recording of emblematic scenes and national types. The references to the instruments of positivist science in such descriptive literature are indicative of a desire for a compelling realism: the achievement of a pure communicable trace which negated its origin as mediated or constructed image. Not surprisingly, the newly enfranchised Mexican writer faced with a decentred world and seeking a kind of vatic transcendence, conceives his interpretative difficulties in terms which allude to the epistemology of vision. The emphasis is on regulating perception and its subjects. The onus on the writer, and the *costumbrista* in particular, is to systematise the imponderables of the shifting point of view. Midway between scientist and magician, he is both the retentive observer and recorder of prosaic minutiae, and the alchemical distiller of the detritus of the multiple and random, from whose measured interventions emerge synthetic emblems – inherent properties denoting Mexican traits and customs.

The nation-building writer in Mexico emulated Walter Scott's antiquarian impulse to collect and legitimise in order to consecrate a subordinated culture. Not coincidentally, one of the first self-professed *costumbrista* pieces is a glossed translation from the English of an article on Scottish customs.[23] Scott's work was widely reviewed, admired for its scenarist detail – the recreative use of costume and props – and for its memorably depictive quality.[24] Part of the appeal of his celebrated ability to paint verbal tableaux that seemed to bring the past vividly to life, was the fact that by popularising history through narrative fiction he had conjured a sense of collective memory. Writers in Mexico were certainly responsive to such effective visualisation, exercised as they were by the difficulty of fostering a sense of collective identity. An interesting consequence of Scott's reception in Mexico is that *costumbrista* writing, in its efforts to characterise a past which could be conceived as 'shared' in the post-colonial period, found itself reduced to historicising the present rather than revisiting a history marked by seemingly ineradicable conflicts. The principal need, according to most of the literary prospectuses, was to effect 'la morigeración social' ['social cohesion'], and the identifiable spectacle and the fixture of living traditions was one way of prefiguring – and thereby promoting – social integration.[25] The literary and pictorial genre of the *cuadro de costumbres* [picture of customs] which emerges as the dominant form during this period played a foundational role in grounding and publicising just such an archive of originary traits. During a period when competing historical mythologies were being devised and circulated to shore up the ideologies of rival factions, *costumbrismo* chose a less combative – but equally affirmative – exegesis of Mexico's cultural palimpsest.

As a genre the *cuadro de costumbres* in Mexico had a genealogy which arguably combined the pictorial strategies developed during the colonial period, with iconographic paradigms of modern European extraction. Typically, the verbal *cuadro* played on the blurred distinction between the notion of the *étude* made from nature and the *esquisse* or compositional sketch.[26] The colonial legacy offered imagistic precedents: *biombos* [painted screens introduced in the seventeenth century], *pintura de castas* [colonial Caste Painting], *bodegones* [still-life paintings] and baroque *retablos* [altarpieces].[27] The proliferation of depictions of local landscapes, generic street scenes and rituals, ethnic classification and allegorical, layered or panelled compositions witnessed in the centuries before independence, attests to a concern with representing Mexican society which betrayed an earlier need for differentiation from the metropolis. There is a qualified adherence to this pictorial tradition in the nineteenth century with the popularity of genre scenes and still lifes. Mexican *costumbrismo*'s descriptive galleries of social types, racial physiognomies, rural and urban customs, collective rituals and spectacles comprised an exhaustive catalogue of archetypal facets which insisted on diversity in unity. The *cuadro de costumbres* delighted in the theatricality of the local in a disrupted post-colonial order, with framing devices which favoured emblematic traditional scenes viewed from balconies, windows, street benches, carriages and theatre seats: crowded marketplaces and central squares, patriotic celebrations and religious processions, rustic entertainments and fashionable promenades were the preferred loci for illustrations of a communal identity in times of crisis (figure 1.3). Guillermo Prieto incidentally confirmed the practice of Mme Calderón de la Barca[28] as a foreign observer when he too recognised the symbolic importance of her preferred vantage point: balconies and 'las ventanas son el punto de transición entre dos públicos

Figure 1.3 Casimiro Castro and Juan Campillo, *La calle de Roldán y su desembarcadero* (1855–6). Private collection.

diferentes' ['windows offer a point of transition between two publics'] – between the largely creole elite and the incipient *mestizo* [mixed race] middleclass and the disenfranchised, populace;[29] between the circumscribed number of reflective observers and the plethoric objects of their observation.

In his own attempt to extol and map the natural resources of newly independent territories, the *costumbrista* writer and illustrator intentionally appropriated the language of enumeration and classification of celebrated romantic travellers and naturalists whose ethnographic sketches often resembled cultural parables on the theme of civilisation versus primitivism. Humboldt and Bonpland's authoratitive summation of the Americas, as well as more contemporary entrepreneur-explorers like John Lloyd Stephens, the engraver and panoramist Frederick Catherwood and popular historians like Prescott, provided suggestive examples of divulgatory enterprises which combined scientific rigour with popular entertainment.[30] Antiquarian investigations undertaken and publicised by such contemporaries marked a growing trend from 1839 in international scientific circles not only to systematise the study of pre-Columbian artefacts but to support the case for polygenesis – the historical possibility of an indigenous American civilisation developing from a non-Western template.[31] This intellectual current, which restored the creative autonomy to Indian civilisations which pre-dated the Conquest, was grist to the mill of liberal writers concerned with exemplifying a synchronic Mexican autochthony.[32] The visual record of classicised ancestral relics was a key component of the magazines which fostered *costumbrismo*. Recently excavated or rediscovered pre-Hispanic sites were illustrated and glossed by a celebratory commentary.[33] These depictions played on the moral association with the *memento mori* – not unlike the pathos ascribed by Romantics to picturesque medieval ruins (figure 1.4). They presented the exhumation of a long-lost, indigenous past as an act of communion with frequently polemical overtones: a sort of reparation for ancient wrongs from which useful parallels could be drawn to the victimisation of the young republic by foreign powers.

With the cumulative avidity demonstrated by inventories of newly conquered domains in the sixteenth century and scientific taxonomies in the eighteenth century, Mexican *costumbrismo* endeavoured to compose pictorially and to historicise the imagined totality – the invisible nation. As an explicatory genre which aimed at the resolution of contradictions which precluded unity, it manifests what might be defined in Hegelian terms as 'appetitive self-consciousness'. The inductive function of emblems had been widely recognised and exploited by republicans in the post-insurgent years, and there were ample precedents at home and

RUINAS DE UXMAL.
(à la luz de la luna.)

Figure 1.4 Anon., *Ruinas de Uxmal (a la luz de la luna)*, *Álbum Mexicano*. CEHM-CONDUMEX.

abroad for a strategy encouraging an emotional identification with visualised ideals.[34] In their attempt to achieve a broad scope and appeal, *costumbrista* writers drew on a recurring number of mostly visual or exhibitionary paradigms from the popular arts and sciences of the period.

The Physiologie Genre and Social Observation

France of the 1830s provided the bestselling, pseudo-scientific and largely satirical *physiologies* by caricaturist Henri Monnier and others, including Balzac, which held up contemporary types, classes and manners to scrutiny in what some termed mimicry elevated to 'intellectual photography'.[35] This genre required mastery of the telling detail which made of the early Balzac a semiotician of the materiality of modern life, with a penchant for telltale furnishing, architectural or physiognomic peculiarities. Guillermo Prieto in particular, of the practitioners of *costumbrismo*, was receptive to this somewhat stockpiling and baggy style of description.[36] In 'Théorie de la démarche' ['Theory of Walking'], Balzac had eulogised ocular fluency as the mark of the modern hero: 'The observer is incontestably the man of genius. All human inventions come from an analytic observation in which the mind acts with incredible rapidity of insights'.[37] Amongst this select fraternity to which the percipient writer belonged, he singled out the quacks and pseudo-scientists as well as the ground-breaking specialists, preferring popularisers such as the phrenologist Gall, the physiognomist Lavater, the hypnotist Mesmer, without excluding the genuine article in the zoologist and paleontologist, Cuvier.[38] All had been engaged in delineating the component structure of the varied objects of their perception. Parisian weeklies like *La Silhouette* (1829–31) and *La Caricature* (1830–5) (Balzac was a contributor to the latter) were repositories of sketches and studies of contemporary life which usually disguised their moral generalisations and humorous criticism behind the dubious objectivity of a 'sociological' approach based on references to statistics and the theories of Gall and Lavater. Mexican illustrated periodicals conceived their intent to characterise contemporary society in similar terms, and adopted comparable strategies. The works of Lavater and Gall were frequently glossed and cited, and their terminology recycled to serve the nation-questing priorities of the journalistic community in Mexico.[39] Preparing to pay homage to the humble *costurera* [seamstress], a Mexican writer speculated waggishly 'estudiaríamos su cara con Lavater, y su cráneo con Gall' ['we shall study her face with Lavater and her cranium with Gall']; another humorous sketch referred to 'la fisiología, o más bien la patología del alacenero' ['the physiology or more precisely the pathology of the stall-holder'], whilst comparing the process of describing such a vernacular specimen to that of zoological or botanical classification.[40] The Lavaterian notion that appearance determines character had, despite the parodic inflation of its application in satirical magazines, a defining influence on the development of literary realism in France. Equally crucial for the pictorial strain which dominated the absorption of this current by Mexican magazines, was Lavater's belief that the painter and the physiognomist were closely related in the task of decipherment (or *criptogamia*, according to one Mexican *costumbrista*).

The Panorama Installation

Although less throroughly prospected than their French counterparts, aspects of British literary and popular culture proved sources of inspiration. Addison's mordant social testimony in *The Spectator* was a frequently cited model for the prospective *costumbrista* writer in Mexico. Dickens's reportorial urban writings (*Sketches by Boz*) were also appreciated as an updated extension of the eighteenth-century tradition of social observation and illustration. Previously unremarked is the extent to which certain forms of popular spectacle provided analogies for the expository work of the *costumbrista* writer in Mexico. The popular entertainment of the panorama installation, which seemingly realised the all-encompassing vision of Bentham's panopticon, is a particularly suggestive example of the kind of assimilative transcription undertaken by the period's writers in Mexico.[41] The panorama combined elements of social engineering with didacticism, in a manner which appealed to the pedagogical streak in Mexican social commentary. Whilst, for the most part, it became a metaphor for the illustrative social compass of *costumbrista* articles, the panorama was also used to signal the hedonism of magazines designed (by men) specifically for the consumption of a largely uneducated female public. The *Panorama de las Señoritas: Periódico Pintoresco, Científico y Literario* [*The Young Ladies' Panorama: Picturesque, Scientific and Literary Periodical*] (1842), for example, emphasised its role as 'puro entretenimiento' [pure amusement], playing imaginatively on the association with a fashionable promenade intrinsic to this popular spectacle.[42]

These illusionistic canvases of landscapes or cityscapes were the height of fashion in the cities of 1830s and 1850s Europe and the United States. The most elaborate often incorporated a dome, a central tower with a circular viewing platform, and even moving scrolls to further enhance the realism of the ambulatory experience.[43] The panorama was frequently promoted as educational entertainment, with entrepreneurs vouching for the scientific exactness of the subject matter depicted. It undoubtedly assuaged the appetite for travel expeditions and primitive quaintness captured in mass-produced engravings and illustrated albums. However, it helped not only to visualise foreign latitudes, but also to satisfy a more parochial need for rootedness amongst the inhabitants of burgeoning European cities. Displaying in minute relief the configurations of national capitals, the panorama cast a totalising gaze on the familiar experienced piecemeal by ordinary citizens. The consumer could thus accede temporarily, and in some cases be literally elevated, to a position of omniscience and collective identification with an iconic site (figures 1.5 and 1.6). *Costumbrista* illustration and verbal sketches sought to re-enact such moments of recognition and communion amongst a Mexican readership.The fact that visitors to a panorama exhibition were often issued with a descriptive booklet to guide and instruct them during their imaginary journey provides a conceptual precedent for the interplay of image and text of the *cuadro de costumbres* – a genre with a marked essayistic tendency.

A notable panorama depicting a view of *Mexico City and Surrounding Country* helped to elevate the international profile of the Mexican Republic in the aftermath of the independence revolutions. Devised by John and Robert Burford, who had succeeded H.A. Barker (the son of the inventor of such installations, Robert Barker), it was on permanent display in a specially designed rotunda in Leicester Square, London, between 1825 and 1827.[44] The breathtaking view and detailed topography were painted by the Burfords from sketches brought back from Mexico in 1823 by William Bullock Jr., whose father published a celebrated account of their sojourn there in 1825 and who exhibited pre-Columbian antiquities in his London gallery to considerable acclaim. The link between the Burford and Bullock commercial enterprises suggests a significant kinship between the panorama and museological displays, which is preserved in the appropriation of such popular vehicles by Mexican peiodicals intent on fostering a *costumbrista* perspective. The centrality accorded to this *View of Mexico City* in the British capital is proof of the novelty value of both the illusionistic device and its unfamiliar subject matter. The panorama was again exhibited in 1853 and finally in 1863. This episode also helps to demonstrate the extent to which, in the process of visualising Mexico, Mexican writers and graphic artists had to contend with an existing body of compelling images produced abroad.

By 1851, when the Great Exhibition of the Works of Industry of All Nations was held in London, the panorama installation, with the addition of polychromed ethnological figures, had not only become a popular part

Figure 1.5 Anon., *The Geometrical Ascent to the Galleries in the Colosseum, Regent's Park* (1829). Guildhall Library, City of London.

of museum displays, but a vehicle for the dissemination of an established ideology relating to colonial control. In the Fine Arts Class at the exhibition, for instance, the U.K. section boasted a series of scenarios with wax figures of natives of Mexico and American Indians, arranged in narratives which purported to exhibit the appearance and customs of semi-savage peoples.[45] Catherwood had erected in the 1840s a panorama based on his explorations in the Yucatán peninsula, into which he had incorporated actual Mayan artefacts. Unlike the waxwork display at the Great Exhibition by Napoleon Montanari, Catherwood's recreation tended to dispute supremacist views of indigenous culture.[46] What Catherwood and Montanari shared was the arrangement of figures and

Figure 1.6 Anon., *Bird's-Eye View from the Staircase and Upper Part of the Pavillion in the Colosseum Regent's Park (1829)*. Guildhall Library, City of London.

objects in a tableau in order to heighten the sense of realism on which the success of these installations was judged. The analogies made to the visual compositional device of the panorama in Mexican *cuadros de costumbres* not only transferred to a degree its imitative poetics (the production of difference through the manipulation of costume, artefacts and physiognomic effigies) but also, paradoxically, its tendency to exoticise colonised peoples. Even whilst the *costumbrista* project was driven by a desire for separation from European traditions, especially since Europe continued to have imperialist designs on Mexico, it nonetheless defined its pursuit of autochthony in terms inflected with those suspect models.

José María Lafragua, who championed *costumbrismo* as part of a Mexican cultural renaissance, collaborated with the historian of pre-Conquest antiquities and Indian codices Manuel Orozco y Berra in producing Mexican guides to the capital of the republic.[47] Published in 1854, they provided a compendium of statistical information, which confirm that panoramas and smaller-scale visual entertainments such as the diorama were indeed popular attractions in Mexico City as elsewhere in the Western world. A list of favourite spectacles in the streets and squares of the once viceregal centre includes a mixture of modern and traditional, lowly and fashionable, pastimes: 'peleas de gallos, *maromas* o juegos de volantines, circo, panorama, diorama, titeres, representaciones por muñecos, en fin otros muchos espectáculos propios para calentar los gustos y todas las condiciones' ['cock fights, acrobatics and juggling, circus, panoramas, dioramas, marionettes, puppet theatre, and in short many other spectacles to appeal to all tastes and social conditions'].[48] The location of the panorama in the arena of popular culture suggested an affinity with *costumbrismo*'s elaboration of a visual vernacular. The metaphor of the panorama carried with it associations to popular performances and theatrical scenarios. It could be used for a particularised description of exteriors, but also the convex interiors of theatres and cafés. The synoptic compass of *costumbrista* sketches not only subsumed the visual aid of the lithograph which often accompanied them – 'Que Dios me tenga de su mano, señor litógrafo, al escribir el presente artículo!' ['May God guide my hand master lithographer when writing the present article!']; 'Antes de todo, fija un momento los ojos en la estampa … el picaresco litógrafo me ahorra el trabajo de describirte el personaje y su vestido' ['Before proceeding, fix your gaze on the print … the mischievous lithographer has saved me the trouble of describing the character and his attire'][49] – but also attempted to evoke the spatial relationship between observer and spectacle experienced in the panorama exhibition. The dramatic moment of revelation is compared to that afforded by the controlled point of view of the popular installation: 'Es México político y social; yo estoy viendo a México, como en un panorama que le comunica vida y acción' ['It is Mexico itself in its political and social guise. I am seeing Mexico City as in a panorama which imbues it with life and movement'].[50] The panoramist's ability to create through a number of contraptions, props and tricks of perspective the illusion of activity – to animate a fixed scenario and enhance its realism – was a skill which writers in Mexico sought to transpose to their stationary *cuadros*.

The Figurative Tradition of Mexican Folk Art

In their investigation of native traditions, some writers drew enabling analogies from folk art, which seemed to offer modest echoes of waxwork museums abroad. Figurines in wax, terracotta and natural fibres, commemorating historical or sacred personages and events or deftly rendered trades and popular types, were produced with syncretic techniques by anonymous craftsmen and sold in the markets of Puebla and Jalisco – singly or in small, compositional dioramas which could take the form of a glass-fronted box.[51] These portable scenarios, autochthonously manufactured and authentically mimentic, complemented the notion of the *cuadro de costumbres* as an exhibit in the broader analogy of the popular magazine to the printed museum, contributing both to the representation of the nation in microcosm and its appropriation by the individual reader-consumer.

The plasticity of period collectibles such as wax figurines of particularised types clearly impressed contemporary writers intent on figuring Mexican autochthony. Manuel Payno, for instance, in the epistolary travel sketches he published in *El Museo Mexicano* (1844), praised the imititative genius of the Pueblan *lépero* or proletarian Everyman: 'posee como nadie en el mundo el sentido de la imitación' ['he possesses like no one else in the world the capacity for imitation'].[52] According to Payno, the singular vernacular culture of the *plebe* [the masses] is vividly embodied in 'los muñecos de cera y de barro' [wax and clay figurines] which were sold in local markets (figure 1.7).[53] The revival of syncretic traditions associated with both profane and sacred iconography, at a time of increasing cultural nationalism, impinged on *costumbrista* writing's visual references, especially in those articles where the peripatetic *costumbrista* sought telling regional detail. The virtually forgotten pre-Hispanic *arte plumario* [images made with feathers], for example, was revived in Michoacán with the manufacture of two-dimensional scenes celebrating the exploits of archetypal *arrieros* [mule drivers] and *chinacos* [cowboy soldiers who fought invading

Figure 1.7 Joaquín Hidalgo, *Charro lanzando* (19th C.), wax figure. Private collection.

enemies].[54] These decorative objects used compositions reminiscent of those found in published travel album illustrations or *costumbrista* engravings culled from popular magazines of the period. An item in *El Museo Mexicano* of 1844 confirms its founders Prieto and Payno's interest in the celebration and conservation of highly figurative local folklore. It describes another popular curiosity known as *Cajitas de entretenimientos* [Little Boxes of Amusements] manufactured in Oaxaca:

boxes usually containing regional sweets adorned with miniature *costumbrista* figures made of a derivative of the *pipirucha* grass (Panicum holciforme) also known as *camelote*.[55] The boxes recreated in considerable detail (including costumes and props) typical rural scenarios with archetypal figures shown in relief or as complete miniature sculptures on three-dimensional pedestals as in a diorama. The popularity of the trade in imitative figures and miniatures, especially amongst foreign visitors, was well established by the time that Jesús Hermosa commends his countrymen's native invention in the statistical manual to the republic of 1857:

> Forzoso es hacer mencion de la admirable facilidad con que en Méjico se trabaja la cera, de la cual se hacen retratos, figuras que representan las costumbres del país, é imitan toda clase de frutas y flores. Tambien merecen particular mencion las figuras que se hacen en barro; de ambas clases se forman colecciones para Europa, donde son muy estimadas.[56]

> [One must mention the admirable facility with which wax is worked in Mexico: they use it in portraits, in figures representing the customs of the country, and in imitating every kind of fruit and flowers. Also worthy of special mention are figures fashioned from clay; both of these types of objects are collected in Europe where they are greatly prized.]

Manuel Payno, in his fictional recollections of mid-century society, provides an illuminating description of the trade in ethnic objects with which his own representational prose had such affinity. In the *costumbrista* novel *Los bandidos de Río Frío*, he recreates the exhibitionary space of *El Portal de Mercaderes* [*The Merchants' Arcade*] in the centre of Mexico City. Describing the cramped box-like stands known as *alacenas*, he coins a compelling image of his own practice as a *costumbrista* writer – the cumulative itemisation of prosaic objects whose function is to embody an indigenous reality:

> ... en el armazón de tablas, hechas de modo que puedan contener la mayor cantidad de objetos posible, se encuentran ... figuras de cera representando chinas, coleadores, indios, fruteros, tocineros, frailes, toreros, indias tortilleras, en fin todos los tipos nacionales perfectamente acabados ... muñecos de trapo de Puebla, que son verdaderos retratos ... multitud de curiosidades y objetos de hueso y madera, y variedad infinita de muchas otras cosas que llenarían un catálogo.[57]

> [... in the framework of planks, constructed so as to contain the greatest possible number of objects, you find wax figures representing *chinas* [the female companions of the folkloric *charro* horseman], riders who fell bulls by the tail, Indians, fruit sellers, bacon sellers, monks, bullfighters, *tortilla*-making Indian women, in short all of our national types perfectly rendered ... rag dolls made of cloth from Puebla, which are veritable portraits ... a multitude of curiosities and objects of bone and wood, and an infinite variety of any number of things that would fill a catalogue.]

The implicit parallels to a national museum exhibit, the box-like portable diorama, a *kunstkammer* (or collector's cabinet), and the link between the transactions of this trade in objects and the constitution of an archive of disappearing traditions, nicely capture the interplay between private and public appropriation which is central to *costumbrista* representational strategies. *Alacena* was also a term commonly used to designate a modest 'bookshop': a stand selling pamphlets, books and printed ephemera (figure 1.8). This usage offers a clear ironic link to the literary profession and the dissemination of its products in a heterogeneous marketplace in

Figure 1.8 Hesiquio Iriarte, *El alacenero*, from *Los mexicanos pintados por sí mismos* (1853–5). CEHM-CONDUMEX.

which they competed with other curios of dubious utility. More suggestively still, in this retrospective work of fiction Payno recycled a patriotic motif characteristic of his early *costumbrista* journalism. He suggested that the objects on display were equal in novelty value to the more celebrated imports known as *Artículos de París* [Articles from Paris]. A new term should be coined for creations of such unrivalled originality: *Artículos del Portal de México* [Articles from the Mexican Arcade]. A punning reference to his own well-known production and advocacy of Mexican *artículos de costumbres* helps to make the point against cultural inauthenticity.[58]

The Camera Obscura and Daguerreotypy

In addition to the fund of pictorial, ethnological and exhibitionary paradigms, *costumbrista* sketch writers evinced an interest in pre-cinematic technology for recording and projecting images: the *camera obscura*, the daguerreotype, the magic lantern and even aerial topography with the use of balloons.

The daguerreotype was introduced to a Mexican public in 1840, with the arrival in Veracruz of the Frenchman Louis Prélier.[59] The interest attracted by this invention in Mexico was not unlike the stir which daguerreotypy and other photographic techniques provoked in European cultural circles and the popular press, convinced as they were of its potential to determine the course of the arts. The association of photography with positivist science, empirical enquiry generally and the quest for absolute visibility is well documented.[60] The parallel development of photography and anthropology has specific resonances in the context of Mexican *costumbrismo*'s typification of vernacular culture. The invention of the panoramic camera in 1845 may have further enhanced the appeal of photography as a metaphor for scientific realism in descriptive literature of the period. Some of the earliest views captured by mechanical means returned to vantage points and subject matter amply exploited by engravers in traveller's albums and *costumbrista* illustrations in Mexican periodicals – the principal port of the republic and the metropolitan cathedral in the capital, for example. It lent further credibility to the tendency by *costumbrista* sketch writers to find equivalences between their representational efforts and those of ocular technology. *El Mosaico Mexicano* of 1840 published an article, part of a growing trend of orientalist topics lifted from French magazines, which recorded the exploits of a travelling daguerreotypist in Egypt.[61] Such photographic travelogues were dubbed 'Excursions daguerriennes' by Parisian publishers and reinforced the notion of the daguerreotype as a memento.[62] Significantly, surviving daguerreotypes in Mexico were often framed in the manner of painted or wax miniatures as well as encased in portable wallets or glass-fronted boxes, prompting understandable analogies between the commemorative object and the historicising aspirations of the *cuadro de costumbres*.[63] Articles on optical instruments such as the telescope and the kaleidoscope followed, confirming an interest in scientific precision of observation as well as illusionism.[64] Others which dwelt on the visual effects to be achieved by the manipulation of perspective complemented this interest in the interplay between optical technology and representation. The strategic distortion of a pictorial subject through the projection of the image, a technique known as anamorphosis, engaged an anonymous contributor to *El Mosaico Mexicano* of 1841. He marvelled at the way in which, depending on the point of view, 'paises, figuras aisladas, animales, flores etc etc ... vistas, por ejemplo, de frente, representan monstruos, y colocándose el espectador en su verdadero punto, son figuras correctas' ['places, single figures, animals, flowers etc etc ... seen from the front, for example, appear to represent monsters, but on placing the spectator at the proper point of view, become accurate images'].[65] Such calculated deceptions reinforced the belief amongst descriptive writers in Mexico that the techniques for presenting subject matter determined how it was finally perceived by a wider audience.

In *El Mosaico Mexicano* of 1837 Isidro Rafael Gondra, in what he accurately termed 'ligero bosquejo del pintoresco puerto de Campeche visto desde el mar' ['a light sketch of the picturesque port of Campeche seen from the sea'], stressed the importance of a distanced perspective whilst comparing his decription to the effects achieved 'delineando con cámara obscura la hermosa vista de aquel puerto' ['delineating with the camera obscura the beautiful view of that port']. His verbal sketch was complemented by a pictorial one of its subject matter by an anonymous engraver, probably Gondra himself (figure 1.9). An optical instrument which since the Renaissance had been associated with landscape painting, the camera obscura was about the achievement of a dominant perspective and the illusions required to effect an 'imitation of nature'. Panoramists, for instance, used this optical device to attain topographical accuracy. By the time that travellers and illustrators like Fredrick de Waldeck and Catherwood included such items in the equipment they brought to Mexico, the camera obscura (and the camera lucida) had become synonymous with the depictive vocation of naturalists and ethnographers – and more generally with the notion of travel as discovery.[66] In the short piece on 'Campeche' for *El Mosaico*, Isidro Rafael Gondra casts himself in the guise of an amateur naturalist in this

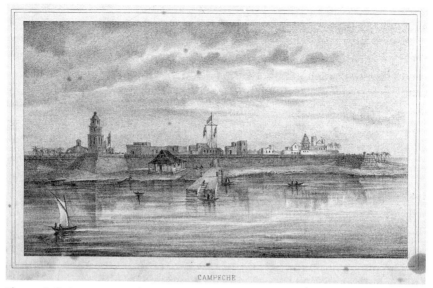

CAMPECHE

Figure 1.9 Anon., *Puerto de Campeche visto desde el mar, El Álbum Mexicano* (1849). CEHM-CONDUMEX.

popular tradition. Actively interested in pre-Hispanic archaeology and in particular the preservation of Maya sites such as Palenque, Gondra refers to his predicament as a writer faced with the task of transcribing the incommensurable. Caught between 'las ilusiones opticas' afforded by technology and the stratagems resorted to by draughtsmen, he abandons himself to ecstatic contemplation of his natural surroundings.[67] The eulogistic tone which dominates the piece suggests a resolution of apparently opposing impulses characteristic of Mexican *cuadros de costumbres*: namely, the invention of what Nathaniel Hawthorne termed the *neutral territory* of romance, 'where the actual and the imaginary may meet, and each imbue itself with the nature of the other', a hybrid construct aspiring towards realism and prone to romantic idealisation, especially as regards landscape imagery.[68]

The oldest collection of daguerreotypes corresponds to the period of U.S. invasion of 1846–8, suggesting another aspect of the new technology which proved a compelling analogue for *costumbrista* writers: namely, its function as a vehicle for the commemoration of historical episodes which helped to construe a national identity through a narrative of epic conflict. Graphic techniques were used to emulate the documentary role of the daguerreotype: a sumptuously illustrated history of the conflict with engravings of battlefields and portraits of military personnel was published in 1848, with similar engravings on a martial theme appearing in illustrated periodicals, which in addition carried uplifting verbal descriptions of the events.

The novel technique of photography was resorted to as a sign of modernity in Mexico, quite apart from the literary analogies suggested by its practical application. The founding editors of *El Daguerreotipo: Revista Enciclopédica y Universal* (1850), the French liberals Alfredo Bablot and René Masson, insisted on the link between the magazine's emblem and its innovative bicultural, sociological approach: 'presentará simultaneamente la imagen complexa de la sociedad universal considerada bajo sus distintos visos y matizadas formas, en todas sus faces y aspectos diferentes' ['it will present contemporaneously the complex portrait of world society under its varied guises and shaded forms, in all its many visages and different aspects'].[69] There is a consequential link between this literary appropriation of daguerreotypy in Mexico and the recycling of scientific paradigms by the *physiologie* genre in 1830s Paris.

Daguerreotypy was about achieving a scientific likeness – investing the transient with an identity that would endure, making the merely temporal historical. The perceived affinity between daguerreotypy and ethnography was undoubtedly one of the more interesting facets of an overdetermined metaphor. Guillermo Prieto, the foremost practitioner of the *costumbrista* genre, writing in 1842, could not resist making a topical analogy between the documentary objectives of his mock-ethnographic piece on Indian *fiestas* [festivals] and the recently introduced photographic medium: 'así como por daguerreotipo' ['thus as in a daguerreotype'], began his detailed description.[70] An extended analogy to a photographic album characterises his *costumbrista* submissions to *El Álbum Mexicano*. Prieto aimed to achieve truthful representations of authentic social types and customs, with a view to preserving their likeness for posterity (including himself in this gallery of historical curiosities): 'Yo pondré en lo sucesivo mi daguerreotipo al frente de otros entes originales, dignos que se conserven sus retratos en *El Álbum*' ['from now on I will place my daguerreotype at the head of other original subjects, worthy of having their portraits preserved in *The Album*'].[71] Prieto was the most accomplished and prolific of the numerous writers adopting the *costumbrista* mode. His persistent advocacy of the genre lent a uniquely reflexive dimension to his *cuadros*, making him a particularly revealing witness in any study of the interplay between *costumbrismo* and nation-building strategies in Mexico. Prieto emphasised the faceted historicity of *cuadros de costumbres*, hence his interest in daguerreotypy's documentary dimension as a source of comparisons. He regarded them as comprising a virtual archive of original traditions, collected by a 'maniático de las costumbres de antaño' ['obsessive aficionado of bygone customs'].[72] His frequent recourse to culinary analogies in his exploration of unmistakable cultural imprints indicates a further ramification of his use of physiognomic paradigms. Prieto draws interestingly on the use made of Lavaterian and Gallist motifs by treatises on national gastronomies, of which Brillat-Savarin's *La Physiologie du goût* [*The Physiology of Taste*] (1825) was the founding example. A Mexican translation appeared in 1842.[73] He casts himself as a devotee of 'el caldo nacional' ['the national stew'], the distinctively hybrid mix of cultural and social elements to which he returned 'con la pobre paleta de mis descripciones' ['with the poor palette of my descriptions'] during a writing career that spanned the century.[74]

Achieving a synoptic point of view was the Mexican *costumbrista* writer's problematic aspiration. Aerial surveys proved an enabling literary analogy, lending a scientific edge to romantic reveries on hilltops. In 1844 Benito Acosta had emulated in Morelia the Montgolfier brothers' own aeronautical achievement. His inspirational feat was commemorated in local paintings and engravings.[75] More spectacular attempts followed with the arrival of the entrepreneurial Frenchman Ernest Petén in 1854. Daumier's humorous depiction of Nadar armed with a camera surveying Paris from a balloon is a celebrated illustration of this pursuit of totalising perspective. The panoramic exhibitions in *México y sus alrededores: álbum por entregas* [*Mexico and its Surroundings: An Album in Instalments*] featured *La Alameda de México tomada en globo* [*The Alameda in Mexico City taken from a balloon*] and *El pueblo de Ixtacalco tomado en globo* [*The Village of Ixtacalco taken from a balloon*] with the balloon in question included conventionally in the depiction (figures 1.10 and 1.11).[76] The assumption of totalising perspectives is a marked trend in *costumbrista* sketches and illustrations of the period. The tension between the first-person testimony and the omniscient perspective of third-person narrative characterises Mexican *costumbrismo*'s play on the mimetic distinctions between a sketch and a photograph, a tension construed as the difference between the application of art and that of science, or individual sensibility and objective scrutiny. Aspiring to the clarity and finished contours of the high ground, Prieto lamented being sometimes thrust into the blinding *vortice* [vortex] or *mezcla* [mixture] of the crowd, in the teeming streets of the capital, by his 'musa pedestre' [pedestrian muse]: 'me agobia el espectáculo' ['the spectacle overwhelms me'].[77] Encounters with *el pueblo*, whose elemental physiognomy he was striving to distinguish and whose vernacular he was intent on transfusing, could, in practice, be all too close: 'No sé cómo salí con vida por observar costumbres: reducido a mi última potencia con un mar de cabezas erizado, mi derredor por codos interrumpido, mi vista por angelitos que cabalgaban en los autores de sus días y con un olor de antigüedad

Figure 1.10 Frontispiece of *México y sus alrededores* (1855–6). Private collection.

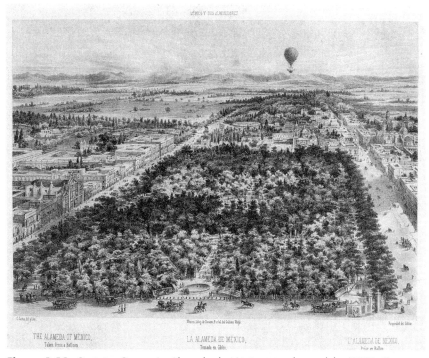

Figure 1.11 Casimiro Castro, *La Alameda de México tomada en globo* (1853–5). Private collection.

nacional, vi frente a frente la comitiva' ['I do not know how I got out alive from my observing customs: reduced to my lowest ebb craning over a sea of heads, my surroundings impeded by elbows, my view by little angels riding on their procreators and with a smell of national antiquity, I came face to face with the procession'].[78] On the other hand, in a separate piece, he extols the omniscience afforded by a bird's-eye view. The closest pictorial analogue in this descriptive passage seems to be, in terms of visual compass, Pietro Gualdi's panoramic vistas of Mexico City and its environs; and in terms of style and mood, romantic vistas in travel albums such as Karl Nebel's, which valued the startling irregularity of the terrain:[79]

Eso de ver una población desde una altura, hundidas en el fondo de una barranca las casas, sobresaliendo las torres, tendiéndose las plazas, serpeando tortuosas las calles, amontonándose las cúpulas de las iglesias, descendiendo como un raudal chozas y casitas … trepando otras habitaciones por la falda del monte, y humeando las cabañas en una quiebra salvaje: esto, la falta de vegetación, la sierra cenicienta de los montes donde hay minas, todo sorprende y mucho más a un mexicano.[80]

[Looking at a town from a great height, the houses buried in the bottom of a ravine, the protruding towers, the squares stretching before you, the snaking of the tortuous streets, the

mushrooming of church cupolas, the huts and small houses descending like a torrent...
other dwellings climbing up the side of the mountain, and the smoking cabins in a wild
crevice: all this, the lack of vegetation, the ashen mountain range where mines are found,
everything is startling especially to the eyes of a Mexican.]

Alternating between the figurative sensibility of the artist's palette and
the sociological acumen of daguerreotypy, Prieto despaired in his articles
of ever producing a faithful copy of the original subject matter of his
observations. 'Tiene una fisonomía propia e incapaz de confundirse' ['It
has its own unmistakable physiognomy'], he insisted, only to concede
defeat: 'La pluma no formará jamas de aquel espectáculo un cuadro
completo, y el lector siempre hallará lánguida y sin vida la copia de tan
poético, de tan animado original … ¡Ah si yo fuera pintor!' [The pen will
never be able to form a complete picture of that spectacle, and the readers
will always find the copy of such a poetic and lively original weak and
lifeless. If only I were a painter!].[81]

Travel Literature and the Picturesque

Prieto shared the widely held assumption that painting and graphic art
(engravings and lithography principally) had proved to be the media that
could most effectively capture and communicate an iconic likeness and
impress the widest possible audience. Writers he admired, like Scott and
Eugène Sue, frequently followed Lavater's own example by studying
extant simulacra rather than engaging in empirical investigations of their
own.[82] Lavater, for instance, had persuaded Henry Fuseli, an artist of
oneiric visions, to contribute illustrations for his bestselling
physiognomic treatise the *Fragmente*.[83] In spite of the fascination with
various kinds of reproductive devices and techniques, *costumbrista*
passages in Mexico not infrequently described and glossed an adjacent
lithograph or engraving. This practice may help to explain why references
to *cuadros* form such a widespread conceit in this particular
manifestation of the genre. The popular travel albums by European and
American artists and travellers (some of the more influential of whom
have previously been mentioned), certainly had a bearing on the
particular *costumbrista* iconography which emerged at a time when few
Mexican writers and artists had the leisure or financial incentives to
brave the perilous byways of their vast country.

There is a good deal of consensus as to the selection of social types
which merit depiction in foreign travellers' anecdotal ethnography and
Mexican periodicals' gallery of national icons. D. Revilla, for instance, in
a series of articles entitled 'Escenas de campo' ['Country Scenes'], cast
an ennobling gaze at different rural types and singled out the 'Herradero'

['Farrier'] in particular as exemplifying 'cierto tipo nacional de nuestros hombres de campo' ['specific national type of our rural men'] (figure 1.12).[84] Rural types had made an impression on foreign artists for their colourful and elaborate costume and their command of traditional equestrian skills. In the 1840 Spanish edition of Karl Nebel's *Viaje pintoresco y arqueológico sobre la parte más interesante de la República Mexicana* [*Picturesque and Archaeological Journey through the most Interesting Part of the Mexican Republic*], a work which was praised by Humboldt, 'Arrieros' were portrayed as romantic figures struggling to control unruly steeds. Claudio Linati before him had, in his celebrated *Trajes civiles, militares y religiosos de México* [*Civil, Military and Religious Costumes of Mexico*] (1828), inaugurated this tendency to personify the primitive nobility of the Mexican populace in mounted horsemen and their variegated working attire. The emphasis on differentiation in European travel albums did provide, paradoxically, a useful source of ethnic particulars for Mexican writers critical of the tendency amongst some of their compatriots to be in cultural matters 'satelites de los otros, sus parodías eternas' ['satellites of others, their eternal parodies'].[85] The objective for Prieto and other like-minded *costumbristas*, such as Manuel Payno, was to publicise an emblematic national character as immediately identifiable and unmistakable, as were

Figure 1.12 Anon., *Escenas de campo, Revista Científica y Literaria de Méjico* (1845). Biblioteca Nacional de Antropología e Historia.

the signs that betrayed a foreigner's provenance: 'con solo ver su postura se diría su nación' ['by only looking at their posture one could tell their nationality'].[86]

The selection and portrayal of properly autochthonous subjects followed a certain aesthetic rationale. The dominant perspective or preferred angle of presentation for the artist and the itinerant *cronista* corresponded to influential notions of the picturesque or *pintoresco*. The earliest eighteenth-century interpretations tended to privilege landscape views which resembled the ideal compositions of Claude Lorrain and Salvator Rosa. In such compositions nature seemed to mimic the Platonic forms of high art. Romantic reworkings of what some had called a system of viewing nature characterised the subject matter in ways which liberated figurative art from the restrictions of classicism. Manifestations of vernacular culture fractured the consensus of what merited artistic representation. The picturesque as opposed to the finished symmetries of the ideal pertained to that which was strikingly anomalous and idiosyncratic. According to William Hazlitt, the picturesque is that which stands out and catches the attention by some striking peculiarity: 'whatever stands out from a given line, and as it were projects upon the eyes, is picturesque'.[87] That an interesting point of vision did not necessarily mean a beautiful one was an essential aspect of this notion.[88] This elevation of irregular forms to the aesthetic realm certainly had liberating consequences for Mexican patriots in the post-colonial era seeking to dignify subject matter that did not accord with any Eurocentric canon of sublimity and beauty. At a time when the challenge was to disprove the notion of nascent republics as merely derivative – bad copies of an unimpeachable original – the application of the concept of the picturesque had resulted in a body of images which helped to visualise the specificities of this hybrid New World.

The notion of the picturesque encouraged the contemplation of eccentricity – in its cultural as well as natural manifestations, contemplation of what Hazlitt did not hesitate to qualify as absorbing 'excrescences' or 'grotesques', which he likened to the hybrid monsters of mythology – satyrs and centaurs.[89] Subjects that had hitherto been considered unworthy of aesthetic treatment became not only visible but particularised and the legitimate substance of literary commentary. A syncretic culture such as Mexico's offered a startlingly various spectacle of irregularities for romantic consumption. It is not surprising that Addison's journalism should have been valued in Mexico as precursor of *costumbrismo*. For his levelling gaze in *The Spectator* seemed to mark a comparable shift of focus to that effected in the arts by the notion of the picturesque.[90]

Romantic essays and figurative art, which were captivated by asymmetry of features whether in landscape, artefacts or human beings, which celebrated the charm of contrasts especially in regard to differences of customs (and more especially costumes) and other manifestations of temporal disjunction in social and cultural development, also carried in their repudiation of a classical aesthetic a criticism of an overcivilised society. This European appetite for the picturesque was often informed by a nostalgia for a Rousseauesque primitivism which expeditionary literature partially assuaged, with its colourful visions of peripheral latitudes. It is largely due to Humboldt's expeditions and the bestselling publications which they generated that the New World on the cusp of insurgency became synonymous with the requisites of the picturesque. His magisterial study of the Americas not only provided scientific data in a compelling personal narrative, but exotic images that were seized upon by the popular press. Of particular interest in relation to the *costumbrista* movement in Mexico is the manner in which Humboldt posed the difficulty intrinsic to the naturalist's project of scientific description.[91] The terms in which he defined the problem of observation, interpretation and transcription, and its possible solution, are closely echoed by Mexican writers such as Prieto, engaged, although with far more modest means, on a similarly ambitious descriptive project.

According to Humboldt, language could not compete with the visual arts: 'Notwithstanding all the richness and adaptability of our language, to attempt to designate in words, that which, in fact, appertains only to the imitative art of the painter, is always fraught with difficulty'.[92] To remedy the insufficiency of language in this field, in *Cosmos* he called on European artists to undertake recording expeditions. Travel writing in Germany was particularly receptive to Lavaterian physiognomic theories in relation to the manifestation of national character. In his *Personal Narrative*, Humboldt praised 'the delineation of the physiognomy of natural scenery' by the widely travelled German painter Johann Moritz Rugendas, whose illustrated travel albums seemed to bear out Lavater's conviction that the physiognomist and the painter were closely related in their objectives.[93] Rugendas, who created an impressive pictorial record of his travels in South America, resided in Mexico between 1831 and 1834. He produced up to 1,600 sketches, views of majestic plateaux, volcanoes and harbours and of folkloric scenes in the capital and the provinces, which would form the basis of the colour illustrations he contributed to Carl Christian Sartorius' *México: paisajes y bosquejos populares* [*Mexico: Landscapes and Popular Sketches*] (1855), and which he would later publish separately in English as *Mexico and the*

Mexicans (1859). The interdependence of a *costumbrista* text and an actual or subsumed illustration in Mexican periodicals, the actualisation of the compound role of physiognomist-painter envisaged by Lavater, is in a sense akin to the solution advocated by the Romantic naturalist.

The *costumbrista* writer in Mexico adopted the mantle of the naturalist and the physiognomist: to particularise social phenomena (or in typical pictorial terms 'matizar aquel cuadro' ['clarify that picture']) and to personify national ideals whilst formulating a descriptive system to account for them. The *costumbrista* work of summation, which regarded itself and was, in effect, a collective effort, shared the Humboldtian Romantic notion of the unity of art and nature, a notion which the *Picturesque Atlas* had exemplified influentially in its attempt to systematise the study of pre-Columbian artefacts, the 'physiognomy' of fauna and flora and the 'configuration of the ground'.[94] The *costumbrista* bent of most Mexican miscellanies of the period bears out a dominant preoccupation with the assemblage of an unprecedented 'Picturesque Atlas' of the autochthonous republic. It could be argued that *costumbrismo* was as much about genuine scrutiny of the post-colonial terrain as it was about the appropriation of the genres and models that had been employed by Europeans to characterise the same subject matter.

The growing number of guides, illustrated travel albums and memoirs on Mexico that were being published in Europe and America, by foreign artists and diplomats such as Karl Nebel, Fredrick de Waldeck, John Phillips and Pietro Gualdi, and which had gained a wider currency in Mexico through reproductions and local editions, as well as through the circulation of the originals and the presence of the artists themselves, prompted a creative riposte from Mexican artists, writers and publishers intent on emancipatory self-definition. Undoubtedly, Pietro Gualdi's architectural vistas with genre details contributed disproportionately to the prominence that such elements acquired in the development of nationalist iconography during this period (figure 1.13); although it could also be argued that his work inserted itself seamlessly in an already existing pictorial tradition in Mexico, dating back to the seventeenth century, which employed topographical vistas of Mexico City as theatrical allegories of viceregal power.[95] In a not dissimilar vein panoramic vistas of the republican capital tended to idealise the degree of symmetry and order of its layout precisely during the period in which its citizens were subject to the effects and daily spectacle of crisis and degradation. Gualdi's collection of urban scenes *Monumentos de Méjico*, first published in Mexico City by Massé y Decaen in 1839–41, proved so popular that a revised second edition was published in 1841–2. The depiction of the administrative heart of the republic seen from rooftops or

Figure 1.13 Pietro Gualdi, *Plaza de Sto. Domingo y Aduana* (1841). BNM.

bell towers served to reinforce an image of orderly government during the calamitous dictatorship of General Santa Anna, a period which the saw the occupation of those same consecrated spaces by the victorious U.S. army. Gualdi actively collaborated (sometimes working on the designs with Nebel) with the magazines which disseminated *costumbrista* trends, although his illustrations for *El Almacen Universal*, *La Ilustración Mexicana* and *El Mosaico Mexicano* were not always attributed. His published lithographs popularised the secular as well as religious sites of nationalist identification (figure 1.14).[96] His presentation of such iconic subject matter provided an intelligible visual precedent for those Mexican *costumbrista* writers, such as Prieto, intent on a composite view made up of indexical fragments. The heightened interest in the symbolic as well as practical utility of cartography and topography is attested to by the lithographs in *La Ilustración Mexicana* and *El Álbum Mexicano*, culminating in sumptuously produced albums such as Casimiro Castro and Juan Campillo's panoramic *México y sus alrededores: colección de vistas, trajes y monumentos* [*Mexico and Its Environs: A Collection of Views, Costumes and Monuments*] (1855–6). Such all-embracing representational works shared the desire expressed in countless editorials to 'nacionalizar' the instruments of perception, representation and production as much as the subject matter depicted and reproduced in the Mexican popular press.

Figure 1.14 Pietro Gualdi, *Santuario de N.S. de Guadalupe* (1841). BNM.

Los mexicanos pintados por sí mismos

The seminal *costumbrista* compilation of *Los mexicanos pintados por sí mismos* [*The Mexicans Painted by Themselves*] (1853–5) is polemical in intent (figure 1.15). Clearly influenced by the example of *Les Français peints par eux-mêmes* [*The French Painted by Themselves*] (1840–2) and *Los españoles pintados por sí mismos* [*The Spanish Painted by Themselves*] (1850), its collection of articles and engravings on recurrent types and trades from urban and rural contexts strikes a proprietorial tone which all of its numerous contributors share. Although there is a good deal of satire in its sundry depictions, *Los mexicanos pintados por sí mismos* was conceived as a riposte to the perceived travesties of 'los ilustrados hijos de Europa que ridiculizan nuestras costumbres' ['the cultivated children of Europe who ridicule our customs'].[97] Although this project does appear as the culmination of a defensive vein which is patent throughout the period's literary discourse, its concern to reclaim local culture from the perceived condescension of foreign commentaries is not blind to the distorting lens of patriotic ambition.[98] The humour of many of the sketches is generated by the spectacle of the affectations adopted by Mexicans seeking to disguise their parochial cultural origins. Guillermo Prieto had, in *El Siglo XIX*, poked fun at those of his countrymen who objected to the often unflattering light in which the *costumbrista* writer cast contemporary society. He detected a strain of *quijotismo* [the Quixotic] delusions of grandeur that 'nos hacen creer más de lo que somos, y siempre queremos ser otra cosa, queremos llamarnos en *ini* o en *oult*, *thon*, en fin, en otro idioma que no sea el

Figure 1.15 Frontispiece, *Los mexicanos pintados por sí mismos* (1853–5) (in colour). CEHM-CONDUMEX.

nuestro, y nos empiezan a hacer insufrible desde el nombre que recibimos en la pila bautismal' ['makes us pretend to be more than what we are, and we always desire to be something else, we want names with 'ini' or 'oult', 'thon', in short in any language other than our own, and has begun to make insufferable even the name we received at the baptismal font'].[99] In this light, the ostentation of Mexicanisms, which is a defining trait of so many *cuadros de costumbres*, was clearly provocative. It is important for a proper qualification of Mexican *costumbrismo* to recognise the extent to which its unquestionable dedication to national aggrandisement was tempered by instructions against self-delusion and mystification. The exaltation of certain editorials should not be taken as proof of a tendency to mythologise Mexico's 'conjunto indescriptible' ['indescribable whole']. The pedagogically minded editors of *El Gabinete de Lectura* [*The Reading Cabinet*] declared that their disseminatory activities should be regarded as 'vindicando ante el mundo nuestra nacionalidad mil veces deprimida' ['defending before the whole world our nationality maligned countless times'].[100] Its descriptive content would aid 'en la reconstrucción del edificio social' ['in the reconstruction of the social edifice']. Similarly, the editors of *El Mosaico Mexicano* launched the second collected volume intent on making it a showcase of Mexican character: 'el nacionalizarlo sera el principal objeto de nuestras comunes tareas' ['nationalising it will be the main objective of our collective efforts'].[101] *Costumbrista* articles and illustrations played a central role in the nation-building strategy of the cultural press; but their iconography was neither formally naïve nor narrowly propagandistic but inflected with a developed critical awareness.

The Magic Lantern

In search of the 'vínculo social' ['social bond'] that seemed to elude governments and legislators, Prieto explored in his *cuadros* the labyrinthine inner city, looking for hidden connections among the inhabitants of the streets.[102] He tried to capture the linguistic verve of the untutored, celebrating the invention of the popular imagination expressed through the neologisms of colloquial speech. He defended the impropriety of fraternising with 'el vulgo' ['the great unwashed'] ('quien se desdeña entonces de ser popular' ['who would disdain to be popular']), convinced that 'las calles de México en su transformación, me ofrecen unas paginas materiales, pudieran ... servir de termometro de nuestros atrasos o adelantos, de nuestras pasiones, de nuestros caracteres' ['the streets of Mexico City in their transformations yield material pages, which could serve as a barometer of our backwardness or our advances, of our passions, of our character'].[103] Rather than a Baudelairean *flâneur*, Prieto cast himself in the more modest, proletarian guise of an itinerant lanternist armed with a rudimentary projector and a fund of curious images. Such a figure inhabited the ambiguous frontier between rural, oral culture and encroaching urban modernity, straddling the parochial and the urbane in a manner which resonated with the mediatory vocation of the *costumbrista* writer.[104] In a humorous sketch which he devoted to 'El pulquero' ['The Pulque Vendor'],[105] a truly aboriginal plebeian figure, Hilarión Frías y Soto invited his readers to scrutinise the familiar subject in an evocation of a lantern show: 'Sigámoslo mirando, pues no es persona capaz de incomodarse porque le hemos colocado tras el lente de nuestra linterna mágica. Adelante.' ['Let us continue to view him, as he is not the kind of person to object to being placed under the lens of our magic lantern. Proceed.'] (figure 1.16).[106] In an article for the *Museo Popular*, Prieto described a typical excursion into the crowded thoroughfares of the capital in search of revealing impressions. He compared the application of the *costumbrista* writer's perception to the effect of light in a magic lantern, delineating the particular contours of vistas, figures and objects whose latent identity would have otherwise remained undifferentiated: 'empolvado y lleno de fatiga, vuelvo del paseo: ha faltado su luz a la linterna mágica que daba vueltas a mi vista' ['covered in dust and exhausted, I return from my walk: the light was missing from the magic lantern that was revolving before my eyes'].[107]

The pre-cinematic slide projector known as the magic lantern provided a suggestive conceit which *costumbrista* writers revisited throughout the century (José Cuellar's series of *costumbrista* novels *La Linterna Mágica* [1889–92] paid homage to this enduring trend).[108] A device which, in its long history, was associated with magic trickery and pedagogy had proved itself an excellent publicising medium. Since the French Revolution lantern shows had provided instructive spectacle or illusionistic sensation (phantasmagoria effects), illustrating scientific lectures, popular storytelling and moral catechisms through visual parables. They had also been turned into vehicles of ideological propaganda and political satire. The painted slides could magnify detail, project amusing fantasies or mordant cartoons, or approximate the magnitude of the panorama in views of landscapes and genre scenes. The first half of the nineteenth century saw the magic lantern's popularity confirmed with the ubiquity of its representation in specialist publications (manuals and educational materials specially designed for the medium) and the popular press. The figure of the itinerant lanternist also had folkloric associations. He was linked to a specific popular trade with frequently rural ramifications, in which artisans and their families

Figure 1.16 Hesiquio Iriarte, *El pulquero*, from *Los mexicanos pintados por sí mismos* (1853–5). CEHM-CONDUMEX.

(conventionally depicted wearing the costume of Savoy) travelled the countryside with a magic lantern strapped to their back. The wandering lanternist became synonymous with a popular form of entertainment with strong communal appeal. These figures could be conflated with the romantically picturesque tribe of nomads comprised by gypsies, minstrels, wandering Jews and stateless bards. Their apparent rootlessness did not diminish their appeal as purveyors of collective images to be imparted at tribal gatherings. The link between the lantern show and the potential for narration, that is to say, for effective transmission and identification, offered a model for Mexican writers seeking a truly popular literary vehicle. Significantly, the frontispiece of *Los mexicanos pintados por sí mismos* (shown in figure 1.15) borrows elements of the established iconography of the magic lantern. Against a rural backdrop, a man on a ladder is shown stretching the sheet that often served as a screen at lantern shows, whilst a group of archetypal figures congregate below. A man standing on the left points with outstretched arm to the central exhibit – the *mestizo* figure of a *china* who alone of those present looks directly at the viewer.[109]

The transformation of the lanternist's trade into a literary metaphor is clearly illustrated by the frontispiece of the satiric 'physiological' compendium *Le Diable à Paris: Paris et les Parisiens* [*The Devil in Paris: Paris and the Parisians*] of 1845, in which the Devil appears in fashionable attire holding a magic lantern whilst straddling a topographical map of the French capital.[110] The young Juan Díaz Covarrubias, a writer who expressed his nationalism through *costumbrista* descriptions, entitled his acerbic, fictional study of contemporary mores *El diablo en México* [*The Devil in Mexico*] (published posthumously in 1860). This explicit borrowing confirms a trend, which although less obvious, is no less evident in older Mexican *costumbrista* writers, namely, a tendency to extract pictorial paradigms from French *feuilleton* publications rooted in the *physiologie* genre. Prieto himself paid tribute to the impact which Eugène Sue's populist and highly pictorial brand of *louche* or *lépero* realism in *Les Mystères de Paris* (1842–3) had on his generation of liberals (José Tomás de Cuetler's *Los misterios de San Cosme* is only one of the numerous progeny engendered in Mexico). Equally resonant was Victor Hugo's celebrated decipherment of the architectural façade in *Notre-Dame de Paris* (1831), which invested the scenic with a contemporary historical resonance. It suggested, to an admiring Guillermo Prieto, that in the historical accretions of topography and architecture the symbolic unity of subject and context could be deciphered: 'la fisonomía de la ciudad es como la de su población' ['the physiognomy of the city is like that of its inhabitants'], he writes in the revealingly titled 'Ojeada al centro de México' ['A Glance at the Centre of Mexico'] of 1842.

Costumbrista Icons

In a lengthy article in the *Revista Científica y Literaria de Méjico* of 1845, in which Prieto defended the need for a nation-conscious literature, *cuadros de costumbres* were praised for their exemplary nation-building potential. Prieto underlined his main concern: the absence of cultural homogeneity. In his appraisal, racial miscegenation had not brought about social integration or a sense of national identification. He decried the essential ambivalence of Mexico's historical legacy: 'siendo los que hoy nos llamamos mexicanos una raza anómala e intermedia entre el español y el indio, una especie de vínculo insuficiente y espurio entre dos naciones, sin nada de común' ['given that those who today call ourselves Mexican are an anomalous race half way between the Spaniard and the Indian, a kind of inadequate and spurious link between two nations, with nothing in common'].[111] It was his view (and that of his generation of liberal reformers and cultural activists) that the composite identity of a prospective *mestizo* nation should be delineated and normalised. *Cuadros de costumbres* would favour particular embodiments of this ancestral hybridity – figures which were familiar, festive and seductive: effective emblems of an emerging autochthony. It is perhaps not surprising that in a country where *guadalupanismo* (the worship of the Virgin of Guadalupe, patroness of Mexico) was undiminished, this evocation of *mestizo* cultural matrices should have assumed largely feminine attributes. Descriptions, engravings and lithographs of the *china poblana* (a typical working-class *mestizo* woman from Puebla known for her colourful attire), or simple proletarian *china*, tend to outnumber those of other regional muses such as the *jarocha* [a woman from Veracruz] (figure 1.17). Similarly, *la chiera* behind her garlanded drink stall was a favourite street dweller in *costumbrista* typologies: 'tipo esencialmente mexicano' ['an essentially Mexican type'] – the Attic muse of poetasters (figure 1.18).[112] These captivating figures inhabited public spaces, squares or markets, exemplifying in the distinctivess of their costume, the vivacity of their colloquialisms, the ethnicity of their physiognomy, and in the particular rituals of their trades, an unproblematic cultural dualism. The *china*, 'esa linda y fresca criatura salida del pueblo' ['that lovely and fresh creature of the common people'], became the muse of those intent on championing a Mexican vernacular: she was untutored but naturally harmonious, with clear rural lineage and yet adapted to the city. A saucy, native beauty cleansed of the signs of savagery or backwardness of that which was

Figure 1.17 Hesiquio Iriarte, *La china*, from *Los mexicanos pintados por sí mismos* (1853–5). CEHM-CONDUMEX.

Figure 1.18 Hesiquio Iriarte, *La chiera*, from *Los mexicanos pintados por sí mismos* (1853–5). CEHM-CONDUMEX.

condemned for deviating from the European standard. Manuel Payno praised her culinary skills, sartorial finesse, musical knowledge and dancing prowess: 'no piensa más que ostentar ese traje nacional tan elegante, tan peculiar de México, tan lleno de gracia y de sal' ['she is only intent on showing off that truly elegant national costume, so unique to Mexico, so full of grace and sparkle'].[113] José María Rivera declared her 'mi tipo nacional y predilecto' ['my favourite national type']: 'la nata y la espuma de la gente de bronce, la perla de los barrios, el alma de los fandangos, la gloria y ambición de la gente de *sarape y monte-cristo* ... la *china* es la legítima y hermosa hija de México ... tan linda como su cielo azul; tan fresca como sus jardines floridos' ['the paragon of bronze-skinned people, the pearl of working-class neighbourhoods, the soul of the fandango dance, the glory and ideal of all wearers of ponchos ... the *china* is the legitimate and beautiful daughter of Mexico ... as lovely as its blue sky, as fresh as its flowering gardens'].[114] In Rivera's opinion, her sincerity and transparency – 'porque la *china* es como Dios la hizo' ['because the *china* is as God made her'] – provided a visible corrective to the artifice of imported European fashions: 'por un lado tenemos a la naturaleza en todo su esplendor y por otro el arte con sus pinturas, sus oropeles' ['on the one hand we have nature in all its splendour, on the other artifice with its paints, glitz and glitter'].[115] With its interest in mediating contemporary *mestizo* elements, literary *costumbrismo* foreshadowed an ideological ascendancy that was to dominate the second half of the century, with the consolidation of Liberal power.

In *costumbrista* writing the *china poblana* (akin to the Hispanic *maja* or *manola* [working-class Castillian beauty]) embodied the virtues of native blood lines. Writers seized on her iconographic celebrity, her association with patriotic rituals both in regard to costume and cuisine. The colours of the republic's flag and that of the founding insurgent army (or *Ejército Trigarante*)[116] – green, white and red – were echoed in her typical attire and in the traditional speciality of *chile en nogada* [stuffed capiscum in a nut-based sauce] for which Pueblan cooks were known. In this conquest of representative subject matter, Prieto and Manuel Payno admired and hoped to emulate in their verbal *bosquejos* [sketches] the work of a local artist from Puebla, José Agustín Arrieta (1803–1874). They championed his still lifes and genre scenes for their regional detail, and genuine popular flavour. Writing in 1843, Payno admired the consummate physiognomic portrait of Arrieta's *China poblana*: the figure is represented in a homely setting but in festive mood. Wearing patriotic colours she smiles invitingly, carrying an appetising platter with an equally patriotic garnish.[117] Prieto compared Arrieta's general *costumbrista* approach to that of Larra, Mesonero Romanos, and Addison. He discerned a similar epigrammatic quality in

Arrieta's canvases: 'que hace reir … con una satira ingeniosa' ['that incites laughter … through its ingenious satire'].[118] In his fondness for pictorial paradigms, Prieto had had occasion to lament that he could not resort to a local Goya to capture the vivacity and variety of the populace and its rituals. Arrieta's reputation rests on his prolific output of *cuadros de comedor* [dining-room pictures], a variation of baroque still lifes or *bodegones*, in which domesticity is itemised and prosaic utensils and foodstuffs are paid solemn tribute. Prieto was particularly taken with a variation on the theme which Arrieta entitled *Mesas revueltas* [*Disorderly Tables*]. These canvases would feature various objects of foreign as well as local manufacture, which vied for space on a table (figure 1.19). Prieto praised the artist's prescience in assembling such an eloquent allegory of the confusion of ideas, values and classes that characterised Mexican society: 'en que está reproducida en la clase media la lucha de costumbres, el pichel de sajonia y el jarro de pico agudo, el plato poblano de pajarito y la azucarera parisiense … una auténtica lucha de costumbres' ['which portrays the struggle of mores in the middle class, the Saxony jug and the traditional terracotta pitcher, the ceramic plate with bird motif from Puebla and the Parisian sugar bowl … a genuine battle of customs'].[119] Prieto frequently exploited the allegorical or scenarist potential of such still-life compositions in his own *costumbrista* articles, in which the contents of 'una mesa revuelta y desordenada' ['a jumbled and disorderly table'] provided an evocative list of disparate objects with hidden affinities.[120]

Figure 1.19 José Agustín Arrieta, *Cuadro de comedor* (n.d.). Private collection.

Prieto insisted that if an intellectual reform were to be effected then *cuadros de costumbres* would play an orientating role precisely as instructive allegories: 'aunque no sea más que poniendo a los ojos del vulgo bajo el velo risueño de la alegoría … este cuadro espantoso de confusión y desconcierto que hoy presentamos' ['although it may only be by putting before the gaze of the ordinary public, behind the enchanting veil of allegory, this terrible picture of confusion and doubt that we now present'].[121] The notion that *costumbrista* articles and illustrations could function as allegorical parables is a revealing one, pointing to the moralising dimension which often informed their social focus and the extent to which detailed observation often had symbolic rather than empirical ends.

Archaeological discoveries and expeditionary literature provided Guillermo Prieto with a final telling analogy for the imagistic strategies adopted by the *costumbrista* in his role as *coaginator* of cultural dichotomies. He suggested that *cuadros de costumbres* could eventually function like symbolic accretions of a lost world, to be decoded by generations to come. These apparently ephemeral journalistic sketches might in time acquire the evocative solemnity of antiquity.[122] Prieto aspires to a hieratic monumentality for the typologies and archetypal landscapes of the *costumbrista* scenario: 'cuando el transcurso de los años les comunique el prestigio que tiene lo pasado y se consideren con la curiosidad que una medalla deforme, o el idolillo de tosco barro, o como el jeroglífico medio borrado de una ruina' ['when the passage of time confers on them the status of antiquity, and they are contemplated with the same curiosity inspired by a damaged medal, a primitive clay idol, or a half-erased hieroglyph on a ruin'].[123] The pathos sometimes conveyed by this pursuit both of differentiation and permanent self-definition is suggested by the strangely spectral still lifes that José Agustín Arrieta, the *costumbristas' costumbrista*, began to paint in the 1850s – years of deepening national crisis. Absorbed by *trompe-l'œil* effects of reflecting and transparent surfaces, his works lost their interest in rendering the corporeal vivacity of those ethnic particulars praised and emulated by *costumbrista* writers. Variously shaped objects of coloured glass were positioned against a mirror, often in candlelight, and Arrieta studied the optical distortions and quasi-phantasmagoric effects of multiplying reflections and complicated perspectives (figure 1.20). The allegorical strain which contemporaries identified in Arrieta's still lifes reminds us that, however humble a genre, the *bodegón* emerged out of a seventeenth-century tradition of 'Desengaño del mundo' ['Disillusionment with the world'], where admonitory images exposed the illusory and fallacious nature of worldly achievements.[124] Images of promiscuous disorder which prefigured Arrieta's 'mesas revueltas' spoke of human *vanitas* and the perishability of all things. And yet the prevalence in subsequent nationalist discourse of *costumbrista* iconography and its descriptive paradigms, a trend which reaches into the twentieth century, suggests that 'lo fugitivo permanece' ['the ephemeral persists'].

Figure 1.20 José Agustín Arrieta, Mesa Revuelta (1857). Private collection.

Notes

1. See C. Monsiváis, 'Prologue', in J.B. Morales, *El Gallo Pitagórico* (Mexico City, 1845; Guanajuato, Mex., 1987), xxii.
2. See e.g. S. O'Reilly et al. (eds), 'Introducción', *Registro Yucateco*, 1 (1845), 3–8 (4).
3. For a satirical treatment of writers' purported neutrality, see Morales, *El Gallo Pitagórico*, 85–6. On the politicisation of the cultural press, see 'Bibliografía: América poética', *El Álbum Mexicano*, 1 (1849), 614–15 (615), and I. Cumplido (ed.), 'Introducción', *La Ilustración Mexicana*, 4 (1854), 1.
4. J.J. Gómez de la Cortina, 'Prólogo', *Revista Mexicana*, 1 (1835), 3–9 (6).
5. There was some scepticism voiced about the real educational value of these encyclopaedic magazines; see J.J. Gómez de la Cortina, 'Necesidad de la critica en las ciencias', *Revista Mexicana*, 1 (1835), 21–3 (21). Questions were also raised about the assumed social benefits of the proliferation of newspapers and magazines; see F. Orozco y Berra, 'Influencia de los periódicos en México', *La Ilustración Mexicana*, 3 (1852), 35–7 (35).
6. On the effects on publishing of civil war and conflict with the U.S.A., see M. Payno and G. Prieto (eds), 'Conclusión', *Revista Científica y Literaria de Méjico*, 2 (1846), 380. On official patronage and censorship, see I. Cumplido, 'A nuestros lectores', *El Mosaico Mexicano*, 2 (1837), 477–8 (477).
7. On the lack of public libraries and the cost of periodicals and pamphlets, see Mme Calderón de la Barca, *Life in Mexico: During a Residence of Two Years in the Country (1839–1841)* (London, 1987), 212–13.
8. On the role of mid-century magazines and the dissemination of scientific knowledge, see E. Trabulse, *José María Velasco: un paisaje de la ciencia en México* (Toluca, Mex., 1992), 52, 61. On the need for popular education, see 'Catecismos y manuales', *El Mosaico Mexicano*, 4 (1840), 169–73 (173). See also A. Staples, 'La lectura y los lectores en los primeros años de vida independiente', in M.T. Bermúdez, P. Gonzalbo, D. Tanck de Estrada et al., *Historia de la lectura en México*, 2nd edn (Mexico City, 1997), 94–126 (100).
9. See the introduction of the populist and philanthropic *El Gabinete de Lectura: periódico literario, ... en particular de la República Mexicana*, 1 (1845), 1–2: 'Por los precios de suscricion [sic] se notará que esta empresa no es de mera especulacion pecuniaria' ['The price of subscription alone indicates that this is not principally a profit-making enterprise'].
10. On the predicament of the writer in search of a readership, see M. Payno, 'Prologue', in F. Calderón, *Obras poéticas de Fernando Calderón*, ed. I. Cumplido (Mexico City, 1844), xiii. For an indication of the kind of readership a successful periodical could hope to have outside the capital, see 'Curiosa relacion … de todos los que se han publicado en Mérida, desde que se estableció la libertad de prensa', *Registro Yucateco*, 1 (1845), 233–7 (235). Subscription was the main source of funding: the top publication in this survey boasted 300 subscribers, while the most popular newspaper had 350.
11. C. Georgel, 'The Museum as Metaphor in Nineteenth Century France', in I. Rogoff and D.J. Sherman (eds), *Museum Culture: Histories, Discourses, Spectacles* (Minneapolis, 1994), 113–21 (113).

12. See I. Cumplido (ed.), 'Introducción', *El Museo Mexicano*, 1 (1843), n.p.n.
13. See I.R. Gondra (ed.), 'Introducción', *El Mosaico Mexicano*, 1 (1836), 3–4: 'sin otro designio que el de formar una coleccion curiosa e instructiva para el uso privado ... los nuevos descubrimientos en las artes y en las ciencias, los sucesos históricos más sorprendentes, los fenómenos naturales ... las descripciones pintorescas de los lugares más célebres del globo, viages, biografías ... poesías puramente mexicanas, y todo género de amenidades formaran el tegido de esta bella coleccion' ['with no other design than to form a curious and instructive collection for private use ... the new discoveries in the arts and sciences, the most surprising historical events, natural phenomena, ... picturesque descriptions of the most celebrated places in the world, travel, biographies, ... entirely Mexican poems, and every kind of amusement will form the fabric of this attractive collection'].
14. Georgel, 'The Museum as Metaphor', 115–16.
15. 'Literatura del siglo diez y nueve', *El Ateneo Mexicano*, 1 (1844), 161–3 (162). Insecurity as to the future of Mexican sovereignty was widespread; see J.J. Pesado (ed.), *Poesías de Manuel Carpio* (Mexico City, 1849), i–viii (i–ii): 'Si está escrito que México, tal como es hoy, deje de existir ...' ['If it is written that the Mexico of today will cease to exist ...'].
16. Originally published in a series of articles for *La Ilustración Mexicana* (1851–3), reproduced in F. Zarco, *Castillos en el aire y otros textos mordaces* (Tlahuapan, Pue., 1984), 73.
17. For a discussion of contemporary ideas about the constitution as a central unifying agent, see R.N. Sinkin, *The Mexican Reform, 1855–1876: A Study in Liberal Nation-building* (Austin, 1979), 9.
18. See J.M. Lafragua, 'Caracter y objeto de la literatura' (first published in *El Ateneo Mexicano*, 1 [1844], 12–13), in J. Rueda de la Serna (ed.), *La misión del escritor: ensayos mexicanos del siglo XIX* (Mexico City, 1996), 69–77.
19. On the need to encourage patriotism, see 'La patria', *El Liceo Mexicano*, 2 (1844), 231.
20. G. Prieto, 'Ojeada a varios lugares de la república: un paseo a Cuernavaca', *Revista Científica y Literaria de Méjico*, 1 (1845), 85–8 (88).
21. Zarco, *Castillos en el aire*, 17.
22. G. Prieto, *Memorias de mis tiempos* (Paris/Mexico City, 1906; Mexico City, 1985), 137.
23. G. Prieto, 'Primer día de año nuevo', *El Museo Popular*, 15 January 1840, 18–19.
24. On the character of Scott's observational realism and its relation to *genre* painting, see R. Humphrey, *Walter Scott: Waverley* (Cambridge, 1993), 103–5.
25. G. Prieto, 'Literatura nacional: cuadros de costumbres', *Revista Científica y Literaria de Méjico*, 1 (1845), 27–9 (29).
26. On the influence of French academic theory on romantic landscape painters, see H. Honour, *Romanticism* (London, 1981; repr. 1991), 63–4.
27. For the subject matter and uses of *biombos*, see E. Umberger, 'The *Monarchía Indiana* in Seventeenth-Century New Spain', in D. Fane (ed.), *Converging Cultures: Art and Identity in Spanish America* (New York, 1996), 46–58; J.J. Klor de Alva, 'Mestizaje from New Spain to Aztlán: On the Control and Classification of Collective Identities', in I. Katzew (ed.), *New World Orders: Casta Painting and Colonial Latin America* (New York, 1996), 58–71.

28. Fanny Calderón de la Barca, the widely published memoirist of Scottish ancestry, was the wife of the influential and conservative-minded Spanish ambassador to Mexico.

29. G. Prieto, 'Corpus. Año de 1842', *Obras Completas*, ed. B. Rosen Jélomer (Mexico City, 1993), II: 111–16 (113).

30. A. von Humboldt, *Essai politique sur le royaume de la Nouvelle-Espagne* (Paris, 1808), *Atlas géographique et physique du royaume de la Nouvelle Espagne* (Paris, 1811), and *Vues de cordillères et monuments des peuples indigenes de l'Amérique* (Paris, 1810) (also known as *Atlas pittoresque du voyage*), which contains sixty-nine engravings, forty-two of which are devoted to Mexican subjects; J.L. Stephens, *Incidents of Travel in Central America, Chiapas and Yucatán* (New York, 1841) and *Incidents of Travel in Yucatán* (New York, 1843); W.H. Prescott, *History of the Conquest of Mexico* (New York, 1843) and *Historia de la conquista de México*, tr. V. García Torres (Mexico City, 1844–46); F. Catherwood, *Views of Ancient Monuments in Central America, Chiapas and Yucatán* (London, 1844).

31. See C.E. Manthorne, *Tropical Renaissance: North American Artists exploring Latin America, 1839–1879* (Washington/London, 1989), 94–5.

32. Lloyd Stephens's *Incidents of Travel in Yucatán* received approving reviews; see F. Diez de Bonilla, 'Arqueologia Mexicana', *El Liceo Mexicano*, 1 (1844), 145. On the interest in the re-evaluation of pre-Hispanic literature which accompanies efforts to salvage the archaeological heritage, see J.M. Tornel, 'Noticias sobre las poesias aztecas', *El Mosaico Mexicano*, 5 (1841), 143–4.

33. See e.g. I.R. Gondra, 'Antigüedades mexicanas', illustrated with an engraving of 'Vista y altura de la fortificacion de Mitlan [in Oaxaca]', and 'Antigüedades mexicanas: Estracto del viaje ...', with a view of the 'palace', *El Mosaico Mexicano*, 2 (1837), 281–4 and 330–4, respectively.

34. On the use of republican emblems, see E. Segre, '*El Iris: periódico crítico y literario* (1826): Republican Exiles and Autochthony in Post-Independence Mexico', *Bulletin of Hispanic Studies*, 74 (1997), 331–50.

35. On the *physiologie* genre, see J. Wechsler, *A Human Comedy: Physiognomy and Caricature in 19th Century Paris* (London, 1982), 33–4, 118. Also, G. Tytler, *Physiognomy in the European Novel: Faces and Fortunes* (Princeton, 1982), 348, 376. On Monnier and Balzac and illustrated magazines, see G. Robb, *Balzac: A Biography* (London, 1995), 169.

36. See e.g. the description of a fashionable interior in 'Algunas niñas que no conozco' (1843) and of popular costume in 'El día de difuntos' (1849), in Prieto, *Obras completas*, II: 188, 474.

37. Wechsler, *A Human Comedy*, 22.

38. For a historical study of Lavater's physiognomical theories and their impact on the development of realism, see Tytler, *Physiognomy*. For physiognomy in Mexican magazines, see 'La nariz o manera de conocer por su figura las inclinaciones de las personas', and 'Diferencias de la especie humana calculadas sobre la linea facial', *El Mosaico Mexicano*, 3 (1840), 180–2 and 449–55, respectively.

39. A review of a Mexican phrenological manual appeared in J.J. Gómez de la Cortina, 'Esposicion sumaria: del sistema frenológico del doctor Gall por José Ramon Pacheco', *Revista Mexicana*, 1 (1835), 383. See also 'Frenologia', *El Mosaico Mexicano*, 1 (1837), 485–7. For an example of explicit use of

phrenological commonplaces in *artículos de costumbres*, see J. de D. Arias, 'El cajero', in M. Herrera Castañeda (ed.), *Los mexicanos pintados por sí mismos* (Mexico City, 1853–5; repr. Querétaro, Mex., 1986), I: 77–86 (79).

40. J.M. Rivera, 'La costurera', and H. Frías y Soto, 'El alacenero', in Herrera Castañeda, *Los mexicanos pintados*, I: 69–76 (75) and 113–17 (116), respectively.

41. *El Mosaico Mexicano* of 1841 devoted several articles to the subject of prison reform; for a discussion of architectural designs based on the preferred English model, the panopticon, see I. Cumplido, 'La carcel de la Acordada en México: modelos para una reforma', *El Mosaico Mexicano* 5 (1841), 145–53.

42. See V. García Torres, 'Introduccion', 1 (1842), 1–2.

43. On the design and spectacle of the celebrated Regent's Park *Colosseum*, see R. Hyde, *Panoramania!: The Art and Entertainment of the 'All-Embracing' View* (London, 1988), 81–4.

44. S. Wilcox, 'El panorama de Leicester Square', in E. Trabulse (ed.), *Viajeros europeos del siglo XIX en México* (Mexico City, 1996), 127–35.

45. A. Yarrington, 'Under the Spell of Madame Tussaud: Aspects of "High" and "Low" in 19th-century Polychromed Sculpture', in A. Blühm (ed.), *The Colour of Sculpture 1840–1910* (Amsterdam, 1996), 83–92 (85–6).

46. Manthorne, *Tropical Renaissance*, 94.

47. See Lafragua, 'Carácter y objeto de la literatura', 74.

48. J.M. Lafragua and M. Orozco y Berra, *La Ciudad de México* (Mexico City, 1987), 282.

49. J.M. Rivera, 'El cómico de la legua', in Herrera Castañeda, *Los mexicanos pintados*, 55–66 (57).

50. Prieto, 'Un día de mis memorias de viaje' (first published in *El Álbum Mexicano*, 1849), *Obras Completas*, II: 527–32 (529).

51. See S. Rubín de la Borbolla, 'Las artes populares en el siglo XIX', in O. Sáenz González (ed.), *Arte Popular Mexicano: Cinco Siglos* (Mexico City, 1996), 69–75.

52. M. Payno, 'Un viaje a Veracruz en el invierno de 1843', *Obras Completas*, ed. B. Rosen Jélomer (Mexico City, 1996), I: 73–7 (75–6).

53. *Ibid.*, 76.

54. Nineteenth-century examples of this popular art are exhibited in the Museo Soumaya, Mexico City. The Museo Franz Mayer has examples from the sixteenth and seventeenth centuries.

55. T. Castelló Yturbide, 'Cajitas de entretenimientos', *México en el Tiempo: Revista de Historia y Conservación*, 13 (1996), 66–71 (70).

56. J. Hermosa, *Manual de geografía y estadística de la República Mexicana* (Paris, 1857; repr. Mexico City, 1991), 45.

57. M. Payno, *Los bandidos de Río Frío* (1889–91), ed. A. Castro Leal (Mexico City, 1986), 60–1.

58. *Ibid.*, 61.

59. O. Debroise, *Fuga mexicana: un recorrido por la fotografía en México* (Mexico City, 1994), 26.

60. See C. Pinney, 'The Parallel Histories of Anthropology and Photography', and B. Street, 'British Popular Anthropology: Exhibiting and Photographing the Other', in E. Edwards (ed.), *Anthropology and Photography* (New Haven/London, 1992), 74–95 (74) and 122–31 (122), respectively.

61. 'El daguerrotipo en el harem', *El Mosaico Mexicano*, 4 (1840), 145.
62. See S. Richter, *The Art of the Daguerreotype* (London, 1989), 6.
63. See J. Bali and V. Hugo Valencia, 'Acervos fotográficos: imágenes de la historia, historia de la fotografía', *México en el Tiempo*, 2 (1994), 45–8 (45). On recorded images of the Mexican-American war, see J. Ortiz Monasterio, 'Los primos del norte', *Luna Córnea*, 13 (1997), 64–71 (64–7).
64. See M. Payno, 'Instrumentos de optica', *El Mosaico Mexicano*, 5 (1841), 243–45.
65. *Ibid.*, 468.
66. See P. Diener, 'El perfil del artista viajero en el siglos XIX', in Trabulse, *Viajeros europeos*, 63–85 (84–5).
67. I.R. Gondra, 'Campeche visto desde el mar', *El Mosaico Mexicano*, 2 (1837), 101–4 (101).
68. Quotation from Nathaniel Hawthorne's *The Scarlet Letter* (1850): Manthorne, *Tropical Renaissance*, 136.
69. 'Prospecto', *El Daguerreotipo: Revista Enciclopédica y Universal* 1 (1850), n.p.n.
70. Prieto, 'Fiestas de indios' (first published in *El Siglo XIX*, 1842), *Obras completas*, II: 60–7 (61).
71. Prieto, 'Daguerrotipo social I', *Obras completas*, II: 512–18 (518).
72. Prieto, 'Domingo de carnaval', *Obras completas*, II: 73–7 (73).
73. E. Romero, *Fisiologia del gusto de Brillat Savarin* (Mexico City, 1842).
74. Prieto, 'Cumpleaños' and 'Ni yo sé qué escribiré', *Obras completas*, II: 100–10 (103) and 78–81 (78), respectively.
75. A. Loya, 'En tiempos de Cantolla', *México en el Tiempo*, 19 (1997), 27–33 (28).
76. C. Castro, *México y sus alrededores. Colección de monumentos, trajes y paisajes dibujados al natural y litografiados* (Mexico City, 1855–6) comprised thirty-eight prints accompanied by descriptive texts by *costumbrista* writers such as Manuel Payno, Francisco Zarco, Hilarión Frías y Soto and Niceto de Zamacois. See G. Jiménez Codinach, 'Casimiro Castro y sus alrededores, 1826–1889', in G. Jiménez Codinach, C. Monsiváis, R. Pérez Escamilla et al., *Casimiro Castro y su taller* (Mexico City, 1996), 27–49 (42–3).
77. Prieto, 'Un sueño de Bodoque, o sea, el matrimonio y el fósforo' and 'Paseo de la Viga', *Obras completas*, II: 154–8 (154) and 89–95 (95).
78. Prieto, 'Fiestas de indios', *Obras completas*, II: 60–7 (63).
79. P. Gualdi, *Monumentos de Méjico tomados del natural y litografiados por Pedro Gualdi, pintor de perspectiva* (Mexico City, 1841). K. Nebel, *Viaje pintoresco y arqueológico sobre la parte más interesante de la República Mexicana, en los años transcurridos desde 1829 hasta 1834* (Paris/Mexico City, 1839) includes by way of prologue 'observations' by Alexander von Humboldt.
80. G. Prieto, 'Manuelita', *Obras completas*, ed. B. Rosen Jélomer (Mexico City, 1994), X: 337–56 (353).
81. Prieto, 'Paseo de la Viga', *Obras completas*, II: 89, 93.
82. Tytler, *Physiognomy*, 174.
83. *Ibid.*, 59.
84. *Revista Científica y Literaria de Méjico*, 1 (1845), 248.
85. Prieto, 'Cartas sobre México', *Obras completas*, II: 237–44 (243).
86. Prieto, 'Cartas sobre México IV', *Obras completas*, II: 258–65 (261).
87. 'On the Picturesque and Ideal: A Fragment', in P.P. Howe (ed.), *The Complete Works of William Hazlitt* (London/Toronto, 1931), VIII: 317.

88. Tytler, *Physiognomy*, 177–8.
89. Hazlitt, 'On the Picturesque and Ideal', 317.
90. See Prieto, 'Literatura nacional: cuadros de costumbres', *Obras completas*, II: 402–7 (402).
91. See L. Mayer, 'Humboldt y sus aportaciones al desarrollo de la geografía y la estadística en México', and J. Labastida, 'Humboldt y la antropología en México', in J.E. Covarrubias (ed.), *Alejandro de Humboldt en México* (Mexico City, 1997), 43–53 and 135–51, respectively.
92. Manthorne, *Tropical Renaissance*, 29.
93. Ibid.
94. See A. Bonpland and A. von Humboldt, *Personal Narrative of Travels to the Equinoctial Regions of America during the Years 1799–1804*, tr. and ed. T. Ross (London/New York, 1851), I: xvii–xviii.
95. See E. O'Gorman, 'Reflexiones sobre la distribución urbana colonial de la Ciudad de México', in *Pasado y presente del Centro Histórico* (Mexico City, 1993), 12–29.
96. A commemorative exhibition of his work was held in the Museo Nacional de Arte, Mexico City, April 1997.
97. Prieto, 'Tlalpan', *Obras completas*, II: 166–74 (169).
98. On the need for social criticism and the *cuadro de costumbres*, see Lafragua, 'Carácter y objeto de la literatura', 74.
99. Prieto, 'Costumbres I', *Obras completas*, II: 56–9 (57).
100. *El Gabinete de Lectura*, 1 (1845), 1–2.
101. I. Cumplido and I.R. Gondra (eds), 'Advertencia preliminar', *El Mosaico Mexicano*, 2 (1837), 3–5 (3).
102. Prieto, 'Un día de mis memorias de viaje', *Obras completas*, II: 527–32 (528).
103. Prieto, 'Costumbres Mexicanas II' and 'Ojeada al centro de México', *Obras completas*, II: 48–55 (51) and 96–9 (97), respectively.
104. See D. Robinson, *The Lantern Image: Iconography of the Magic Lantern, 1420–1880* (London, 1993), 9–10.
105. *Pulque* is an alcoholic drink of pre-Hispanic origin derived from the agave plant. In the nineteenth century it was consumed predominantly by the working classes and the poor.
106. H. Frías y Soto, 'El pulquero', in Herrera Castañeda, *Los mexicanos pintados*, I: 25–32 (27).
107. Prieto, 'Costumbres Mexicanas I', *Obras completas*, II: 39–47 (43). See also G. Prieto, 'Apuntes de Fidel en un viaje a Zacatecas en agosto de 1842', *Obras completas*, ed. B. Rosen Jélomer (Mexico City, 1993), V: 31, in which the *linterna mágica* is compared to a purifying visual filter.
108. See M. Glantz (ed.), *Del Fistol a la Linterna: Homenaje a José Tomás de Cuéllar* (Mexico City, 1997).
109. The frontispiece is reproduced in J.N. Iturriaga, *Litografía y grabado en el México del XIX* (Mexico City, 1994), I: 128.
110. Robinson, *The Lantern Image*, 54.
111. Prieto, 'Literatura nacional', 27–9 (28–9).
112. H. Frías y Soto, 'La chiera', in Herrera Castañeda, *Los mexicanos pintados*, I: 15–22 (21). This drinks stall was particularly associated with Holy Week festivities.

113. Payno, *Obras completas*, I: 76.
114. J.M. Rivera, 'La china', in Herrera Castañeda, *Los mexicanos pintados*, I: 121–31 (122).
115. Ibid., 123.
116. 'The Army of the Three Guarantees' purported to defend independence, union and religion.
117. See E.C. Morales (ed.), *Homenaje nacional a José Agustín Arrieta, (1803–1874)* (Mexico City, 1994), 95–8.
118. Ibid., 98.
119. Ibid., 95.
120. Prieto, 'Angelita', *Obras completas*, X: 325–8 (328).
121. Prieto, 'Literatura nacional', 27–9 (29).
122. Ibid.
123. Prieto, 'Corpus. Año de 1842', *Obras completas*, II: 111–16 (111).
124. See P. Cherry and W.B. Jordan, *Spanish Still Life from Velázquez to Goya* (London, 1995), 21–2, 116–17.

Chapter 2

An Italicised Ethnicity:
Memory, Renascence and Visuality in the Literary Writings of Ignacio Manuel Altamirano

Los habitantes del sur componen la parte menos civilizada y más vengativa de la república, poblada de indios y mulatos, aún muy inclinados al robo y a la desobediencia.[1]

[The inhabitants of the south comprise the least civilised and most vengeful part of the republic, peopled by Indians and mulattos, still very inclined to robbery and disobedience.]

Ignacio Manuel Altamirano's[2] polymathic writing on the subject of the scripted nation in the post-intervention years (after the defeat in 1867 of Archduke Maximilian's occupying imperial army) is preoccupied by notions of inception, severance and lineage – in a language freighted with references to republican neo-classicism, insurgent patriotism and ethnic origin. The established tendency to regard him as a diligent, eclectic consolidator (rather than an innovator) and the architect in cultural matters of an aesthetic status quo which complemented the monolithic and prescriptive Eurocentric liberalism of the Porfiriato (1876–1910), needs to be revised in favour of a more complex intelligibility.[3] It may well be that it is Altamirano's adoption of a deceptively mainstream vocabulary of patriotic endeavour and telluric pride in his inaugural publications which has led some literary historians to overestimate the degree to which he embraced generational continuity, or advocated doctrinal conformity, and to accord a formal centrality to his work that it did not naturally enjoy nor sought to cultivate in its fundamentals.[4] Altamirano was undoubtedly receptive to the image of the civic poet as tribal visionary, coined topically by Joaquín Baranda in 1866: 'el poeta ... órgano de las naciones ... como la columna de fuego en el desierto debe caminar delante de los pueblos para señalar la senda que conduce á la tierra prometida del orden, de la libertad y del honor' ['the poet ... organ of the nations ... like the column of fire in the desert must lead the people, guiding them to the path which leads to the promised land of order, liberty and honour'].[5] His early post-war literary reviews are full of missionary zeal, conceiving of literature as an apprenticeship in prophetic nationalism.[6] But his signposting developed subsequently into a more oblique prospecting of the margins, in pursuit of a violated and concealed homeland rather than a complaisant investiture of the pro-European and urbane middle ground of the *Pax Porfiriana* [the dictatorship of General Porfirio Díaz]. Personal geography impinged decisively on the figuration of a national culture sourced internally by a receding, ignored, pre-industrial rural 'elsewhere', which Altamirano had occasion to call 'el *quid ignotum*'.

This chapter will attempt to show how Altamirano's preoccupation with the configuration of an autochthonous subject, and his interrogation of ethnic identity in the post-colonial era, assumed the form of intellectual autobiography. The quest for an appropriate representational strategy, which exercised him throughout his life as an essayist, poet, novelist, art critic and cultural activist, centred on problems of transcription and translation in the complex web of internecine and transatlantic cultural transactions in which Mexico had been historically enmeshed. For Altamirano, of Indian parentage, having been inducted into Spanish in his teens, and in adulthood having fought against the imperial French army and Mexican monarchists, the notion of translation afforded an ambivalent metaphor for conversion and interpretation. In his work the problem of authentic articulation could be described conceptually as placing more importance on the intersemiotic than the interlingual: the first implying a transpositional quality and a double competence, the other belonging to the category of reformulation tending towards a single kind of expression.[7] I shall argue that his advocacy of national autochthony was not predicated on the assumption of cultural homogeneity, but was explicitly resistant to redemptive notions of hybridity coined by a preceding generation of *costumbrista* writers – a generation of liberals for whom an allegorised *mestizo* ethnic identity provided an integrative paradigm for national culture. The prevailing notion of the *mestizo* as a cultural composite was not egalitarian although apparently inclusive. It tacitly subsumed the indigenous into a sterile, symbolic role while lending vigorous ascendancy to the European lineage.

Literary historiography in Mexico during the latter half of the Porfiriato virtually canonised Altamirano in his lifetime as 'el maestro' ['the Master'], founder and president of epoch-making literary fraternities and cultural societies.[8] He was regarded as the magisterial precursor of a modernising sensibility, which spliced insurgent autochthony with a cosmopolitan orientation in the *post bellum* transactions between metropolitan Europe and the developing Mexican republic. Interestingly, his elevation to symbolic status, as a kind of totemic figure of nationalist discourse during the era of 'order and progress', foreshadowed the obsolescence of his ideas and the effective silencing of his political voice in the 1880s.[9] This process paralleled the codification in public monuments and historical painting of an allegorised Aztec matrix – a euphemistic ethnicity – as part of a representational policy which severed the link between signifier and signified of previous descriptive strategies in Mexican literature and illustration. Literary *cuadros de costumbres* had sought to emulate reproductive media such as etching, engraving and lithography in order to democratise the national image and realise the dream of widespread visual literacy. Altamirano's public persona became implicated in the disjunction which emerged between the Porfirian consecration of an Aztec Golden Age, a selective gallery of enlightened emperors and tragic warriors to which the pathos of archaeological remains lent romantic credibility, and the debased conditions of contemporary Indian life. His resistance to this policy of ethnic estrangement is notable in his promotion of Mexican cultural autonomy, in which visualisation and description were dominant concerns.[10] It was a crucial part of Altamirano's general project as a nation-questing writer to make Indians and Indian culture 'appear' – to make it visible – against a background of such limited and stereotypical images as were prevalent at the time of his writing.

Since the Reform era (1855–60), photography had played an important role in visualising the nation and increasing the visibility of its subjects. Cognisant of this, Altamirano saw its potential for mass-produced scenic description, which he hoped would help to determine a national field of perception: 'para sacar vistas diferentes que la fotografía multiplica hasta hacerlas populares' ['in order to produce different views which photography can multiply until they become popular'].[11] He was equally alert to photography's use in portraiture and sociological typologies (figure 2.1). The image-conscious Imperial Court under Maximilian had ushered in the age of the *cartes de visite*.[12] The camera and the photographic studio seemed to guarantee the construction and dissemination of a voluntary identity. Even the usually satirical *La Orquesta* in 1866 hailed the technology as an instrument of popular empowerment: 'es una representación de la democracia artística ... el fotógrafo echando abajo esa aristocracia de las imágenes ha llegado a ser el tipo de esa ley que iguala a los señores con los plebeyos' ['it represents

Figure 2.1 Antíoco Cruces and Luis G. Campa, *Vendedor de pieles curtidas* (c.1870), *Carte de visite* from a popular series of collectible images of *costumbrista* types. FINAH.

democracy in the arts ... the photographer overturning the aristocracy of images has come to embody the law which makes masters and workers equals'].[13] Yet paradoxically, in Mexico at the height of its popularity in the 1870s and 1880s, photography's verism, the factual visibility of its subject matter, the exactness of detail and mass communicability of data in all fields of government and intellectual enquiry, increasingly disqualified it as a paradigm of a visualised national identity.

As a social metaphor photography offered the conceptualisation of the world as a series of collections and promised a methodology of seeing.[14] Although clearly indexed internecine racial and cultural heterogeneity did provide evidence of a knowable social order during a period of urban-industrial change, such differentiation did not accord with the myth of achieved collective integration, a homogenised prototype, promoted by the Porfirian administration. The production and accumulation of anthropological photographs, conflated scientifically with collections of criminal and medical photographs, assuaged instead a tendency to define Indian ethnicity in pathological terms (figures 2.2 and 2.3). Such compendiums abetted the fossilisation of contemporary Indian cultures, which were subsumed into archaeological relics requiring extensive decipherment, or subjected to Spencerian diagnosis, from the mid-1860s, as specimens of endemic retardation and decline, whose extinction might be accelerated by infusions of European blood lines (figure 2.4).[15] From the vantage point of his obligatory Indian ethnicity, Altamirano himself was to become a living exhibit or edifying parable of the triumph of civilisation over barbarism.

Yet despite the condescension and neo-colonial complicity of the ethnographic gaze, Altamirano was one of the few who in the 1870s continued to prioritise the need for empirical veracity in representational media, favouring an investigative strain which sought, in nation-conscious, self-referential literature, the evidential detail of 'exactitud fotográfica': 'la verdad de las descripciones, que son como fotografías de la vida en México' ['the truth of such descriptions, which are like photographs of life in Mexico'].[16] His inclusion of untranslated but italicised Nahuatl nomenclature in his descriptions of the rural periphery, differentiating a highly localised native lexicon from both the dominant *mestizo* vernacular and universal specification in Latin, can be seen as more than simply conforming to typographical conventions and as indicative of a similar kind of resistance to cultural centralisation.[17] The italicised words are embedded and contained in the text but not smoothed over or entirely assimilated. It is a form of quotation – of both incorporating the original and preserving its 'alien' intractability – which provides a resonant analogy to Altamirano's more general coming to terms with his bilocated cultural and ethnic identity. This is incorporation that resists homogenisation.

Altamirano's championing of observational writing echoed to a degree the descriptive imperative which had guided the nation-building strategies of *costumbristas* such as Manuel Payno, Guillermo Prieto and Francisco Zarco up to and beyond the Reform period, whilst focusing on the subjects omitted in their depictive, and supposedly inclusive panoramas: 'Prieto, lo mismo que todos, ha evitado de propósito hacer

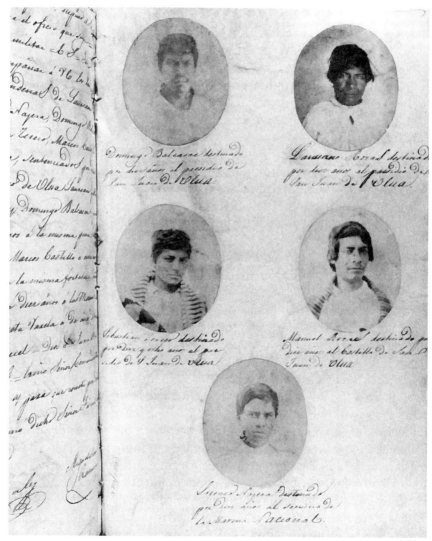

Figure 2.2 *Domingo Balcazár, Laureano Rosas, Sebastián Cereso, Manuel Rosas y Lorenzo Nájera primeros presos retratados con motivo de un asalto cometido en la ciudad de México en 1854* (c.1859), penal album attributed to Colonel José Muñoz. AGN.

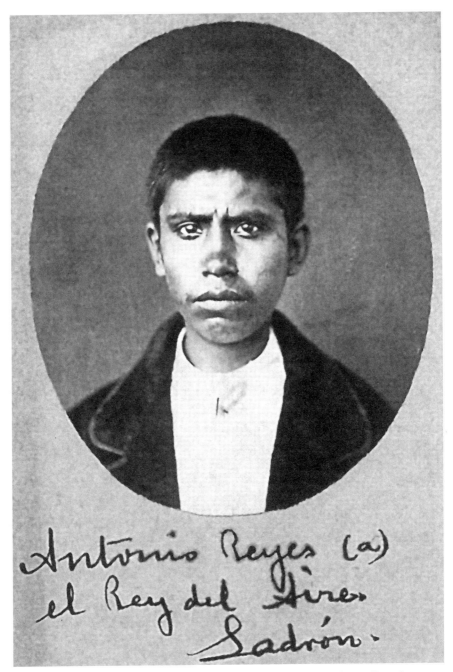

Figure 2.3 *Antonio Reyes, 'El Rey del Aire', Ladrón,* forensic portrait from *Albúm de presidiarios* (Mexico City, 1860–5), attributed to Joaquín Díaz González. FINAH.

Figure 2.4 *Indian Couple with Cage* (c.1865) on the theme of native decline and primitivism, attributed to François Aubert. FINAH.

penetrar a su musa en el mundo sombrío y melancólico de la raza indígena, aislada de ellos por la lengua y, a su parecer, alejada de la poesía de la miseria' ['Prieto, just like all the others, has intentionally avoided letting his muse enter into the sombre and melancholy world of the Indian race, isolated from them due to language and, in his view, too distant even from the poetry to be found in destitution'].[18] The figurative vein in *costumbrismo*, which had borrowed visual, technical and plastic metaphors from the graphic arts, popular exhibitionary installations, the natural sciences and daguerreotypy, gave way, during Altamirano's creative maturity, to a more synthetic, aesthetically mediated and theoretically predetermined articulation of communal space and identity in literature. The gradual systematisation of the discourse of science, and the increasingly specialised dissemination of literature and art propitiated a decline in interdisciplinary eclecticism and an insistence on formal purity which aided the consolidation of a formulaic nationality in literature – a tendency peculiarly prevalent in the so-called 'naturalist' novel. Altamirano resorted to photography tactically whenever he was intent on exposing prepackaged *aperçues*. In 1871 he praised the veracity of a novel accordingly: 'es una fotografía y no una pintura convencional' ['it is a photograph and not a conventional painting'].[19]

For Altamirano photography came to be linked, through his declared interest in spiritualism, with the evocation of imperishable ancestral traces. He likened ethnic memory to nebulous 'impresiones [que] se fijan en la imaginación como en una *negativa* imborrable' ['impressions (which) fix themselves in the imagination like in an indelible negative'].[20] His rather slanted advocacy of 'realismo' in artistic production should be taken less as a declaration of positivist conviction, and more as a desire for a restoration of the invisibly present, the actually variegated 'virgin' ground of autochthonous settlement – self-generating and self-sustaining. His cultural nationalism, in which the recurrent term *virgen* becomes synonymous with authenticity, sought to actualise those aboriginal elements which he regarded as foundationally latent, conflating the singularity of *mi pueblo* [my village] with the forging of *el pueblo mexicano* [the Mexican people] through literary and artistic practice or teaching.[21]

Conversely, in the debate over the nature of his legacy, Altamirano was emblematically significant for cultural nationalists after the Mexican Revolution (1910–16), especially in the *Indianist* [pro-Indian aesthetic] 1930s, seeking to salvage evidence of a prescient, articulate Indian ethnicity resistant to wholesale co-option by cultural imperialism of European or 'yanqui' extraction. For instance, in 1934 the novelist and screenwriter Mauricio Magdaleno paid homage to Altamirano's racial monumentality, aestheticising precisely those physical characteristics which had been denigrated in his lifetime when he was compared to 'un ídolo de barro por lo feo' ['as ugly as a clay idol']: 'El tipo físico es hermoso en la plástica, y ya de suyo posee calidades de estatua. Bronceado y nudoso, de firme pelambre negrísima ... Soberbio tipo indígena de inequívoca gleba, tan legítimo como la aridez desamparada de los yermos de cactus' ['The physical type is beautiful in its plasticity and already possesses the qualities of a statue. Bronze-like and gnarled, with solid jet black hair ... A superb Indian type of undeniable native origin, as legitimate as the bleak aridity of the cactus wastelands'].[22] Magdaleno's perception of Altamirano's inherently sculptural traits remind us of how perennial has been the tendency to treat him as an incarnation of an abstract ethnicity which could be commemorated publicly (figure 2.5).

Throughout his multifaceted career as a writer, pedagogue and politician, he posited a discursive notion of national identity which in practice advocated the development of a universal aesthetic style – an austere Mexicanised classicism suspicious of the baroque hybridity, which he dubbed 'literatura hermafrodita', and introversion of colonial figures such as Sor Juana Inés de la Cruz.[23] He sought to disentangle the deterministic coupling of essence and appearance in the socially divisive hierarchy of ethnic classification which had traditionally impinged on efforts to picture or describe the nation, and which had been revitalised by Darwinian positivism from the mid-1860s.[24] Altamirano's most interesting contribution to the pursuit of origins in nationalist discourse is the manner in which he sought to render the ethnic particular congruent with a totalising definition of a polygenetic/polygenous homeland. Also notable was his attempt to distinguish semantically between the originary and the original in the discussion of cultural autonomy. The former pertained to the source matter of derivation, what amounted to a *natural* substratum; the latter to its modern cultural reformulation. An offshoot of this preoccupation with the lexicon of inception was his legitimating compression of the term 'indígena' to mean simultaneously 'Indian' and 'native' against the widespread usage which split 'Indian' from original inhabitant (or 'autochthonous premise') to designate a generic racial physiology. In his fiction and quasi-ethnographic social sketches, this epistemological aspiration was expressed as a problem of representation and linguistic cognition – of how to make the adjectival a substantive absolute, of how to express particularity in the general, of how to make the non-European visible and communicable on its own terms. These questions had been addressed before – notably in the 1830s and 1850s in the periodical press – but

Altamirano's was not merely a reprise but an internalisation of the discourse into his own exegesis of his displaced, Indian/Nahua identity.[25] In personal as well as intellectual terms, the problem was of how to be 'esencialmente mexicano' ['essentially Mexican'] in Spanish, of how to be an Indian without costume, how to reinvent an exhaustively ethnologised racial persona in the dominant ideological currency.[26]

Figure 2.5 Studio of Cruces y Campa, portrait of Altamirano (c.1866). Museo Nacional de Historia.

Throughout his public life, Altamirano was subjected to physiognomic scrutiny in the illustrated press, where the genre of satiric *physiologies* popular in the 1830s and 1850s had become receptive to positivist delineations of racial character in photography, museum exhibits, world fairs and commemorative civic monuments.[27] In his more confessional poetry, where he expresses his sense of displacement and cultural 'orphanhood', as in his political oratory, Altamirano explicitly addressed his Indian ancestry with reference to his appearance during a period which saw the proliferation of a visual culture and the dominance of ocular paradigms in relation to questions of national identity: 'Yo soy un indio como nadie feo ... / Os repito, soy hijo de esos parias que habitan las oscuras serranías, / que construyen sus chozas solitarias / en las selvas más tétricas y umbrías' ['I am an Indian ugly like no other ... / I repeat, I am the son of those pariahs who inhabit the dark mountain ranges, / who build their solitary huts/in the most dismal and shade-filled forests'].[28]

With equal persistence his opponents caricatured the perceived evolutionary disparity between his reputation for aesthetic refinement and erudition, especially his classical education and advocacy of popular progress, and his physical resemblance to widely disseminated images of unpacified frontier savages (or 'indios bárbaros' ['savage Indians']), ethnological exhibits of primitive tribes, illiterate rural peons, and even criminological photographs of an Indian underclass (figures 2.6 and 2.7). For these critics he was the incongruous personification of a barbarous ethnicity attired in the trappings of civilisation. In 1878, for instance, a

Figure 2.6 Alfredo Laurent, *Seri Indians from Tiburón Island* (1892), State of Sonora. FINAH. The subjects fell under the category of *indios bárbaros*, nomadic or living in remote communities, resistant to acculturation and central government.

revealing caricature cum satirical poem appeared in *Mefistófeles: Semanario Burlesco Ilustrado* [*Mephistofeles: Illustrated Satirical Weekly*] (figure 2.8). It purported to cut down to size Altamirano's exalted public persona as well as to question his reputation for radical independence by pointing to the disjunction between his cultural and political prestige and the debased reality of his racial appearance:

Figure 2.7 François Aubert, *Vendedores de pollos* (1860s). Musée Royal de l'Armée, Brussels. The Indians' trade along with their ethnic clothing, rudimentary artefacts and burdened or crouching posture inscribed their subaltern status while framing them as exportable curiosities.

Filósofo le llaman, y soldado,
Orador, diplomático, y poeta
Maestro de escritores sin chaveta,
De todos los gobiernos abogado;

Ha obtenido los nombres de arrogante,
De libre pensador, de ilustre ateo,
De sábio, de sublime, de gigante.
¿Y qué es en realidad? Hombre pigmeo,
que por sus obras se parece a Dante,
Y á un ídolo de barro por lo feo.[29]

[They call him philosopher, and soldier,
Orator, diplomat, and poet
Teacher of writers with a screw loose,
Lawyer to every government;

He has earned the titles of 'arrogant',
'free thinker', 'distinguished atheist',
'wise', 'sublime', 'colossus'.
And what is he in reality? A human pigmy,
Who through his oeuvre resembles Dante,
And through his ugliness a clay idol.]

Recourse to archaeological imagery based on unearthed artefacts and other pre-Hispanic salvage became widespread in the satirical press to discredit or ridicule figures of authority of Indian descent, most notably presidents Benito Juárez and Porfirio Díaz. This form of public unmasking acknowledged the increasing institutionalisation of the pre-Hispanic legacy in state collections and academia while revisiting the polemic about the aesthetic value and exemplarity of such material for the modern republic. Legitimate political concerns about undemocratic practices and repression of free speech could lead to racist insinuations which treated such manifestations as if they were naturally sourced by a strain of native barbarism embodied in the governor of Indian origin.

Altamirano's response to pejorative racial stereotyping, often by political detractors, was to develop out of his preference for pictorial description an *epidermic* chromatic scale which effectively equated authenticity in literature, 'con su color americano propio' ['with its own American colour'], as well as moral and patriotic rectitude with the much maligned 'el oscuro de mi semblante' ['the darkness of my appearance'].[30] Altamirano had first tried this defensive strategy in his

Figure 2.8 Anon., caricature of Altamirano in *Mefistófeles* (1878). HN.

political satire against the presidency of Benito Juárez, himself a Oaxacan Zapotec, sometimes caricatured inexactly as the monolithic Aztec god of war and sacrifice, Huitzilopochtli.[31] He deflected racist slurs which dubbed him 'el negro' ['the black man'] to distinguish him from his associate, Ignacio Ramírez, a *mestizo* known as 'El Nigromante' for his atheism, by insinuating that Juárez, the conqueror of the white invader, had in the aftermath of victory betrayed his Liberal mandate and all legitimate Mexicans unaffected by creole *extranjerismo* [the embracing of foreign values]: 'Ganaron los blancos y perdieron los negros ... La raza caucásica está de triunfo. El Nigromante y yo lamentamos esta nueva victoria de los ojos azules y de los cabellos rubios' ['The whites have won and the blacks have lost ... The Caucasian race is triumphant. The 'Nigromante' and myself regret this new victory by the blue-eyed and blond-haired'].[32]

Portraits of Altamirano in press graphics tended to emphasise the singularity of his racial imprint and the unusual political ubiquity of his persona by depicting him in profile with a rare degree of physiognomic accuracy informed by studio photographs. In collective scenes, his darkened figure served to articulate a compositional chiaroscuro in which he appears as the necessary point of contrast, allowing the other non-Indian figures to emerge into the limelight. His is usually the only overtly pigmented face in a crowd of political affiliates of varied backgrounds. In a late caricature from a satirical gallery of 'Celebridades mexicanas' (1885), Altamirano is depicted wearing generic Indian costume notable for its proletarian informality (rolled-up shirt sleeves combined with the unsartorial *jorongo* [poncho]) with one hand resting on an ill-defined pre-Hispanic stone head (figure 2.9). His other hand holds a giant feather quill in the manner commonly associated in colonial iconography with the exotic savage or the allegorical body of the native continent. With its interest in the materials of ethnic difference the composition as a whole is reminiscent of an enthnographic exhibit with telltale props to emblematise a local curiosity. The parodic eulogy that is printed at the foot of the image alludes to Altamirano's classical erudition, which the portrait echoes in its classicising gestures while contesting his ability to transcend his lowly Indian background despite the steadfast pride of his demeanour. The anonymous author plays with the idea that appearances can be deceptive only to reinscribe the racist axiom that the exceptional case proves the rule of Indian subalternity – especially as regards aesthetic desirability: 'Ignacio M. Altamirano / Poderosa inteligencia, / vasta instrucción, gaya ciencia, / el Mexicano Tirteo / seduce por su elocuencia / y subyuga ... por lo feo' ['Ignacio Manuel Altamirano / Potent intellect, / vast erudition, poesy, / the

Figure 2.9 Anon., caricature of Altamirano in *La Actualidad* (1885). HN.

Mexican Tyrtaeus (a patriotic poet) / who seduces through his eloquence, and subjugates … through his ugliness'].[33]

Altamirano consistently denounced misrepresentations and falsifications of Mexican culture by foreign writers, artists and even studio photographers, as well as criticising a tendency amongst the cultivated elite and the middle class to reproduce or graft subserviently alien models and genres in an attempt to Europeanise an unpalatable autochthony: 'ya basta de repeticiones fastidiosas y pueriles' ['enough of irritating and puerile repetitions'] when the universal trend amongst emancipated nations 'aspira a despojarse del arreo imitativo' ['aspires to divest itself of the yoke of imitation'].[34] His critique of inauthenticity, his disabused perspective on contemporary representational strategies, was clearly informed by a highly self-referential dimension, for any essentialist conception of a post-colonial Mexican identity entailed an evaluation of the Indian component, which in Altamirano was an embodied locus of meaning. It could be argued that Altamirano's advocacy of Mexican cultural autonomy was rather more defensive than conciliatory, intent on appropriating the representational means and ideological tools to define indigenous subject matter at a time when increasingly sophisticated technologies were being deployed to circumscribe the nature of the 'Indian problem'. Conscious of the manner in which, in the wake of Maximilian's execution, Europe demonised Mexico with allusions to its inherent, racially specific barbarism, Altamirano urged a campaign of visual affirmation: 'Corremos el peligro de que se nos crea tales como se nos pinta, si nosotros no tomamos el pincel y decimos al mundo: "Así somos en México"' ['We run the danger of being thought to be the same as we are portrayed, if we do not ourselves take up the brush and tell the world: "This is the way we are in Mexico"'].[35] In his apparently commemorative novel *Clemencia* of 1869, he polemicised what he regarded as the residual traces of colonial 'pigmentocracia' and Manichean prejudice within the ranks of the liberal forces fighting Maximilian. The same year, while commending the academic painter José Obregón's attempt in *El descubrimiento del pulque* [*The Discovery of Pulque*] to illustrate and thereby aestheticise a foundational episode from dynastic Indian history, Altamirano pointed to the conventional rendition of the ethnic protagonists who were depicted anachronistically as noble *mestizos*.[36]

Whilst others, such as the philologist and sociologist Francisco Pimentel, were intent on historicising the Indian subject and advocating 'una raza de transición' which would engender a fully Caucasian modern Mexico, or extracting malleable exotic material which could be showcased at Universal Exhibitions, such as the sculptor Jesús Contreras, Altamirano activated personal memory. He engaged in a remembrance of ancestral beginnings which not only inserted the Indian presence into a dystopian present but offered a potential corrective to the rhetorical exaltation of Aztec antecedents by institutionalised creole-inflected history.[37] Against those nationalists who urged 'que los indios olviden sus costumbres y hasta su idioma mismo' ['that Indians should forget their customs and even their very language'] in order to homogenise culture and racial identity by fomenting collective amnesia amongst the Indian peoples, in *Paisajes y leyendas, tradiciones y costumbres de México* [*Landscapes and Legends, Traditions and Customs of Mexico*], Altamirano revisited his Indian childhood, memorably evoking the precise configuration of place, and tracing the vibrant roots or degraded vestiges of pre-conquest culture in communal festivities and rituals throughout the republic.[38] Whilst it could not be said that in this 'living archive' he paid unqualified tribute to every aspect of indigenous culture or the elements of a pre-conquest order, including language, which had survived colonialisation and pervaded contemporary society, he did restore to centrality and make uniquely pertinent that which had been marginalised in Porfirian ideology and administration, or which had been subordinated by reform liberals, such as Guillermo Prieto, who expressed their populism through a celebration of a *mestizo* vernacular. Altamirano's explicit adherence to a literal *Tierra patria* [*Homeland*] in his exploration of nationhood should be regarded as a tacit acknowledgement of his Indian background. For as Enrique Florescano has more recently reiterated, 'este vínculo con la tierra ... pedazo de tierra claramente delimitado, bendecido por el espíritu vigilante de los ancestros que descansaban en el propio suelo, y protegido por los dioses creadores del cosmos' ['this bond with the land ... with a piece of clearly bounded ground, blessed by the watchful spirit of the ancestors who lie in that very soil and protected by the gods who created the universe'] characterised the social structure and ethnic identity of pre-Hispanic communities in Mexico.[39] Altamirano refers suggestively to the importance traditionally accorded to memory in the articulation of collective identity when he cites a piece of Indian lore, thereby contextualising his own acts of remembrance: 'la facultad de la *memoria* que un antiguo llamaba la *custodia de todo*' ['the faculty of *memory* that an ancient called the *guardian of all things*'].[40]

The experience of the most recent liberation struggle against a dynastic European monarch cast a rather overdetermined conceptual shadow on the lexicon of those advocating cultural emancipation. For instance, in 1868 Altamirano urged 'es la ocasión, pues, de hacer de la bella literatura una arma de defensa' ['it is the time, then, to make of beautiful literature a defensive weapon']; and in 1872 he deplored that in cultural matters 'todavía no nos hemos atrevido todos a dar el "grito de Dolores"' ['we have not all yet dared to give the insurgent cry of freedom'].[41] Although in the aftermath of war Altamirano's declamatory language resonates with the familiar conceits of Mexican liberal reformers – the need for integration and intellectual homogeneity – with whose work he was conversant, his point of view on questions of racial destiny and modernity was subtly divergent and personalised (figure 2.10). Whilst it could be argued that the 1830s, 1840s and 1850s witnessed the emergence in liberal circles of an emblematic and increasingly assimilated hybridity, a redemptive popularisation of *mestizo* iconography in the arts, in the 1860s and 1870s Altamirano problematised this consensual identity by publicising in an unconventional way the problems of Mexican self-definition in relation to his own Indian ethnicity. He turned his awareness of the discursive uses of contemporary anthropology and his study of the early Spanish *cronistas* [chroniclers] into a process of autobiographical validation which partially reversed denigrating typologies.

Altamirano's membership of the cultural society known as Liceo Hidalgo, of which he became president, would have ensured a first-hand experience of the influential proponents of such ethnic characterisations. Principal amongst these figures was Francisco Pimentel whose reputation as a scholar had been established by his *Cuadro comparativo de las lenguas indígenas de México* [*Comparative Frame of the Indigenous Languages of Mexico*] (1862) (which, unusually for a work published in Mexico, had attracted good reviews from the European academic establishment). More provocative in relation to Altamirano's ethnic identity was Pimentel's *Memoria sobre las causas que han originado la situación actual de la raza indígena de México y medios de remediarla* [*Report on the Causes of the Current Condition of the Indian Race in Mexico and Its Remedies*] (1862), in which contemporary Indians were defined as obstacles to progress and the forging of a Mexican nation predicated on unity. According to Pimentel, a wealthy *hacendado* [landowner], Indians were demonstrably 'egoístas' because 'isolationists': wholly engrossed in the preservation of their lands, customs and languages, they had no sense of civic duty or loyalty to the nation. He acknowledged their aptitude for manual labour and imitation, whilst pointing to their secretiveness, idolatry, physical and moral degeneration, and their natural lack of intellectual ingenuity.[42] Uninclined to rational thought, 'embrutecidos y degradados' ['made brutish and degraded'], only full assimilation by way of transitional *mestizaje* [miscegenation] could save a race unable to cure itself. In such a dangerously polarised country, faced with the stark choice of '¡matar o morir!' ['to kill or die!'], Pimentel, who praised Maximilian for his enlightened paternalism towards the Indians, discarded the genocidal option adopted by the U.S.A. in favour of *transformación*, a term associated with social Darwinism,

Figure 2.10 Anon., portrait of Altamirano during the military campaigns against the Habsburg occupation (c.1860s). Museo Nacional de las Intervenciones. The loose-fitting outfit is strikingly similar to that made famous by Giuseppe Garibaldi's liberation legionaries in South America and Italy, casting him in the mould of a revolutionary renegade.

which entailed a philanthropic extinction of the domestic alien.[43] Altamirano's introspective scrutiny should be regarded as a riposte to just such a critique that pitted the future welfare of the Mexican nation against the continued survival of a non-European ethnic identity, for in his poetry, fiction and literary criticism Altamirano provided the individualised substance for a conceptualisation of the nation which in his terms was 'más genuina, es decir más indígena' ['more authentic, that is to say more native'].[44] The public scope of this effort was to counteract 'cierta repugnacia para conocer el país nativo' ['a certain repugnance for knowing one's native country'], to make familiar a localised terrain and its circumambient detail, which for Altamirano had precise familial connotations, from which to forge a mythic, bilocated common source.[45]

Born into an unacculturated, monolingual Indian family in the remote mountain town of Tixtla in the state of Guerrero, until the age of fourteen Altamirano was a member of an ethnic majority whose loyalty to the pre-conquest past impinged decisively on the syncretic forms that Catholic conversion assumed. In Altamirano's fiction and poetry, the mountains of his childhood figure prominently as the last preserves of the conquered Aztec nobility and its fallen civilisation, and as the sites of his own visionary, dominant marginality. The mountain heights sacred to the pre-conquest Nahuas, still venerated as Catholic shrines after Christianisation, in Altamirano's metaphorical geography offer spiritual resistance to the crude materialism and *extranjerismo* of urban modernity.[46] These are the vantage points of true autochthony: the spaces in which some saw evidence of residual savagery. Unlike the celebrated landscapes by the positivist painter José María Velasco, in which the vast mountains and volcanoes of the central valley of Mexico are distanced monuments, testimony to pictorial self-aggrandisement during the Porfiriato, Altamirano evokes a terrain which is neither depopulated nor inscrutable, but perhaps equally paradigmatic.[47]

The *Tierra Caliente* [*The Burning Land* or *The South*] (which included Morelos as well as Guerrero), was a part of post-independence Mexico notorious for interracial conflict, virulent anti-Spanish agitation in the 1850s and Indian agrarian rebellions. It figured as a kind of proscenium of the struggle for 'descolonización' which was to last the century.[48] In his poetry, Altamirano pointedly celebrated 'el elemento indígena, la belleza nacional' ['the indigenous element, the national beauty'] of a region which had been cast as the repository of anarchy, bloodthirsty savages and degenerate half-breeds by those advocating a European reconquest of Mexico.[49] Opinion in Spain regarding ethnic identity in the ex-colony crystallised in 1858, two years after the massacre of Spaniards in a number of local *haciendas* [estates]: 'La raza hispano-mejicana, en su degeneración actual ... no puede sostener el peso de la nacionalidad ... las diez y seis razas salvajes que abriga en su seno, más degeneradas que ella todavía no pueden comunicarle estos elementos de existencia, su regeneración ha de tener distinto origen' ['The Hispano-Mexican race, in its current state of degeneration ... cannot sustain the burden of nationality ... the sixteen savage races which it harbours, even more degenerate than itself cannot provide those elements essential for its existence, its regeneration must have a different source'].[50] Not only did Altamirano recast the ground of interethnic conflict into a bucolic scenario of native innocence and pacific organicity, in poems which combined classical regularity with a delight in Nahuatl vocabulary for flora and fauna, but these 'pequeños cuadros de los paisajes del sur para mí tan queridos como que allí se meció mi cuna' ['small paintings of those landscapes of the south which I cherish so deeply for they saw me from the cradle'] provided the conceptual bearings of the cultural renascence he envisaged from the pages of literary magazines in the late 1860s.[51] This sensual land, of generative abundance, was the forgotten place of origin. The fact that Altamirano situated the premise of authenticity in Indian soil, tacitly arguing that originality entailed an inclusion of such an element however transfigured or reworked, must surely constitute his reply to those who insisted that colonised Indians were essentially imitative rather than creative, incapable of invention or self-renewal.

In choosing the title of his famous literary magazine, *El Renacimiento* [*The Renaissance*], in 1869, the frontispiece of which depicted a phoenix rising from the flames (figure 2.11), Altamirano sought to encourage associations to the 'reconstrucción' of Italy and the 'resurrección' of Greece, spiritual homelands of his republican neo-classicism.[52] The term 'renacer' ['rebirth'] and 'renacimiento' ['renascence'] in relation to literature had appeared in previous reviews of his which pointedly omitted the term 'regeneración'.[53] An ubiquitous commonplace of nation-questing journalism in the 1850s, it had become identified with the ideology of ultramontane conservatives who had supported European intervention and Maximilian's empire. The fact that the title similarly avoided the qualifier 'Mexicano', which had been an obligatory token of nationalist orientation in the organs of a previous generation (*El Museo Mexicano*, *La Ilustración Mexicana*, *El Mosaico Mexicano*, etc.), may be part of the depoliticisation of cultural discourse, which was one of the stated intentions of the magazine. The conciliatory sentiment was directed both at home and abroad. The contents manifested an inclusivity in which works of European, Mexican, North and South American provenance were accommodated in a spirit of universal egalitarianism.[54] In practice this challenged the hierarchy between the periphery and the centre, the civilised and the underdeveloped in relation to cultural production.

There is a curious irony that clearly did not escape the acutely self-conscious Altamirano when, in 1890 towards the end of his life, he received an invitation to address the VIII Americanist Congress in Paris as the official delegate of the august Sociedad de Geografía y Estadística (figure 2.12). He was tacitly operating in his dual capacity as both

Figure 2.11 Frontispiece of *El Renacimiento: Periódico Literario* (Mexico City, 1869). HN.

Figure 2.12 Felipe and Manuel Torres, portrait of Altamirano, reproduced in *La Ilustración Mexicana* (1893). BNM. The dedication to the photographers points to his concern with misrepresentation: 'en señal de afecto y agradecimiento por este magnífico retrato, que es mejor que los que me han hecho en esta ciudad los fotógrafos franceses' ['as a token of affection and gratitude for this wonderful portrait which is better than those made by French photographers in this city'].

anthropological exhibit and scholarly interpreter, in a neat self-referential conceit which amounted to an act of empowerment. After all, his status as an Indian relic was a widely circulated visual joke in the Mexican opposition press. In 1889 *El Hijo del Ahuizote* published a mordant lithograph under the title *Bocetos de la Exposición Universal. Sección de Antigüedades Indígenas* [*Sketches of the Universal Exhibition. Section of Indian Antiquities*] which satirised the longevity of Porfirio Díaz's presidency and that of his long-term supporters, including Altamirano whose democratic credentials were tarnished by association.[55] The accompanying text in cod Nahuatl dubbed him 'Altamiranplumiviejoxtle' as part of a wider critique of Indianist rhetoric in the showcase of national culture sponsored by the Díaz government. In Altamirano's opening speech – with surely a knowing allusion to recent history between the European power and Mexico – he referred to himself apologetically as 'le premier indien demi-civilisé qui vient en France' ['the first half-civilised Indian to come to France'], thanking the host nation 'de tout ce qu'elle a fait pour notre progrès scientifique et moral' ['for all she has done for our scientific and moral progress'], the deprecatory irony of 'demi' constituting, I would suggest, a vindication of the irreducible and untranscribable rather than an ingratiating admission of subalternity.[56] Altamirano's work is importantly engaged upon such vindication, and with articulating a sense of bilocation rather than binarism, in ways that have not been sufficiently recognised. Through his work of verbal description and illustration, and as a critic of the representational efforts of others, Altamirano recovered the original vocation of native scribe or

Tlacuilo (in Nahuatl), to depict and to write: to write is to depict; to depict is to write.

Notes

1. Official report from the Spanish representative in Mexico to the Secretary of State in Madrid, 29 September 1855: R. Falcón, *Las rasgaduras de la descolonización: españoles y mexicanos a mediados del siglo XIX* (Mexico City, 1996), 33–4.

2. Born in Tixtla, Mexico 1834; died in San Remo, Italy 1893.

3. See E. Enríquez Fuentes, 'Altamirano, nuestro contemporáneo: entrevista con Nicole Giron', *Tierra Adentro*, 82 (1996), 41–7; R. Hernández Monroy, 'Ignacio Manuel Altamirano, crítico literario', in J. Rueda de la Serna (ed.), *Historiografía de la literatura mexicana: ensayos y comentarios* (Mexico City, 1996), 89–106.

4. See C. González Peña, *Historia de la literatura mexicana. Desde los orígenes hasta nuestros días* (Mexico City, 1928); J. Jiménez Rueda, *Historia de la literatura mexicana* (Mexico City, 1928) and *Letras mexicanas en el siglo XIX*

(Mexico City, 1944). For an ironic view of his canonisation, see H. Batís, 'Maestro de la nación: los hijos de Altamirano', *Unomásuno*, 4 December 1984, 2.

5. J. Baranda, *Obras* (Mexico City, 1900), 24.

6. I.M. Altamirano, *Revistas literarias de México (1821–1867)* (Mexico City, 1868).

7. See R. Jakobson, 'Aspects linguistiques de la traduction', in N. Ruwet (ed. and tr.), *Essais de linguistique générale* (Paris, 1963), 78–86.

8. See e.g. E. de Olavarría y Ferrari, *El arte literario en México: noticias biograficas y críticas de sus más notables escritores* (Madrid, 1878); *Velada literaria en honor de Ignacio M. Altamirano* (Mexico City, 1889); V. Agüeros, *Escritores mexicanos contemporáneos* (Mexico City, 1880); L. González Obregón, *Breve noticia de los novelistas mexicanos en el siglo XIX* (Mexico City, 1889); M. Sánchez Mármol, *Las letras patrias* (Mexico City, 1902); S. Moreno Cora, *La crítica literaria en México* (Orizaba, 1907).

9. For the impact of positivism on Mexican political culture, see C.A. Hale, *The Transformation of Liberalism in Late Ninenteenth-Century Mexico* (Princeton, 1989).

10. For a speech in defence of Indian civic rights, see I.M. Altamirano, *Obras completas*, ed. C. Sierra Casasus and J. Sotelo Inclán (Mexico City, 1986), I: 326–45 (336).

11. On visualisation and photography, see I.M. Altamirano, *Obras completas*, ed. J.L. Martínez (Mexico City, 1988), XII: 90.

12. See P. Massé Zendejas, 'Tarjetas de visitas mexicanas: retratos de Cruces y Campa', *Luna Córnea*, 3 (1993), 49–53, and *Simulacro y elegancia en tarjetas de visita: fotografías de Cruces y Campa* (Mexico City, 1998), 110–22.

13. E. Acevedo and F. Ramírez (eds), *Testimonios artísticos de un episodio fugaz, (1864–1867)* (Mexico City, 1995), 171.

14. See M. Warner Marien, *Photography and Its Critics: A Cultural History, 1839–1900* (Cambridge, 1997), 125, 129. On the social uses of photography in Mexico, see O. Debroise, *Fuga mexicana* (Mexico City, 1994), 30–44.

15. On positivism and photography, see G. Rodríguez, 'Miradas sin rendición' and E. Flores, 'Los hombres infames', *Luna Córnea*, 13 (1997), 25–31 and 55–63 respectively.

16. *Obras completas*, XII: 61.

17. See 'La Semana Santa en mi pueblo': *Obras completas*, ed. J.J. Blanco (Mexico City, 1986), V: 37–54.

18. *Obras completas*, XII: 241.

19. Ibid., XII: 236.

20. *Obras completas*, V: 37.

21. See e.g. *Obras completas*, XII: 36: 'La poesía y la novela mexicanas deben ser vírgenes, vigorosas, originales, como lo son nuestro suelo, nuestras montañas, nuestra vegetación' ['Mexican poetry and the novel must be virginal, vigorous, original like our soil, our mountains and our vegetation'].

22. M. Magdaleno, 'Dos cabezas indias', *El Libro y el Pueblo* (January 1934), 1–12 (9), and 'Altamirano', *El Nacional*, 12 December 1933. In a similar vein, see writer and ethnologist F. Benítez, 'Apuntes para una biografía de Ignacio Manuel Altamirano', *El Nacional*, 30 August 1938.

23. *Obras completas*, XII: 37. On Sor Juana as a model for women writers, see 'Carta a una poetisa' (1872), in I.M. Altamirano, *Obras completas*, ed. J.L. Martínez (Mexico City, 1988), XIII: 42–69 (68). For critical reception of Sor Juana's work, see *Composiciones leidas en la velada literaria que consagró El Liceo Hidalgo a la memoria de Sor Juana Inés de La Cruz* (Mexico City, 1874).
24. For 'polémicas darwinistas' and Spencer on the Mexican Indian, see E. Trabulse, *Historia de la ciencia en México* (Mexico City, 1997), 226–7 and 231 respectively.
25. See e.g. F. Zarco, 'Estado de la literatura en México', *La Ilustración Mexicana*, 3 (1852), 5–8.
26. *Obras completas*, XII: 223–4.
27. For delineations of Indian identity promoted by the Mexican Academy of Art, see S.G. Widdifield, *The Embodiment of the National in Late Ninenteenth-Century Mexican Painting* (Tucson, 1996).
28. *Obras completas*, ed. S. Reyes Nevares (Mexico City, 1987), VI: 157–62, (160–1).
29. C. Barros and C. Sierra, *Ignacio Manuel Altamirano: iconografía* (Mexico City, 1993), 77.
30. *Obras completas*, VI: 157; 12: 36.
31. E. Acevedo, 'Los hombres del lápiz y la pluma: la prensa oposicionista de 1869 a 1877', in E. Acevedo and F. Ramírez (eds), *La fabricación del estado, 1864–1910* (Mexico City, 2003), 90–109 (103).
32. *Obras completas*, ed. C. Monsiváis (Mexico City, 1987), VII: 70–7, (77).
33. Barros and Sierra, *Ignacio Manuel Altamirano*, 79.
34. *Obras completas*, XIII: 48, 176.
35. *Obras completas*, XII: 38.
36. M. Tenorio-Trillo, *Mexico at the World's Fairs: Crafting a Modern Nation* (Berkeley/Los Angeles/London, 1996), 121.
37. See F. Pimentel, *Dos obras*, ed. E. Semo (Mexico City, 1995), 173. For Jesús Contreras, see Tenorio-Trillo, *Mexico at the World's Fairs*, 105–12.
38. Pimentel, *Dos obras*, 169. I.M. Altamirano, *Paisajes y leyendas, tradiciones y costumbres de México* (Mexico City, 1884).
39. E. Florescano, *Etnia, estado y nación: ensayo sobre las identidades colectivas en México* (Mexico City, 1997), 38–9.
40. 'La Semana Santa en mi pueblo' (1880), in *Obras completas*, V: 37.
41. *Obras completas*, XII: 38; XIII: 64.
42. Pimentel, *Dos obras*, 162–4.
43. Ibid., 173.
44. *Obras completas*, V: 121.
45. *Obras completas*, XIII: 228.
46. This term appears in his review 'La literatura en 1870', published in *El Federalista* in 1871; see *Obras completas*, XII: 230–6.
47. See Altamirano's allegorical *La Navidad en las montañas* [*Christmas in the Mountains*] (Mexico City, 1871).
48. Falcón, *Las rasgaduras de la descolonización*, 103.
49. *Obras completas*, XII: 191, 216.
50. Falcón, *Las rasgaduras de la descolonización*, 36.

51. Altamirano's comments appear for the first time in 1880 in the third edition of *Rimas*; some of the poems were written in the 1860s. See *Obras completas*, VI: 31–6.
52. H. Batís (ed.), *El Renacimiento: periódico literario* (Mexico City, 1869; repr. 1979). For comparisons to Greece and Italy, see Altamirano, *Obras completas*, XII: 227–8.
53. Altamirano, *Revistas literarias de México*, 3: 'Decidamente la literatura renace en nuestra patria' ['Decidedly literature is being reborn in our motherland']. Pedro Santacilia had twinned the idea of 'el renacimiento de la literatura' ['the rebirth of literature'] with national self-affirmation in *Del movimiento literario en México* (Mexico City, 1868).
54. See H. Batís, *Índices de 'El Renacimiento'* (Mexico City, 1963).
55. Acevedo and Ramírez, *La fabricación del estado*, 260.
56. Barros and Sierra, *Ignacio Manuel Altamirano*, 164.

Chapter 3

Visualising Mexico:

The Interplay of Graphic Arts and Film in the 1930s and 1940s

Debemos, pues mexicanizarnos en el buen sentido del vocablo. No vestirnos de charros y de chinas poblanas, pero no renegar tampoco de lo que constituye el fundamento de nuestra personalidad histórica.[1]

[We must then Mexicanize ourselves in the positive sense of the term. Not by donning the costume of typical cowboys and Pueblan Maidens, but neither by denying what constitutes the basis of our historical character.]

As is well known, the turbulent years spanning the 1930s and 1940s in Mexico witnessed the apogee of a widespread cultural nationalism. The politicisation of the arts and the pursuit of cultural 'authenticity' was accompanied by a number of recurring tropes: a concern with the recuperation and use of popular culture; the celebration of ethnicity; the sublimation of the rural landscape as site of violated origins; the official elevation of folklore as the unmistakable signature of a syncretic *mestizo* nation; and finally, the recasting of national history into an edifying spectacle: an epic marked by revolutionary struggle against dictatorship, institutionalised racism and Western economic and cultural imperialism.

This preoccupation with the articulation of emblematic nationalist narratives did not, contrary to expectation, interact easily with the presiding government's doctrine, or always meet with the consensus of a mobilised, patriotic public. Nor did the intellectual or artistic community coalesce behind the banner of the civic-minded, declamatory aesthetic and exclusivity of an enabling *mexicanismo* [Mexicanism]. The emergence of a fully fledged indigenous cinema in this period has to be seen in the context of increasingly sophisticated debates about the function of art in mass culture, and the discerning critique of competing *mexicanismos* in the press, which frequently included satirical treatment of the perceived excesses of cultural jingoism. The problematisation of the concept of national identity was informed by the fundamental conflict between tradition and modernity that underpinned political debate in the post-revolutionary years. The cinematic image proved a potent extension of this polemic, providing ideologically-inflected allegories, synthetic metaphors and distinctive visual styles, which influenced as well as absorbed current topics, partly fulfilling what the poet and critic José Juan Tablada, writing in 1927, regarded as the cinema's proven role as a 'Tabloid newspaper for the illiterate masses'.[2]

The 1930s and 1940s, the era in which Mexican cinema came of age, were marked by the radicalisation of political debate, the expansion of urban centres, and the restructuring of the rural economy and traditional order: a period which includes the Máximato [regime] of Plutarco Elías Calles (1924–8, 1929–35) with its marked anti-clerical, authoritarian and centralist tendencies; the visionary presidency of Lázaro Cárdenas with its sweeping agrarian and social reforms (1934–40); the expropriation of foreign oil companies (1938); the influx of republican refugees from the Spanish Civil War; the controversial granting of asylum to Trotsky (1937); and the momentous signing of the Mexican-U.S. pact for the duration of Second World War. It is perhaps fairly unsurprising to find that during a time of displacement and reform, a rapid review of the titles of films produced in Mexico in 1937 and 1938 reveals a predominance of films set in an idyllic countryside unaffected by social change.[3] And if the experience of accelerating urbanization disorientates and dissolves the once-fixed parameters of daily life, it is hardly anomalous that a director and producer with conservative affiliations like Juan Bustillo Oro should enjoy box office success with the nostalgic *costumbrismo* of *En tiempos de don Porfirio* [*In the Times of Don Porfirio*] (1939/1940) or *México de mis recuerdos* [*The Mexico of my Memories*] (1944), sunny films set during General Porfirio Díaz's long-lived dictatorship. Or that such a common touch should have been brokered by his earlier adaptation of the nineteenth-century novel by the Porfirian liberal writer, General Vicente Riva Palacio, *Monja y casada, virgen y mártir* [*Nun and Wife, Virgin and Martyr*] (1935), a popular historical melodrama in the style of feuilleton novels, the prototypes of modern radio serials and comic books. Stranger perhaps, that attempts at a less strident, cautiously critical nationalism, like Fernando de Fuentes's revisiting of the Revolution through the adaptation of Rafael F. Muñoz's gritty novel *¡Vámonos con Pancho Villa!* [*Let's go with Pancho Villa!*] (1935), admittedly tempered by the financial support of Cárdenas's populist government, should have failed to persuade the viewing public.

The thawing in relations between the capitalist Colossus and the Revolutionary Exemplar in effect ushered in an unprecedented era of cross-border collaboration between the hegemonic Hollywood film industry and the under-resourced, badly equipped handful of Mexican companies struggling to secure a national audience.[4] Since the newsreels and dramas based on the revolution of 1910, Mexico, as reconstituted in American celluloid,[5] had provided and would continue to provide the visual trappings of an imaginary foreign cultural essence that paradoxically set the standard iconography for a Mexican cinema concerned with the exemplification of the autochthonous. The impact of what one contemporary Mexican film critic referred to as 'mexicanismo a la yanqui' ['Yankee Mexicanism'] cannot be underestimated, and certainly informed the work of emerging Mexican directors either concerned with finding a corrective to the formulaic travesties of Hollywood or keen to adapt this conventional visual language in home-grown productions, with a view to capturing the established national market and expanding beyond, to Hispanic America.[6] Hollywood offered choreographed pseudo-folkloric pageants of singing *charros* passionate *señoritas* of indeterminate ancestry – celluloid cultural hybrids, part castanet-wielding *manola* [stereotype of Castilian femininity] and part dusky, *china poblana*; mustachioed and *sarape*-laden [poncho-covered] bandits and posses of anonymously picturesque extras wearing the standard *sombrero* in impossibly festive or improbably destitute markets. It fashioned or recycled stereotypes that (despite the scrutiny of the Mexican censors) became familiar incarnations to the growing, cinema-going audience of the pervasive *mexicanidad* [Mexicanicity] of political and cultural rhetoric.

A diet of the eccentric fruits of American *Cinelandia* [*Movieland*] did lead to rather unpatriotic resistance to Mexican productions that attempted to replace cosmetic *pintoresquismo* [picturesqueness] with a sombre and quasi-mystical evocation of a corrupted rural arcadia. The following celebrated example can serve as an instructive parable: when the sometime Hollywood Latin dancer and B-movie villain turned proselytising director, Emilio ('El Indio') Fernández, previewed his classic film *María Candelaria* (1943), this new attempt to introduce a subject alien to the staple narrative repertoire established by Hollywood – the elegiac, aestheticised depiction of a tragedy in a rural Indian community – the Mexican audience vociferously rejected what it clearly considered an act of cinematic heresy. Their outrage may at least in part be attributed to the implausible casting of the aristocratic, *castizo* [of pure ethnic descent] beauty Dolores del Río as the persecuted village maiden (figure 3.1), an actress more familiar to Mexican audiences for her glamorous portrayals of exotic women in Hollywood dramas and musicals: films such as King Vidor's *Bird of Paradise* (1932), where she played 'a native' of 'the Southern Seas' or in *Flying Down to Rio* (1932) by Thorton Freeland, where she played a sedentary but decorative Brazilian aristocrat to Fred Astaire and Ginger Roger's footloose couple. On the other hand, the stylish director Fernando de Fuentes had enthused the public at home and abroad with the potent cocktail of festive *ranchero* [country] music, folkloric dance numbers and revisionist nostalgia of *Allá en el Rancho Grande* [*Down on the Great Ranch*] (1936), which led the poet Xavier Villaurrutia to coin the term for this nascent costume

Figure 3.1 Gabriel Figueroa. Dolores del Río as the Indian maiden María Candelaria in *María Candelaria* (1943).

genre – *cine mexicano pintoresco* [Mexican picturesque cinema] (figure 3.2).[7] The more acerbic film critic Cube Bonifant (aka 'Luz Alba'), dismissed the incongruities of this trend-setting film, which had invented 'una alegre vida de campo llena de música citadina, de charros de automóvil e inclusive de democracia' [a gay rural life full of city music, automobile cowboys, and even a touch of democracy'].[8] In a previous article, she had provocatively suggested that national productions rivalled Hollywood in parading '*mexicanismos falsos*' ['false Mexicanisms'], films which she later derided with the generic title *mexicanadas* [kitsch Mexicana].[9] In a prescient newspaper article, entitled 'México en la pantalla' ['Mexico on Screen'], published in 1917, the writer and critic Carlos González Peña noted the characteristic omission of *el pueblo bajo* [lower classes] from the contemporary screen. He explained this systematic rubbing out as a prudent tactic adopted by directors to placate a hostile local audience, who invariably ridiculed the appearance of anything purporting to signify plebeian or vernacular culture. He wondered whether the discouraging conclusion to be drawn from such representative fiascos was that 'nuestros país no es presentable sino "a la europea"' ['our country is only presentable if cast in a European mould'], not withstanding a populist Revolution. The dilemma for the aspiring director and patriot was how to 'embellecer artísticamente a nuestro pueblo bajo. No hay estética posible ante el calzón y el sombrerazo' ['beautify through artistic representation our lower classes. There is no possible aesthetic to be drawn from common long johns and outsized sombreros'].[10] However, the actor Mario Moreno was to transform

Figure 3.2 Still from *Allá en el rancho grande* (1936).

derision into indulgent complicity with his immensely popular comic creation: *Cantinflas*, the ubiquitous punning scapegrace *lépero* / everyman, whose untutored ingenuity in the face of innumerable setbacks celebrated the resilience of *el pueblo bajo* and *mestizo* popular culture.

The muralists, photographers and engravers that emerged in the wake of the Revolution were to disprove González Peña's reservations spectacularly, making of 'el calzón y el sombrerazo' the internationally recognised insignia of an aesthetic of solidarity, although the question of the actual scope and popular reception of their prosaic visual currency was problematic at the time and remains a debated issue (figure 3.3). The pictorial language fashioned by artists as diverse yet complementary as Diego Rivera (1886–1957), José Clemente Orozco (1883–1949),

Figure 3.3 Anon., illustrated cover of *México: Revista Quincenal de asuntos e ideas de interés general*, 15 April 1924, (in colour). Private collection.

Leopoldo Méndez (1902–1969), Tina Modotti (1896–1942) and Paul Strand (1890–1976) evinced the predominance of Indianist physiognomy, the secularization of mundane images of the labouring poor, the distilled primitivism of ancestral landscapes, the framing of archetypal collective ritual, the pregnant abstraction of traditional artefacts and the portentous telluric shadows of pre-Columbian and tribal architecture and sculpture.

From this outpouring of iconic images of a richly imagined national essence, and the Mexican traditions which underpinned the work of Rivera and his contemporaries, national cinema borrowed a number of formal paradigms: (a) monumental, public mural art provided a potent analogy for the giant silver screen. Mural narratives had taken over the pedagogic mission that belonged to literature in the nationalist cultural programme of the previous century; (b) graphic art lithographs, engravings and woodcuts suggested another enabling analogy. Rooted in the popular printing tradition of illustrated *corridos* [musical ballads], miracle stories, penny dreadfuls, *ejemplos* [instructive parables], satirical cartoons and *calaveras* [skeletal cartoons], this graphic work was exemplified by the artist revered above all others by the avant-garde, José Guadalupe Posada (1852–1913).[11] The immediate appeal of its simplified and stylised compositions, the apocalyptic binarism of black and white, seemed to offer an antidote to the mystifications of 'local colour' and the foreign distortions of the picturesque; (c) the photographic image: its transfixed reality, lending permanence to the elusive yet essential elements of collective experience. Combining poetic licence with documentary realism, photography in Mexico struck a fine balance between the trappings of the village studio and the transcendent objectives of a testimonial art, as practised by Tina Modotti and Manuel Álvarez Bravo; and (d) most seductive by far, the nineteenth-century pictorial tradition of the *cuadro de costumbres*, sketches of social types, racial physiognomies, customs, an exhaustive catalogue of fragments – or *mosaico* – insisting on diversity and unity, emblematic traditional scenes, the theatricality of the local in the decentred universe of post-colonial Mexico. This genre attempted to compose and lend coherence to the endemic heterogeneity of a destabilised cultural and political order, to picture that invisible totality – the nation. The knowing sequence of folkloric *cuadros* that characterised so many of the films of the period borrowed a well-tried technique to similar ends (figure 3.4).

The seminal films of Emilio Fernández (1904–1986) are perhaps the most original, internationally celebrated and controversial of those produced in the so-called 'Golden Age of Mexican Cinema': they exemplify the successes and limitations of the dominant pictorial style, as well as the pitfalls of a nationalist aesthetic. His long, fruitful

Figure 3.4 Still from *La zandunga* (1937), directed by Fernando de Fuentes.

collaboration with the mercurial Gabriel Figueroa (1907–1997), the outstanding cinematographer of his generation, culminated in the development of a highly stylised imagistic vocabulary in black and white, distilled out of a compendium of references to the work of artists concerned with cultural regeneration and national specificity.[12]

Iconoclastic and self-mythologising, Fernández discovered his vocation and ethnic destiny amidst the costumes, sets and props of Hollywood's kitsch *mexicana*: he made instructive if ultimately unsuccessful attempts at incarnating the imaginary Mexico between 1926 and 1934. In two 1930 B-Westerns, *Oklahoma Cyclone* and *The Land of Missing Men*, he played the revealingly anglicised 'Panchez [sic] Gomez' and the anonymous 'Lopez' respectively. The same year saw him appear as a dancer in a musical comedy by the Catalan musician Xavier Cugat, which astutely gathered the dominant Hispanic stereotypes in a single film with the disarming title of *Charros, gauchos y manolas* [*Mexican Cowboys, Argentinian Horsemen and Castilian Dancers*], part of Hollywood's failed attempt at an exportable Spanish-speaking cinema. In 1932 he bolstered the rows of exemplary Latin males in the crowded *carioca* dance number in *Flying Down to Rio*, and played a '*mestizo*' in *The Western Code*. When in later life, as a consecrated, pistol-wielding actor ('el charro negro' ['the cowboy in black']) and director he boasted in an interview that: 'Ni los mexicanos sabían como era México hasta que yo se los enseñé' ['Not even the Mexicans knew what Mexico was like until I showed them'], it is tempting to regard his own foundational mythologies as emerging out of the humiliating acquaintance with Hollywood's thoroughgoing caricatures.[13] His monolithic, sombre designs repudiated the frivolous colour in film generated by the consumer phenomenon that his friend the muralist David Alfaro Siqueiros (1896–1974) dismissed as 'Mexican-curios chic'.[14] Having danced with Olga Falcón the *mexicanísimo* 'jarabe tapatío' [Guadalajaran folk dance] in Fernando de Fuentes' folkloric smash *Allá en el Rancho Grande*, it is not surprising that he seized on the unfinished but highly suggestive work of Eisenstein's and Tissé's *¡Qué viva México!* (1931), for a vision of a transcendent grandeur absent in his experience of Mexico in film. The transformation of Dolores del Río from Hollywood starlet specialising in foreign sirens to Mexican muse and superstar, sacred icon of the national film industry, owes a great deal to Fernández's cleansing of her image from the cosmetic exoticism of Hollywood, to glamorous incarnation of the Mexican sublime. Invariably lit and framed by Figueroa's baroque chiaroscuro, her classical face under a humble but hieratic *rebozo* [shawl], lingered in the national imaginary as the expression of an ideal Mexican femininity, aspiring to be natural and indigenous, yet belonging to the realm of Platonic ideas (figure 3.5).[15]

It is Fernández's lyrical evocations of a timeless yet tragically flawed rural Mexico that established his reputation for a polemical, highly

Figure 3.5 Gabriel Figueroa. Dolores del Río and Pedro Armendáriz in *María Candelaria* (1943).

personal *indigenismo* [pro-Indian discourse]. His films, from *Flor Silvestre* [*Wild Flower*] (1943) to *Río Escondido* (1947), *Pueblerina* (1948) and *Maclovia* (1948), posited a symbolic Indian identity and peasant culture rather than the attentive scrutiny of cultural difference proposed by the ethnographic cinema of American pioneers like Robert Flaherty. His long-standing scriptwriter, the left-wing novelist Mauricio Magdaleno, recalling his collaboration on *María Candelaria*, set in a notional Xochimilco, judged the plot implausible and the cinematic treatment of the subject false: 'yo pensaba que la historia de *María Candelaria* era falsa … Lo que más me molestaba … era su folklorismo' ['I thought that the story of *María Candelaria* was false … What I most disliked was … its folkloricity'].[16] Fernández, on the other hand, was rightly convinced that the work would seduce the sceptical artistic intelligentsia wary of what it viewed as the parochial and reactionary pastiche of rural society in Mexican films critical of social reform. Significantly, Fernández's first starring role on his return from Hollywood had been in *Janitzio* (1934–5), directed by Carlos Navarro and shot by the American Jack Draper, a knowledgeable admirer of Eisenstein's work, on location in Michoacán. Fernández played the noble Zirahuén, an Indian fisherman cheated of his livelihood and fiancée by a corrupt white merchant (figure 3.6). His subsequent work as a director

Figure 3.6 Emilio Fernández as Zirahuen in *Janitzio* (1934).

combined ideological parables with the exaltation of native beauty in what he acknowledged was 'this great desire to mexicanize the Mexicans, for we are becoming americanised'.[17] At the end of his life he compared his *oeuvre* with his friend Diego Rivera's spiritual reconquest of Mexico through kilometres of patriotic mural art and paintings that had elevated *los de abajo* [the underdogs]. Rivera had revealed the timeless heart of the nation to be where Fernández had known it to be hidden '[in] rural things [which] have always been the same, always, always'.[18]

Gabriel Figueroa's association brought a cultured aesthetic eye to bear on Fernández's passionate allegories. Internationally renowned for his work with Luis Buñuel, John Ford and John Huston, as well as every significant Mexican director (winning his first international prize for *Allá en el Rancho Grande*), Figueroa's collaboration with Fernández coincided with a deep-seated admiration for the social and aesthetic scope of contemporary Mexican graphic art. The artists' collective founded in 1937 and known as *El Taller de Gráfica Popular* (TGP) included the charismatic Leopoldo Méndez, and at various times collaborated with Siqueiros, republican exiles, and the salient writers and artists of the period producing pamphlets, broadsheets, albums, illustrated books, educational materials and posters.[19] Champion of a robust, civic art committed to political agitation for change, accessible to the illiterate disenfranchised masses, Leopoldo Méndez, according to Figueroa, initiated him in 'el aprendizaje de lo que era mexicano' ['apprenticeship in all things truly Mexican'] through his powerful engravings.[20]

Méndez had harboured a dream, which was finally realised in his collaboration with Figueroa in five of Fernández's films, including *Río Escondido* (1947) and *Pueblerina* (1948): the production of graphic murals.[21] The translation of this dream to celluloid marked the fusion of a populist aesthetic with the primacy of the photographic composition in film. Leopoldo Méndez was commissioned to produce an album of ten engravings based on *Río Escondido*, a film which told the tragic but edifying story of an enlightened rural teacher's struggle against a tyrannical local *cacique* [local tyrant]. Méndez had interpreted the topical subject some years previously (1938–9) for the TGP, in seven lithographs based on newspaper reports of the persecution and murder of government-appointed rural teachers.[22] The project intended to pay homage to the martyrs of progress but also to vindicate the government-subsidised *Misiones culturales* at a time when they were being denounced as outlets for inflammatory Communist propaganda.[23] According to Figueroa, Méndez was shown the edited film and responded selectively to the cinematography and the subject matter to provide narrative imagery of his own:

> Los grabados para el cine los hacía con la conciencia de que se iban a agrandar e interpretaba la historia para poder hacer el grabado. Nunca copiaba, si acaso en alguna forma estaba influido con el contenido de la película él lo interpretaba, porque no me iba a copiar la fotografía.[24]

> [He would prepare the engravings for the cinema in the knowledge that they would be magnified and he interpreted the narrative in order to come up with an image. He never copied. If he happened to be influenced by the content of the film, he always interpreted it because it was never his intention to copy my cinematography.]

The engravings for the film were photographed and projected in the title sequence on the giant screen, acquiring the dimension and finality of a mural. The scope of Méndez's images was rather more prefatory and eye-catching than the static decorative background to a title sequence might suggest. Figueroa pointed out that their inclusion had a practical aim which took advantage of Méndez's virtuosity as a communicator who dramatised abstract ideas for a popular readership through pamphlets, manifestos, posters, crusading magazines and educational manuals (figure 3.7). The intrusive didacticism which advertised Fernández's authorship saw the engravings of scenes of feudal exploitation and barbarism as having an

Figure 3.7 Leopoldo Méndez, *El dueño de todo [The Owner of Everything]*, engraving for *Río Escondido* (1947).

initiatory role for the cinema audience (figure 3.8). The director envisaged a dynamic interaction between the projection of the engravings and the public. Méndez offered a forceful visual digest of the themes which would begin to shape audience response to the civic-minded tragedy about to unfold on the screen. Both Figueroa and Fernández were interested in replicating the monumental spectacle afforded by Rivera's and Siqueiros's secular piety, which made an emotional appeal for ordinary people's minds. Their lofty cinema borrowed effects from, as well as paid homage to, the *Escuela Mexicana* [Mexican School] in the arts:

> era totalmente nueva la posibilidad de ver ampliado un grabado a ese tamaño, era un verdadero mural ... Quiero destacar que la función de los grabados no era sólo realzar la destreza y creatividad del grabador, pues la gran fuerza que tenían los grabados de Leopoldo a nosotros nos ayudaron dramáticamente para preparar el público. Al público ya no le pescaba de sorpresa el drama de la película pues con los grabados ya había entrado en calor, pues se le había dado una síntesis de la película.[25]

> [The possibility of seeing an engraving enlarged to that size was totally new, it became a true mural .... I would like to emphasise that the function of the engravings was not only to showcase the skill and creativity of the engraver because the power of Leopoldo's engravings helped us to prepare the public through their drama. The audience anticipated the drama of the film because, thanks to the engravings, they had warmed to its themes since they had been presented with a synopsis of the film.]

The highly composed nature of Figueroa's dramatic images seem almost to be designed to be extracted as stills. Ironically, motion pictures

Figure 3.8 Leopoldo Méndez, *El bruto [The Brute]*, engraving for *Río Escondido* (1947).

for Fernández-Figueroa aimed to achieve the plenitude and definition of the perfect frozen shot: every frame a finished composition, fixed in time, a monument to a national essence (figures 3.9 and 3.10). If the illusion of permanence was the final objective, the source of some of Figueroa's most accomplished effects – Paul Strand – had paradoxically attempted to surpass through his camerawork the static fixity of the mural as a medium of mass communication.[26] Commissioned by the Cárdenas government to produce a series of divulgatory films for a specifically Indian audience, only *Redes* (directed by Fred Zinneman) was completed in 1934 before the programme was abandoned. Following Eisenstein's much-vaunted example, most of the actors were amateurs, to inject a gritty realism and authenticity to this uplifting tale of the principled rebellion and solidarity of a community of fishermen faced with exploitation and a corrupt police force. Significantly, unlike Strand and Eisenstein, Fernández's public authentication of native culture resulted in the substitution of revelatory physiognomic portraits of the untutored and the unwashed, for lingering close-ups of the desirable, flawless visages of the universal tinsel *mestizas*, María Félix, Dolores del Río and Columba Domínguez. These now legendary actresses wore on screen the symbolic trappings of a national ethnicity, an elegant sartorial reconditioning of ethnography which revised the much more flamboyant investiture of popular costume by the artist Frida Kahlo, friend of both Dolores del Río and María Félix.[27]

Figure 3.9 Gabriel Figueroa, scene from *Río Escondido* (1947).

Figure 3.10 Gabriel Figueroa, scene from *Río Escondido* (1947).

In the pursuit of an enabling 'mexicanismo auténtico' ['authentic Mexicanism'], Figueroa's influential cinematography adapted Eisenstein's metaphor for the binarisms of Mexican culture: the traditional, syncretic *sarape*, with its bold mesh of contrasting patterns, had inspired the stylised motifs and contrasts in light and shadow of Eisenstein's archetypal Mexican scenes. But whilst his position as a sympathetic tourist had led Eisenstein to attempt to capture Mexico's 'violentos colores',[28] Figueroa had adhered to an elemental formula drained of superficial colour in the belief that, as he said in an interview: '... el pueblo mexicano no tiene color. Las camisas y los calzones de manta, el sombrero de petate y los rebozos negros de las mujeres. No hay color, solo en las fiestas sale el colorido muy barroco, pero en general el pueblo está despojado de color' ['... common Mexican people are not colourful. The shirts and long johns made of plain cloth, the sombrero made of natural fibre and the women's black shawls. There is no colour, only during celebrations do very baroque tonalities emerge, but in general ordinary men and women are divested of all colour'].[29] Figueroa and Fernández constructed a much-emulated concept of authenticity out of the slippery division between the rainbow gaiety and quaintness of the tourist object and the sombre-hued nobility of the original, popular garment.

The now canonical films of Fernández-Figueroa, partly based on an analogy with the graphic arts and on a non-cinematic pictorial tradition, produced images representative of national identity which were themselves to become fetishised in a manner they were hardly designed to prevent. Concerned with undoing Hollywood stereotypes, they sought lasting visual archetypes. A contemporary Mexican artist, Javier de la Garza, lifted stills from Fernández-Figueroa's *La perla* (1945, released 1947) – of statuesque fishermen shown in profile against a vast cloud-filled sky – copying them on canvas in lurid, painted colour in an unwittingly parodic homage (figures 11 and 12).[30]

De la Garza emerged as one of the better-known exponents of a mid-1980s trend in painting, dubbed *Neomexicanismo*, with cross-border appeal in the art market. He – along with Dulce María Núñez, Julio Galán, Elena Climent and others – revisited the techniques, styles, tropes and iconography of the golden age of Mexican cultural nationalism from a perspective which often diluted ironic tribute to visual monoliths and a coarse-grained vernacular with a self-referential nostalgia for figurative traditions. The critic Osvaldo Sánchez encapsulated well this neo-expressionist phenomenon and its reception in Mexico:

Un Bad painting nutrido de kitsch urbano, de íconos populares, de fantasías oníricas, de nostalgia retro y de emblemas nacionalistas, a veces con aditaciones de objetos y de símbolos a medio terreno entre el artefacto y el collage ... Había mucho entusiasmo por este regreso *light* al contexto simbólico nacional, tal vez en la esperanza de que la expresión cultural funcionara como corrector a las derivas globalistas de las políticas institucionales.[31]

[A sort of Bad painting drawing on urban kitsch, popular icons, oneiric fantasies, retro nostalgia and nationalist emblems, sometimes with the additions of objects and symbols halfway between artefact and collage ... There was a great deal of enthusiasm for this diet-*light* return to the context of national symbolism, perhaps in the vain hope that cultural expression might act as an antidote to the globalising sympathies of governmental policies.]

In the case of de la Garza, the appropriation of a visual archive of the classic and the banal centred on the Mexican film heritage. By excising stills from Fernández-Figueroa vehicles he rendered the highly pictorial cinematography of the originals literal through a painterly reconversion which reframed what in the films was the repeated stilling of motion to create an iconic picture. Under his treatment the austere symmetries and tonal restraint of Figueroa's aesthetic of authenticity becomes overpainted in folkloric technicolour, falling somewhere between the humble hand-coloured photographic memento and the reverential excess of Jesús Helguera's commercial calendars depicting Mexican myths and types. A similar treatment of a scenic still from *Enemigos* [*Enemies*] (1933), Figueroa's early collaboration with director Chano Urueta, crops the original and transforms Figueroa's sombre-hued blanket enveloping a

Figure 3.11 Gabriel Figueroa, scene from *La Perla* (1945), directed by Fernández.

Figure 3.12 Javier de la Garza, *La Perla* (1945) (in colour).

recumbent woman into a multi-coloured tourist trophy (figures 3.13 and 3.14). The copied image in its capacity as fetishised object levels the grand manner of Fernández-Figueroa's classicizing style by yielding to the impurities of popular consumption and taste. In some respects de la Garza's false replica is revealing of a widespread misreading of the pictorial rhetoric generated in the 1930s and 1940s in some film and art. It fails to see beyond the often contrived and hieratic black-and-white compositions to the underlying fibre of resistance which complicates the simplification of cultural identities constructed in celluloid. An American critic like Mackinley Helm, in personal contact with art circles across the border, presciently pointed out to a prospective 1941 exhibition audience in the U.S.A. how 'unmexican' art by modern Mexican artists would appear precisely because it sought to distance itself from the 'Mexico Picturesque' of foreign travel books and albums:

> For every native painter working conscientiously at home, five migrating Americans have portrayed the Mexican scene, of whom time and again it has been said, in our country, that their pictures are more 'Mexican' than those produced by the Mexicans themselves ... The generality of Mexican painters, having an almost morbid aversion to the picturesque, characteristically approaches subject matter inwardly.[32]

Figure 3.13 Gabriel Figueroa, still from *Enemigos* (1933), directed by Chano Urueta.

Figure 3.14 Javier de la Garza, *Enemigos* (1933) (in colour).

When Figueroa spoke of allying himself with Méndez's graphic *mística* [mysticism], he was acknowledging the struggle towards a quality of *inward* truth rather than outward appearance that created a poetic blurring of observation and abstraction on the screen. The cinematographic pursuit of sculptural moments, which had the density and permanence of some endangered primal essence, describes a strategy of defence rather than blithe affirmation. An overtly and problematically Indianist film such as *María Candelaria* contains within the implausibilities of its casting and scenarios a preoccupation with the social impact of representation and misrepresentation – in which it is implicated – which has been largely overlooked. It is a composite portrait of María painted by an itinerant city artist, in which he combines studies of her draped bust with sketches of nude Indian models, which precipitates her tragic downfall. The well-meaning but improvident artist soils what he most admires. The explicit Marian imagery which accompanies the figure of the misconstrued Indian woman points to the unresolved tensions between the ideal and the compromised reality which typify the visualisations of rural Mexico on screen. The novelist and scriptwriter José Revueltas made a suggestive distinction, when discussing Fernández's films in 1950, between a legitimate poetic distortion and an arbitrary poetic distortion of reality.[33] The 'reiterada distorsión' manifest in Fernández-Figueroa films and in much of the art that inspired their visual language, turns on this fine and often imponderable distinction.

María Candelaria defines itself textually in the opening sequence as a story salvaged from the forgotten margins of national life in the year before the outbreak of the Mexican Revolution: 'Una tragedia de amor arrancada de un rincón indígena de México, Xochimilco, en el año de 1909' ['A tragic love story torn from an indigenous corner of Mexico, Xochimilco, in 1909']. The explicatory subtitle introduces the symbolic historical referent which frames the critique of racial discrimination, juridical corruption, educational neglect, exploitative labour and cultural misconceptions to which the Indian community is shown to be subject at the hands of a despotic government and local merchants. We are dealing with a romantic parable with a coercive moralising structure rather than a documentary fiction or a piece of social realism. But, if this presentational preamble alludes implicitly to the conventional 'Causes of the Revolution' theme that had motivated many pictorial reconstructions intent on dispelling back-sliding nostalgia and reinforcing identification with a just and heroic struggle, it also serves to underline its equally overt concern with the very representation of the past and ethnic identity.[34]

The next filmic passage involves a sequence of single close-up shots of celebrated Aztec statues of female deities, from national archaeological collections, culminating in a dramatically cropped frontal shot of a contemporary Indian woman's face filling the screen. The pace of the editing (by Gloria Schoemann) leading up to the all-encompassing racial physiognomy is marked by a processional decorum emphasising the physicality and potent presence of these stone effigies.[35] The rhythm quickens markedly with the dissolve from this final cropped visage to a spatial arrangement of ancient sculpted features in a frieze exhibited next to the same Indian exemplar now restored to a less oneiric size. The visual blur that is resolved into the contiguity of flesh and stone faces effects through its acceleration a spatiotemporal confluence which was held to be key to an understanding of contemporary Indian identity: the proximity of an ancient past existing durably and palpably in the present characterised modern perceptions of Indian alterity, influenced by Manuel Gamio's archaeo-anthropological model for promoting a racially integrated nation.[36] María Candelaria, the audience will be told, epitomised a pre-contact dynastic Indian beauty surviving into a post-conquest world marked by acculturation and miscegenation: '... esta indígena tenía la belleza de las antiguas princesas' [... this aboriginal woman had the beauty of the ancient princesses]. She is described as 'la esencia de la verdadera belleza mexicana' ['the essence of authentic Mexican beauty'], making explicit the sense in which this figure is the personification of something abstract: the recuperation of an ideal aesthetic consanguinity. In the context of this visual reinvigoration of a pre-Hispanic heritage it is unsurprising to discover that the most salient stylistic device of the film will be the composed stillness of lingering shots of the 'Indian' protagonists in close-up or seen from low angles erect on the raised banks of the canals so that their figures acquire the qualities of statues on a pedestal. The telluric qualities associated with the hieratic and frozen movements and postures of Lorenzo Rafael (played by Pedro Armendáriz) in particular and María Candelaria, although her bearing is more cloyingly expressive, are exemplified in a scene in which the chaste couple appear ascendant in relief against something akin to a celestial backdrop. The cloud-filled skies of the film play on a pictorial tradition of mystical landscapes where spirituality resides in the evocation of airy altitudes. From this spiritualised vantage point the characters express their unbroken attachment to the land in poetic terms of refined simplicity (echoes of Ramón López Velarde's celebrated paean to a homely motherland in 'La suave patria' ['The Gentle Homeland']): '... aquí nacimos los dos y aquí hemos vivido siempre ... esta es nuestra tierra, que bella, que suave' ['... here we were both born and here we have always lived ... this is our land, how beautiful and gentle']. The faux naïve blend of pigeon Spanish and archaic native syntax, which is meant to convey the verbal distinctiveness of modern Indian speech, is a stylistic affectation which, along with references to the imagery of prestigious Mexican and foreign visual artists (Saturnino Herrán, Rivera, Roberto Montenegro, Strand, Modotti, Eisenstein), betrays the high cultural aspirations of this would-be popular film.

Lorenzo Rafael adopts the remote, impassive manner, and a near mineral ponderousness of movement, that were commonly taken to represent the natural behaviour of Indians. For influential intellectual visionaries such as José Vasconcelos, who saw in the spectacle of speed the transformative power of modernisation, this apparent physical stasis served to denote the arrested development and resistance to change of all isolated and unmixed Indian groups.[37] However, under Fernández's direction, the verbal and gestural restraint of María Candelaria's loyal defender is meant to enhance the character's manly nobility, his racial dignity and unbending, inner strength. Lorenzo Rafael's stoical forbearance, captured by close and medium shots of his stationary persona, is mistaken for cunning stealth by the villainous merchant who displays the typical racial prejudices and anti-Indian phobias of his class. The defiant, clenched profiles and obdurate expressions of tortured or defeated yet unvanquished Indian figures to be found in Siqueiros's large-scale depictions of struggle and suffering from the 1930s (including a heroic portrait of the assassinated Revolutionary agrarian leader Emiliano Zapata) provide the mould for Lorenzo Rafael's most characteristic postures, which exude a natural integrity unaffected by his abject condition. The obsidian mask-like plasticity of Siqueiros's suffering proletarian or peasant Indian mothers and physically broken male workers, with thick angular brush strokes carving out jutting racial bone structures, offers an artistic model for the embodiment of targeted oppression.[38] It is ironic that the compilatory picture-making of *María Candelaria*'s visual borrowings and citations should have neutralised the perspectival dynamism that Siqueiros increasingly sought to inject in his easel and mural work, partly influenced by the spatial projections and transformative mobility that he admired in 'motion pictures'.[39] Although there is a dramatic crane shot of a kneeling Lorenzo Rafael in front of the local church, Figueroa tends not to exploit troubling angles or diagonals, preferring conventional framings that emphasise the iconicity of the projected image. Despite – or perhaps precisely because of – the tribute paid to his work in the film,[40] Rivera publicly criticised the petrifying camera work, its all too visible framing as well as the conventional recreations of village spaces, glaring anachronisms and inaccurate staging of artistic practice:

... ni los camárografos tuvieron la felíz ocurrencia de fotografiar el Mercado en mañana de tianguis, prefiriendo hacer escenas en uno más convencional, lleno de puestos fantásticos, absurdos, que yo jamás he visto ... y la fotografía a base de blanco y negro, sin matices, con momentos demasiado lóbregos junto con otros en que la luz rompe e inunda la escena, resulta monótona e inmóvil. La cámara apenas si tiene movimiento.[41]

[... nor did it occur to those behind the camera to photograph the market scene during an actual market-day morning, preferring instead a more conventional set, full of unreal stands, absurd ones, that I have never seen ... and the photography, based on black and white, without tonal variation, with moments of excessive lugubriousness and others in which the light breaks and floods the scene, proves to be monotonous and static.]

As a colourist who celebrated the variegated spectacles of popular culture to be found in markets and festivals, Rivera objected to Figueroa's bold graphic simplifications and dramatic lighting which imposed an austere aesthetic symmetry and conferred a self-conscious sublimity to what the painter considered a condescending rural fantasy that divested popular culture of its vitality and irreverence.[42] Apart from the prominence given to the still image on the big screen, Rivera also seems to have disliked those residual elements of a discredited pictorialist aesthetic in painting and photography that he detected in the design of the film.

It is interesting to note that although both Siqueiros and Rivera admired the innovations and defended the artistic credentials of modernist photography in Mexico in the 1920s (especially the use of the close-up and the work of Weston and Modotti) and used creative and journalistic photographs by others to construct some of their compositions and portraits, they retained a traditional sense of painting's superior calling as a synthetic and revelatory medium capable of greater breadth, universality and durability.[43] If genuine art does not reproduce the visible but makes the visible, then photography's replicative mechanism restricted its scope and autonomy, although it could serve to modernise painting by cauterising away the last gauzy remnants of pre-Raphaelite symbolism. For these social realists, photography was principally a purveyor of veracity, a factual medium that could be directed by a cultivated and discriminating eye. Rivera and other film critics objected to the artificiality or artfulness of the cinematographic image in *María Candelaria* in terms which suggest that photography's natural evidentiary property had been corrupted: 'No deja de ser bonita la fotografía de *María Candelaria*, pero falsa' ['The photography in *María Candelaria* is certainly pretty, but false'].[44]

The elevation of the humble and ordinary peasant farmer, although from a community uniquely tied to forms of cultivation of Aztec origin (the floating *chinampas* [man-made islands]), assumes a particular scheme of points of view which produce the formal hauteur of Fernández-Figueroa's representation of Indian culture. The pre-Columbian pedigree of this man-made environment is part of its attraction as an emblematic geography. The oblique inclusion of foreign tourists visiting the intricate waterways to marvel at the idiosyncratic customs and picturesque panorama situates these locations within the bounds of itineraries charting a clearly differentiated cultural identity. As a reviewer of the film noted approvingly in 1944: 'Xochimilco, el sitio al que pudiéramos llamar más "fotogénico" de nuestro país' [Xochimilco, the place that we could call the most "photogenic" in our country].[45] The key collective scenes on the water combine expansive semicircular long takes with figures moving from the horizon into shot followed by a sequence of individual close-ups of silent Indian villagers seemingly chiselled against the sky, standing motionless with impenetrable expressions. The stony impassivity of their demeanour and the arrested camera serve both an aesthetic and a dramatic purpose when the entire village takes to canoes in order to intercept María Candelaria and prevent her from violating her exile as a 'polluted' member by reaching the market to sell flowers to pay her debt to the store-keeper. This petrean quality helps to typify a communal attitude which adds to the pathos of the outcast maiden subject to the unfeeling persecution of her own people while stressing the trope of pre-Hispanic stone archetypes come to life.[46]

It is not merely that the Indian figures in the film appear sculptural, it is the cinematography itself that is sculptural in the sense that it makes images of Indian characters that imitate the look of photographs of statues. The cinematography raises indigenous figures into a definite category of canonical images and by so doing aspires to place itself as well as its subjects into a high art tradition which includes photography as well as painting. It alludes to and redeploys images belonging to the tradition of photographed Aztec sculpture which had helped to visualise a nationalist agenda from the 1870s onwards. In the 1920s and 1930s analogue photography acquired a documentary value for Mexican artists and scholars through its apparently objective visual archive of pre-Columbian statues and edifices, from cropped, close-up details to full-volume representations. Such descriptive photography provided the source material for an imaginary museum of autochthony which promoted an Indianist cultural identity predicated on the exaltation of a largely sculptural corpus. An admiration for unearthed pre-Columbian ceremonial statuary and stone or clay artefacts played a significant part in the reimagining and objectification of indigenous subjects in the visual arts and sculpture in the foundational decades of twentieth-century cultural nationalism. Photographers made a living from reproductions of canonical and contemporary fine art and pre-Columbian objects so that the process of replication could involve multiple layers of representation with a capacity for cross-pollination between creative media. For example, the prominent avant-garde photographer, still-man and cinematographer, Agustín Jiménez (1901–74), not only reproduced paintings by Rivera and other artists such as Carlos Mérida (1891–1984) whose work explicitly revisited the so-called primitive Indian heritage, but also the work of contemporary sculptors inspired by ancient monuments such as Oliverio Martínez (1901–38) and Mardonio Magaña (1866–1947).[47] Portraits of pre-Hispanic sculpture by well-known photographers as well as of contemporary art works influenced by its plasticity became a popular genre in a 1930s periodical press intent on sharing a Mexico-centred visuality with its middle-class readership. The physical presence of sculpture, its volume and density, offers a paradigmatic experience for the stately camera work of Figueroa, which aspired to give formal solidity to the flickering celluloid image.

The control of lighting in the film throws up intriguing analogies with the methods used to photograph three-dimensional works of art. In order to achieve a clean and unmistakable contour the recurrent backdrop of white clouds floating in a serene sky provides the equivalent of the white cloth that early photographers were recommended to place at one side of a statue 'to reflect back the sun's rays and cause a faint illumination of the parts which would otherwise be lost in shadow'.[48] In order to avoid strong shadows, which might confuse the subject, a better delineation could be obtained in cloudy weather, according to early experiments with specimen sculpture. In Mexican ethnographic photography Indian 'specimens' were posed in front of white cloths so as to bring into relief the generic profile, the general form over the distracting surface particulars. The fallen sheet of light effect helped to diffuse the depth of contrast that in black and white images could black out the features of dark-skinned models. If we turn to the film's cinematographic strategies – the tonal contrasts, the still camera work, the compositional symmetries, the frontality of poses, the elevating angles, the close-ups of silent faces and motionless torsos – we discover the underlying purpose of Fernández and Figueroa's collaboration: that of turning Indian beings into imperishable works of national art. Naturalism, which might reinscribe ethnic and cultural polarities, is overtaken by a finely calibrated aestheticising approach in order to craft the visual materialisation of a national form. The lapidary aesthetic may well also turn the relation between spectator and screen characters cast as living sculpture into one associated with the contemplation of other consecrated simulacra, whether of a civic, museological or religious kind.

In *María Candelaria* the Eisensteinian visual conceit of collapsing temporal distinctions by juxtaposing a classic archaeological remain with an ethnographic specimen to celebrate the inherent racial nobility and cultural monumentality of the descendants of pre-Hispanic empires, acknowledges what had become a conventional imagistic strategy for elevating a traditionally subordinate subject. The shots frequently resemble, with their photographic and pictorial fixities, those tableaux vivants in which life imitated art and the actors duplicated sculpted and painted figures.[49] They are conceived as individual aesthetic manifestations that can be excerpted and rehung in a private anthology of indicative or striking images. The eloquent reticence embodied by Lorenzo Rafael extends to encompass the quality of silent stills that many sequences retain. According to Figueroa's testimony, his collaborations with Fernández always followed an unusual pattern in which the positioning of the camera and the actors was decided by the cameraman rather than the director.[50] The latter explained the effect he wanted to achieve and the former interpreted the ideas, developing the formal language that lent their films their explicitly artful design. Given Figueroa's professional antecedents in photographic studio portraiture, advertising and as a still-man, it is perhaps unsurprising that he developed a focal style which drew attention to its artistic contrivance with highly manipulative lighting of faces, interiors cast in painterly chiaroscuros and the overly composed placing of people and props. A serious collector of paintings with a passion for pre-Columbian figurines, Figueroa explained revealingly in later life that he approached problems of framing and perspective first from a pictorial rather than technical angle.[51] The compositional allusions to easel and mural work on Indian themes by leading artists, such as Rivera (a friend and associate of Fernández and Figueroa) and Roberto Montenegro (1885–1968), inform the gestures, poses and scenarios of the film and follow naturally from this representational premise, for both these artists (as in the case of many of their contemporaries) were champions and avid collectors of pre-Hispanic artefacts and folk art, depicting Indian singularity through the evidence of its ancient as well as contemporary material culture. A didactic antiquarianism provides the infrastructure for the portrayal of indigenous culture.[52]

It is worth remembering that nation-conscious artists such as Saturnino Herrán (1887–1918) and the early Rivera had attempted to 'indianise' the figurative heritage of the European Renaissance, combining identifiably European representational techniques and styles with unmistakable vernacular subjects, whether of popular, mythological, historical or archaeological extraction, in an attempt to evidence cultural fusion in Mexico through its distinctive and lasting permutations.[53] When discussing the construction of a classically denuded and anti-picturesque visual aesthetic in Figueroa's cinematography, it is worth considering the extent to which it is based on a homage to a particular strain of cultural nationalism with a marked symbolist bent originating in the first decade of the twentieth century. The impersonation of a pure-blood Indian by Dolores del Río needs to be seen in the context of the integrationist ideal advocated by Gamio, the pre-eminent archaeologist of the post-Revolutionary decades, in which the imitative and Eurocentric middle classes were reconciled with a living Indian heritage: '… hay que forjarse – ya sea temporalmente – un alma indígena' ['… we must forge for ourselves – even if only temporarily – an Indian soul'].[54] The aesthetic consequence of this was to be a harmonisation of 'la producción artística del indio y del individuo de la clase media' [the artistic production of the Indian and the middle-class individual] that entailed the blending of high and low, ancient and contemporary, colonial and revolutionary forms of culture. The film unwittingly provides a retrospective of an Indianist figurative aesthetic which by the 1940s was regarded as conventional and dated in experimental artistic circles. In 1945, the year of *María*

Candelaria's release, Siqueiros launched his polemic against the fossilisation of modern Mexican art production in terms which illuminated the film's cultural anxieties. His critique helped to contextualise Figueroa's excisions and stylisations during a period of artistic transition and crisis:

> Las fuentes profundas de la tradición mexicana no están en los aspectos superficiales, en las expresiones pintorescas, en pueriles 'fórmulas de mexicanidad' tales como 'el color de las blusas de la indias' (color de origen industrial extranjero), o 'el color con que los indios pintan sus casas' (consecuencia obligada de un retraso industrial), o el empleo de estilos provenientes, arqueológicamente, de la escultura autóctona.[55]

> [The deep sources of the Mexican tradition are not to be found in superficial aspects, in picturesque manifestations, in puerile 'formulas of mexicanicity' such as 'the colour of Indian women's blouses' (colour of foreign industrial origin), or 'the colour with which Indians paint their houses' (the unavoidable product of industrial backwardness), or the archaeological use of styles from autochthonous sculpture.]

The figure of María Candelaria is cast in a number of postures and activities which by the 1940s had become archetypal in pictorial narratives and photography intent on capturing the elemental cultural forms typifying rural Indian life by imitating 'timeless' clay and ·stone representations. So the willowy Dolores del Río is seen bent over a *metate* [stone mortar] grinding corn as in Rivera's and Siqueiros's depictions of *molenderas* [women grinding corn], emphasising the eternal plasticity of a squat shape found in pre-Hispanic sculpture of domestic life. She is shown sitting weaving outside her hut at a traditional loom as in mass-produced postcards by C.B. Waite and anthropological illustrations such as Ernest Gruening's in *Mexico and Its Heritage* (1928), and, in a long shot, paddling her picturesque canoe full of flowers as if bringing to life one of the collectible wax figurines of types, trades and customs which had been popular curiosities and mementoes since the nineteenth century. When she carries her flowers to market, the basket on her back tilts forward so that the blooms crown her face as she bends under the weight in a frontal, close-range composition favoured by Rivera in numerous works featuring flower-sellers.[56] Although the shots associated with the arrival of the fugitives in the local market are lit festively as in Rivera's more decorative compositions, this mood is short-lived and off-set by the lyrical, nocturnal passages on the water which reprise the melancholy theme attached to flowers as *vanitas* symbols made famous by Saturnino Herrán's *La ofrenda* [*The Offering*] (1913), which evoked the mystical piety of a group of Indians carrying bundles of Day of the Dead marigolds in a *trajinera* [traditional canal barge or canoe].[57] The shots of anonymous Indian workers unloading produce on the quay while the rapacious merchant Don Damian looks on dwell on bronzed, muscular, nude torsos bent under substantial loads in a variation on the theme of *cargadores* or builders shifting materials to be found in Herrán's male Indian nudes and allegories on labour, in Tina Modotti's distilled images dignifying the working poor, or in an early mural by Roberto Montenegro profiling the construction of a new social order.[58] It is revealing of the cinematography's purist inclinations that those mass scenes which most clearly resemble an orchestrated folkloric pageant, the procession to the village church for the blessing of the animals ceremony, turn seamlessly into shots of a barbarous crowd bent on violent retribution. The shift from the orderly procession of brightly festooned village faithful to baying mob can be read in aesthetic terms, rather than as part of the film's undoubted social critique, to reveal Figueroa's repudiation of the contrived gaiety of local colour in pursuit of the sombre shades of a high cultural seriousness engaged with the force of a tribal identity perceived alternately as authentic and primitive, generative and destructive, beautiful and grotesque.

After the opening sequence of archaeological emblems, the next wide-angle shot in the film transforms the gallery of significant ancestral objects (including, of course, the photographic portrait of the prototypical Indian matrix) into subjects and props in a contemporary artist's studio. The unnamed *maestro* sitting at his easel before a mixed audience of Mexican and foreign journalists and admirers is engaged in painting a native model next to her archaeological double, but here as in the rest of the film, except for this opening inclusion of a hazy glimpse of a figurative sketch, the viewer is never afforded a full view of the canvas and its subject matter. We see the elect artist ('... siempre me he interesado por los indios' ['... I've always taken an interest in Indians']) at work constructing an image in the full glare of public curiosity. The artist makes clear to his audience that he is not interested in literal identity. The full-length nude portrait of an Indian woman which when spied through a window provokes the indignation of the villagers, who chase and finally stone to death the alleged original for her shameless exhibitionism, is only ever seen from the back or at a blind angle by the cinema audience. The film effectively provides, as its eponymous title suggests, the missing portrait through a foundational analogy between cinematographic representation and depictive strategy: film and painting are conflated as expressive media, aiming to revisualise a long-traduced common identity. María Candelaria, 'una india de pura raza mexicana' [an Indian woman of pure Mexican race], according to the painter, steps out of the ill-fated frame which has been locked from sight in an attic into renewed, moving visibility through the complicities of film and art. The fictional artist, who is white and middle-class, explains to his biographer that the Indian woman was the uncanny 'materialización' ['materialisation'] of an ideal fashioned by his imagination. María Candelaria's status as a living simulacrum, a compelling blend of artistic figurations and ideals, is confirmed by the aesthetic borrowings and simulations of the camera work. The incomplete visualisation of the painted portrait introduces the speculative shadow of the cinema audience's participatory myth-making: the interiority of image-making is as evocative as the evidenced representation.

Although overlooked by critics, the film thematises the difficult interethnic transactions which underpinned the emergence of a pro-Indian aesthetic in the Mexican artistic avant-garde (especially in Rivera, Montenegro and Fernando Leal (1896–1964)), intent on translating the lowly and abject through a lofty diction into a new aboriginal classicism. The artist and critic Jean Charlot (1898–1979), an important member of this avant-garde, was to recognise how admiration for the way the Mexican Indian supposedly 'take[s] his stand in nature with a kind of artless camouflage' turned into an aesthetic which purged and simplified indigenous subjects until they attained the lapidary ideality of Attic monuments: 'sometime throughout the years 1920–1925, an ideal Mexican type was evolved that has already become a classical art form, as shorn of paraphernalia as was the Greek nude man'.[59] Figueroa's cinematography reprises this modern legacy, while the filmic narrative charts its problematic trajectory, its naïve interventions and manipulations through a rural melodrama.

The film unfolds through a series of declamatory retrospective framings. These denote the way regressive perspectives power the reflexive subtext of the film: we move from the historical assignation of the subtitle to the spot-lit gallery of pre-Columbian statues, to the parallel ancient and living models in the atelier, to the artist in front of his easel, to the atavistic space of the attic with its enigmatic canvas, to María Candelaria herself in situ. The plot relies on the unlocking of suppressed recollections by the famous artist who, in youth, unwittingly caused the downfall of his ideal female Indian model by looking at her too closely and making this gaze public. One of the unnoticed self-referential aspects of the film is the way in which it makes visible the controversial power of the gaze in interethnic encounters and exchanges in which it is implicated. Don Damian expects Indians to approach him with downcast eyes and never to raise their gaze to engage as equals in commercial transactions ('tu que me ves aborigen!' ['What are you looking at Indian!']): he stares and dictates, they listen passively without meeting his gaze and comply; the social and economic inequities that afflict the

Indian population are reflected in the unequal exchanges of words and glances. The power of the gaze is made explicit in scenes where Lorenzo Rafael pleads for the quinine to which the ailing María Candelaria is entitled and the camera cuts between silent close-ups of the imperious merchant and the humbled claimant which stress the disjunct eye-lines.

María Candelaria is an illegitimate orphan ostracised by her people and expected to remain out of sight. Her orphanhood and exilic position are as significantly symbolic of her marginality as is the cultural distance that divides her from the middle-class artist and would-be patron. According to the film's much-criticised poetic anthropology, public invisibility is part of the punishment visited upon her for the sins of the mother who, as prostitute, made her body a public spectacle and scandal. María Candelaria's untouchability in the eyes of the villagers is turned into a badge of purity and otherworldliness by the artist and Figueroa's camera, concerned to reveal the beauty concealed behind an ordinary downcast *rebozo*. Her character displays the qualities of a conventional femininity in her relation with Lorenzo Rafael: modesty, abnegation, obedience. She readily offers to muddy her face as a form of concealment to guarantee that she will be overlooked when moving through the market. She is frequently veiled by or wrapped in a *rebozo* (notably unlike her vociferous female opponent in the village), the essentialist garment par excellence, synonymous with the pious mexicanicity of kneeling supplicants and repentant sinners. It is significant that the fictional artist's final aim is to paint María Candelaria as a full-length classical nude shorn of all layers, rid of all paraphernalia. Representation is predicated on exhibition and display, reminding us that the exposure which the artistic avant-garde sought to promote for Indian subjects required in practice a controversial immodesty in its female models. (In a tantalisingly congruent scenario in the mid-1920s Rivera and Weston did have occasion to strip the avant-garde's favourite authentic Indian artist's model, Luz Jiménez, of most of her characteristic ethnic garments in two notable nudes in order to capture her natural monumentality, rather than her folkloric identity, through a cleansing of surface particulars in pursuit of originary form.[60]) The presence of compliant Indian models in the studio who fail to persuade María Candelaria to follow their example introduces an interesting ambivalence in the film as regards the propriety to be observed when representing and viewing Indian women.

The philanthropic tenor behind the visualisation of the underdog and the outcast is intensified, beyond its obvious incarnation in the artist, to include the manifestation of the sacred in art. In a climactic scene at the end of the film María Candelaria seeks refuge from her persecutors in the village church, where she comes face to face with her idol and artistic double, the sublime paragon of femininity represented in paint, wood, stone or plaster with whom she has been associated through the transfigurations of the camera lens. Despairing in front of the high altar with its full-length statue, and in the presence of the priest, she accuses the Virgin of abandoning her faithful and innocent followers. Unseeing, oblivious to their suffering, why does she never cast her celestial gaze in their direction?: '... tus ojos nunca bajan a mirarnos' ['... you never lower your gaze to look upon us']. The priest enjoins her to notice the tears apparently flowing from the statue as evidence of the Virgin's empathy. One might say that the metaphor of the sentient statue neatly encapsulates the tensions in the film's cinematography between a monumental plasticity and a therapeutic sentimentality, between Figueroa's representation and Fernández's signification, between representing things or their effects. If we consider *María Candelaria* as a synoptic archive of the construction of national visuality itself, based on the film's pictorial, sculptural and photographic borrowings and reflexivity, it is tempting to conclude that the celluloid image became supplanted by what might be termed the ethic of photo-sculpture, where rituals of commemoration, the presence of material memory and the solemnity of death made a virtue of fixity and traceable contours.

Notes

1.   X. Sorondo, 'Necesitamos mexicanizarnos', *Revista de Revistas*, 18 September 1932, n.p.n.
2.   J.J. Tablada, 'La abeja de la crítica y la "tiple-jazz" (1927)', in A. Miquel (ed.), *Los exaltados: Ántología de escritos sobre cine en periódicos y revistas de la ciudad de México (1896–1929)*, (Guadalajara, Mexico, 1992), 53; A. de los Reyes, *Los orígenes del cine en México (1896–1900)* (Mexico City, 1984), 162–63.
3.   E. de la Vega Alfaro, 'Origins, Development and Crisis of the Sound Cinema (1929–64)', in P.A. Paranaguá (ed.), *Mexican Cinema* (London, 1995), 84.
4.   C.J. Mora, *Mexican Cinema: Reflections of a Society, 1896–1988* (Los Angeles/London, 1989).
5.   M. de Orellana, *La mirada circular: el cine norteamericano de la Revolución mexicana, 1911–1917* (Mexico City, 1991).
6.   Miquel, *Los exaltados*, 204.
7.   P.I. Taibo I, *El Indio Fernández: el cine por mis pistolas* (Mexico City, 1986), 72.
8.   *Ibid.*, 63.
9.   E. García Riera, *México visto por el cine extranjero: 1894–1940* (Mexico City, 1987), 210.
10.   C. González Peña, 'México en la pantalla (1917)', in Miquel, *Los exaltados*, 65–6.
11.   According to José Clemente Orozco, 'Al igual que los verdaderos grandes artistas,

Posada es una admirable lección de sencillez, humildad, dignidad y equilibrio' 'Like all the really great artists, Posada offers an admirable lesson in simplicity, humility, dignity and balance', cited in *José Guadalupe Posada: Ilustrador de la vida mexicana* (Mexico City, 1963; repr. 1982), 75. See also A. Rodríguez (ed.), *José Guadalupe Posada: 150 años* (Mexico City, 2003).

12. L. López Argoutia, 'México en la lente de Gabriel Figueroa: Entrevista', *Vice-Versa*, 5 (1993), 34.

13. Taibo I, *El Indio Fernández*, 56.

14. *No hay más ruta que la nuestra* (Mexico City, 1945), 71–2.

15. E. Fernández described Dolores del Río as 'la mujer distintiva de nuestra patria … "la flor más bella del ejido"'; see E. García Riera, *Emilio Fernández (1904–1986)* (Guadalajara, 1987), 47.

16. Taibo I, *El Indio Fernández*, 81.

17. J. Tuñón, 'Emilio Fernández: A Look Behind the Bars', in Paranaguá, *Mexican Cinema*, 184.

18. *Ibid.*, 184.

19 R. Tibol, *Gráficas y neográficas en México* (Mexico City, 1987).

20. M. de Orellana, 'Palabras sobre imágenes: entrevista con Gabriel Figueroa', *Artes de México*, 2 (1992), 51.

21. Fernández-Figueroa's other films were *Un día de vida* (1950), *Rosa Blanca* (1953), and *La rebelión de los colgados* (1954) with director A.B. Crevenna.

22. See L. Méndez, *En nombre de Cristo … han asesinado a más de 200 maestros* (Mexico City, 1939).

23. H. Prignitz, *El Taller de Gráfica Popular en México (1937–1977)*, tr. E. Siefer (Mexico City, 1992), 128. See also B. Garduño Pulido, L. González Matute, S. Morales Mora et al., *Misiones culturales: Los años utópicos, 1920–1938* (Mexico City, 1999).

24. G. Figueroa, 'Untitled', in I. Rodríguez Prampolini (ed.), *Leopoldo Méndez: Artista de un pueblo en lucha* (Mexico City, 1981), 39–44 (42).

25. *Ibid.*

26. J.D. Oles, 'México en veintitantas tomas: la obra mexicana de Paul Strand y Anton Bruehl', *Luna Córnea*, 1 (1992–93), 73–8.

27. R. Tibol, *Frida Kahlo: An Open Life*, tr. E. Randall (Albuquerque, 1993), 83.

28. García Riera, *México visto por el cine extranjero*, 190.

29. 'Un pueblo despojado de color', *Artes de México*, 10 (1990), 48.

30. A.R. Sánchez Lacy, 'Homenaje o exageración', *Artes de México*, 28 (1995), 22–5.

31. A. Arteaga, O. Sánchez and R. Stearns, *Mexico Now/México Ahora: Point of Departure/Punto de Partida [arte contemporáneo en México]* (Columbus, Ohio, 1997).

32. M. Helm, 'The School of Mexico City', in *Modern Mexican Painters: A Loan Exhibition of Their Works Organized by The Institute of Modern Art* (Boston, 1941), 10–15 (10, 12).

33. 'El cine mexicano', in J. Revueltas, *Obras completas*, ed. E. García Riera (Mexico City, 1981; repr. 1991), XXII: 135–7 (136).

34. See Rivera's panels *El capataz* [*The Foreman*] and *La liberación del peon* [*The Liberation of the Peon*] from the mural cycle of the Secretaria de Educación Pública (1923–8) on the social struggles of the Mexican people and their distinctive vernacular culture. On the theme of *La tierra liberada* [*The Liberated*

Earth] and agrarian revolution, see the panel *Formation of the Revolutionary Leadership* in the chapel of the Universidad Autónoma de Chapingo (1926–7), depicting the oppression of mine workers and peasants.

35. After *María Candelaria* Schoemann went on to edit twenty-two other films by Fernández.
36. See M. Gamio, *Forjando patria, pro-nacionalismo* [1916] (Mexico City, 1960).
37. See excerpts from Vasconcelos's *Indologia* cited in V. Magdaleno (ed.), 'El problema del Indio', published in the influential cultural organ *Universidad: Mensual de Cultura Popular*, 7 (August 1936), 5:

> ... aquellas tribus que han quedado apegadas a su lengua y costumbres, encerradas dentro de los medios reducidos y remotos de los valles y las serranías, se encuentran hoy como si hubiesen perdido toda conciencia, pues no queda impune el pecado de sustraerse a la corriente general de la vida. La ley del espíritu es el cambio perpetuo hacia adelante. Por eso los que se aislan y apegan a una sola tradición reniegan de la ley del espíritu y como que recaen en la ley de las cosas físicas, y la esencia del hombre no tiene la calidad simple de la piedra.

> [... those tribes which have continued to cling to their language and customs, enclosed within the narrow and remote environments of valleys and ranges, find themselves today as if they had lost their very consciousness, for the sin of withdrawing from the general current of life does not go unpunished. The law of the spirit demands perpetual change forwards. Hence those who isolate themselves and adhere to a single tradition reject the law of the spirit as if succumbing to the law of material things, and the essence of man does not have the simple quality of stone.]

On Vasconcelos and 'la genuina nacionalidad', see G. Sheridan, *México en 1932: La polémica nacionalista*, (Mexico City, 2004), 31.

38. See e.g. *El entierro del obrero* [*Worker's Burial*] (1922), *Madre proletaria* [*Proletarian Mother*] (1929*)*, *El tormento* [*The Torment/Torture*] (1930), *Accidente en la mina* [*Accident in the Mine*] (1931), *Madre campesina* [*Peasant Mother*] (1939).
39. For a discussion of Siqueiros's theory of 'pictorial cinematographic art', see M. Carmen Ramírez, 'The Masses are the Matrix: Theory and Practice of the Cinematographic Mural in Siqueiros', in O. Debroise, J.D. Oles and M.C. Ramírez, *David Alfaro Siqueiros: Portrait of a Decade, 1930–1940* (Mexico City, 1997), 68–95.
40. For Rivera's influential depictions of Xochimilco and its canals, see his canvas *Flower Day* (1925) connected in subject to the panel *Friday of Sorrows on the Canal of Santa Anita*, Court of the Fiestas, Education Ministry (SEP) which arranges flowers, canoes, tree-lined banks and pilgrims in a close-knit composition of diagonals, horizontals and verticals.
41. Rivera cited in García Riera, *Emilio Fernández*, 54.
42. See Rivera's Court of the Fiesta's panels (1923–4) in the Ministry of Education mural cycle, where popular religious and secular festivals are depicted including the folkloric *The Ribbon Dance*, the carnivalesque *The Burning of the Judases* and the hieratic *The Corn Festival*.

43. For Siqueiros's review of Weston and Modotti, see 'Una transcendental labor fotográfica. La exposición Weston – Modotti', *El Informador*, 4 September 1925, 6. See also Rivera's 'Edward Weston and Tina Modotti', *Mexican Folkways*, 2 (1926), 16–28. For Siqueiros on photography's documentary realism, see 'La función de la fotografía' [1945], in R. Tibol (ed.), *Textos de David Alfaro Siqueiros* (Mexico City, 1998), 70–6 (72): 'La fotografía, como debemos saberlo todos, ha transformado en prueba documental lo que antes sólo fue hipótesis … La fotografía ha dado a la expresión "comprobación científica" un sentido de realidad indiscutible' ['Photography, as we surely all know, has transformed what was previously merely a hypothesis into documentary evidence … Photography has given to the expression "scientific proof" the ring of incontrovertible reality'].

44. Pseudonymous film critic cited in García Riera, *Emilio Fernández*, 53.

45. Alfonso de Icaza cited by García Riera, *Emilio Fernández*, 50.

46. On the hieratic imagery of the Indianist avant-garde, see C. Monsiváis, 'La toma del poder desde las imágenes (el socialismo y el arte en México)', in R. Pérez Escamilla (ed.), *Estética socialista en México, siglo XX* (Mexico City, 2003), 23–31 (30).

47. See C.A. Cordova, *Agustín Jiménez y la vanguardia fotográfica mexicana* (Mexico City, 2005), 36–7 (on Magaña) and 130–42 (on pre-Hispanic architecture and folk artefacts).

48. William Henry Fox Talbot cited by J. Snyder, 'Nineteenth-Century Photography of Sculpture and the Rhetoric of Substitution', in G.A. Johnson (ed.), *Sculpture and Photography: Envisioning the Third Dimension* (Cambridge, 1998), 21–34 (23).

49. For a discussion of the 'tableau' as visual paradigm, see R. Barthes, *Image, Music, Text*, tr. S. Heath (London, 1977), 69–78.

50. See A. Isaac, *Conversaciones con Gabriel Figueroa* (Guadalajara, 1993), 30–1.

51. Ibid., 19.

52. On Montenegro and popular 'primitivism' see K. Cordero Reiman, 'La invención del arte popular y la construcción de la cultura visual moderna en México', in E. Acevedo (ed.), *Hacia otra historia del arte en México: La fabricación del arte nacional a debate (1920–1950)* (Mexico City, 2002), 67–90 (88–9). For Rivera, modernism and pre-Hispanic models, see B. Braun, *Pre-Columbian Art and the Post-Columbian World: Ancient American Sources of Modern Art* (New York, 1993), 185–249.

53. On the relation between Gamio and Herrán, the first illustrator of the pre-Hispanic murals at Teotihuacan, see M. León Portilla, 'Manuel Gamio y el indigenismo', in E. García Barragán (ed.), *Saturnino Herrán: Jornadas de homenaje* (Mexico City, 1989), 107–20.

54. Gamio, *Forjando patria*, 25.

55. D.A. Siqueiros, *No hay más ruta que la nuestra*, 72.

56. See C.B. Waite's *Mexican Woman Grinding Corn* in J.K. Turner, *Barbarous Mexico: An Indictment of a Cruel and Corrupt System* (London/New York, 1911), 116; the photograph of an Indian woman *Weaving the faja* in E. Gruening, *Mexico and Its Heritage* (London, 1928) n.p.n.; and Rivera's oil paintings *Flower Seller* (1926), *The Flowered Canoe* (1931), *Nude with Calla Lilies* (1944) and his 1938 pastel and charcoal studies *Profile of Indian Woman with Lilacs*, *Indian Woman with Marigolds*, *Profile of Indian Woman with Calla Lilies*.

57. On Herrán and symbolism in Mexico, see F. Ramírez, 'El simbolismo en México', in I. Henares Cuellar, F. Ramírez, R. Velásquez Martínez del Campo et al., *El espejo simbolista: Europa y México, 1870–1920* (Mexico City, 2004), 29–59.

58. See R. Montenegro's *La Fiesta de la Santa Cruz y Resurrección*, also known as *La reconstrucción de México por obreros e itelectuales* (1923–24).

59. See J. Charlot, 'Painting and Revolution' [1951] in *An Artist on Art: Collected Essays of Jean Charlot*, 2 vols (Honolulu, 1972), vol II: *Mexican Art*, 3–11 (10).

60. See Edward Weston's back view of an upright *Luz desnuda* [*Nude Study of Luz*] (1926), Rivera's nude seated figure modelled on Luz in the crowning panel of the Chapel of the Universidad Autónoma de Chapingo fresco cycle *La tierra liberada o El paraíso reconquistado* [*The Liberated Earth or Paradise Regained*] (1926–7) and his preparatory sketch *Nude with Braided Hair* (1925). For a discussion of this ubiquitous Indian model, see B. Garduño Pulido, 'Luz Jiménez en el muralismo mexicano', in B. Garduño Pulido, A. Hijar, J. Villanueva Hernández et al., *Luz Jiménez: Símbolo de un pueblo milenario, 1897–1965* (Mexico City, 2000), 37–53.

61. On photo-sculpture, see M. Garza, *Foto-Escultura: A Mexican Photographic Tradition* (Albuquerque, 1998).

Chapter 4

Reframing the City:
Images of Displacement in Urban Films and the Visual Arts of the 1940s and 1950s

La ambición de las amas de casa de tener una cocina integral nació en los salones cinematográficos.[1]

[The housewives' ambition to own a fully fitted kitchen was born in cinema auditoriums.]

Alejandro Galindo's romantic comedy *¡Esquina ... bajan!* [*At the Corner ... Getting Off!* or *Corner Stop*] (1947) is set in the vertiginous world of Mexico City's buses and expanding transport arteries, against a background of criss-crossing vertical skylines and widening horizontal vistas (a perspectival web due in part to the appearance of *super manzanas* [*Super Blocks*] and flyovers). With its conceit of a hurtling, overcrowded collective vehicle it captures the headlong rush to modernisation, the *desarrollismo* [developmentalism] staged spectacularly in the boom years between 1940 and 1950,[2] a decade in which the nation's capital witnessed the most rapid rate of population growth in its history: 5.7 percent per annum, from 1.7 to 3 million inhabitants.[3] Such an influx and expansion prompted the inception of a notion of the capital based on the experience of economic and social change. Mexico City in its guise as 'la ciudad de los viajeros' ['the city of travellers'] constitutes a threshold for the displaced and a theatre of the transitory, as well as a passageway to modernity.[4] By the end of the 1950s the multiplying web of arteries has become a convoluted *mandala* whose metaphorical applicability no longer holds the promise of a central destination. The urban locations of a film like Ismael Rodríguez's *El hombre de papel* [*The Paper Man*] (1963) are shot so as to conjure patterns of ceaseless, aimless activity, most memorably in an aerial shot of coursing traffic in the complex, repeated design of a super-junction.[5]

Motion without finality, mobility without a corresponding social fluidity, seems to be the cinematographer's disabused conclusion on the preceding decade's exploitation of the motif of transport and modernisation.

In the heady 1940s and 1950s the associative armature of new construction and its attendant textures – scaffolding, ordnance surveys, architectural maquettes, consecrated materials like steel, concrete, cement and acrylic paints, motorway bridges and tentacular junctions, the omnipresent building site and demolition crew – impinges conclusively on the visual codification of the capital in the media and the arts (figure 4.1). Galindo's classic film, a success at the box office, belies with its carnivalesque visions the blueprint of government engineered and directed urban restructuring (figure 4.2).[6] He offers his knowing audience unruly motorcades, duplicitous competitors, bellicose or abused travelling citizenry, parenthetical homesteads and underground revelry,

Figure 4.1 Nacho López, *Mexico City from above*, from the series *Pasos en las nubes* (1951). FINAH.

harrying traffic and overcrowding. The title, *¡Esquina bajan!*, which cites the typical instruction shouted to the driver along routes with no predetermined or fixed stops, plays suggestively on the theme of unregulated and non-consensual modernisation, especially as the gags revolve around the litigious, wayward *chofer* played by the muscular David Silva (of *Campeón sin corona* [*Champion without a Crown*]

Figure 4.2 Publicity poster of *¡Esquina bajan!* (1948) by F. Rivero Gil (in colour). AFG.

[1945] fame) who is usually reluctant to accede to either the passengers' legitimate requests or his loyal conductor's directions.[7]

Similarly, in cinema, photojournalism, pictorial art and illustration of the period the visualisation of the state-prescribed trajectory from the traditional socioeconomic order to full-scale industrial urbanisation and modern technologies (an indeterminate and finally inconclusive transition) assumes the form of a parable-like narrative oscillating between metropolitan initiation and vestigial ruralism. The strategies deployed for framing the actual or aesthetically reconstituted city in graphic media and the moving image show a surprising degree of convergence, cross-pollination and transcription. It is interesting to note that the response to economically driven cultural change and atomisation is a reaffirmation of visual production's synthesising role and the inherent interrelation and unity of the arts. The premise of such fusion and complementarity is the 'image' in the age of technical reproduction and mass transmission. The novelist and screenwriter José Revueltas advanced this equation in an influential article, 'Lugar del cine en el arte' ['The Place of Cinema in the Arts'], published in *Anthropos* in 1947.[8]

Revueltas argued that cinematic practice exemplifies the Heraclitean axiom of 'la estabilidad móvil, como el reposo en movimiento' ['mobile stability, like rest in motion'].[9] Cinematography's essential character – 'estabilidad de la inestabilidad' – naturally predisposes it to be an instrument for the representation of a process of modernisation understood in dialectical terms.[10] Its relation to the subject of temporal change on which it reflects is tautological. Cinema *is* the experience of modernity, according to Revueltas, not merely a useful analogue. Its operation is poetic rather than empirically descriptive: terms such as *descomponer* [to separate or split], *transformar*, *interpretar*, *yuxtaposición* [juxtaposition] recur in a text which confirms the continuing influence in Mexico of Sergei Eisenstein's theory of montage.[11] Revueltas's exposition suggests that cinema as art is alert to the medium's potential for visual discontinuity and pre-empts unintelligibility through *rhythm*, by which he means the construction of patterns of imagistic counterpoint. The presumed distinction between 'la fotografía fija y [la] fotografía en movimiento' ['still photography and photography in motion'] is a fallacy, according to Revueltas, and he cites the work of the eminent photographer Manuel Álvarez Bravo (1902–2002).[12] The latter's honed shots, equivalent to arrested cinematic images, '[ofrecen] el signo puro, la *ecuación* lírica precisa, la *síntesis* heroica y acabada' ['(offer) the pure sign, the precise lyrical *equation*, the heroic and perfect *synthesis*'].[13] Not coincidentally, Álvarez Bravo during the 1940s had begun to collaborate in a number of films (it is presumed principally as a stills photographer), and was a close friend and associate of the outstanding *camarógrafo* [cameraman] Gabriel Figueroa and various directors, including Alejandro Galindo (1906–1999) and the internationally acclaimed Emilio Fernández.[14] In the 1940s both Álvarez Bravo and Figueroa taught in the Instituto de Artes y Ciencias Cinematográficas, providing an aesthetic orientation based on distilled antinomies in black and white to such incisive urban photographers of the period as Nacho López (1924–1986).[15]

The intersection between mural, giant screen and easel painting in the configuration of urban panoramas evidences a growing receptivity to modern architectural paradigms. Discourses about the role of architecture in national development and the forms it should assume are centre stage in the 1940s.[16] Preoccupations about the modernisation of space provoke nation-conscious questions about place and identification. Juan O'Gorman (1905–82), the influential modernist architect, muralist and socialist, resorts with discursive pointedness to a traditional pictorial genre and methodology to make visible his notion of autochthonous, synchronic development of the nation's capital.[17] He delineates the expanding city in a panoramic painting, *La Ciudad de México*, in which it is framed with specific reference to the tradition of colonial and nineteenth-century representations taken from *azoteas* [terrace roofs] and belltowers: every building is differentiated and particularised by the celebrated transparency of light (figure 4.3).[18] In the foreground, the magnified hands of the artist/architect as *Homo faber* hold up an early Spanish map of the valley and its settlement, which provides a point of historical reference and temporal gauge superimposed over a receding, increasingly vertical cityscape. In the furthest horizon the totemic volcanoes of the Popocatépetl and Iztaccíhuatl encircle the valley and city in a familial embrace which maintains a proper balance between nature and culture. Above the bottom edge of the painted surface a commemorative legend in a scroll reads: 'Aquí se presenta el corazón de la Ciudad de México tal y como se ve desde arriba del monumento de la revolución en dirección al oriente' ['Here is depicted the heart of Mexico City as it actually appears from above the monument to the Revolution looking eastward'].[19] On a scaffolding towers the truly modern popular hero – an indigenous-looking *albañil* [brick-layer/builder] holding a blueprint and flanked by the instruments of his craft. The specific reference to the vantage point from which this limpid cityscape is articulated, the 1933 monument commemorating the Mexican Revolution of 1910, does more than attest to figurative realism. It turns perspective into a symbolic viewfinder. Acknowledging the inferred point of the painting's inception, the triumphal archway from which the centre of the capital is represented allows the infrastructure of O'Gorman's vision to

Figure 4.3 Juan O' Gorman, *La Ciudad de México* (1949) (in colour). MAM.

become as apparent as the armature of the buildings under construction he depicts. It is the proletarian revolution which provides the framework for modernisation and which tacitly frames the erection of modernist buildings in a foundational space. This celebration of work in progress, the building of an egalitarian and prosperous Mexico, amounts to a corrective to O'Gorman's own dystopian *Monumento fúnebre al capitalismo industrial* [*Funereal Monument to Industrial Capitalism*] (1943), in which a fantastic amalgamation of spewing factories creates an involuted and suffocating citadel. Painted in 1949 by a member of the 1930s avant-garde, this resolutely humanist vision of progress, orderly and rooted in a respect for the labourer as artisan, contrasts with a more explicitly allegorical treatment of the subject from the same year.

Significantly entitled *Río revuelto* [*Turbulent River*] (1949), José Chávez Morado's city is seen as generic, an agglomeration of the tropes of the rhetoric of progress. Here the signs of modernism are anarchically omnipresent whilst the reality of modernisation is shown to be a fallacious currency of myths and deceptions: a pornographic commercialism made up of billboard advertisements for dentures, stockings, cigarettes.[20] Chávez Morado (1909–2002) articulates a visual critique of the process of capitalist modernisation which he had denounced the previous year as corrosive of national organicity and autonomy: 'Este sello es para mí el símbolo de una nueva agresión, y así tenemos cine y música Coca Cola, arquitectura Coca Cola, gráfica y plástica Coca Cola' ['This brand is for me the symbol of a new aggression and so we have Coca Cola cinema and music, Coca Cola architecture, Coca Cola graphics and art'].[21] The painting showcases commonplace urban motifs conceived as scenes culled from the reproductive media – scenes which are predicated on the juxtaposition of old and new, Utopia and reality. In Chávez Morado's multiple take on modernity as myth and reification the prime consumers and spectators are represented as a hypnotised cinema audience – entertained by the menace and *relajo* [clamour] of popular culture: the naked corpse of a woman in a squalid room; a sinister silhouette of an armed man in the inevitable darkened doorway; rural migrants scrounging a living as beggars; a protest march by a workers' union; a traditional *pulquería* [pulque bar]; metal scaffolding; cement; *cargadores* [loaders]; *obreros* [workers]; imported cars; packed buses with paperboys hitching a free ride on the back. Such composite, multi-sequential constructs provide evidence of the logocentricity to which image production was widely subject. Explicitly or implicitly, representations of contemporary urban reality used interpretative *motifs* as an organisational principle and index of legibility.

In film and photography the explicatory text or subtext was often clearly invoked with the use of illustrated books as paradigms for an episodic narrative or triptych; or with painted or printed apothegms smuggled onto vehicles as connecting proverbs and premonitory warnings foreshadowing events, as in Ismael Rodríguez's *Nosotros los pobres* [*We the Poor*] (1947) (figure 4.4) and Luis Buñuel's *El gran calavera* [*The Great Madcap*] (1949) (figure 4.5), where trucks and vans publicise messages on plaques or through loudspeakers, which acquire unsuspected meanings as they move through the plot and locations.[22] Such vehicles – whose obligatory participation in films and photographs is usually attached to rituals of capitalist exchange, displacement and the perilous experience of cultural and social dislocation – become a *vicus* of didactic transmission and circulation (or parodic deflation, as in Buñuel's surrealist bus and tram, in *Subida al cielo* [*Gone to Heaven* or *Mexican Bus Ride*] [1951] and *La ilusión viaja en tranvía* [*Dreams Travel on the Train*] [1953], respectively).[23] They come to embody the visible process of *transculturación*, understood as both domestic and international intervention: hegemony from the metropolitan centre and Westernisation of U.S. or European extraction. The conflating of advertising jingles, proverbs and irreverent *albures* [puns] in a kind of visual pastiche of

Figure 4.4 Still from *Nosotros los pobres* (1947).

silent film textual gloss, propaganda and catechism signals an ironic awareness of the dominance of rhetoric and pedagogy in the official patronage of culture and modernisation. As Gabriel Figueroa admitted, 'las películas recurrieron a los diálogos explicativos o literarios' ['films resorted to explanatory or literary dialogues'], but cinema's responsiveness to the modalities of political rhetoric did not preclude, as many have assumed, an ironic manipulation of such scriptural elements: irony, I would argue, was a common structural device in representational strategies which engaged with the discourse of modernity and not, as has too readily been concluded, a critical resource exclusive to Buñuel.[24] If schools and hospitals are the redemptive symbols in Emilio Fernández's humourless, dystopian vision of modernising Mexico City as theatre of corruption and exploitation, most notably in *Salón México* (1948), films such as *Maldita ciudad* [*Damned City*] (1954) by Ismael Rodríguez (who termed it a 'drama cómico'), have some fun at the expense of the stock elements of such didactic, highbrow melodramas even as they knowingly contribute to the mythologisation of the metropolis.[25]

In the mid-1940s and 1950s photography had found its principal outlet in magazine illustration and reportage. Photographs 'told a story': glossed an ideal interior where modernist elements coexisted with traditional domestic artefacts in lifestyle magazines (such as *Femina*, *Femenil*, *Orquídea*, *Revista de Decoración*, *La Familia*); provided corroboration for

Figure 4.5 Still from *El gran calavera* (1949).

a sociological thesis or visual data for deductive exploitation as well as deferential material to stoke the growing *presidencialismo* in the Mexican media such as in *revistas* [magazines] (*Siempre!*, *Mañana* or *Novedades*) and newspapers (*Excélsior* or *El Universal Gráfico*).[26] Such mass circulation organs published photographic essays by Héctor García (1923–) and Nacho López, the two most influential photojournalists of the post-Revolutionary era.[27] Nacho López in particular became the chronicler of 'la modernidad desarticulada' ['dislocated modernity'], producing work throughout the 1950s on ironic themes which targeted official populism such as *Sólo los humildes van al infierno* [*Only the Poor Go to Hell*] (1954), on criminals and the police; or in a more descriptive vein *Tianguis* [*Street Market*], on the persistence of traditional street markets, and *Periféricos y viaductos* [*Ring Roads and Viaducts*], on the new configurations of space and mobility; on *Trabajadores ambulantes* [*Street Sellers*], which captured the transactions of the invisible majority living off the detritus of capitalism or servicing its urban nuclei (figure 4.6); or insisted on a foundational dualism in the series *México de noche* [*Mexico by Night*] and *México de día* [*Mexico by Day*], an ironic *son and lumière* show exploring the scenarios and underbelly of modern living.[28] The series *Disolución social* crystallised the fears generated by state-propelled development through visual anecdotes of social disjunction.[29] In fact during this period of visible as well as envisaged change in public space the reproductive arts – especially photography and cinematography – intersect influentially, as practitioners reflect on the evidential traces of a transformation whose identity they are seeking to configure legibly and often ironically.[30] In this context, the black-and-white differentials and chiaroscural gradation of Agustín Jiménez's individual trajectory from constructivist photography to stills photography (most notably for Fernando de Fuentes) and then to cinematography (on films by Luis Buñuel: *El Bruto* [*The Brute*], *Abismos de pasión* [*Wuthering Heights*], *Ensayo de un crimen* [*The Criminal Life of Archibaldo Cruz*]) can be regarded as exemplary.[31]

The process of emblematic characterisation, for example, selected topical landmarks such as the new Nonoalco bridge. This architectural monument was exhaustively photographed by professionals such as the Hermanos Mayo and Juan Rulfo, incised by engravers of the *Taller de Gráfica Popular*; shot by cinematographers like Gabriel Figueroa for Emilio Fernández's drama *La bienamada* [*The Loved One*] (1951), and figured in films from the period by Bustillo Oro and Miguel Morayta. It came to represent the frontier between the urbanised city and 'la ciudad perdida' ['the lost city'], a passage to the 'horizonte de la desesperanza' ['horizon of despair'] – the peripheral latitude of the uprooted, inhabited

Figure 4.6 Nacho López, from *Un día cualquiera en la vida de la ciudad* (c.1955). Fondo Nacho López, FINAH.

by the *sombras* [shadows] and *fantasmas* [ghosts] – rural migrants and disenfranchised citizens – that haunt the lenses of both Rulfo and Nacho López.[32] Ángel Bracho's black-and-white lithograph, *El puente (de Nonoalco) y el tilichero* [*The Nonoalco Bridge and the Rag-and-Bone Man*] (1944) captures the disjunct social reality of urban restructuring (figure 4.7). A peddler making a meagre living by salvaging and reselling the broken or discarded paraphernalia of middle-class interiors rests on his toy-sized cart. There he sits leaning against its motley contents, his back to the viewer, with his elementary hand-pulled contraption while above him yawns the impressive symmetrical body of the new bridge which has cut a swath through the landscape, its giant pillars supporting the modern viaduct receding to the horizon with its invisible vehicular transit. Although placed at the centre of the composition, between the pillars, the *tilichero* is marginality incarnate,

Figure 4.7 Ángel Bracho, *El puente (de Nonoalco) y el tilichero* (1944). Museo Nacional de la Estampa.

inhabiting the underground corridors of the ascending metropolis. He is portrayed turning to cast a slanted gaze at something outside the picture rather than looking straight ahead down the gullet of the structure stretching menacingly before him. The obliquity of his attention suggests that his priorities lie outside the construction which encases him, pointing to a lack of temporal confluence between form and subject. At the foot of the pillars, in the shadow of the bridge, as if dwarfed and side-stepped by capitalist modernisation, sit figures wearing overalls and *rebozos* evoking the workers and rural migrants whose traditional poverty remained an unbridgeable gap in the social fabric. They dwell in an interstitial limbo, being culturally displaced as well as economically marginalised.[33]

If new building complexes such as hospitals and educational establishments (Hospital de la Raza, Ciudad Universitaria) are key reference points in the symbolic architecture of the progressive city, providing allusive backgrounds or actual locations for films, *esquinas* [corners] and crossroads become recurrent compositional vantage points for photographers intent on capturing points of transition and disjunction in the city's human traffic. In 'Cíclope' ['Cyclops'], one of his experimental 'fotopoemáticos' ['photo-poems'] in which images inspire a textual gloss, Nacho López suggestively evokes the urban photographer's oblique yet incisive penetration:

Auscultando las sombras
descubro formas ondulantes
vaivenes entre gentes y episodios
rincones de la vida cotidiana.
Encrucijadas y redes apremiantes
alfileteadas casas por varillas en cruz
cíclope retratista del poliendro humano.[34]
[Taking soundings from the shadows
I discover undulating forms
comings and goings between people and episodes
corners of daily life.
Pressing intersections and networks
houses pinned by crossed bars
photographing Cyclops of the human polyhedron.]

Héctor García's 1947 photograph *Entre las ruedas del progreso* [*Caught between the Wheels of Progress*] (figure 4.8) is a study in bilocation – a recurrent motif in the graphic arts of the period.[35] An older man whose rural provenance is unmistakable, clasping a small girl by the hand, dashes through an opening between gargantuan American vehicles in the teeming centre of the capital. In *Entre el progreso y el desarollo* [*Between Progress and Development*] (1950), a barefoot peasant boy stands between the gleaming chrome bumpers of two parked cars (figure 4.9). Figures pressing through fissures in lines of traffic; solitary individuals carrying outsize loads across dusty avenues in a blur; or skimming at a tangent across tarmac making a faint trace in an avenue yawning to infinity, are images more constructed than captured by such photographers. Rulfo's scepticism accentuates this figurative strain with photographs of the city that dwell on interstices – the spaces between and betwixt. Surprising camera angles produce the *nowhere* of shadowy citizenry caught between rail tracks, compressed and fleeting between stationary train carriages or setting out from precarious verges and corners: these are inhabitants with little purchase on their surroundings.[36] A noticeable device, especially prevalent in Nacho López, which may owe a great deal to the lighting techniques pioneered by Figueroa in early collaborations with Fernández in the cinema, is the depth of contrast achieved by 'separación entre el primer plano y los fondos' ['the separation between close-up and backgrounds'].[37] The illusion of three-dimensionality of such a procedure is again predicated on a kind of visual

Figure 4.8 © Héctor García, *Entre las ruedas del progreso* (1947).

caesura and *découpage*. In the context of deliberations about the election and use of perspective in representations of the urban environment, one might venture to suggest a tactical correlation between a bus's penetrative journey through a cross-section of the city and the focal diagonals slicing open in depth the dense mass of construction.

The circular journey from the congested, populous centre to an increasingly indeterminate periphery of Galindo's rocambolesque vehicle in *¡Esquina ... bajan!* (the terminal is located in a barren plain) posits a circuitous journey unlike that of the orderly tram lines it traverses. It parodies good-humouredly, in the grounded vernacular of 'Línea Zócalo, Xochicalco y Anexas', the triumphalist rhetoric of accelerated development, whilst positing a notion of grassroots solidarity which resists the perceived rapacity and egocentricity of transnational capitalism.[38] A similar notion of cultural resistance based on communal solidarity informs his rather more discursive treatment of the subject of

Figure 4.9 © Héctor García, *Entre el progreso y el desarrollo* (1950).

cross-border transactions in *Espaldas mojadas* [*Wetbacks*] (1953). At a time in which the Mexican cinema industry enjoyed state support, the preferred locus of this exemplary but troubled apprenticeship in the ideology of *desarrollismo* quickly assumed topographical and architectural specificity. If cinema was to provide a virtual education in the topoi of Western modernity, the proletarian *vecindades* [neighbourhoods] and *barrios* [districts] of the *comedia* and *melodrama* 'arrabalero' ['of the poorer quarters'] problematised the journey to full industrialisation whilst helping to exorcise the individual trauma of transition in the dislodged populace. The genre showcased the phenomenon of rupture within familiar parameters. Absorbent conduits of massive immigration from the countryside, traditionally occupying the sites of the capital's foundation, the colonial *traza* or grid superimposed on pre-Hispanic urban design, these proletarian neighbourhoods became highly symbolic configurations – not to say accretions – of ancestral space at a time in which domestic interiors and collective dwellings were undergoing radical redevelopment or being demolished. High-density officially sponsored tower blocks known as *multifamiliares* by architect-entrepreneur Mario Pani (erected in 1949, 1952, 1962) come to publicise notions of modern living and redemptive modernity to an increasingly receptive mass audience during the *sexenio* [six-year term] of President Miguel Alemán (1946–52). Under government auspices the 'Plan regulador de la Ciudad de México', dubbed *proyectazo* ['Super Plan'] by the press, proposed an ambitious conversion of the city centre to better reflect what the poet and *cronista* Salvador Novo regarded as housing's need for temporal contiguity with the pace of development 'que la adapte al medio urbano y social, mutable y constantemente renovado' ['which should be adapted to the urban and social environment which is changeable and constantly subject to renewal'] (1946).[39] A commentator in the mass circulation daily *Excélsior* hailed the construction projects in terms which register a shift of emphasis from a redistribution of wealth to a centralised redistribution of space in the public domain: 'está destinado a revolucionar en nuestro medio el concepto mismo de habitación y a convertirse en el experimento colectivo más importante que se haya llevado a cabo … obra constructora de un México mejor, del nuevo México que debe interesarnos a los hombres que estamos vivos, el México de mañana' ['it is destined to revolutionise in our context the concept of housing itself and to become the most important experiment in collective living that has been tried … a foundational work for a better Mexico, the new Mexico that must interest the men of the present, the Mexico of tomorrow'].[40] The epic conflict between old order and new which had animated the visual rhetoric of the 1920s and Cardenismo in the 1930s still dominated by Revolutionary ideology and agrarian reform, gives way to a nationalist struggle whose visual lexicon is informed by the paraphernalia and methodologies of embodied progress.[41] This is a struggle imagined in architectural juxtapositions and scenarist/scenographer binarisms, in keeping with the felicitous aperçues of 1920s photographers such as Tina Modotti (and later Lola Álvarez Bravo), who used montage to frame cultural and economic dualism in terms of startling contrasts in the streets of the capital.[42]

In their designation of metropolitan folklore, urban films frequently retain a fondness for *costumbrista* typologies, more usually associated with the *comedia ranchera* [rural comedy of manners, often musical], transposed to a subtly incongruous setting or ambience. A common formula of course is the *charro* who travels to the big city, giving ample scope for scenic binarisms, but tending to result in a focus which is retrospective and nostalgic (figure 4.10).[43] A more reflective vein incorporates a collage citation which creates an interesting tension between established modalities of seeing and representation and the attempt to portray something incommensurate with established archetypes, a homage to the pictorialist anecdotes in which text and image illustrated and corroborated each other in self-contained simulacra, in a manner less valedictory than one might expect. Mexican films continued to be receptive to the exploration of national folklore which marked the

1920s and 1930s, not necessarily through ethnographic fantasy or indigenist spectacle, but through a related kind of celebration of ancestry which focused on the medium itself as a form of folk art. Directors seemed to want to visibly restore the nexus between stationary picture and the evolution of the moving image predicated on such paradigms drawn from the domain of popular culture – genre paintings, postcards, comic strips, with subject matter drawn from songs, pulp magazines and cheap

Figure 4.10 Publicity poster for *Del rancho a la capital* (1941) (in colour). AFA.

novels.[44] They were intent, perhaps, on historicising contemporary vernacular culture through a negation of filmic modernism, whilst upholding cinema as a vehicle which promoted (in the words of Panofsky) 'dynamic contact between art production and art consumption'. In the case of directors proficient in both rural and urban genres, such as the ambidextrous Ismael Rodríguez (1917–2004), intertextuality is often humorously self-referential, as in *Maldita ciudad* (1954) (figure 4.11), where a respectable provincial family uproots itself to the capital and the bipolarity of urban and rural melodramas, highbrow civicism and lowbrow populism are entertainingly lampooned, with occasional digs at his own productions. Significantly anti-modernist yet wary of traditionalist mystifications, Rodríguez's film taps into popular incredulity at Mario Pani's regenerative notion of the *multifamiliar* as the architectural hypothesisation of modernised 'patrias chicas' ['little homelands'] and 'aldeas' ['villages'].[45]

Shot in the *multifamiliar* Alemán (highrise complex), which had been inaugurated in 1949 with nationalist pomp and folkloric choreography (figure 4.12), the film subsumed the polemic which *El Universal Gráfico* had spearheaded that same year against state-sponsored 'palomares' ['pigeon cages']. It is worth remarking that the official presentation of the new architectural complex contrived to splice together emblematic folkloric spectacle and modernist backdrop in a compositional ensemble rendered popular in cinema musical comedies such as Raúl de Anda's *La reina del trópico* [*The Queen of the Tropics*] (1945), where the crisis of displacement from country to city resolves itself choreographically. Such knowing manipulation offers an instance of the kind of aesthetic confluence which characterised the interplay between architecture and film in the discourse of modernisation and its preferred exhibitionary paradigms.

From its pages, *El Universal Gráfico* had encouraged ironic speculation as to the future production of a national film on such a topical subject as public housing, to be entitled 'Nosotros los amontonados' ['We the overcrowded'] in a back-handed tribute to Rodríguez's box office hit *Nosotros los pobres* (1947). Five years later Rodríguez directed a film that might have been imagined by the prescient satirist in *El Universal Gráfico*, but did so in a manner which exposed the increasingly diagrammatic and self-explanatory semiotic conventions for representing the city-country dichotomy on the screen.

In the earlier *Nosotros los pobres* the paradigm of pictorial illustration and apothegmatic text become structural devices of plot and representation. Two ragged street urchins scavenging in the city's *bajos fondos* [lower reaches] extract a mouldy, illustrated book from a rubbish bin: the film opens with this casual leafing through established

Figure 4.11 Publicity poster for *Maldita ciudad* (1954) by Raúl Martínez Cacho (in colour). AFA.

simulacra, and goes on to recycle the physiognomic types of the plates in a series of interconnected *cuadros* – creating a neo-*costumbrista* spectacle where popular archetypes combine with topical detail. The framing device is reminiscent of the publication of popular illustrated books or *feuilleton* narratives in serial parts, which invited both composite assembly – the completed sequence could be taken apart and

Figure 4.12 Inauguration of the *Multifamiliar Alemán* (1949). AGN.

bound in different orders – and non-consecutive reading subject to the practice of flipping back and forth which is intrinsic to the perusal of books with plates. The rubbish bin itself, with its circular aperture disgorging heterogeneous matter and relegated objects, is less of a repository of cultural memory (or a cache of *artículos de costumbres*), than a self-reflexive camera obscura where the subjects of representation are drawn not from nature or a putative objective reality but sourced from prefabricated representations. The circularity of the conceit of the fortuitous bin which initially expels and finally ingests the evocative illustrated book underwrites Rodríguez's urban *geste* in a style which is clearly resistant to the purported modernity inherent in cinematographic 'discontinuity' and motion. The rubbish bin acts as a vision machine for the reproduction of well-thumbed genres. It is a film less concerned with the articulation of the city as transformative motion through purely visual means than a pursuit of arrested *tableaux vivants*, theatrical and logocentric. In relation to the enactment as well as the portrayal of urban modernity in Mexican films, and the static, contemplational plasticity of *Nosotros los pobres*, it is interesting to compare the strategy advocated by the Bauhaus's Laszlo Moholy-Nagy in his scheme for the film project *Dynamic of the Metropolis* (1921–2), where traditional figurative paradigms are superseded by the visual dynamic of cinematography.[46]

In the extensive use of diagonals in photographic compositions, Moholy-Nagy had already challenged the pursuit of a parallel symmetry between the photographic frame and its subject matter – an identification which Rodríguez's editing still tried to achieve on the screen.[47] In his typographically discontinuous scenario, where a montage of images and words creates a cognitive tension for the reader/spectator, Moholy-Nagy insists on the optical conception of duration through spatiotemporal juxtapositions, and on non-logical or consequential visual narrative which invites an unscripted and non-scriptural perception. He opts for 'optical action, optical arrangement of tempo' instead of 'literary, theatrical action'. His notion of 'dynamic of the optical' (not unlike Eisenstein's montage in practice, but explicitly resistant to synoptic reading) requires 'much movement, some heightened to the point of brutality'.[48] Moholy-Nagy's scenario also entailed an interactive notion of visual reception on the part of the spectator – what he termed *a dynamic insertion* into the visual action gestating the metropolis on the screen. In Mexico, where the pictorial remained for the most part attached to a figurative imperative, rather than perspectival experiments and compositional abstractions, the reformulation of ideas about image reception seems not to have surfaced specifically in discourses about cinema or by cinematographers, but in the constructivist experiments of photographers such as Tina Modotti and Agustín Jiménez, and in the commentaries which they inspired in the pages of cultural supplements such as *Revista de Revistas* and arts magazines such as *Forma, Contemporáneos* and *Mexican Art and Life* in the late 1920s and 1930s, and subsequently in avant-garde periodicals like *Espacios: Revista Integral de Arquitectura y Artes Plásticas* [*Spaces: Integrated Magazine of Architecture and the Plastic Arts*] (1948–58), founded by two architects, in the context of a broader discussion of technological innovation and its application in the arts, design and construction.[49] The argument against the assumption of a necessarily inert (and compliant) spectator emerges out of a concern to revolutionise architectural space as well as muralism's flattened pictorial narratives. One would do well to remember, in relation to this latter critique of what was purported to exemplify modern Mexican art, that the exegetical tendency of cycles produced in the populist 1930s was not so far removed in execution from the earliest murals from the colonial period, which sought to replicate black-and-white woodcut illustrations, substituting the walls of monasteries for the pages of ecclesiastical books as a form of popular catechism.[50]

The integration of the *artes plásticas* – a premise popularised by the Bauhaus and Le Corbusier – was clearly regarded by the contributors of *Espacios* (including Manuel Álvarez Bravo, the artist Rufino Tamayo and the architect Luis Barragán) as a prerequisite for a modern conception of urban development and aesthetic validity.[51] It is no coincidence that in an article published in 1948 in the first issue of *Espacios*, the artist, muralist and political activist David Alfaro Siqueiros introduces his critique of the place of the spectator in traditional visualisation as part of his advocacy of a 'plástica unitaria/integral' ['unified/integral aesthetic'].

Spatial configuration, as he understood it, entailed 'una composición y una perspectiva que se realizan considerando al espectador no como una estatua, o como un autómata que gira sólo en su eje fijo, sino como un ser que se mueve en una topografía y en un tránsito correspondiente' ['a composition and perspective that are realised by treating the spectator not as a statue or as an automaton who only moves in a fixed axis, but as a being who moves in correspondence with topography and trajectory'].[52] Siqueiros's radical notion of what might be termed a *desplazamiento ubicuo* [ubiquitous displacement] required both multiple perspectives and multidisciplinarity, in a total aesthetic experience. In contrast, Rodríguez's film with its adherence to pictorial paradigms that insisted on the logocentricity of the image, effectively seems to reject the film medium's offer of a less discursive syntax than the verbal for conjuring the crisis of modernity. The spectator, as it were, occupies a fixed seat aesthetically as well as physically.

The fabular element within the plot of *Nosotros los pobres* prescribes the staging of a happy outcome after a catalogue of misfortunes from the archive of Mexican melodrama, but the ending is less conclusive and rather more self-deprecating, resistant to scriptural rhetoric and officially required optimism than film historians have allowed. The pair of presumably illiterate urchins, disenchanted with their find, discard the illustrated narrative, returning it to a pile of detritus whose centrality perhaps denotes the in-built obsolescence of cultural products in the capitalist metropolis – not unlike pictorial allegories of capitalism such as Chávez Morado's, or Frida Kahlo's *My Dress Hangs There* (1933), in which an overflowing garbage container indicts American consumerism and the commodification of culture. This might be a gesture of predictable moral turpitude on the part of two marginalised youngsters, or of incomprehension based less on immaturity or a culpable misreading than on the inability to read at all. The premises of the filmic conceit are themselves fallacious. The found book is an empty analogue and its fictionality absolute. The ambiguous circularity of the film's ending has the paradoxical effect of delaying moralising closure, perhaps anticipating a more critical response to populist myth-making on the part of the aspiring proletarian consumer, if it did not advertise its patent artifice and delight in play.

An instance of strategic reconversion of genre elements occurs in *El ropavejero* [*The Old Clothes Dealer*] (1946) by Emilio Gómez Muriel (1910–1985).[53] A director with a marked textual bent and an interest in theatre, Gómez Muriel's initiation into cinema was as an editor for whom film could be defined in terms of meaningful language: 'una serie de trozos unidos que van creando una frase; fundamentalmente es la palabra, y la sucesión de ella forma la frase' ['a series of linked fragments that create a phrase; basically it is the word and its sequence which forms the phrase'].[54] The picaresque *léperos* scavenging on the margins between civilisation and barbarism demonised by the colonial and Porfirian imaginary, are rehabilitated through the comic persona of Joaquín Pardavé (1900–55), an ingratiating hero of the *patria chica* [parochial homeland]. A spontaneous defender of basic values, conviviality, communal living, *tianguis*, honourable poverty, self-deprecating humour – he solicits and hawks his used wares in the streets, with the same piercing cries of pre-Revolutionary society recorded nostalgically by Antonio García Cubas in *El libro de mis recuerdos* [*My Book of Memories*] (1905). An astute recycler of the detritus of predatory capitalism – whilst clothing himself in its disparate ordure and disjecta – he brings a disabused perspective to bear on the trappings of modern bourgeois prosperity, and turns base metal into edifying aphorisms. Gómez Muriel's comic alchemist had a nineteenth-century precursor in the itinerant and equally pungent *trapero* [ragman] of folk memory. The *trapero*'s trade was to gather discarded clothing and rags for the paper mill where such used and soiled fabric would be transformed into various grades of paper for writing, printing and packaging. Mexican satirists were attracted to this trafficker in dirty linen, supplying low and corrupt matter that would be fermented in a *pudridero* [rotting vat] and turned into the stuff of official inscription and communication: '¡El papel! Fórmanse con él libros y periódicos, es decir la luz y la oscuridad, la verdad y la mentira ... se cambian las costumbres y se trastornan los imperios! Y todo esto proviene de sucios trapos, de harapos abyectos recogidos por la noche en los basureros de las callejuelas' ['Paper! Books and newspapers are made from it, that is to say light and darkness, truth and falsehood ... customs are changed and empires overturned! And all this has its origin in filthy rags, wretched tatters collected by night from the rubbish tips of the alleyways'].[55]

El ropavejero's lowly mobility is polysemous: culpable in its affinity with notions of vagrancy and mendicancy, and restorative in its recirculation of traditional cultural currency. Nothing is lost or conclusively expelled whilst the 'ropavejero' functions as a conduit in a city which has become a shifting nexus rather than a stable hierarchy. His covert transactions with other archetypally liminal figures – serving maids and cooks – establishes an interesting exchange of metaphorical commodities in the form of costumes and customs which finally questions the reconstituted social hierarchy in the proscenium of modernity – Mexico City. Initially spoken to from folkloric balconies and modernist second-storey widows, seen from above, the personification of *los de abajo* and framed as such, *el ropavejero* draws the camera down to a ground level in a clearly signalled specular descent. If focal distance can be conceived analogically in ethnographic photography as a measure of cultural primacy, a condescending perspective on the subaltern, then the progressive shift to close-up, frontal and full shots and spatial contiguity sets out to level through cinematic spectacle the aboriginal with the hierarchy factored into the stratified cityscape, viewed as a series of façades. In its deft allusions to modernisation as authoritarian deception and architectural spectacle, the film deploys modernist villas and residential *fraccionamientos* [real estate development] of suburban developments like architect Luis Barragán's exclusive Jardines del Pedregal de San Ángel (1948–50), as elegant sets for the scheming and dissolute – and in later films, in psychological thrillers such as *El hombre sin rostro* [*The Man without a Face*] (1950), by Juan Bustillo Oro, for a dysfunctional élite in charge of policing the modern metropolis.

Emilio Gómez Muriel's ludic treatment of marginality in 1946 is counterposed by photographic images, from the same period, of entrapment, subordination and arrested development. Images such as those by Héctor García, where insolvent *cargadores*, as ubiquitous as landless beggars in the graphic arts of the period, carry the weight of other people's commodities like sculpted medieval Atlantes or misericords; where a destitute child finds a temporary refuge, completely enclosed in a crevice in a wall of concrete (figure 4.13); where a beggar is transfixed, crouched, eating rubbish (figure 4.14).[56] Marginality here does not lend itself to discursive recuperation and festive redeployment, but points to a conceptual vacuum through its wilful misreading of an encoded, visualised modernity predicated on new construction with its symmetries, textures and materials. Photographers like García, López and, less consistently, the Hermanos Mayo, in effect mounted a virtual campaign against the falsely visible – a mystificatory trend in cinema production which directors like Alejandro Galindo condemned as the elevation of 'el convencionalismo a la categoría de definición profunda' ['banality raised to the category of essential definition'].[57] At the end of the 1950s it is as if the film medium's very modernity, as much as its rendition of modernisation, has become subject to suspicion and disenchantment. Its *dynamisation of space*, the aesthetic experience of motion through identification with the lens of the camera, is regarded as a false promise of empowerment and change. Any notion of purposeful, redemptive mobility – social or political – other than the increasingly banal experience of displacement, is a calculated deception to which cinema's narrative trajectories, controlled locomotion and modernist mythology is tacitly complicit. Nacho López, a visionary of fusion in the graphic arts, regarded contemporary photography, and photojournalism in particular, as the proper avenue for an aesthetic reinvigoration of national cinema and cleansing of its lens of distorting rhetorical filters. Engaged like photography in synoptic exposition, such films would undertake constant experimentation with the substance of representational strategies, conjuring through the moving image a latent reality. This was to be a divulgatory process which López imagined to be akin to the violent irruption of something too long repressed ('una realidad latente se vuelca en movimiento' ['a latent reality erupts into movement']).[58] In 1957 he was advocating a *perspicuous* vision: a

Figure 4.13 © Héctor García, *Niño en el vientre del concreto* (1949).

Figure 4.14 © Héctor García, *Comiendo basura* (1947).

representational aesthetic which would foster understanding through the revelation of visible connections 'para decir las cosas de nuestro existir en un lenguaje más claro y directo' ['to relate the aspects of our life in a language which is clearer and more direct'],[59] thereby instituting a critical acuity at the very centre of the image-making process. Paradoxically, in pursuing the possibility of *transparent* communication López seemed to desire to contemporaneously re-establish photography's claim to a pure, unmediated trace and refine its interpretative scope through its manufacture of images, as well as to disengage photographic arts from what in modernism had become a trend to be assimilated into a commodity culture. Interestingly, López's call for an integrated aesthetic of the lens may have appeared to a generation of Mexican modernists as tantamount to depriving both the still and motion picture cameras of independence as instruments of figuration, by seemingly subordinating them to the representational strategies of pre-existing media such as painting and theatre. In 1939 a piece in *Artes Plásticas* (probably by Álvarez Bravo), offering an appraisal of new directions in representation, had seized on cinematography's groundbreaking potential for formal emancipation from the tradition of painting and theatre – in effect the eliding of the 'composición de cuadro' ['pictorial composition'].[60]

The counterpoint between a collectivity conceived vertically, as in tower blocks and *multifamiliares*, and the articulation of civic life as levelling horizontality, as in public transport, bridges and *supermanzanas*, provided a perspectival model based on intersection and interpenetration for representational strategies which dwelt on the contemporary experience of change – the mutability of the cultural and social order emblematically configured in public spaces. The quest for visual resolution in cultural production (be it film, photography or architecture) which was exercised by the redesignation of traditional notions of place and provenance, reveals an interpretative trend: the symmetrical oppositions of previous discursive strategies are reformulated into something akin to a sociological conceit. As Monsiváis has suggested, 'lo *mexicano* va siendo, cada vez más, el cemento de las tradiciones rurales y urbanas en las vecindades capitalinas' ['"the typically Mexican" progressively becomes the cement of rural and urban traditions in the capital's neighbourhoods'].[61] The notion of an accommodating synthesis of social and cultural elements previously conceived in an oppositional relationship forms part of an aesthetic of convergence which paralleled to a degree official invocations of 'unidad nacional' ['national unity'] in pursuit of development.

Luis Buñuel's *El río y la muerte* [*Death and the River*] (1954) is a film which uses the iconography of displacement, its specific oppositional topographies and discursive syntax, to compendious (and perhaps ambiguously parodic) effect. It relates the story of a young, thoroughly urban, disabled doctor forced to confront a disturbing, predatory family history in the provinces. He undertakes a parabolic retrospective journey from Mexico City to the riverside place of origin (not coincidentally called Santa Bárbara with its association to the civilisation versus barbarism formula of regionalist novels) – a return which serves to confirm the redemptive distance travelled from underdevelopment. A member of the class of professionals which had become synonymous with desirable modernity in official mythology, the focus of 'el optimismo clasemediero' ['middle-class optimism'] of a new genre of urban comedies in cinema, he is unexpectedly summoned back from the capital where he has found education, order and prosperity, to the southern backwater which had witnessed the quasi-extinction of his family through a cyclical blood-feud:[62] a telluric legacy predicated on tribalism, a masculinist tradition of duels, revenge and superstitious faith which he had hoped to escape. This was a blighted heredity which had its equally compelling equivalent in a cinematic genre. *El río y la muerte*'s hyperbolic treatment of stock motifs of national cinema which had been accorded the gravitas of *calidad* [quality] and international recognition –

namely, edifying rural dramas, patriotic and *progresistas*, where violence formed part of folkloric spectacle – suggests an ironic self-referentiality at play, not unlike that essayed by *Maldita ciudad*. Statistics suggest that the escape from the mystifications of rural melodramas and folkloric musicals was being effected by the industry in the 1950s, albeit intermittently and strategically. The film historian García Riera has suggested, for instance, that the recourse to the *cine ranchero* against the trend to *urbanise* the national screen proposed escapist fantasy, or controlled displacement, to distract from the reality of economic hardship.[63] The film's narrative structure relies heavily on *flashbacks* instituting a metaphorical counterpoint which constructs a discursive viewpoint. Generically, the film is explicitly regressive (it features, for instance, one of Fernández's hieratic autochthonous beauties, Columba Domínguez). It is based on a didactic novel by Manuel Álvarez Acosta, *Muro blanco sobre roca negra* [*White Wall on Black Rock*], the title of which neatly encapsulates the allegorisation of graphic binarisms in visual narratives, and the way in which the arts provided a representational syntax for literature. Such manipulative contrasts were especially evident in the collaborations of Fernández-Figueroa's rural tragedies, Leopoldo Méndez's *Taller de Gráfica Popular*, with its pungent delineations of social inequalities in black and white, and the disjunctive visual ironies achieved by the young Nacho López through his adoption of directorial techniques for lighting a scene in his earliest *foto-ensayos* [photo-essays]. The latter's framing and sequencing of shots in *Noche de muertos* [*Night of the Dead Rituals*], for example, his first piece for *Mañana* in 1950, starts with the equivalent of a cinematic *establishing shot* and moves to lapidary close-ups.[64]

El río y la muerte culminates bathetically in reconciliation between the rival families and competing rural and urban traditions, restoring the protagonist to synchronic plenitude, his pastoral vocation vindicated as he is wheeled across and through the modernist vistas of the newly constructed Ciudad Universitaria (1950–2), itself the resolution of aesthetic debates that pitted international modernism against a strongly pictorial cultural nationalism. The wheelchair movements – a dependent form of locomotion in the film – choreograph a specular map of the gaze (and the operation of directorial perspective). In the background the centrally located main library building, with its monumental geometric volume overlaid by O'Gorman's pointilistic two-dimensional mural – a mosaic of pre-Columbian mythic motifs, masks and emblems from Mexican and human history – provides a telling example of humanist logocentricity in image production. The façade of the modernist building provides a giant screen for a totalising narrative of cultural origins, the film's closing shots in effect reflecting through their own captious narrative an ironic homage to a consecrated representational discourse.

For modernists such as the Mexican *estridentistas* (1922–5)[65] and Moholy-Nagy in the 1920s, the mechanical, technical methods of photography and cinematography ushered in a new representational optical form which would challenge the primacy of traditional pictorial paradigms (based on the Renaissance), and which would be receptive to the passage of deconstructive modernity (through abstraction, for instance). In practice, film and photography in 1950s Mexico, which addressed urban and technological modernisation, inflected by journalism and pedagogy, suggest that the verist exactitude of the lens (based on the notion of the technical rather than sensory eye) becomes subject to literary *captionalisation*. The contingent moment becomes subject to narrative recuperation and an integrative imperative which ran counter to the discontinuity of actual urbanisation, but which was in keeping with its official ideology. Formal cross-pollination imbued urban scenarios in film and photographic essays with the lingering paralysis of the valedictory trace, whereby in the immediacy of a staged or captured moment the future subsists, interpretatively framed for consumption like the most portable of cased daguerreotypes or the most literary of portable museums. Such apparent encapsulating stasis does not, as Walter Benjamin observed, preclude 'an irresistible urge to search such a picture for the tiny spark of contingency, of the Here and Now, with which reality has so to speak seared the subject'.[66] Or, as one might say, to search for the *memorias del porvenir* [memories of the future] in the spectacle of modernity – the strategies of visualisation rather than the visualised matter of an archaeology of seeing.[67]

It may well be that the intersection of elements which plays such a crucial role in photographic compositions, cinematic narrative, architectural practice and theory in the 1950s does not so much generate a single, unified perspectival space or convergent perception but a recurrent poetic conceit akin to Nacho López's 'Cycoplean eye' by which cultural identity is reconstituted (rather than evidenced) through stilled disjunctions and crossed trajectories.[68] Arguably the paradigm of the still photograph itself, understood as conflating filmic and photographic visualisation by Revueltas, may owe its appeal as a model of representational modernity to its origin as a temporal excision from a visual narrative. For each depicted element is but a single transitory and transitional phase of motion which is only seen imaginatively – through what is visibly absent but experienced as requisite. Implicit in the still photograph is the expectation of succession which may or may not be developmental: a fitting metaphor for the speculative and often recursive trajectories of modernisation. Such urban photography which, despite its frequent non-conformism, sought to inspire loci of collective identification could be conceived as enacting with its 'momentary fixities' an inconclusive passageway for the viewer.[69] For, intriguingly, the viewer would experience both displacement and transition in the effort required to see the transitory through, rather than in, still images of urban reality.

Films Cited

La reina del trópico (dir. Raúl de Anda, 1945)
El ropavejero (dir. Emilio Gómez Muriel, 1946)
Nosotros los pobres (dir. Ismael Rodríguez, 1947; released 1948)
¡Esquina ...bajan! (dir. Alejandro Galindo, 1948; released 1949)
[*Hay lugar para dos* (dir. Alejandro Galindo, 1949), sequel of the above]
Salón México (dir. Emilio Fernández, 1948; released 1949)
El hombre sin rostro (dir. Juan Bustillo Oro, 1950)
Maldita ciudad (dir. Ismael Rodríguez, 1954)
El río y la muerte (dir. Luis Buñuel, 1954)
El hombre de papel (dir. Ismael Rodríguez, 1963)

Notes

1. A conversation with Alejandro Galindo in 1974 in Mexico City; see B. Reyes Nevares, *Trece directores del cine mexicano* (Mexico City, 1974), 56.
2. For 'desarrolismo', see C. Monsiváis, 'Sociedad y cultura', in R. Loyola (ed.), *Entre la guerra y la estabilidad política: el México de los 40* (Mexico City, 1990), 259–80 (263).
3. A. Ballent, 'El arte de saber vivir: modernización del habitar doméstico y cambio urbano, 1940–1970', in N. García Canclini (ed.), *Cultura y comunicación en la ciudad de México*, 2 vols. (Mexico City, 1998), I: 65–131 (70).
4. See A. Castellanos, N. García Canclini and A. Rosas Mantecón, *La ciudad de los viajeros: Travesías e imaginarios urbanos: México, 1940–2000* (Mexico City, 1996).
5. The film was shot by Gabriel Figueroa and included visual references to images coined by the photographer Manuel Álvarez Bravo, his friend and sometime collaborator – esp. *Tumba reciente* [*Recent Tomb*] (1933), *Fábula del perro y la nube* [*Fable of the Dog and the Cloud*] (c.1935) and *Quema dos* [*Fire II*] (1957).
6. For stills of the film, see C. Bonfil and C. Monsiváis, *A través del espejo: el cine mexicano y su público* (Mexico City, 1994), 89–90; J. Ayala Blanco, *La aventura del cine mexicano en la época de oro y después* (Mexico City, 1993), 95. The publicity poster for the film by the Spanish exile Francisco Rivero Gil is reproduced in R. Agrasánchez, Jr (ed.), *Carteles de la época de oro del cine*

mexicano/Poster Art from the Golden Age of Mexican Cinema (Mexico City, 1997), 121.

7. *Campeón sin corona* (1945, released in 1946), directed by Alejandro Galindo, has been credited with having encapsulated cinematically the psychology of the *pelado* – Mexico City's archetypal proletarian underdog. See Ayala Blanco, *La aventura del cine mexicano*, 175–9.

8. J. Revueltas, 'Lugar del cine en el arte', *Anthropos*, 1 (1947), 2–10 (2). The full title reads *Anthropos: publicada por elementos de la Escuela Nacional de Antropología e Historia y el Centro de Estudios Circuncaribes*. It described itself as 'una publicación con el próposito de difundir conocimientos e ideas entre los grupos de orientación popular de la cultura' ['a publication whose object is to spread knowledge and ideas among those groups connected to popular culture'] and as having no political affiliation.

9. Ibid., 2–10 (2).

10. Ibid.

11. For a discussion of Eisenstein, art and film in Mexico, see e.g. E. de la Vega Alfaro, *Del muro a la pantalla: S.M. Eisenstein y el arte pictórico mexicano* (Mexico City, 1997). For a translation of Eisenstein's theory of montage, see A. Aragón Leiva (tr.), 'Sergio Eisenstein: montaje', in M. Durán (ed.), *Antología de la Revista Contemporáneos* (Mexico City, 1973), 294–304, first published in *Contemporáneos*, 35 (1931).

12. Revueltas, 'Lugar del cine', 5.

13. Ibid., emphasis added. For a monograph on Álvarez Bravo which includes the photograph *Un poco alegre y graciosa* discussed by Revueltas, see S. Kismaric (ed.), *Manuel Álvarez Bravo* (New York, 1997), 185.

14. Manuel Álvarez Bravo directed his only known full-length film *Tehuantepec* in 1934. In an interview he dated the period of his film collaborations between 1943 and 1959; see A. Castellanos and M. García, 'Encuentros con el fotógrafo Manuel Álvarez Bravo', *Kalías: Revista de Arte*, 15–16 (1996), 122–30 (128).

15. See A. Castellanos, 'Espacio y espejo', in Castellanos et al., *La ciudad de los viajeros*, 43–55, (50). On Nacho López and Mexico City, see A. Arnal and P. Massé, 'Nacho López: cronista en blanco y negro', *Luna Córnea*, 8 (1995), 32–9; C. Monsiváis, 'Before the Flood: Nacho López and Hector García', *Aperture*, 153 (1998), 40–2. See also the interview with Álvarez Bravo in T. Cooper and P. Hill, *Dialogue with Photography* (Stockport, 1998), 183.

16. See G. Boils, 'Arquitectura y producción del espacio social', in Loyola, *Entre la guerra y la estabilidad política*, 321–38.

17. Juan O'Gorman regarded his encounter with Diego Rivera's mural art and defence of autochthonous popular traditions as a conceptual apprenticeship from which emerged his own advocacy of an organic Mexican modernism in architecture. See A. Luna Arroyo, *Juan O' Gorman: Autobiografía, antología, juicios críticos y documentación exhaustiva de su obra* (Mexico City, 1973).

18. For pictorial representations of the city in the colonial era and in the nineteenth century, see *Pasado y presente*, with essays by E. O'Gorman, J. Manrique and T. del Conde.

19. The painting is part of the national collection of the Museo de Arte Moderno in Mexico City.

20. The oil painting is on show at the Antiguo Palacio del Arzobispado in Mexico City as part of the *Pago en Especie* collection of Mexican art. Chávez Morado was a founder member of the collective *Taller de Gráfica Popular* (1936), which promoted printmaking on subjects such as the exploitation of the poor, Western imperialism and the need for popular literacy. He was professor of lithography from 1945 to 1947 at the Escuela de Artes del Libro, having been appointed director of the fine arts section of the Ministry of Education in 1940. See his allegorical *La gran ciudad* [*The Great City*] (1948), in which the personified Indian motherland is perforated and exploited, encircled by aeroplanes with the expanding cityscape threatening the horizon, in L.-M. Lozano (ed.), *José Chávez Morado: En memoria* (Mexico City, 2004), 30–1; and his painting *Calle en construcción con letrero* (1959), in J.L. Cuevas, E. Krauze, R. Tovar y de Teresa et al., *Pintura Mexicana 1950–1980: homenaje a Fernando Gamboa* (Mexico City, 1993), 51.

21. Ballent, 'El arte de saber vivir', I: 65–131 (108), originally published in *Espacios*.

22. For a discussion of Buñuel's films in the Mexican genre, see E. Segre, 'Cultural Nationalism and Buñuel in Mexico, 1946–1955', in J. Macklin (ed.), *Convivium: Festschrift for Ronald Cueto* (Leeds, 1997), 265–97.

23. On the subject of public transport and the urban imaginary, see e.g. photographs by Manuel Álvarez Bravo, *Las ruedas* (*c*.1933) and *Ángeles en camión* (1930) and those by Nacho López of the series *La Venus fue de juerga por los barrios bajos* (1953).

24. A. Isaac, *Conversaciones con Gabriel Figueroa* (Guadalajara, 1993), 20.

25. For a critical synopsis of the film, see E. García Riera, *Historia documental del cine mexicano* (Mexico City, 1993), VII: 189–90.

26. On the history of photojournalism and its modalities, see O. Debroise, *Fuga mexicana* (Mexico City, 1994), 140–69.

27. Modelled on *Life* magazine, *Hoy*, *Mañana* and *Siempre!* (founded in 1937, 1947 and 1953 respectively) dominated the period from 1937 to 1960. See J. Mraz, *Nacho López y el fotoperiodismo mexicano en los años cincuenta* (Mexico City, 1999), 43–4. On the legacy of López and García, see J. Mraz, *La mirada inquieta: nuevo fotoperiodismo mexicano: 1976–1996* (Mexico City, 1996), 22. *Fotoreporteros* from 1920s and 1930s included Enrique Díaz and Manuel Ramos.

28. See A. Castellanos, 'Nacho López: los rituales de la modernidad', *Alquimia*, 2 (1998), 7–11. See also the retrospective monograph by C. Carrillo Trueba and J. Lépez Vela, *Nacho López: los rumbos del tiempo* (Mexico City, 1997).

29. On the representational scope and responsibilities of photography, see N. López, 'Mi punto de partida', *Generación*, 9 (1996), 13, a special issue entitled 'Fotoperiodismo: un enfoque generacional'.

30. For Nacho López's active interest in cinematography, which culminated in a number of documentary projects for the Instituto Nacional Indígenista and publicity shorts in the 1960s, see C. López, 'Nacho López: un artista multidisciplinario', *Generación*, 9 (1996), 10–12. For López's interaction with neo-figurative tendencies, see S.M. Goldman, *Contemporary Mexican Painting in a Time of Change* (Albuquerque, 1995), 169–78.

31. See S. Albiñana, 'Agustín Jiménez', in S. Albiñana and H. Fernández (eds), *Mexicana: Fotografía moderna en México, 1923–1940* (Valencia, 1998), 102–37.

32. See J. Tuñón, 'La ciudad actriz: la imagen urbana en el cine mexicano (1940–1955)', in Castellanos et al., *La ciudad de los viajeros*, 48; the exhibition catalogue in M.I. Roqué and A. Sánchez (eds), *La ciudad de Juan Rulfo: Textos y fotografías de Juan Rulfo* (Mexico City, 1996). Nacho López printed some of Rulfo's rediscovered negatives of Mexico City from the 1940s and 1950s for the Bellas Artes exhibition of 1980. The area of Nonoalco also figures in Rulfo's story *Paso del Norte*, where it is associated with rail transport, exploitative labour and displacement. See M. Giménez Cacho, 'Juan Rulfo, fotógrafo', *Luna Córnea*, 6 (1995), 50–5. For images of Mexico City between 1940 and 1992, see A. Castellanos, J. Mraz, L. Ortiz Monasterio et al., *Foto Hnos Mayo* (Valencia, 1992), 113–15.

33. The image is reproduced in L.-M. Lozano (ed.), *Arte moderno de México, 1900-1950* (Mexico City, 2000), 166. For an equally disenchanted perspective from a member of the TGP, see Alfredo Zalce's etching *México se convierte en una gran ciudad* (1947).

34. Emphasis added: N. López, 'Fotopoemáticos', *Generación*, 9 (1996), 16–18.

35. See H. García, *México sin retoque* (Mexico City, 1987), 30, with an essay by Elena Poniatowska, and *Camera oscura* (Mexico City, 1992).

36. The theme of displacement and migration is as prevalent in Rulfo's photographic subject matter as it is in his fiction. As an itinerant salesman he was particularly receptive to the visual signs of transition. Some of the images from the 1950s were commisioned by Goodrich/Euzkadi for the travel guide *Caminos de México*, while others were published in the magazine *Ferrocarriles Nacionales*. See E. Billeter, C. Fuentes, M. Glantz et al., *México: Juan Rulfo fotógrafo* (Barcelona, 2001).

37. Isaac, *Conversaciones con Gabriel Figueroa*, 19.

38. In later life Alejandro Galindo regarded himself as something of a heretic when articulating a social critique on the screen. In the 1970s he claimed that film in Mexico 'Está encorsetado entre el capitalismo y las izquierdas' ['It is held in a straitjacket by capitalism and the left wing'] (Reyes Nevares, *Trece directores del cine mexicano*, 36).

39. Ballent, 'El arte de saber vivir', 72.

40. Ibid.

41. For the articulation of a revolutionary aesthetic in Mexico City, see *Grupo de Pintores ¡30-30!*, founded in 1928, who adopted the iconic weapon of the Mexican Revolution as their insignia. For manifestos and other illustrated facsimiles, see L. González Matute (ed.), *¡30-30! contra la Academia de Pintura? (1928)* (Mexico City, 1993).

42. See *La elegancia y la pobreza* [*Elegance and Poverty*] (c.1928) in S.M. Lowe (ed.), *Tina Modotti: Photographs* (New York, 1995), Fig. 95; *El sueño de los pobres* [*The Dream/Sleep of the Poor*] (n.d.) in J.J. Blanco, M. Fernández Perera, L. Zapata, et al., *Lola Álvarez Bravo: Recuento fotográfico* (Mexico City, 1982), 38.

43. See e.g. Raúl de Anda's *Del rancho a la capital* [*From the Farm to the Capital*] (1941).

44. For film as folk expression, see E. Panofsky, 'Style and Medium in the Motion Pictures' (1937/1947), in I. Lavin (ed.), *Erwin Panofsky: Three Essays on Style* (Cambridge, MA, 1995), 93–125 (95).

45. See L. Noelle Merles, 'The Architecture and Urbanism of Mario Pani: Creativity and Compromise', in E.R. Burian (ed.), *Modernity and the Architecture of Mexico* (Austin, 1997), 177–89.
46. 'The intention of the film *Dynamic of the Metropolis* is not to teach, nor to moralise, nor to tell a story': L. Moholy-Nagy, *Painting, Photography, Film*, tr. J. Seligman (London, 1969), 122–37 (122), an English translation based on the 1967 German facsimile edition. *Malerei Fotografie Film* was originally published in 1925 in the *Bauhausbücher*, vol. VIII.
47. Ismael Rodríguez either edited most of his films himself or collaborated in the process. He claimed to enjoy this aspect of film-making most of all despite his polymathic training and involvement as 'proyeccionista, editor, laboratorista, técnico de sonido, fotógrafo, argumentista, distribuidor y hasta exhibidor' ['projectionist, editor, lab technician, sound engineer, photographer, scriptwriter, distributor and even exhibitor'] (Reyes Nevares, *Trece directores del cine mexicano*, 60). For examples of Moholy-Nagy's perspectival diagonals, see A. Haus, *Moholy-Nagy: Photographs and Photograms* (London, 1980).
48. Moholy-Nagy, *Painting, Photography, Film*, 123.
49. Modotti's industrial abstractions *Telphone Wires*, *Tank No. 1* and *Labour 2* appeared in R.M.E., 'Obras de Tina Modotti', *Forma: Revista de Artes Plásticas* 4 (1927), 30–3. See also F. Toor, 'Exposición de fotografías de Tina Modotti', *Mexican Folkways*, 5 (1929), 192–5; J.A. Rodríguez, 'La gramática constructiva de Agustín Jiménez', *Luna Córnea*, 2 (1993), 72–9. For Álvarez Bravo's organic abstractions, see 'Fotografías de Manuel Álvarez Bravo', *Contemporáneos*, 33 (1931), 136–9; for Salvador Novo's speech, see 'El arte de la fotografía', *Contemporáneos*, 33 (1931), 165–72; for reproductions of Man Ray's, see 'Rayografías de Man Ray', *Contemporáneos*, 13 (1929), 257–61.
50. See J. Favrot Peterson, *The Paradise Garden Murals of Malinalco: Utopia and Empire in Sixteenth-Century Mexico* (Austin, 1993), 65, 70.
51. See C. Alvarado Lang, 'La necesidad de conjugar todas las artes plásticas con un sentido integral', *Espacios*, 1 (January 1949), n.p.n.
52. Ibid., 81.
53. For a retrospective interview, see M.A. Fulgueira, *Cuadernos de la Cineteca Nacional: Testimonios para la historia del cine mexicano* (Mexico City, 1976), III: 77–87.
54. Ibid., 78.
55. H. Lenz, *Historia del papel en México y cosas relacionadas (1525–1950)* (Mexico City, 1990), 148, first published in J. Pizzetta, *Historia de un pliégo* (1875).
56. Reyes Nevares, *Trece directores del cine mexicano*, 43.
57. *Comiendo basura [Eating Rubbish]* (1947), *Diálogo de cargadores [Conversation between Loaders]* (1948), *Niño en el vientre de concreto [Child in the Concrete Womb]* (1949 or 1952), *Descargando harina en San Juan de Letrán [Delivering Flour in San Juan de Letrán]* (1951).
58. López, 'Nacho López', 11.
59. Ibid.
60. M. Álvarez Bravo, 'Cine', *Artes Plásticas*, 1 (1939), n.p.n.
61. Monsiváis, 'Sociedad y cultura', 259–80 (269).

62. E. García Riera, *Breve historia del cine mexicano: primer siglo, 1897–1997* (Mexico City, 1998), VII: 188.
63. Ibid., 187–8.
64. For the influence of the classics of indigenist cinema on López's early framing of ethnic subject matter, see Mraz, *Nacho López*, 65–70.
65. *Estridentismo* was an irreverent artistic movement headed by the poet Manuel Maple Arce and included painters such as Fermín Revueltas, Leopoldo Méndez, Jean Charlot and Ramon Alva de la Canal. Strongly influenced by Italian Futurism, it was anti-academic and celebrated urbanisation, industrial architecture, modern means of communication, and technological innovation.
66. W. Benjamin, *One Way Street and Other Writing*, ed. and trs. E. Jephcott and K. Shorters (London, 1979), 43.
67. For Walter Benjamin on photography, see ibid., 243.
68. For a revisionist study of theories of perspective, J. Elkins, *The Poetics of Perspective* (Ithaca/London, 1994).
69. For Octavio Paz on Álvarez Bravo, see O. Paz, *Essays on Mexican Art*, tr. H. Lane (New York, 1993), 266–74.

Chapter 5

Allegory, Self-Reflexivity and Irony:

A Photographic Genealogy

It is a misunderstanding to think that with the material possibility of learning a technique
... that automatically this knowledge will produce insight.[1]

Photography in Mexico has been an instrument of surface definition and critical unmasking: it has both helped to circumscribe visual identity and to interrogate the construction of such imagery and the gendering of ethnicity through persistent figurative tropes (consider, for instance, the gallery of archetypal *Malinches* [after the celebrated Indian interpreter and lover of the Conquistador, Hernán Cortés], *Tehuanas* [Zapotec women from the Isthmus of Tehuantepec], *Chinas poblanas* and Indian Madonnas of 1920s and 1930s nation-conscious art, photography and film).[2] Self-reflexive, ironic strategies in relation to the photographing of indigenous subjects characterise the work of an influential number of contemporary women photographers who have sought to mark the visible signs of image-making interventions to create perceptual difficulties for the viewer. Their provocative work draws on a little-recognised legacy of ludic reflexivity, experimentation and self-doubt bequeathed by those Mexican photographers who from the 1920s through the 1950s had been jointly exercised by the conceptual and the political problem of visual identity and intrigued by the production of visuality itself. This chapter offers a contextual, comparative study of the questing work of Mariana Yampolsky and Graciela Iturbide in relation to that of predecessors Nacho López and Lola Álvarez Bravo, as well as making reference, by way of contrast, to the more ambivalent case of Flor Garduño.

The chapter takes as its starting point an expository conceit. It emerges out of curiosity induced by the startling conjunction of photographic images collected without apparent design, scattered on my table. Their fortuitous contiguities prompted questions about the interplay between certain techniques and genres of figuration and the representational strategies adopted by Mexican women photographers whose work seemed to situate itself in the interstices between such disciplines. The functional moment of exposure in photography which produces an immediate *memento mori* is problematised in work which focuses on indigenous communities that for the most part have naturalised the invasive technology into practices of self-representation fostered by the itinerant village photographer, the local studio and, most recently, the cheap Instamatic.[3] The photograph's status as cultural object as much as its experimental objectivity seems to exercise both Mariana Yampolsky and Graciela Iturbide's 'ethics of seeing'.

As spectacle the chance display of images on the table had something of the studied unobtrusiveness of a seventeenth-century *trompe-l'œil* painting of a letter rack, the allegorical pungency of a nineteenth-century *costumbrista mesa revuelta* [disordered table still life] and the eye-catching disjunctions of surrealist collage or montage.[4] The notion of the photograph as facsimile and inventory complicated by an ironic self-reflexivity seemed to provide a partial explanation for what struck me as a quasi-acquisitive and curatorial interest by Mexican women painters and photographers in the presence and order of things.[5] A recurrent concern with the genre of still life, the framing device of the box, for instance, as cabinet of curiosities, domestic *alacena* [dresser], votive niche and home altar, theatrical camera and camera obscura, as well as with mortuary studio photography and the painterly illusions of *trompe-l'œil* is peculiarly prevalent in their work.[6]

A reflective engagement with modes of representation and exhibition and with interdisciplinary citation is evidenced perhaps most intriguingly in the work of Mariana Yampolsky (1925–2002) (figures 5.1, 5.2 and 5.3). She was a notable engraver and draughtswoman, whose important work in the *Taller de Gráfica Popular* collective (1945–58) pre-dated and facilitated her adoption of photography (in the mid-1950s) as her preferred medium of re-presentation.[7] Versed in architectural design and space, and a photographer of both modernist and vernacular structures, Yampolsky was an editor, curator and photographic illustrator of unsurpassed book compilations on the folk art traditions of Mexico.[8] She was also instrumental in promoting the historical study and conservation of Mexican photography, helping to set up the national archive in Pachuca. Her formal trajectory might be conceived as re-enacting the original proximity between graphic arts such as engraving, lithography and photography itself; a paradigmatic affinity which explains the

Figure 5.1 Mariana Yampolsky, *Alacena* (1974). Courtesy of © FCMY.

original adoption of a conceptual terminology culled from pictorial reproductive techniques.[9] Even Yampolsky's otherwise eccentric interest in buildings resonates with the early history of the photographic subject as still object.

Of contemporary Mexican photographers, she was the most preoccupied by what might be termed the anthropology of photography, its cultural formulations as opposed to theorising its operation. She admits to having been influenced by Franz Boas, her great-uncle, although in an indeterminate way.[10] His anthropological concept of cultural pluralism countered the Eurocentric evolutionary model, 'shifted the ground of inquiry from a search for signs of inherited difference to an investigation of how foreign material was taken up by a people and modified by pre-existing ideas and customs'.[11] The tension between reproduction and production when photography is operated ethnographically is superseded in Yampolsky by co-representation (with its pictorial antecedents) in

Figure 5.2 Mariana Yampolsky, *Trampantojo (Trompe-l'œil)* (n.d.). Courtesy of © FCMY.

Figure 5.3 Mariana Yampolsky, *Retratos* (1976). Courtesy of © FCMY.

which the photographer is the recording surface imbricated by the subject. Her statement in an interview that 'No soy yo que toma la foto, soy un simple negativo' ['It's not me who takes the photograph, I'm simply a negative'] is perhaps best understood as alluding to the need for receptive disempowerment on the part of the photographer.[12] To be utterly receptive is a rigorous kind of passivity (figure 5.4).

Graciela Iturbide (b. 1942), on the other hand, channelled her literary vocation into the imagistic narratives afforded by cinematography before opting for the poetics of the still image and perspectival authorship.[13] She is a 'method photographer', getting to know the subject (as if studying for a role in which one assumes an unfamiliar identity) through complicitous immersion, part of the scene yet coaxing elements into place (figure 5.5). The shutter clicks at the moment of synoptic accretion, having found the 'look'.[14] Conversely, to expose the subterfuge of photographic neutrality, she sometimes resorts to visible framing, *mise-en-abîme* and other telling signatures or even 'thumbprints' of directorial intervention and mediation (figures 5.6 and 5.7).

Flor Garduño's allegorical proclivities, her practice of 'darle una arregladita a la realidad para que se parezca a mis particulares sueños' ['rearranging reality a little so that it resembles my particular dreams'] openly admits to 'algo de pintora frustrada' ['something of the frustrated painter'] in the framing, composition and manipulation of the print.[15]

Figure 5.4 Mariana Yampolsky, *Mazahuas*, State of Mexico (1989). Courtesy of © FCMY.

Figure 5.5 © Graciela Iturbide, *Na' Marcelina*, Juchitán, Oaxaca (1984). Courtesy of Graciela Iturbide.

Figure 5.6 © Graciela Iturbide, *Serafina*, Juchitán, Oaxaca (1985). Courtesy of Graciela Iturbide.

Figure 5.7   © Graciela Iturbide, *Lagarto*, Juchitán, Oaxaca (1986). Courtesy of Graciela Iturbide.

The fact that Garduño (b. 1957) also makes Joseph Cornell-like boxes, fantastic showcases and collages, which unlike her photographs are not for public view, is more than merely tangentially related to the formation of the 'realidad compuesta' ['composite reality'] (in her own words) of her work on indigenous peoples, predicated on a very personal form of ethnographic decontextualisation.[16] She is the least concerned with the effacement of the marks of the photographer's culture, or with effecting transparency by making you forget her presence (figure 5.8). In her symbolic arrangements, Indians make available to Westernised perception the vertiginous ancestry of a syncretic nation: '... voy con los indios, porque ahí me encuentro al ser humano que todavía se deja ver, se deja percibir en momentos, en situaciones, en actitudes que yo siento ancestrales, viejísimas, comunes; pertenecientes a todos, aunque nosotros ... ya las vivimos como perdidas' ['... I go with the Indians because there I find myself before a human being who still allows himself to be seen, on occasion allows himself to be perceived, in situations, in attitudes that I feel to be ancestral, very old, common; belonging to all, although we ... now experience them as lost'].[17] The notion of the photograph as *memento mori*, with its familial and commemorative uses, imposes itself although the reality at stake is an imaginary construction.

My (reworked) assemblage of 'found' images included the following five photographs.

Two were C.B. Waite's mass-produced postcards of Indian types and customs.[18] The first, captioned 'Indias de Tehuantepec', consists of a full-frontal posed shot of three women wearing their distinctive regional costume (figure 5.9). One stands, crowned by a defining prop of a *jícara* or brightly painted or lacquered gourd, a receptacle for carrying and displaying food – a fitting visual pun perhaps for her role as deposit and conduit of signification. The image has been literally overwritten by the sender of the postcard, whose comments confirm the image's illustrational purpose, its replication of the Indian's subalternity through the exercise of reproductive technology and the extent to which the scenic Indian functioned as a differentiating emblem of place, a commodity like an *artículo de costumbres* or curiosity which could be readily exported and exhibited and a receptive surface for inscription.[19] The legend in the second does not define the Indian women by provenance, but by their typical trade, that of *deshiladoras* [unpicking threads from a fabric to form an open-work which is then embroidered] (figure 5.10). The women and their frames have been positioned in such a way that the stretched squares of textile which they are embroidering provide a convenient space for inscription. The shawl-clad women, seen in profile, have been arranged as if they were decorative elements in the margin of a page. The

Figure 5.8   © Flor Garduño, *Agua o Mujer amuzgo*, Valle Nacional, Oaxaca (1983). Courtesy of Flor Garduño.

Figure 5.9 Charles B. Waite, *Indias de Tehuantepec* (1906) (in colour). FINAH-SINAFO.

design of the postcard image presupposes the interplay of text and image, an assumption which inscribes the photograph within the space of writing, upholding the paradigmatic link of the photograph to the text and print of nineteenth-century discourse.[20]

The third of my found images by *fotorreportero* [photographic reporter] Enrique Díaz is a publicity photograph of a cabaret show from 1929 provocatively entitled, at the height of cultural nationalism, *Mexican curios*, which uses as a backdrop the recreated interior of a store.[21] It seems to offer a parodic compendium of exhibitionary paradigms, from the diorama to the altar (figure 5.11). Three women dancers pose in front of a painted *alacena*, exhibited like colourful objects in the cabinet; above them in a niche, moulded figures (possibly articulated) of folkloric musicians and dancers signal a popular entertainment. Various autochthonous artefacts, including a chest from Olinalá, are depicted with the exactitude of an ethnological catalogue, although arranged in decorative motifs. Disproportionately life size, a traditional toy of horse and rider made of natural fibre stands like a gigantic equestrian statue, whilst behind it its painted analogue flanks the *alacena*. Before this composite *retablo* [altarpiece/tableau], stand the three dancers, arms akimbo, wearing intriguingly abbreviated, art deco interpretations of vernacular costume. The women operate on the same level of signification as the other simulacra that construct the scene, so that the photograph is ostensibly a facsimile of art-made objects and, inductively, of different forms of representation.

Figure 5.10   Charles B. Waite, *Deshiladoras* (1906) (in colour). FINAH-SINAFO.

Figure 5.11   Enrique Díaz, *'Mexican Curios'* (1929), Teatro Lírico. AGN.

Fourth in the assemblage is Edward Weston's photograph of Federico Marín, Jean Charlot and Tina Modotti from *c*.1924 to 1926 (figure 5.12).[22] The symmetry of the composition, the three sitting at an angle, allows both the delineation of distinguishing profiles and the expanse of Modotti's back to be exposed as a drawing surface for Charlot's draughtsman's pencil (he was an artist in his own right although an assistant to Diego Rivera, producing an impressive mural cycle of his own).[23] Marín's spectacles direct the specular curve to the point of inception on Modotti's back. The potential references to forms of reproduction and representation are multiple and interpenetrated: Modotti was model and muse to both Weston and the muralist Diego Rivera: the distilled formalism of Weston's studies of her nude in an abstracted space contrasted with Rivera's allegorical treatment of her, on the walls of a civic building, as the embodiment of generative telluric forces.[24] Modotti's informal apprenticeship with Weston led to her becoming a professional photographer, shifting from the position of observed object to autonomous subject, wielding the apparatus which was customarily associated with scientific objectivity and knowledge. One of her first projects was photographing the murals of Rivera and Orozco for publication in illustrated cultural magazines (co-founded by Rivera).[25] Charlot was also helping to disseminate the work of the muralists through a series of descriptive articles for the same or similar magazines.[26] In Weston's photograph, Modotti's figure has become the locus (in her guise as model and material) of reproductive techniques which were regarded as rivals in mimesis, with photography usually subordinated to pictorial art for being mechanically produced. Weston seems to be toying discursively with the classic definition of photography as 'The Pencil of Nature' (the title of William Henry Fox Talbot's celebrated exposition), with the pictorial metaphor referring to clarity, contour, resolution and finish.[27] This formulation considered the photographic image as the product of nature's art rather than of human design. In this context, Modotti fulfils the role of specimen object in a demonstration of photography's self-reflexivity. In Weston's abstract studies of things, the photograph obviates verbal description and defies the kind of visual literacy which characterised Rivera's pictorial narratives of race and nation. Modotti moved away from facsimile reproduction of art works to a visual autonomy which sought the *photographic* over the *artistic*: free from 'the distortions or manipulations … of photographers [who] still seek "artistic" effects, imitating other mediums of graphic expression', as she wrote in an article for Rivera and Frances Toor's *Mexican Folkways* in 1929.[28]

Figure 5.12 Edward Weston, *Federico Marín, Jean Charlot and Tina Modotti* (c.1924–6). © 1981 Center for Creative Photography, Arizona Board of Regents.

Lastly comes the photograph of a circus act or peep-show entitled *Mujer florero* [*Woman-vase*] by Guillermo Robles Callejo based on *trompe-l'œil* illusionistic effects (figure 5.13).[29] The spectacle of a fantastic hybrid, a living collage of still life and portrait, seamlessly combines the organic and the manufactured, in a ludic tribute to feminine beauty and the language of flowers. This truncated head emerging like an exotic bloom from amidst an arrangement of roses is reminiscent of Grandville's acerbic engravings of women as botanical specimens and of a topsy-turvy modern world in which the objective and the subjective transmogrify, both ornaments and implements assuming human physiognomy and autonomy. The photograph serves to corroborate the ingenious theatrical deception predicated on the credulity of the eye and the allegorisation of gender. The photograph frames the encased article of visual consumption, the *Mujer florero*, in a reflexive movement which attests to its own status as a simulacrum.

It is perhaps too easily assumed from the vantage point of current post-colonial and post-modern *knowingness* that the interrogative strain which favours ironic play, ambiguity and formal scepticism in relation to identity is a contemporary (and rather belated) phenomenon in Mexican representational, reproductive and exhibitionary arts. In effect work by contemporary photographers like Mariana Yampolsky and Graciela

Figure 5.13 Guillermo Robles Callejo, *Mujer florero*, Gran Circo Beas (1920s). Centro de la Imagen, Mexico City.

Iturbide subtly explores interdisciplinary slippages between pictorial art, testimonial journalism, filmic ethnography and popular traditions of the *memento mori* as spectacle and artefact. Through such paradigmatic citation they acknowledge the way in which a previous generation of Mexican photographers had problematised the notion of the medium as an analogue of realism. Figures as different as Nacho López and Lola Álvarez Bravo (1907–93), whose work was subject to the editorial cutting, cropping and narrative gloss of the magazine and newspaper page, and who actively fostered interaction between the reproductive arts, were acutely aware of photography's involvement in the contemporary politics of representation, alert to the logocentricity of image production and adept at counter-manipulation. Photographs were primarily displayed within the syntax of the page, shaped by a pictorial frame, graphic plate or tablet and disseminated by way of the illustrated text in book or magazine format. The continuing vogue of commercial studio portraiture at the time confirmed the persistence of the notion of photography as the conflation of family album and portable museum of nineteenth-century illustrational writing.

From the mid-1950s, photography in Mexico becomes increasingly self-reflexive, especially in its relation to Indian culture, in response to the institutionalisation and discursive ubiquity of national anthropology.[30] The traditional links between ethnography and the camera came into critical view. For since its introduction in the 1840s, the camera in Mexico had played an instrumental role in shoring up and corroborating taxonomies of race and cultural difference, both in practice and as a model for visualisation and reproduction. Anthropologists in the 1950s and 1960s were intent on deconstructing mystificatory ethnographic archetypes and nationalist conceits sourced by nineteenth-century *costumbrismo*. Fernando Benítez in his multi-volume divulgatory *Los indios de México* resorted to the camera itself, with photographer Marino Benzi, to help undo the legacy of distorted visualisations in which it was implicated. Photography evidenced a growing unease with the homogenising tendency of cultural nationalism in the 1920s and 1930s for which *indigenismo* had provided an *escenografía* of emblems, props and styles to configure a highly pictorial Mexicanist aesthetic, and to which photography had provided its own archival fixities. Photographers such as López contributed to the disaffected scrutiny of the impact of modern technologies and urban-driven, *desarrollista* [developmentalist] ideology on popular culture, encouraging a valedictory perception of the variegated rural veins of 'el México profundo' [essential/in depth Mexico] – a disabused perspective which in Juan Rulfo's photography becomes a structuring melancholy.[31] In the 1950s and 1960s, the systematisation of 'objective' methodologies for knowing (rather than visualising) a particularised and inclusive autochthony, as in the case of the Benítez project, provided a strategy against the fallacies of *pintoresquismo* [the conventionally picturesque] and *folklorismo* of the 1920s and 1930s which implicated photography in its guise as documentary inventory. Nevertheless, would-be correctives to earlier ethnographic fantasies did tend to subordinate the investigative photographic image to the textual gloss. During this period, amongst its most salient and questioning practitioners, there was an acute sense of photography's historicity – both in the sense of the history of its applications and genres and the foundational temporality implicit in its exercise. Nacho López and Lola Álvarez Bravo were consequently engaged in renegotiating the criteria of visibility as well as the modalities of visualisation.

Aware of the mystifications of the ethnographic gaze in the nineteenth century, the discursive aestheticisations of cultural nationalism in art and film of the 1930s and 1940s and the compelling archive of captious or abstract definitions produced by foreign photographers (Lumholtz, Brehme, Strand, Cartier-Bresson), photo-essayists like the now still influential Nacho López struggled to redefine the boundary between science and art, between *re-production* and *production*. López advocated a 'conciencia óptica' ['optical conscience'] predicated on testimony and critical engagement to obviate 'el fotógrafo-turista … [quien] dispara su cámara como rifle, sin ninguna consideración, buscando lo sensacionalista y la "barbarie mágica"' ['the tourist-photographer … (who) shoots with his camera as if it were a rifle, without regard, searching for the sensationalist and "magical barbarism"'].[32] López personalised the practice of photography (negating the presumed inhumanity of the 'mechanical eye'), acknowledging the disturbing complicity with forms of oppression and exploitation – whether through positivist racial typologies, exotic exhibits or telluric allegories of place and provenance – in which the medium had been historically enmeshed. He elevated the notion of *enlace* [connection], as a corrective to the camera as 'instrumento de agresión' [weapon], into a metaphor of filiation and *intercomunicación* which informs the conduct of the photographer in Indian communities whilst privileging framing which insists on patterns of convergence (over those of alterity).[33] López publicised his highly manipulative directorial approach as a kind of auterism where self-inscription was an ethical statement. The darkroom afforded him the opportunity to construct visual hyperbole of delineated contrasts – a technique for configuring 'lo transcendente en lo intranscendente', the latent essence in the transitory particular. The Indian, as marginalised substratum of a syncretic culture, provided the test of moral integrity in which the photographer cast himself in a parable akin to that of the prodigal son, with the transcendence of the ego presaged by the transformative perception of the subaltern, ancestral other. The conversion is propitiated by the focal exercise required in 'looking'. López's introverted camera becomes as self-enclosed as a confessional, an inhabited space rather than an instrument. The darkroom becomes the laboratory of enhancement, of spiritual salvation and self-knowledge, as in a seventeenth-century diagram of the pre-photographic camera obscura as a darkened chamber where the artist has withrawn from the world for the purpose of attending better to it.[34] However, López's acute self-referentiality, less detectable in his photographs than his writing might suggest, did serve a useful purpose in exposing the unquestioned superstitions (and myths) of contemporary photography, and to that extent there was a divulgatory impulse behind his diagnostic case study:

> Poner el ojo en el visor fotográfico, encuadrar al sujeto y oprimir el botón, es fácil si se piensa que lo folclórico es el motivo principal. Ellos están tras las rejas, nosotros fuera. Si invertimos la imagen, los cautivos somos nosotros. Atrapados en otra realidad, concebimos un mundo imaginario acorde a los prejuicios de una clase social que no penetra en ese mundo 'mágico' (idea-cursi-poética) sólo descarnada por la injusticia, hambre, represión, aislamiento e insalubridad prevalecientes.[35]

> [Placing one's eye in the viewfinder, framing the subject and pressing the button is easy if one thinks that the folkloric element is the principal objective. They are behind bars, we are on the outside. If we invert the image, we are the captives. Trapped in another reality, we conceive an imaginary world in keeping with the prejudices of a social class that does not penetrate into the 'magic' world (a sentimental poetic cliché) represented exclusively by the injustice, hunger, repression and isolation which are prevalent.]

López's fidelity to the integrative paradigm of visualisation, which he termed the operation of the photographer's 'Cyclopean Eye', has, unsurprisingly, attracted condemnation from cultural critics and historians in Mexico engaged in 'esa guerra sin cuartel por la legitimidad de la mirada' ['that merciless struggle for the legitimacy of the gaze'] of which the Indian subject continues to provide the locus of gestation.[36] According to such sceptics, despite his self-deprecating acuity and the focal deference of adopting a 'distancia respetuosa' ['respectful distance'] in relation to the ethnic communities he photographed, López in practice replicated 'la visión dominante' of nationalist discourse: an official discourse which invested Indian cultures with the fixity of atemporal effigies serving to commemorate a homogenised and mythologised ethnicity, whilst confirming their status as repositories of obsolescence. López is in this light an instructive case: his ethical scruples,[37] reflexivity, egalitarian humility and dissident engagement do not of themselves provide a textual antidote, a kind of inbuilt public disclaimer, to the aesthetic of the image or the synoptic potency of the composition. Nor do they provide a ready solution to the imponderables of cultural transcription, consumption and reformulation based on unequal transactions. He was seemingly held captive (in his own words) by the mythology of ancestry, the appeal of a facsimile of origins: the physiognomic imprint on paper served as a consecrating shroud of the invisibly latent. In this sense, the Indian subject is the negative ground of development, and the photographer's intervention the enabling premise of the actualisation of an ethnic identity habitually subsumed, expectant potentiality awaiting recognition from an external source. The materiality of photographic production becomes a metaphorical ritual in which restitution is effected through the investiture of the marginalised with visibility: this is testimony as indeterminate compensation for the dispossession and injustice perpetrated over centuries. The perceived complicity of the camera with a modernity threatening the integrity of ethnic traditions and unique communal modalities suggests that López enacted a difficult (exculpatory) homage, in which the notion of the predatory camera was primarily an expression of the photographer's own anxieties rather than of native diffidence.

Lola Álvarez Bravo, whose work inspired rather than influenced that of Yampolsky, explained her orientating aspiration towards 'lo popular' as defensive, a form of *rescate* [recovery], based on a rejection of what she regarded as institutionalised misrepresentations which she termed 'lo popular de grito y sombrerazo' ['of patriotic yelling and outsize sombreros']: orchestrated civic spectacle in which the indigenous was merely the recording surface for a rhetorical autochthony.[38] Interestingly, for her *lo popular* was the indigenous but not necessarily the ethnically particular. Her notion of 'lo popular profundo' ['deep popular culture'] as a corrective to the *mirada engañada* and *engañosa* [deceived and deceiving gaze], which dwelt on superficial manifestations of difference, may itself be based on an essentialist premise. Arguably its true interest lies, however, in demonstrating the way in which photography seemed to provide an antidote to an incurious ocularism (but not by dint of its supposed technological neutrality). *Profundidad* [depth] in this critique of superficiality is a spatial metaphor which implies cognitive penetration of the merely apparent or the optically configured, not unlike a seventeenth-century exhortation to contemplative reflection over visual consumption and credulity. She proposed an inductive 'tercer ojo' ['third eye'] which combined 'el hallazgo y la búsqueda' ['the find and the search'].[39] Both Nacho López and Lola Álvarez Bravo decried the commodification of national identity, the interplay between Mexican curio and familial heirloom in image-making, which frequently manifested itself through embodiments of feminised ethnicity. Lola Álvarez Bravo especially (close friend of artists Frida Kahlo and María Izquierdo, whom she photographed extensively) was well versed in the defensive use of representational strategies, exhibitionary paradigms, costume and genre, in relation to the configuration of gender and ethnicity as ironic spectacle.[40] It is in her work that we can trace the proximity of object and objectification in which the still photograph is imbricated – a speculative rather than affirmative modality which distinguishes in turn the work of Yampolsky and Iturbide (and which is arguably absent from Garduño's). Nacho López's disabused self-questioning (and theorising) in relation to the ethnic subject can be regarded as providing an inescapable experiential context which informs the 'resistant complicity' of their camera work: that is to say, for Yampolsky and Iturbide's often explicitly problematised relation to their subject matter, which seeks and is wary of 'identificación-compenetración' ['identity-empathy'].

One of Lola Álvarez Bravo's photographs, *La patrona* (1960s), with its awareness of iconographic connotation and forms of reproduction and representation, is particularly suggestive of the issues I have been exploring in relation to identity and the practices and strategies of photography (figure 5.14). It may serve as a concluding testament to the nature of the affinity between her interrogative eye, reflexivity and ludic play and the work of contemporary women photographers who either openly, as in the case of Yampolsky, or tacitly acknowledge the significance of her endeavour and its visual legacy. The title of the photograph of a covered market stall display of printed scarves lit from behind makes ironic play on the sacred and profane allusions of the word *patrona* to employer/mistress, patron saint and pattern or model. The photographic composition frames the display duplicating the design of the stand exhibiting copies of the eulogised *Reina y Madre de México* [Queen and Mother of Mexico], *Reina de los cielos* [Queen of Heaven], *Felicidad de México* [Mexico's Joy], *Vínculo celestial* [Celestial Bond] and patriarchal ideal of femininity. Hanging on a visible line across the frame, the two linked scarves imprinted with the exhaustively reproduced image of the Virgin of Guadalupe have a membranous, diaphanous quality lent by the light of the background illuminating the gloom of the market interior. Like the images cast by the nineteenth-century pre-cinematic magic lantern slide projected onto a hanging cloth, the element of illusionistic play or phantasmagoria imbues the suspended scarves with the air of the conjured 'supernatural'. The photograph seems to re-enact, in a demystificatory prosaic setting, the miraculous apparition of the autochthonous Virgin of Guadalupe to the Indian Juan Diego: in order to prove the truth of her earlier visitation to doubting clergy, her image appeared on a *lienzo* [cloth] displayed by Juan Diego (he is conventionally portrayed in a kneeling posture holding up the cloth to an enraptured audience). The seventeenth-century Mexican poet Carlos de Sigüenza y Góngora captured the sense in which the miraculous was predicated on the very plasticity of the Virgin's final apparition as a divine simulacrum: 'Una Copia, una Imagen, un Traslado de la reina del Cielo más volado' ['A copy, an image, a transposition of the Queen of the most distant heaven'].

Figure 5.14   Lola Álvarez Bravo, *La patrona* (1960s). © 1995 Center for Creative Photography, The University of Arizona Foundation.

Figure 5.15 © Graciela Iturbide, *La Verónica, patrona de la fotografía* (1982), Ecuador. Courtesy of Graciela Iturbide.

As semblances of a venerated icon commemorating divine revelation, the manufactured scarves offer themselves to scrutiny rather than contemplation. Further parallels suggest themselves between the visual pun of the *Guadalupanas* and the rituals of analogue photography itself: in the darkroom, for instance, where a sheet of photographic paper is hung up to dry after undergoing the development process in order to allow the impression appear from the original negative. Or with the sacred shroud or Veronica on which the physiognomy of the dead Christ is said to have imprinted itself – a *memento mori* or sacred relic of his passage on earth. The slippages between evidential trace, replica, *memento mori*, copy, illusion and mechanical reproduction which the perusal of Lola Álvarez Bravo's *La patrona* prompts in the attentive viewer may help to explain why Graciela Iturbide had occasion to title one of her own photographs *La Verónica, patrona de la fotografía* (1982) (figure 5.15). In Lola Álvarez Bravo's exemplary photograph, appearance and production are intimately conflated in a form of still life in which the genre's usual compositional contrivance gives way to the deceptive casualness of a moment of ironic observation.

Notes

1. Mariana Yampolsky in conversation with the author, Tlalpan, Mexico City, April 2000.
2. For an example of the gendering of ethnic identity in the avant-garde, see the mural panel *Alegoría de la Virgen de Guadalupe* [*Allegory of the Virgin of Guadalupe*] (1923) by Fermín Revueltas (1901–35) in C. Zurian, *Fermín Revueltas: Constructor de espacios* (Mexico City, 2002), 82.
3. For the regional penetration of studio photography and practices of ethnic self-definition, see C. Monsiváis (ed.), *Foto Estudio Jiménez: Sotero Constantino, fotógrafo de Juchitán* (Mexico City, 1984), and '"Así nos gustaría ser en el caso de que no fuéramos así": los estudios fotográficos', *Luna Córnea*, 3 (1993), 54–61; *Alquimia*, 4 (1998); C. Canales, *Romualdo García: un fotógrafo, una ciudad, una época* (Guanajuato, Mexico, 1990). For an anthropological project in which individuals from Indian communities were 'armed' with cameras in order to provide a photographic chronicle of daily life manipulated from their perspective, see C. Duarte (ed.), *Camaristas: Fotógrafos mayas de Chiapas*, (Mexico City, 1998).
4. For a discussion of 'mesa revueltas' and Mexican *costumbrismo*, see above in Ch. 1.
5. Particularly in the case of the composite allegories, still lifes of fruit and other foodstuffs, representations of home altars, domestic *alacenas* and theatrical stages in the paintings of María Izquierdo and Frida Kahlo in the 1930s and 1940s. These are works which play with exhibitionary paradigms, mannequins, vitrine props, votive art and other popular genres of representation, including

photography, in ironic exploration of identity and creative agency. See e.g.
Naturaleza muerta con cámara fotográfica, the series of *alacenas*, *altares* and
naturalezas vivas in E. Ferrer, *The True Poetry: The Art of María Izquierdo*, (New
York, 1997). Kahlo's *bodegones* rework seventeenth-century motifs associated
with *vanitas* and *desengaño del mundo*.

6. See e.g. Yampolsky's *Alacena, Trampantojo, Última mirada, Osario* and *Milpa de espejos* in M. Yampolsky, *Imagen – memoria*, ed. F. Reyes Palma (Mexico City, 1999), 27, 37, 119, 123, 131, and F. Reyes Palma and N. Schnaith (eds), *Mariana Yampolsky* (Salamanca, 1995), 12. On Iturbide's visible framing in *Na'Marcelina, Serafina, Lagarto*, see G. Iturbide, *Images of the Spirit* (New York, 1996), 11, 45, 77, and in *La Verónica, patrona de la fotografía* (Fig. 15), see G. Iturbide, *Sueños de papel* (Mexico City, 1988), 64; on her use of *mise-en-abîme* in photographs for 'Los ojos de Graciela Iturbide: dieciséis fotografías', see E. Poniatowska, *Luz y luna, las lunitas* (Mexico City, 1994), 97–111, and *Seri*, see G. Dehesa (ed.), *México indio: Testimonios en blanco y negro* (Mexico City, 1994), 159.

7. The 1998 retrospective of her work held in the Centro de la Imagen, Mexico City, included engravings produced during her membership of the *Taller de Gráfica Popular* from 1945 to 1958 – helping to restore an unjustly neglected facet of her creative output. Yampolsky's graphic work (for books, manuals, magazines and pamphlets) had been featured in international exhibitions of the *Taller*'s engravings throughout the 1950s.

8. See e.g. the two volumes which Yampolsky co-edited with the founder of the *Taller de Gráfica Popular*, Leopoldo Méndez, and for which she provided photographic illustrations: *Lo efímero y lo eterno del arte popular mexicano* (Mexico City, 1971). On vernacular architecture, see e.g. M. Yampolsky, *La casa en la tierra* (Mexico City, 1981), *La casa que canta* (Mexico City, 1982), *Haciendas poblanas* (Mexico City, 1992), and *The Traditional Architecture of Mexico* (London, 1993). She also published work on the house and garden designed by Surrealist collector Edward James in Xilitla, San Luis Potosí, and on the seminal Mexican architect, Luis Barragán. In 1989 she was curator of the *Memoria del tiempo: 150 años de fotografía en México* exhibition at the Museo de Arte Moderno, Mexico City; see F. Reyes Palma (ed.), *Memoria del tiempo: 150 años de fotografía en México* (Mexico City, 1989).

9. C. Armstrong, *Scenes in a Library: Reading the Photograph in the Book, 1843 –1875* (Cambridge, MA, 1998), 115.

10. In April 2000 the author discussed this issue with Yampolsky in an interview, in which autobiographical anecdotes about her family and formative years pointed to the centrality of Franz Boas (the brother of Yampolsky's grandmother). She inherited a number of pieces from Boas's ethnographic collection.

11. C. Farago (ed.), *Reframing the Renaissance: Visual Culture in Europe and Latin America, 1450–1650* (New Haven, 1995), 76.

12. Yampolsky, *Imagen*, 14. On the Indian community with which she had long-standing links, see M. Yampolsky, *Mazahua* (Toluca, Mexico, 1993).

13. See the interview with Iturbide in Dehesa, *México indio*, 131.; also C. Patterson and M.S. Peden, *Out of the Volcano: Portraits of Contemporary Mexican Artists* (Washington/London, 1991), 169, and Iturbide's autobiographical essay in A.

Hopkinson (ed.), *Desires and Disguises: Five Latin American Photographers* (London/New York, 1992), 65–9.

14. See G. Iturbide, *Juchitán de las mujeres* (Mexico City, 1989) and *En el nombre del padre* (Mexico City, 1993). For work which has explored displacement, travel and landscape, see P. Ortiz Monasterio (ed.), *India – México: Vientos paralelos: Graciela Iturbide, Raghu Rai, Sebastião Salgado* (Mexico City, 2002) and G. Iturbide, *Travel Notebook* (Mexico City, 1999).

15. Dehesa, *México indio*, 92.

16. For a discussion of the problematic role of photography in anthropological discourse, see Pinney, 'Parallel Histories', 74–91.

17. Dehesa, *México indio*, 92.

18. F. Montellano, *C.B. Waite, Fotógrafo: Una mirada diversa sobre el México de principios del siglo XX* (Mexico City, 1994), 198–9.

19. For the *Tehuana* in Mexican visual culture, see L.M. Lozano (ed.), *Del Istmo y sus mujeres: Tehuanas en al arte mexicano* (Mexico City, 1992) and *Artes de México*, 49 (2000).

20. For the uses of photography in nineteenth-century Mexico, see T. Matabuena Peláez, *Algunos usos y conceptos de la fotografía durante el Porfiriato* (Mexico City, 1991); Massé Zendejas, *Simulacro y elegancia*; R. Casanova and O. Debroise, *Sobre la superficie bruñida de un espejo: Fotógrafos del siglo XIX* (Mexico City, 1989).

21. See E.X. de Anda Alanís, *Art Déco: un país nacionalista, un México cosmopolita* (Mexico City, 1997), 120. For period images of actual Mexican curio shops and folk art exhibitions, see J. Oles, *South of the Border: Mexico in the American Imagination* (Washington/London, 1993), 85, 111, 129. On Díaz see, R. Monroy Nasr, *Historia para ver: Enrique Díaz, fotorreportero* (Mexico City, 2003).

22. A vintage gelatin print reproduced in J. Riley and A. Rowley, *Tina Modotti: Photographs* (New York, 1997), plate 2.

23. His surviving mural *La masacre del Templo Mayor* in the Ex-Colegio de San Ildefonso, Mexico City was executed in 1922, the year he began his friendship with Weston.

24. Weston's most famous nude studies of his model date from 1923 to 1924. In 1925 Modotti posed for Rivera's mural *The Liberated Earth and Natural Forces Controlled by Man* in the Universidad Autónoma de Chapingo (1926–7), inspiring the *Virgin Earth* and *Germination* figures.

25. For Modotti's originally untitled modernist studies, *Staircase, Telephone Wires, Tank No. 1* and *Labour 2*, see R.M.E., 'Obras de Tina Modotti', *Forma: Revista de Artes Plásticas* 4 (1927), 30–3. Her photographs *Frescoes of José Clemente Orozco in the National Preparatory School* appear in *Mexican Folkways*, 4 (1928), 194–9, and *Contemporáneos*, 8 (1929), 24–31, although some were taken in 1926. Her 1926 photographs of Rivera's mural cycles include the allegorical figures for which she had been a model. See M. González Cruz Manjarrez, *Tina Modotti y el muralismo mexicano* (Mexico City, 1999), 111–12. Rivera himself wrote a laudatory review: 'Edward Weston and Tina Modotti', *Mexican Folkways*, 2 (1926), 16–28. Modotti photographed Charlot and he drew a portrait of her and one of Weston in 1924.

26. In the 1920s Charlot collaborated with *Forma* and *Contemporáneos* as well as *Mexican Folkways*. From 1923 he defended muralism in the Mexican press. See

J. Charlot, *An Artist on Art: Collected Essays of Jean Charlot*, 2 vols. (Honolulu, 1972) and J.A. Álvarez Lima, G. Estrada, D. de la Torre et al., *México en la obra de Jean Charlot* (Mexico City, 1994).

27. For a discussion of *The Pencil of Nature* (1844–46), see Armstrong, *Scenes in a Library*, Ch. 2.

28. T. Modotti, 'Sobre la fotografía/On Photography', *Mexican Folkways*, 4 (1929), 196–8 (196).

29. Reproduction of the original shown in the exhibition 'Gran Circo Beas', photographs of a travelling circus by Guillermo Robles Callejo (Puebla, 1891–1934) at the Centro de la Imagen, Mexico City, 19 March to 3 May 1998.

30. In *Fuga mexicana*, 117, Olivier Debroise has pointed to a tendency to underestimate the close links between photography and anthropology from the 1920s to the 1950s. My own awareness of these links has been significantly informed by conversations (since 1990) with the anthropologist/archaeologist Doris Heyden, second wife and assistant of Manuel Álvarez Bravo (and close friend of Mariana Yampolsky), who was herself a published photographer in the 1940s. For a timely discussion of the patronage of photography by official institutions such as the Instituto Nacional Indigenista (founded in 1948) and the Escuela Nacional de Antropología e Historia, see A. Bartra, A. Moreno Toscano, E. Ramírez Castañeda, *De fotógrafos y de indios* (Mexico City, 2000).

31. See e.g. Nacho López's *fotoensayos* in 'Noche de muertos', *Mañana*, 18 November 1950, 34–41, and 'Sólo los humildes van al infierno', *Siempre!*, 19 June 1954, 20–5, 70. For an anthology of his work on Indian culture, see N. López, *Los rumbos del tiempo*, ed. J. Lépez Vela (Mexico City, 1997).

32. His theoretical writings are cited extensively in Mraz, *Nacho López*, 205. See also C. Naggar and F. Ritchin (eds), *Mexico through Foreign Eyes, 1850–1990* (New York/London, 1993) and above Ch. 3.

33. Mraz, *Nacho López*, 76.

34. For a discussion of the camera obscura as metaphor, see S. Alpers, 'The Studio, the Laboratory and the Vexations of Art', in P. Galison and C.A. Jones (eds), *Picturing Science: Producing Art* (London/New York, 1998), 405.

35. N. López, *Los Pueblos de la Bruma y el Sol* (Mexico City, 1981), 8. For his work on anthropological projects with the INI, see his photographs in G. Aguirre Beltrán, A. Caso, A. Salas Ortega et al., *Los centros coordinadores indigenistas* (Mexico City, 1962).

36. See Yampolsky, *Imagen*, 44.

37. López, *Los Pueblos*, 8: 'Las imágenes de este libro son sólo una tímida aproximación al pueblo mixe que me permitió compartir algo de sus vivencias, siempre a distancia respetuosa' ['The images of this book are only a timid approximation to the Mixe community who allowed me to share their experiences, always at a respectful distance'].

38. Blanco et al., *Lola Álvarez Bravo*, 103, which includes interviews by Manuel Fernández Perera, José Joaquín Blanco and Luis Zapata. See also O. Debroise, *Lola Álvarez Bravo: In Her Own Light* (Tucson, 1994). Yampolsky was a student of Lola Álvarez Bravo's at San Carlos. In October 2000 in an interview with the author, Yampolsky recalled how the *maestra* (as she addressed her), unusually for

her, encouraged her student to use the darkroom facilities of her own professional studio in the Zona Rosa district of Mexico City. For a compressed discussion of Yampolsky's professional antecedents and their relation to her photography, see E. Poniatowska, 'Preface', in M. Yampolsky, *La raíz y el camino* (Mexico City, 1985), 5–10.

39. Blanco et al., *Lola Álvarez Bravo*, 12–13.
40. See S. Grimberg (ed.), *Lola Álvarez Bravo: The Frida Kahlo Photographs* (Dallas, 1991) and the catalogue of the important exhibition *Mujer x mujer: 22 fotógrafas* (Mexico City, 1989), 16–17, with a preface by Elena Poniatowska.

Chapter 6

The Poetics of Skin:
Surface and Inscription in Contemporary Photography

If Joan Fontcuberta is right in his contention that photography 'ha vivido bajo la tiranía del tema: el objeto ha ejercido una hegemonía casi absoluta' ['has existed under the tyranny of subject matter: the object has exercised an almost complete hegemony'], then one of the more intriguing traits of contemporary Mexican photography's apparent rupture with such a tradition, in its productive oscillation between 'el objeto y el concepto', has been its continuing interest in the figurative photographic object and the remastering of its identity,[1] a proclivity which, although interrogative, has tended to maintain photography's reach 'dentro de los límites estrictos de represeutación, sólo excepcionalmete violados' ['within the rigid limits of representation, infringed only very rarely'], as a recent Mexican critic observed.[2] I would like to posit tactically a visual installation of my own to explore the maziness of some current photographic practice.

Like players in a specular game devised in the 1930s, *What is it? Photo-Puzzle*, post-modern photographers in Mexico 'are invited to wander round and try to name the objects' which consist of 'a set of *distorted* photographs' which have been ' laid about the house, hall or garden' or, one might add, to update the analogy somewhat, invited to stray through museum, cinema, magazine, advertising, television and family album of extant simulacra.[3] In this period game, modernist manipulation of perspective, cropping, decontextualisation and lighting effects scrambles and scatters the habitual lexicon of the visibly real, in a set of (rather hazy) black and white images on numbered cards. Competitors pore over the reproductions of mysterious originals and engage in hypothetical associative play which will soon be curtailed by the restoration of correct, standardised perception with the final disclosed identity of objects. The instructions read: 'The first player to return a completely correct list, in accordance with the solutions below will be the winner'. In this case the restored order of things and system of corresponding representations is comprised by an arbitrary collection of unremarkable mass-produced utensils, whose mystery will deepen with the incurable obsolescence of their design and use. The melancholy list includes 'spring armbands, coal hod, shoe tree, tie clip, telephone dial, coal hammer' etc. In this game, I would suggest, 'everyone's a winner' for the visual restoration of identities is not effected visually but deferred to the invisible resource which informed the practice of deduction: a fund of prior knowledge based on inducted resemblances and correlations. For experimental photographers in Mexico, on the other hand, the specular game serves to expose the epistemology of vision and reproduction. On closer inspection, in photography nothing is as obvious as it seems. Consequently, the quest for Mexican photographers turns on exploring disruptively the configurations of representational discourse without re-establishing a figurative hegemony predicated on fixed ontological codifications of their own. In a sense, in the Mexican application, 'everyone is a loser', for the surfeit of assembled or disassembled visual matter speaks of dissolution and loss/release of graspable identities: the reward in their 'game' is not order but ambiguity. In Mexican photography of the 1990s, one detects an inclination towards disruption of the already represented rather than rupture of the visible (as in the case of the surrealists). Photographic abstraction or nihilism perhaps seem inconceivable and unpracticable gestures in an environment exercised by issues of cultural identity and personal agency raised by the Tratado de Libre Comercio [The North American Free Trade Agreement (1994)],[4] democratisation of the one-party state, the Zapatista [EZLN or Zapatista Army of National Liberation] uprising in Chiapas,[5] and globalisation. The risk in any specular game or installation is that it may be received and perhaps obliquely conceived as a pedagogic exercise with a discursive conclusion at its end.

Of an older generation, the photographer Mariana Yampolsky, who was working until her death in 2002, introduces a suggestive variant to the reflexive paradigm of my installation which helps to signal the tensions in contemporary photography in Mexico.[6] In a recorded conversation she remembered the formative antipathy she felt for the kind of guessing games based on manipulated photographs (of which the already mentioned table game is a representative sample). *Trompe l'œil* riddles encountered in illustrated magazines such as *Look* and *Life* in close proximity to 'straight' photographic essays, portraits and advertisements were a source of malaise and frustration. The reasons she gave for her antipathy, partly to do with the panoptic deception of the shot and partly with the superficiality of a photograph's glossing of reality, provide an inroad into the subject of this chapter: the problem of surface in contemporary Mexican photography, a problem which, as the above example suggests, predates the current generations' distinctive engagement with it. For Yampolsky photography is both all surface – that is, about appearance and literally flat – and defined by a lack of surface, as in a lack of distinguishing material texture. In her reflections she alluded to the analogical relation between photography and skin, based on their perceptual affinities as recording surfaces:

> [in analogue photography] There is a visual rather than a tactile surface and that visual surface has to be varied – it has to substitute the tactile. In nature the varied surface exists and is so important that you could not recognise an object if it had no surface. Think of the surface of a human being – not only does it give an impression to someone looking from afar – for if we didn't have skin we wouldn't exist – it protects the very essence. It registers.[7]

Yampolsky seems to believe in the necessary correlation between surface and content, what we might term the configuration of immanent identity, and yet distrusts the finished contours of the visible afforded by photography – a nice paradox, which has drawn her to focus on the materiality of textured surface in studies of untouted vernacular architecture and the quasi-geological accretion of plant forms. Her photographs reflect on the contrasting organic grain and mesh of hand-made walls and the layered fretwork of botanical membranes – or probe the *trompe-l'œil* reflectivity of glass, water and semi-transparent tissues which have been handled – without ever actually violating the surface of still negative or print. Her quasi-physiognomic external views of houses have a permeable quality often resembling membranous or callused envelopes, stretched hides, pockmarked or adipose skin.[8] The focal resolution accentuates the *density* of infrastructures rather than the *depth* of metaphysical revelation. In a luminous photograph, *Agave de papel* [*Paper Agave*] (1991) (figure 6.1), the peeling of a pellucid *maguey* [agave] skin against the light enacts a sloughing of a representational subject ritualised by nationalist iconography.[9] Raised to view like an offering, the exposed fleshy rawness conjures an ontological unsheathing that takes us back to the paradox of Yampolsky's surface *rapture* (rather than rupture). Interestingly, few of the younger experimental photographers in Mexico have taken the route of deliberately rubbing the actual negative or print against the grain of physical reality in pursuit of an ironic imprint through frottage. In avant-garde photographic work, manipulation and distortion can often be rendered disturbingly seamless, not to say polished, especially with recourse to digital technology – an interesting recuperation/reification of the language of severance and transgression.

The aim here then is to explore the links between epidermis, surface and physiognomy in contemporary Mexican photography, which is engaged in problematising the formal and thematic exploration of identity in the post-essentialist period, in its capacity as both mediated presence and trace plasticity. From the mid-1990s (non-journalistic) Mexican photography has been increasingly conceptual, ludic, interdisciplinary, spectacular and interested in construction, collage and dissemination, as well as its own historical archive and practical anthropology.[10] There has been an ideational shift, propitiated in part by the challenge of digital image-making and the attendant debate of digital versus analogue amongst practitioners and theorists of photography: a shift from the fixity of the image as nostalgic recuperation or defining exposure, figurative or documentary objectifications, to a performative gestation in which the photographic image is mindful of its materiality as disembodied trace or expended carapace. The influential work of Gerardo Suter (b. 1957) can help to showcase this deconstructive tendency to pollute Mexican photography's vocational transparency by embracing interdisciplinary construction.[11]

Figure 6.1 Mariana Yampolsky, *Agave de papel* (1991), Ixtacamatitla, Puebla. Courtesy of © FCMY.

Suter's mock early twentieth-century archaeological-naturalist travel album *El archivo fotográfico del profesor Retus* (1986) (Suter spelled backwards) is a fictional narrative of exhumed origins by way of a series of 'vintage' images. With its sepia-aged and 'distressed' prints of monumental pre-Columbian ruins (as portentous architectural details or panoramic overviews), he inverts the metaphor of archaeology as an ontological excavation that ruptures surface to extract and restore a lost 'truth'. The series of photographs ironically resurfaces the mythic loci of Mexicanised cultural identity. He invents a provenance for this collection of rediscovered documentary prints as part of the exhibition's narrative, images yielded supposedly by a suitcase in the ruins of a building struck by the 1985 earthquake.[12] Through this literary device, akin to the lost chest, ark, or 'lumber room', the commonplace equivalence between photography and a portmanteau visual memory is museologically choreographed. The reproduction not only displaces the real but dramatises the distance between the photograph and its historicity as temporal trace. As a photographer he is interested in myth-making rather than historical or archaeological salvage. Suter revisited pre-Hispanic mythology, the domain of nationalist anthropology, through its colonial residue in the explicatory interplay of text and image of the Mexican codices. His celebrated staged/tableaux enactments of recollected illustrations from codices – pictorial texts commissioned by and compiled under the vigilant tutelage of Catholic missionaries – pose the body of a model as the surface of inscription. Totemic figures, masked or painted with grainy pigments, allude to barely remembered ancestral deities lit gloomily in darkened cameras.[13] Suter plays with the notion of photographic reincarnation of the sacred in ways that allude to the centrality of iconic presence in Mexico's syncretic religious discourse. The primacy of grated or caked skin in Suter's photographic tableaux manufactures a fantastic ethnography, in which epidermis and costume elide, giving way to a symbolic parchment or vellum of ancestral signifiers. Through the gigantism of the 'blow-up' print, fetishised props and faux arcana, he points to photography's complicit *escenificación* [staging] of originary mythologies – neatly implicating the racial typologies and mystificatory primitivism of identity politics in Mexico.

Suter's mixed-media installations using digital image, still photograph, film, object placement and projected text have coined the interdisciplinary hybridity of a work such as *El libro de las circulaciones* [*The Book of Circulations*] (1999–2000), in which the exhibition space becomes an initiatory conduit with multiple bifurcations.[14] The interactive slippages factored into such displays point to a semantic *reubicación* [relocation] of photographic discourse which is freighted with a sense of photography's mordant obsolescence and its 'baroque' (in the sense of composite and theatrical) visual eloquence. The gestural scratches on the print, which he sometimes includes, claw the surface into view in a manner that seems to have become a widespread conceptual shorthand in younger contemporaries. In Suter's work, however, these smooth creases and craquelure marks are traces of interference or extraneous disturbance rather than graphic additions to the approximation of the subject or a form of personal graffiti. They are not so much signatures of the real as prefigurations of the corrosive temporality to which the unstable material, like skin, is subject.

Equally pungent in this reorientation of photographic discourse and space has been the work of Pedro Meyer (*b*. 1935). His conversion to new imaging technologies has entailed a fascinating and very public reconversion of his own well-established analogue material.[15] As provocative editor and founder of the groundbreaking, bilingual website magazine and multiplex gallery <zonezero.com>, he has provided what amounts to a regular explicatory *crónica* cum notebook of work in progress.[16] He has deployed digitalised montages of photographic images in a polemical reworking from his own analogue archive, a symbolic act of self-desecration and de- and reconstruction. In effect, this amounts to a canny redeployment of the dadaist technique of dialectical montage from the 1920s in pursuit of his own 'documentary fictions', predicated on ironic social observation on such topical themes as the phenomenon of migration between Mexico and the U.S.A. or the expansion of consumer utopias in the U.S.A.[17] Actively bilocated, living and working on both sides of the northern border, Meyer uses state-of-the-art reproductive technology to refine the acuity of his critique of free-market capitalism, and to relocate the artist from traditionally subordinated cultures into the fluidity of the worldwide web.[18] His publicised abandonment of the darkroom and advocacy of digital photography are a response to what he decries as the monolithic discourse of analogue photography in Mexico – a critique directed in particular against the verist essentialism of the so-called 'non-manipulated' image. Meyer mischievously equated the 'apertura/e' in photographic practice which he spearheads with the belated defeat of the authoritarian one-party system at the national elections in Mexico.[19]

Clearly both Suter and Meyer deal with issues which characterise what has been called the 'post-photography' of a medium haunted by the spectre of its own demise.[20] Like many valedictory enterprises, this has entailed the scrutiny of the myths underpinning photography's epistemology. But it would be credulous to take self-proclaimed heretics on their own terms: a speculative, reflexive modality is already present in the work of such classics of Mexican photography as Manuel Álvarez Bravo, Nacho López and Lola Álvarez Bravo, working from the 1920s to the 1970s. It is a speculative line less experimentally signalled or explicitly formulated, but nonetheless vibrantly present in work by older contemporaries working in more traditional book and magazine formats, like Mariana Yampolsky, and found also in the disabused relation to ethnic subjects in her work and in those of other, younger practitioners such as Graciela Iturbide, Maya Goded (b. 1967) and Yolanda Andrade (b. 1950), who have scavenged the preferred paraphernalia of visual identities, masks, costumes and banners in urban and rural locations in order to provide startling antidotes to folkloric voyeurism.[21]

Nor is reflexivity in photography naturally confined to a self-styled, loquacious urban avant-garde of professionals: the Chamula Indian photographer Maruch Sántiz Gómez (b. 1975), one of a growing number of published photographers from officially designated 'minorities', provides a poignant perspective on the practice of photography as cultural inscription in which ethnic subjects have provided the visual materiality of autochthony. Gómez's *Creencias (de nuestros antepasados)* [*Beliefs (of our ancestors)*] (1998) illustrates beliefs about the material world with an interplay between traditional Chamula sayings, (Chol) lexicon and excerpted photographic images of circumambient things.[22] On the one hand, it is indubitably commemorative as well as inflected in terms of reception with a pre-existing anthropological literacy; on the other, it includes a discreetly allusive amalgam of text and image which complicates the standard metaphor of photography as 'un espejo de la memoria' ['a mirror of memory'], and brings this (Western) *creencia* into view. The Spanish translation to the entry 'Nen' [mirror], reads like a warning against the 'narcissistic' seduction of reflected appearance. Taken from a dominant perspective looking down, the accompanying photograph is of a square reflective pane (rather than a conventional *espejo*), inclined so as to mirror the grainy surface of the ground. The object of the photograph is differentiated from the rest of the flat, homogenous ground only by the delineated contours of the frame roughly repeated in the symmetry of the edges of the printed shot. What we gaze at is a doubled surface without apparent subject, an *escritura de las apariencias* [writing of appearances], as photography has been dubbed, without identifiable *sustantivos* but only the intangible sign of its reflectivity. Or perhaps what is framed and pointedly not there is the ubiquitously visualised *ausente* [absentee] of Mexican history, the non-conceptual indigenous person. The translated line reads: 'Es malo vernos en el espejo en la noche, porque se tapa uno la vista' ['It is bad to look at ourselves in the mirror at night because our sight is covered'].[23] In my reading of this ambiguously reflexive juxtaposition of surfaces, the 'videntiary' [*vidente*] and 'evidentiary' [*evidente*] properties of photography are captured. The oscillation between the fabular and the scientific, absence and presence, of the mirror as optical device depends on its cultural use and the elided subject draws attention to this troubling vacuity at its core. Fontcuberta's playful division of photographers into *narcisos* (those seduced by apparent reality) and *vampiros* (the less deceived who nevertheless desire the congruity of the image) is tested by an image which seems to issue from a discursive elsewhere.[24] Sántiz Gómez's visual aphorism can be read as a kind of photographic morality tale about the 'blindness' of ocularist traducing of (ethnic) identity.

Jorge Camarillo's mordant manipulated self-portrait offers a much more self-conscious take on ancestral memory, using collage as a visual pun about cultural identity. [25] The neatly constructed image refracts in multiple allusions. The folded page of an English-language newspaper's two-page spread on 'The Olmec', one of the oldest pre-Hispanic civilisations, is held up as a textual screen, a comparative indexical table, and a publicity shot. The divided photographic reproduction of a gigantic stone head from the archaeological find in La Venta (Tabasco) is held up so as to be superimposed on the photographer's face, creating a composite although seamless mask of personal physiognomy which is also an ironic replica of an ancestral artefact. Just noticeable is the laboratory glove which sheathes the hand holding the edge of the specimen, sample or exhibit offered up in this dissection of alterity. Camarillo's composition attests to the museological impulse in the construction of self-image to which photography lends the unsettling fixity of a *naturaleza muerta* or still life. Cultural archetype, racial typology and Lombrosian mug-shot[26] *fade in* the 'freak show' display of character representation.[27] Camarillo offers a reworking of disassociative collage in relation to the photograph's reputed capacity to evidence a containable identity, which is both representative and irreducibly singular. Along with the allusion to a palimpsest of textual visualisations, the duality of the collage design is itself an ironised conceit drawing on the discourses of syncretism and *mestizaje* of Mexican anthropology and visual and literary culture in the first half of the twentieth century. Possibly there is an iconographic reprise of one of the 'tres grandes' ['three greats'] of Mexican muralism, David Alfaro Siqueiros's own critique of what he regarded as the exploitative standardisation of the Indian as living relic in 1930s representational nationalism. In the painting *Etnografía* (1939) he indicted the discriminating discourse of social science in the service of authoritarianism: a generic *campesino* [farmer], defined by his costume, with the hieratic posture of an archaeological exhibit, stares out in a nearly full-length frontal composition, the lower half of his legs significantly truncated by the picture plane. His face is – rather than wears – an imprecise pre-Hispanic mask. The discursive ubiquity of the mask in paradigmatic speculation on the nature of Mexican psychology from the 1920s to the 1950s (Ramos, Paz) is well known, and Camarillo's self-figuration is pointedly banal. His inclusion of the mesh of a *petate* (or woven reed mat) as a backdrop to his bust operates as a kind of *guiño* [wink] to the closely observed studies of emblematic folk materials and objects in the foundational discourses of 1920s photography in Mexico. In the influential work of Edward Weston and Tina Modotti, for instance, such textures and materials (especially patterned weaves) were simultaneously the exhibitionary ground and the subject matter, scenic prop and sign of the significant other.[28]

In an interview from the mid-1990s, the near-centenarian photographer Manuel Álvarez Bravo (1902–2002), who was considered the official embodiment of modern Mexican photography, provided an interesting perspective on his own longevity through an analogy between sloughed or flayed skin, photographic representation and personal identity as masquerade:

> I came upon the image of a flayed saint who was holding his skin in his hands. And I thought of the pre-Columbian god Xipe-Tótec, *El descarnado [The Fleshless One]*, and almost automatically the idea came to me of how people shed an artificial skin – and then put it on again. I have made various photographs exploring this idea, Xipe nudes not holding their skin, but their clothing in their hands ...[29]

The poetics of skin alludes to thematic formulation in which the prominence of skin is treated as the locus of cultural and ethnic inscription and accretion; and to material reflexivity in photography with membranous analogues of reproductive technology ghosting or simulating the negative print on paper or plate in the form of visual or tactile traces. Álvarez Bravo's invasive exposures and concealments – his *Xipe* rituals – are informed by the ocular *gestes* familiar to surrealism: those peelings back of eye lids, those rotating inwards of eye balls, or those slicing of corneas into new apertures. Graciela Iturbide harvests a gathering of such perceptual conceits when she turns to a literal theatre of piercing, slicing and peeling in a series of photographs on butchery in village life. Unpicking a potent visual legacy, Iturbide photographs a peeled goat membrane being hung up to dry on a line like an undergarment, in the domestic rituals of slaughter in which women are the executioners (figure 6.2).[30] This is an unobtrusive act of photographic commemoration which humorously slips into the frame the spectre of its own rites of passage as

Figure 6.2 © Graciela Iturbide, *Piel*, from her *En el nombre del padre* (1993). Courtesy of Graciela Iturbide.

reproductive technology. From the series entitled *En el nombre del padre* [*In the Name of the Father*] (1993) (later published as a book) on Mixtec women's seasonal slicing, disembowelling, skinning and quartering of goats in Huajapan de León (Oaxaca), the shot of the woman hanging a dissected empty vessel is a two-fold *Xipe* moment. It points to the wielding of both the scalpel and the speculum in circumcisions which trouble patriarchal gender roles and hierarchy, reaching beyond the rustic anecdote to Iturbide's own darkroom apprenticeship with Álvarez Bravo, the master of excision and splicing (and reputed to be the 'father' of Mexican photography). Álvarez Bravo had occasion to practise his metaphysical disclosures through the morphology of semi-clad, bandaged or otherwise shrouded female bodies. In his photographs from the 1930s and 1940s we find models (and not infrequently wives) – recumbent in the simulated inanity of sleep, the grotesque rictus of death, or reconstituted through the arranged abandon of a hand-made dress crumpled on a chair.[31] It could be then generalised that Álvarez Bravo's own consecrated corpus of photographs has been gradually and widely dissected in his lifetime by a generation of photographers seeking to rescue the possibility of severance or sample the meaning of continuity.

This chapter has been interested in the slippages between formally different uses of surface analogues in current photography. Compare, for instance, Iturbide's tacit symbolism with the documentary journalism of Agustín V. Casasola in the 1920s; or Iturbide's use of skin as photographic membrane along with other tissues and fabrics whose opacity or compromised transparency offer two-way windows on the mediations of photography. And then turn to the neutral grey studio backdrop associated with the photography of 'simple' presence.[32] The quality of 'thereness' in Agustín V. Casasola's forensic display *Preso en el hospital Juárez* [*Prisoner in the Juárez Hospital*] (1925), is somehow sustained by the empirical demonstration implicit in the stretched sheet behind the slouched Indian detainee posed in profile as in a eugenicist diagram (figure 6.3).[33] The torn sheet of Casasola's penal display in turn acquires disturbing echoes when seen in conjunction with the *lienzo* or *verónica* shroud-like imprint of Manuel Álvarez Bravo's solipsistic photograph *La gran interrogación* [*The Great Question Mark*] (*c.*1972).[34] Here the revelation of the absent real is effected through a T-shirt imprinted with a faded question mark hanging from a tree like a spent case or discarded skin: we see a fabricated but unsourced token of identity,[35] an image which resonates further in Iturbide's *La Verónica, patrona de la fotografía*, her homage to the evidentiary 'magic' of photography and its faith in revelation (see figure 5.15).[36]

This chapter has also been interested in the textuality of the body as surface. Silvana Agostoni's series *Topografías* (1998) and *Fisonomía* (1997) use the body's skin as defining contour and cyphered parchment-ground, canvas map or engraver's plate.[37] Agostoni effectively incarnates her critique of visual determinism by filleting the differentiated configurations and documented singularities of discourses that sought to standardise perception and typologise ethnic, moral and gender particulars. The body is treated as draughted physical geography – a Utopian map of an habitable place, the displaced residence of a fractured or transitory identity.

The ink-blotted photographs of Adriana Catalayud (b. 1967) continue this conceptual emphasis on the readability and 'navigability' of figurations of the body. Her calligraphic series *Monografías* (1996) offers splayed, flattened full-length women, front and back in adjacent panels like dried specimens in a book.[38] In *Cuerpo disperso* [*Dispersed Body*] and *Cuerpos sutiles* [*Subtle Bodies*] she also plays with the *exquisite corpses* of surrealist drawings with assembled androgynous figures shaped by convoluted formations of wrinkled, folded or pendulous skin. Alluding reflexively to the literacy of bodily representations, the splayed or compressed bodies are imprinted with anatomical engravings of

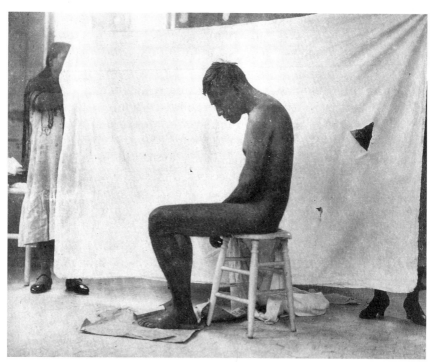

Figure 6.3 Agustín V. Casasola, *Preso en el hospital Juárez* (1925). FINAH-SINAFO.

internal organs or other diagrammatic cyphers which are only partially visible. Catalayud enters her work into the baroque theatre of a Western tradition of anatomical iconography based on duality, and by so doing pays a more widespread debt in contemporary photography to Frida Kahlo's own absorption of medical illustration, a visual tradition in which binaries such as surface and content, aesthetic and praxis, concealment and revelation have been articulated through the female form, which has been treated simultaneously as a pedagogic vessel, a reproductive 'fábrica' and an ideal measure of beauty defined by harmonious proportion and smoothness.[39] The charcoal background against which Catalayud's bodies seem pinned (like bits of paper images on a board) is depthless. Contrary to the pictorial chiaroscuro of anatomical realism, which uses contrast to create an illusion of volume and three-dimensional form, the matte blackness exposes the surfaces like the thinnest of sliced membranes in formaldehyde. In *Cuerpos sutiles* Catalayud also reimagines oriental mysticism and the notion of a cosmic sexuality centred on an impalpable 'inner body' stripped of the illusory bonds of space and time regarded as merely the confluence of subjective projections. The title of the series seems to evoke a central notion of Tantric Yoga, 'The Subtle Body', which is the non-corporeal ('inner') sensory experience afforded by carnal interpenetration. The photographed body, which Catalayud has overwritten with diagrammatic symbols and arcana, does not so much evidence its detachable materiality and knowability as rarify further the notion of its singularity and personhood to the brink of transparency.

Similarly, Tatiana Parcero's series *Cartografía interior* (1996) plays with the superficiality of analogue technology and the myth of the penetrative gaze (figure 6.4).[40] Parcero (b. 1967) draws attention to the optical stategies of cropping, microscopic magnification and telescoping of the body and its parts, in order to tease the myth of visual resolution as an aid to true sight and knowledge. In an earlier stage of the project, *El mapa de mi cuerpo* [*The Map of My Body*], she spliced fragments of her body, anatomical diagrams and ancient codices, turning her skin into the layered contact paper of the material world as sign and image. In Elena Eherenwald's suture-incised *Mujeres fragmentadas* [*Fragmented Women*] (1996), *la matriz* [womb] of the image of a female nude is torn but rendered seamlessly.[41] By drawing attention to the seamless polish of the representation of 'defilement' on the photographic surface, Eherenwald (b. 1959) also hints at the difficulty of effecting a subversion of gendered representations in her chosen medium: the attempted deconstructive violation is seemingly resisted by the homogeneity of the female as identifiable photographic entity. In a lighter vein, Mauricio Alejo's composite *La cadera de mi esposa* [*My Wife's Hip*] (from his series *Asuntos domésticos*) [*Domestic Matters*] (1996–7) uses photographed wallpaper as an exhibitionary ground on which an X-ray of a female pelvis is pasted with scribbled annotations and the exclamatory arrows of an improvised diagram.[42] Alejo (b. 1969) offers an ironic inflation of the kind of proprietorial *machismo* whose vaunted penetrative reach appears to reduce woman to an impersonal anatomical analogue.

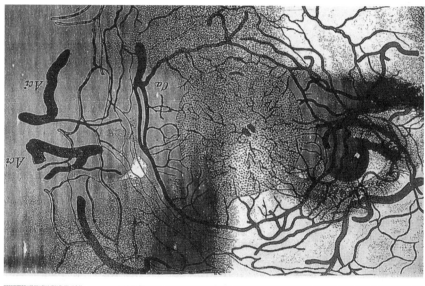

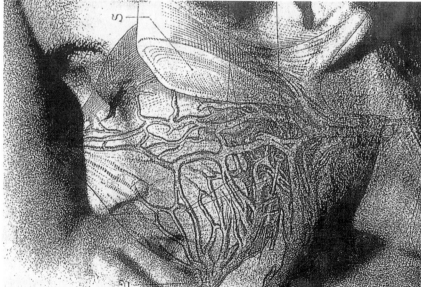

Figure 6.4 Tatiana Parcero, *Untitled*, from the series *Cartografía interior* (1996). Courtesy of Tatiana Parcero.

Conversely, the series *Historia en la piel* [*History on Skin*] (1996–7) by Federico Gama (b. 1963) is interested in popular appropriations of skin for the inscribing of personal codices.[43] His black-and-white prints narrate the eccentric brand of epidermic nationalism to be found in tattoos. The skin in Gama's images offers the obverse of superficial identity: its significant graffiti hints at unsuspected cultural depth amongst the illiterate and outcast.[44] The use of body inscriptions in urban counter-culture entails a performance and ironic *cosificación* [commodification] of personal and tribal identity, constructing an embodied history for the displaced and the transient – the alternative corporeal textuality of the *indocumentados*. In *De mi sangre y cuerpo* [*Of my Blood and Flesh*] a man holds up defiantly a close-up photograph of his baby – a portrait which is level with its tattooed replica on the arm angled at the camera.

Paradoxically, perhaps the closest we come to abstraction is in Laura Cohen's deft transposition of the reflexivity of the *vanitas* pictorial genre.[45] Her minimalist still lifes tend to dwell on the way photographic images dematerialise the tactile world. In her work, permeable and impermeable surfaces are exposed to natural sunlight or illumined so as to shear the differentiated grain and elude the imprint which is so crucial, for instance, to Yampolsky's visual tactility (figure 6.5). Through her camera refracted light is given a membranous adhesiveness which delineates and separates the spectral airiness of things, lending a

Figure 6.5 © Laura Cohen, *Fuerza de gravedad* (1992). Courtesy of Laura Cohen.

momentary *espesor* or density in the surface of the paper still. Cohen (b. 1956) believes that 'La luz también es una parte importante de mi iconografia. La utilizo como si fueran palabras' ['Light is also an important part of my iconography. I use it like words'].[46] In effect, Cohen's words and images offer a paraphrase of one of the original pictorialist definitions of photography as 'painting with light'. A further comment about her still lifes has a wider relevance: 'Las fotos no son sobre los objetos' ['Photos are not about objects']. For one might argue that this last statement comprises the underlying *advertencia* [admonition] of contemporary Mexican photography's suggestively occluded vision of things: a photography of the 'mirada *écorché*' ['flayed gaze'] (to borrow a term from the history of anatomical display) in which the play of reflexivity, not material presence, is exposed by the shedding and sheathing of identities. An interesting epistemological interplay has emerged between the analogue medium's meditation on itself as material inscription (where signs are seemingly inseparable from the surface that carries them) and the digital encoding (the 'bricolage' effect) and simulation of such chemical inscription which, in effect, entails an electronic configuration detachable from material sources. Engaged in what photographer Víctor Flores Olea calls a 'trabajo lúdico de pruebas y contrapruebas' ['ludic work of trials and counterproofs'], contemporary conceptual photography's experimentation has revisited the positive origins of the medium even as it applies itself to a dismantling of representational orthodoxies based on such a tradition.[47] The concept and the object elide in the involuted curiosity of some Mexican photography.

Notes

1. J. Fontcuberta, *El beso de Judas: fotografía y verdad* (Barcelona, 2000), 19–33 (21).

2. J.A. Molina, 'Entre el objeto y el concepto: la buena fama de la fotografía construida', *Tierra Adentro*, 102 (2000), 58–63 (63).

3. *What is it? Photo-Puzzle: It's educating-interesting* (London, n.d.).

4. The NAFTA-TLC which promoted economic integration between Mexico, Canada and the U.S.A. came into effect during the controversial neo-liberal, pro-privatisation presidency of Carlos Salinas de Gortari.

5. The EZLN led by 'Subcomandante Marcos' originally represented disenfranchised farmers and Mayan Indians in the struggle for social justice and democracy. It launched an armed revolt in 1994. Its appeal grew amongst the urban working class and those elements of the middle-class media seeking social and political reforms and the modernisation of the one-party state. It has its stronghold in the southern states of Chiapas. The EZLN has been engaged in peace negotiations with successive governments.

6. Yampolsky's work is internationally known and collected. Her publication and exhibition record in Mexico, the U.S.A. and Europe is extensive. Her work was included in the *Tina Modotti and Edward Weston: The Mexico Years* exhibition at the Barbican Art Gallery, London in 2004. An 'Homenaje Nacional' to celebrate her work was held at the National Museum of Anthropology, Mexico City in 2002–3; see A. Castellanos, E. Poniatowska, F. Reyes Palma et al., *Homenaje Nacional a M. Yampolsky* (Mexico City, 2002).

7. Yampolsky in conversation with the author, 3 April 2001, Tlalpan, Mexico City.

8. See M. Yampolsky, *Casas de tierra* (Mexico City, 2000) and E. Álvarez-Buylla Roces and M. Lavín (eds), *Formas de vida: plantas mexicanas vistas por M. Yampolsky* (Mexico City, 2003), a posthumous edition of her work.

9. For the reproduction of this photograph and other studies of the archetypal *maguey* [agave], see Yampolsky, *Imagen*, the catalogue of her 1998 retrospective exhibition with texts by E. Ferrer, E. Poniatowska, and F. Reyes Palma; Álvarez-Buylla Roces and Lavín, *Formas* (2003).

10. A key marker of innovation in Mexican photography was the 1996 exhibition *Fotografía construida* [*Constructed Photography*] in the Museo de Monterrey. A curatorial interest in the 'tradition of the new' traced construction from canonical figures (e.g. Manuel and Lola Álvarez Bravo) to contemporary exponents (e.g. Tatiana Parcero and Gerardo Suter).

11. For other 'deconstructive' photographers, see E. Ferrer, *A Shadow Born of Earth: New Photography in Mexico* (New York, 1993), which includes work by Pablo Ortiz Monasterio, Germán Herrera, Eugenia Vargas and Adolfo Patiño. See also A. Ruy-Sánchez, 'El fundamentalismo fantástico del arte joven de México', *Universidad de México: Revista de la Universidad Nacional Autónoma de México*, 508 (1993), 24–8.

12. Images of this series are reproduced in G. Suter: *Labyrinth of Memory* (New York, 1999), plates 1–10. For Suter on photography as a form of memory, see G. Suter, 'Una forma de memoria', *Alquimia*, 9 (2000), 38.

13. For examples from the series *Códices* (1991), see *Tonalamatl, Tlaloc, Tlapoyahua*, and *Inscripción* (1989) in Suter, *Labyrinth*, 14, and plates 22, 27 and 21, respectively.

14. The multimedia exhibition was held from September 1999 to January 2000 in the Museo Amparo, Puebla, Mexico. See G. Suter, *Circulaciones* (Puebla, Mexico, 1999), the 'catalogue' designed by Suter for the exhibition with an essay by Karen Cordero Reiman. For his 1996 installation *Geografía de la memoria*, see Suter, *Labyrinth*, plates 34–6.

15. See e.g. P. Meyer, *Espejo de espinas* (Mexico City, 1986), with an introduction by Carlos Monsiváis, in the now classic *Colección Río de Luz*, launched by Fondo de Cultura Económica to showcase Mexican analogue photography (including Nacho López, Héctor García, Mariana Yampolsky, Graciela Iturbide, Víctor Flores Olea, Rafael Doniz).

16. See B. Ruiz, 'El laboratorio terminó: entrevista con Pedro Meyer', *Tierra Adentro*, 105 (2000), 69–72; P. Meyer (ed.), 'Fotografía tradicional vs. fotografía digital', *ZoneZero*, Editorial 28 (March 2001): <http://zonezero.com/editorial/editorial.html>.

17. See J. Green, 'Pedro Meyer's Documentary Fictions', in M. Haworth-Booth (ed.), *Metamorphoses: Photography in the Electronic Age* (New York, 1994), 32–7. For examples of reconversion of analogue images, see P. Meyer (ed.), 'Hacia una redefinición de la fotografía documental', *ZoneZero*, Editorial 22 (April 2000): <http://zonezero.com/editorial/editorial.html>.

18. See P. Meyer, *Truths and Fictions: A Journey from Documentary to Digital Photography* (New York, 1995), with an essay by Joan Fontcuberta; also reproduced on CD-ROM (Voyager, 1995). See also Meyer's groundbreaking CD-ROM *I Photograph to Remember* (Voyager, 1991), and for his computer-generated images, see P. Meyer, 'Inside the USA', in T. Ziff (ed.), *Between Worlds: Contemporary Mexican Photography* (London, 1990), 46–57.

19. See P. Meyer (ed.), 'Sobre la cuerda floja', *ZoneZero*, Editorial 25 (July 2000): <http://zonezero.com/editorial/editorial.html>.

20. See G. Batchen, 'Phantasm: Digital Imaging and the Death of Photography', in Haworth-Booth, *Metamorphoses*, 46–51 (50).

21. For Maya Goded's unprecedented exploration of black culture, see M. Goded, *Tierra negra: fotografías de la costa chica en Guerrero y Oaxaca, México* (Mexico City, 1994). For Andrade's long-standing interest in urban *masquerades*, see R. Tibol (ed.), *Die Schrift. Mexikanische Fotografen 13x10* (Frankfurt, 1992), 22–5; Ziff, *Between Worlds*, 105, 113–14, 125; Y. Andrade, *Pasión mexicana* (Mexico City, 2002).

22. Sántiz Gómez participated in the *Proyecto Fotográfico de Chiapas*, set up in 1992 by Carlota Duarte, director of the Archivo Fotográfico Indígena. Some of her images also appear in Duarte, *Camaristas*.

23. M. Sántiz Gómez, *Creencias (de nuestros antepasados)* (Mexico City, 1998), 76–7.

24. See Fontcuberta, *El beso*, 35–51 (40–1).

25. See Camarillo's 'portfolio' of five images in the index of 'experimental' works in 'Autorretrato', *ZoneZero*: <http://zonezero.com/...olios/experimental/ camarillo/ 1en.html>.

26. Cesare Lombroso was an influential Italian criminologist, who through bestsellers such as *L'uomo delinquente* [*Criminal man*] (1876), devised a 'foolproof' system for diagnosing criminal types through recognisable physical signs or 'stigmata'. A bank of degenerate or atavistic features was supplied by photographic records of individuals who displayed the characteristic physiognomic and phrenological signs of a criminal predisposition. See D. Pick, *Faces of Degeneration: a European Disorder, c.1848–1918* (Cambridge, 1989).

27. For diagnostic sciences and photography, see M. Kemp and M. Wallace, *Spectacular Bodies: The Art and Sciences of the Human Body from Leonardo to Now* (London, 2000), 124–47.

28. See e.g. Tina Modotti's frontal study of a Mexican mask (*c*.1926), one of her illustrations for *Idols Behind Altars* (1929), reproduced in M. Hooks, *Tina Modotti: Photographer and Revolutionary* (London, 1993), 130.

29. F. Kaufman, 'An Essay of Memories (based on interviews with Manuel Álvarez Bravo, Winter 1996)', in M. Álvarez Bravo, *Photographs and Memories* (New York, 1997), 4–13 (11).

30. Iturbide, *En el nombre*, n.p.n. Some of the images are reproduced with individual titles, unlike the original publication, in Iturbide, *Images*, 16–23.

31. See *La buena fama durmiendo* [*The Good Reputation Sleeping*] (1939), *A la mañana siguiente* [*Morning After*] (1945), and *Retrato ausente* [*Absent Portrait*] (1945) in Kismaric, *Manuel Álvarez Bravo*, 123, 179, 183, respectively; and *Retrato desagradable* [*Unpleasant Portrait*] (1943) in Álvarez Bravo, *Photographs*, 35.

32. For a discussion of the 'impartiality' of mechanical intervention and representation of the body, see J. Elkins, *Pictures of the Body: Pain and Metamorphosis* (Stanford, 1999), 155–60.

33. Reproduced in A. Castellanos (ed.), *Memoria fotográfica de México* (Madrid, 1998), n.p.n. The photo-journalist Agustín V. Casasola's 'forensic' archive chronicles crime, punishment and deviance in 1920s and 1930s Mexico City in photographs of violent deaths, prisoners, suspects, prostitutes, homosexuals and the application of science in punitive and clinical regimes. See P. Ortiz Monasterio (ed.), *Mirada y memoria: Archivo fotográfico Casasola, México 1900–1940* (Mexico City, 2002), 146–79.

34. Reproduced in the pamphlet of the exhibition held in the Galería Juan Martín, July 1975, Mexico City. For Álvarez Bravo's recurrent interest in sheets, paper and other *envoltorios* [bundles], see *Juego de papel* [*Paper Games*] (1926–7), *La tercera caída* [*The Third Fall*] (1934), *Las lavanderas sobreentendidas* [*The Washerwomen Implied*] (1932), *Sábanas número 1* [*Sheets No. 1*] (1933), *Guadalupana, mantel* [*Virgin of Guadalupe Table Cloth*] (1940s), *Sábana caída* [*Fallen Sheet*] (1940s), *La abuela, nuestra abuela* [*The Grandmother, Our Grandmother*] (1945), in Kismaric, *Manuel Álvarez Bravo*, 44–5, 83, 91, 104, 127, 128, 163, respectively.

35. For the analogy between the *Verónica* and photography, see the interview with the important photographer Héctor García in C. Pacheco, *La luz de México: entrevistas con pintores y fotógrafos* (Mexico City, 1995), 271–2: '… hay una especie de magia, de milagro no resuelto racionalmente en el prodigio de la fotografía. El paño de la Verónica y el manto de Cristo son puntos para referirme al milagro' ['… there is a kind of magic, something of the miracle which cannot be rationally explained in the marvel of the photograph. The cloth of Verónica and the shroud of Christ are points which allude to the miracle'].

36. Iturbide, *Sueños*, plate 64.

37. Agostoni's work is featured in *Octava bienal de fotografía* (Mexico City, 1997), 66–9; *Fotoseptiembre* (Mexico City, 1996), 232; J.A. Rodríguez, 'Fotografía mexicana de hoy', *Tierra Adentro*, 105 (2000), 35–48. See also Agostoni's dossier of images in the index of 'experimental' works in 'Región abdominal', *ZoneZero*: <http://zonezero.com /… folios/experimental/ agostoni/1en.html>.

38. Catalayud's work appears in *Fotoseptiembre*, 100, *Muestra de fotografía latinoamericana* (Mexico City, 1996), 210–11, Rodríguez, 'Fotografía mexicana', 35–48, and *Octava bienal*, 60–1.

39. See L. Jordanova and D. Petherbridge, *The Quick and the Dead: Artists and Anatomy* (London, 1997); illustrations include *An Anatomical Virgin and Child* (18th C.), *Petal Venus* (with foetus) (17th C.), wax female figurine-containers in classical poses with lids (18th C.), and detachable flaps on paper female figures cast as muses (16th C.).

40. Parcero's work is reproduced in *Fotoseptiembre*, 139; *Muestra*, 88–9; J.L. Barrios Lara, 'Cuerpo fragmentado', in J.L. Barrios Lara, I.M. Benítez Dueñas, K.

Cordero Reiman et al. *El cuerpo aludido: anatomías y construcciones, México, siglos XVI–XX* (Mexico City, 1998), 172–81 (179), a catalogue of a groundbreaking and influential exhibition on figurations and constructions of the body. See also T. Parcero, 'Interior Cartography/Cartografía interior', *Southward Art: Latin American Art Review* 2 (2001), 116–17, 120–9, with an essay by Laura Batkis; Parcero's dossier of images (with a personal statement) in 'Cartografías', *ZoneZero*: <http:// zonezero.com/...iones/fotografos/ tatiana/default.html>. For a discussion of Parcero's video work, see E. Ganado Kim (ed.), *Las transgresiones del cuerpo: arte contemporáneo de México* (Mexico City, 1997), 13–29.

41. See Eherenwald's work in *Muestra*, 102–5.

42. See Alejo's work in *Octava bienal*, 70–3, and in Rodríguez, 'Fotografía mexicana', 35–48.

43. For a reproduction of Gama's *Historias en la piel*, see K. Cordero Reiman, 'Síntomas culturales: cuerpos del siglo XX en México', in Barrios Lara et al., *El cuerpo aludido*, 89–109 (101), and *Octava bienal*, 110–13.

44. In the late 1980s Graciela Iturbide focused on body inscription in street gangs of Los Angeles and Tijuana. Mariana Yampolsky's work on migration and the transformation of popular culture in the 1990s shows an interest in graffiti and pictures on skin.

45. See L. Cohen, *Obra reciente* (Mexico City, 1997) and J. Oles, 'Ensayos en el estudio/Tested in the Studio', in Cohen, *Obra*, 3–7. Cohen's work is featured in Ferrer, *Shadow*, 116–21; *Muestra*, 224–7; *Octava bienal*, 86–7; J.A. Rodríguez, 'Nuevos paisajes, nuevas proyecciones de deseos', *Tierra Adentro*, 105 (2000), 62–8 (63). See also O. Debroise (ed.), *Laura Cohen: albercas* (Mexico City, 2005).

46. See Cohen's dossier of images (with a personal statement) in 'Naturaleza muerta', *ZoneZero*: <http://zonezero.com/...ciones/fotografos/cohen/ default.html>.

47. See Flores Olea's series of photographs *Eros en el espacio virtual* in <http://zonezero.com/exposiciones/fotografos/vfo/default2.html>.

Chapter 7

The Hermeneutics of the Veil in Photography:
Of *Rebozos, Sábanas, Huipiles* and *Lienzos de Verónica*

The *huipil*: sometimes the cotton is heavy and coarse, sometimes so finely spun as to be filmy and semi-transparent. When the cloth is woven with a gauze technique, it is frequently net-like.[1]

El rebozo, que se ha convertido en un tema de interés histórico por las dudas respecto a su origen, fue una prenda de uso obligado para las mujeres desde el siglo XVI. Es un manto que se usa para tapar la cabeza, cubrir los hombros y semiocultar el rostro.[2]

[The *rebozo*-shawl, which has become a subject of historical interest because of the doubts about its origins, was an obligatory garment for women since the sixteenth century. It is a mantle which is used to cover the head and shoulders and to partially conceal the face.]

The veil's reiterated visibility in Mexican black-and-white photography is as multilayered as its material trace is two-dimensional. It operates in a field of metaphoric semblance whose fantasmic formal architecture is guessed at and de-formed in retrospect – evading 'the now of knowability'[3] often associated with photography's eliding of reproduction and recognition. Take, for example, Antonio Reynoso's moving sculpture on hanging lines, at once spatialised and aspatial, sheathing and shifting a homely courtyard.[4] In another image, torn and gap-eyed sheets and canvas billow to shape a vacuum.[5] Or consider Mariana Yampolsky's nebulous bridal carapace *Fantasma [Ghost]* (n.d.), a facsimile in absentia of an eye-catching disappearance (figure 7.1).[6] In Manuel Álvarez Bravo's *Las lavanderas sobreentendidas [The Washerwomen Implied]* (1932) sheets hung out to dry over giant agaves overlay the monument-defining, death-defying drapery of neo-classical sculpture (figure 7.2).[7] As a perceptual conceit the veil stretches to the periphrases of sacred speech and metaphysical exegeses, turning the commonplace cloth – the *sábana*, [sheet], *mantel* [tablecloth], *huipil* and *rebozo* – into something meaningful

Figure 7.1 Mariana Yampolsky, *Fantasma* (n.d.), Oaxaca. Courtesy of © FCMY.

through being overlooked. The interplay of presence and absence
characterises its formal entanglement with photography and pictorial art.
Consider curtain and drapery as scenic barriers 'to conjure up the
transports of illusion'.[8] Turn to Pliny's celebrated narrative of the
competition between the two painters Parrhasios and Zeuxis, cited in
Western art history as a parable of realism, a key text for the illusionistic
spectacle of *trompe-l'œil* and the metaphysics of 'fallen vision' in the still
life genre:

> Parrhasios and Zeuxis entered into competition, Zeuxis exhibiting a picture of some
> grapes, so true to nature that birds flew up to the wall of the stage. Parrhasios then
> displayed a picture of a linen curtain realistic to such a degree that Zeuxis, elated by the
> verdict of the birds, cried out that now at last his rival must draw the curtain and show his
> picture. On discovering his mistake he surrendered the prize to Parrhasios, admitting
> candidly that he, Zeuxis, had deceived only the birds, while Parrhasios had deceived
> himself, a painter.[9]

Photography has been rehearsing this false unveiling from its inception as
an offshoot of the graphic arts, ghosting specular expectations and
spectating within the spectacle itself. Take a suggestive piece of
anecdotal evidence regarding 'El Gran Lente' ['The Great Lens'], the
studio of popular photographer José Antonio Bustamante in 1930s to
1950s Fresnillo. He used the standard props and accoutrements of

Figure 7.2 Manuel Álvarez Bravo, *Las lavanderas sobreentendidas* (1932). Familia
Álvarez Bravo y Urbajtel.

theatrical illusion, the 'mise-en-scene', the 'cortinas, telones y paisajes'
['the curtains, backcloths and scenery'] but the symbolic or illustrational
cloths also had a practical application as filters and screens in controlling
the play of light and shadow, regulating the economy of the seen and the
unseen and the staging of appearance: 'El estudio era como todos: Un
salón con sus cortinas, telones y paisajes … . Las cortinas en un estudio

son esenciales: cortinas de terciopelo, de franela, blancas' ['The studio was like all the others: a reception room with its curtains, backcloths and scenery … Curtains in a studio are essential: velvet curtains, made of flannel, white'].[10]

If we further extend the Parrhasian analogy with its simulated drape to the seventeenth-century Spanish 'mystical *trompe-l'œil*' (e.g. Francisco de Zurbarán's Veronicas and crucifixions and their anonymous Mexican imitations), one might argue that photography has transposed the dialectic between the *engaño* and *desengaño* [deception and disillusionment] of visionary painting. For through the contrivance of the still life's effect of the real, the spectator was given access to the transcendent in a visual confrontation with the sacred – the uncircumscribable other.[11] Mexican photography's scenography of drapery and the veil seems haunted by the aposcopic gestures of a tradition of religious Christian painting in which 'sight' and its exertions was a central theme: the Resurrection, Transfiguration, Ascension and Assumption are cited or renegotiated in a double movement which imbricates the problem of unifying immanence and transcendence as regards manifestations of identity with that of photography's very production of images.[12] When Henry Fox Talbot sought to describe the evidentiary mimicry of 'photogenic drawing' (or photography) in 1839, he devised an exemplum not unlike Pliny's parable of pictorial realism but replaced the illusory curtain with an open-work fabric of linen:

> To give an idea of the degree of accuracy with which some objects can be imitated by this process, I need only mention one instance. Upon one occasion, having made an image of a piece of lace of an elaborate pattern, I showed it to some persons at the distance of a few feet, with the inquiry, whether it was a good representation? When the reply was 'That they were not to be so easily deceived, for it was evidently no picture, but the piece of lace itself'.[13]

Talbot's influential notion of a material manifestation delineating itself spontaneously on the chemically sensitised surface of a sheet of paper was tacitly freighted with the Christian discourse of otherworldly impressions and traces on equally fragile and adherent surfaces. The genre of spiritualist photography which purported to record the materialisation of spirit identities effectively recycled the spectacle of the divine imprint and unwittingly parodied the photographic production of images itself. The medium often sat in a theatrical cabinet flanked by curtains. Ghostly physiognomies supposedly delineated themselves through and on gauze-like cloths unaided. According to Cesare Lombroso's testimony, suspicions of artifice were raised by the apparitions' tendency to make themselves known through contact with the psychic's skirt or 'behind the material stuff of draperies, such as the portières of the medium's cabinet'.[14] A photograph by Baron von Schrenck-Notzing, one of many purporting to show the phenomena of materialisation, has a medium in full net-like veil, head bowed, while in the foreground a makeshift sudarium hovering not so mysteriously over her lower body carries a delineated portrait of a responsive spirit.[15]

The privileged return to the motif of the Veil of the Veronica and its variation, the *lienzo* [cloth] of the Guadalupana, in work which explicitly cites or simulates allusively across generations of Mexican photographers, is more than simply a recursive aesthetic unafflicted by mutability. It intersects with photography's epistemology of appearance (Fox Talbot spoke in neo-Platonic terms of 'the art of fixing a shadow') and the secular and religious dramaturgy of the immaterial and 'marvellous'. See the appeal of this exhibitionary paradigm in Bernice Kolko's women shouldering a statue of the Saint displaying the sudarium from 1955[16] and in Yolanda Andrade's *El martirio* [*The Martyrdom*] (1987), where a diminutive Veronica is partially obliterated by a placard-sized veil.[17] The sudarium's syntax of bodily secretions dignifies the absorbing and absorbent quality of the photographic. Graciela Iturbide made the link between the interceding deified mantle of collective rituals and photography's own mystical devotions by entitling her photograph of Holy Week pilgrims *La Verónica, patrona de la fotografía*.[18] It is worth remembering that the *lienzo* of the Veronica, a consecrated relic carrying the material imprint of the divine visage, served in theological discourse to legitimise 'el culto de las imágenes' ['the worship of images'] in opposition to Reformation iconoclasm. No wonder then that it should serve as a talisman for Mexican photography's figurative imperative.

In a work by the most testimonial of photographers, Héctor García, the imprinted cloth does not follow 'el camino de la imagen dentro del espejo, cuando no existe imagen real que reflejar' ['the path of the image in the mirror, when no real image exists to reflect'].[19] Instead, in his poignant photomontage of 1972 (figure 7.3), the visage of a suffering Christ with half-closed eyes is replaced by Zapata's photogenic death mask, which is a reproduction of a newspaper image by J. Mora.[20] In this mortuary shot, the name of the assassinated revolutionary leader is scrawled on the print like a forensic identity tag, tagging what for some has become a holy relic. The evidence of Zapata's mortality is woven into a *mortaja* [shroud] through which he is transfigured and perpetuated as myth. It seems possible that in García's *La Verónica* photography's deadly complicity is offset by its recording of forms of resistance to its own empirical exploits. The Zapata image is superimposed on a hand-made cloth, which also bears the identity stamp 'Hecho en México' ['Made in Mexico'], and is

Figure 7.3 © Héctor García, *Verónica* (1972).

held up by an Indian 'Saint Veronica' screened behind it, branded in turn by the shot. Her eyes, radiating wrinkles of feeling, and those of an alert boy over her shoulder make the eye contact which the supine Zapata, of Mora's image, was guaranteed never to return. In the image's compositional economy, the return of the gaze exposes the photographer to ethical scrutiny and self-abasement – even as a return from death is promised to the faithful. Even allowing for the distinctive differences in practice and formal execution, for instance, as in the witnessing as opposed to the recreation of mystical devotions, we find that in Manuel and Lola Álvarez Bravo, Héctor García, Bernice Kolko, Yolanda Andrade, Rafael Doniz, Graciela Iturbide and Pedro Meyer what is perhaps effected is a melancholy or burlesque valediction to a kind of faith: the belief in the ontological immanence of the photograph as defining trace as an 'end in itself' and the acknowledgement of its status as merely a 'transitive episode'. It is interesting to note that the tacit parallel made between the circulation of the sacred icon and the 'imagología' of a manipulated consumerist visuality places the photographer in a penitential role.

It may be recalled that one such form of photographed reverential self-castigation, the *Manda* [*Offering/Gift*], requires the faithful to wear a hood, a symbolic blindness which is a sign of abjection/infamy, a plea for exculpation and the correction of wayward perception. See the anonymous 1937 shot of just such an act of public contrition[21] and the images of Mariana Yampolsky[22] and Rafael Doniz on such auxiliary figures engaged in seeing the unfathomable, yearning for the rapture afforded by rupture which made St Teresa desire not 'to ever open my eyes again'.[23] Pedro Meyer's fixation with the veiled and shrouded in his analogue work in the 1970s and 1980s, part of his thematising of resistance to photography's collusion with hegemonic identity politics, could be said to foreshadow the crisis of belief which led to his abandonment of the darkroom in favour of digital photography and image-making.[24] With humorous portentousness, the swollen semi-permeable veil of *El velo negro* [*The Black Veil*] (1975) darkens the frame with the secret terror of an unknown thing (figure 7.4). With its fine mesh, the veil bends and closes upon what it wants as the shadow of death precedes and envelops the subjects of photography's roving apprehensions. In *La dama del lunar y sus amigas* [*The Lady with the Beauty Spot and Her Friends*] (1982), gradations of visibility are netted and displayed as in the stages from blank to increasing resolution and delineation on the surface of the coated paper, as it swims into view in the developing trays (figure 7.5). In *Anteojos detrás del velo* [*Glasses behind the Veil*] (1980), an unyielding eyelid muffles the heightened attentiveness of the four-eyed Argos (figure 7.6).[25]

Figure 7.4 © Pedro Meyer, *El velo negro* (1975). Courtesy of Pedro Meyer.

Figure 7.5 © Pedro Meyer, *La dama del lunar y sus amigas* (1982). Courtesy of Pedro Meyer.

Figure 7.6 © Pedro Meyer, *Anteojos detrás del velo* (1980). Courtesy of Pedro Meyer.

The dramatic effect on an audience of the veil's ambivalent semiotic can be gauged in the forum of justice and retribution, the Mexico City law court, during the sensational trial of the suggestively named Magdalena Jurado of 1922. Being tried for the murder of her husband, she appeared before the court, the public gallery and newspaper photographers wearing a thick head veil:

> Magdalena causó sensación y estupor al entrar: vestía completamente de negro. De un gorro, del mismo color, se desprendía un grueso velo, también negro, que escondía 'su pena y su mortificación', 'llegó paso a paso hasta el banquillo del acusado, sin que nadie pudiera conocer sus impresiones, a no ser por el menudito andar y los movimientos descompasados que se le observaban'.[26]

> [Magdalena's arrival caused astonishment and a sensation: she was dressed completely in black. From a hat of the same colour fell a thick veil, also black, which concealed her 'shame and mortification', 'step by step she reached the defendant's bench without anyone being able to discover her feelings, apart from what her dainty walking and exaggerated movements suggested to the observer'.]

The female defendant directed the penal gaze, obtrusively catching the eye of her judges while manipulating the associative disharmony of the veil – between ingratiating self-mortification and alluring evasion, chaste modesty and carnal effrontery. Some of the published shots catch her peering sideways from beneath the veil, smiling knowingly at the male photographer, anticipating the prurient interest of her soon-to-be readers.

The veil as sudarium, shroud and envelope/wrap signifies revelation and concealment, transparency and opacity, the embodied and the immaterial, the liminal and the universal, essence and appearance, the temporal and the timeless, depth and ephemerality, tactility and the intangible, the enclosed and the limitless – in a surfeit of always inferred but also always deferred content. Turning to another classic manual for representing ideas through pictorial manifestations, the entry for the *The Rational Soul/Anima Rationalis* in Hertel's illustrated edition of Cesare Ripa's *Iconologia*, a Mexican translation appearing as late as 1866, reads:

> The personification of the Soul is a female figure draped in white, the colour of purity, the colour which is supposedly not made up of any other colours, just as the soul is not composed of anything earthly. Her head is covered with a transparent veil, since the soul, according to St Augustine ... is invisible to human eyes. Through the veil, the woman is seen to be beautiful, since God, the source of all beauty and perfection, created man in his own image ... although the soul has no form or body, it must be represented thus to men, who can perceive things only through their senses.[27]

Photography's spirit machine simulates the otherworldly in the rhetorical gradations of white and black, negative and positive impressions, lighting effects to rival the most painterly chiaroscuros. The diaphanous reminds us that 'light is the insubstantial foundation of the world' and that photography enjoins specular peregrinations through intervisual communication and experience that is 'siteless'.[28] Like the spiritual exercises of religious faith, it requires a high level of participatory visualisation of the viewer, a 'mystical witnessing' that folds back on interior visualisation as if restoring the pre-imagistic darkness of the darkroom; stilling the lens shutter on the click of shut.[29] It averts and invites dis-closure. Consider finally the sixteenth-century representation of the ancient Roman patron goddess of childbirth, Lucina, a female figure sheathed in full body veil resembling 'a limbless sack' – shrouded from view, her presence pregnant like a parenthesis, represented as wholly enveloped due to the shame attendant on her gestating condition.[30] This reminds us of the veil's double, the membrane, and photography's contemplation of its own membranous adhesion to the surface of things. In Mariana Yampolsky's *Madre* (*c*.1980s) (figure 7.7), the gauze-like *huipil* heavy with child helps to imagine the inside out.[31]

Figure 7.7 Mariana Yampolsky, *Madre* (n.d.), Cuetzalán, Puebla. Courtesy of © FCMY.

Manuel Álvarez Bravo's *Guadalupana, mantel* [*The Virgin of Guadalupe Table Cloth*] (1940s) (figure 7.8) clothes a still-life vessel of fruit with a porous filter of textile.[32] The homely is often cast as the most metaphysically pregnant in the mystical still-life genre. The sacred Marian image picked out through gaps in the fabric borrows its own precarious visibility from the play of light and chequerboard contrasts. For Manuel Álvarez Bravo, photography drops on the material world and snags it in an insubstantial filmic trace – which you can see through as well as in. For Mariana Yampolsky, the net-like semi-transparencies of homespun white fabric lets out more than it holds in, in a respectful elision of the Indian subject which lends a deftness and delicacy to her engagements that has not been sufficiently recognised.

This study hopes to show that the potential for reflexivity of veils and drapery in Mexican photography is complemented by photography's metaphorisation of some of the ritual postures of its own traditional practices. Take, for example, the ducking of the photographer's head beneath a black drape, giving the impression of a blinded figure before the picture is shot, or the feminisation of the aperture of the lens as a bodily orifice (rather than the usual analogy to the human eye) – as a voracious mechanical vagina dentata.

Figure 7.8 Manuel Álvarez Bravo, *Guadalupana, mantel* (1940s). Familia Álvarez Bravo y Urbajtel.

It seems that the veil in even the most self-consciously ludic, reflexive or symbolic Mexican photography introduces a point of incongruity as regards the evidentiary exposure supposedly afforded by mechanical reproduction. In other words, it points to the black hole which empties ontological form and disturbs habitual analogic thinking. Not even the dramaturgy of photography itself played out in front of the camera through pantomimic surrogacy and transference, as in Manuel Álvarez Bravo's, Mariana Yampolsky's and Graciela Iturbide's meditative *mise-en-abimes*, can conclusively allay the fear of the inconsequential, fitful and random that haunts photography's conjuring of appearances.[33] In Yolanda Andrade's *La espera* [*The Wait*] (1978), for instance, a shrouded form in a room is fixed in dejected expectation of photography's mythic revelations, inertly awaiting an unsheathing that the medium's veiled transparencies can't deliver.[34] The call of the veiled one – the promise of being in abeyance – probably explains Rafael Doniz's dwelling on the connotative nexus of a life-size shrouded statue carried in procession. The muffled figure circulates in his *Casa Santa* [*Holy House*], (c.1986) a memorable book on the house of spiritual retreat and pilgrimage where popular faith comes to exercise its corrected vision, which offers virtually a compendium of the use of cloths, veils and drapery in the spectacle of popular faith in Mexico.[35]

In a little-cited original work on nineteenth-century photographic portraiture (1938), Enrique Fernández Ledesma introduces the reader through a verbal proscenium to a gallery of familial ghosts.[36] He describes the passage as an intersubjective experience with salvific powers for both the viewer-reader and the simulacra of the dead 'de un México fugado ya'/'de un México extinguido' ['of a Mexico which has already vanished'/'of a Mexico which has become extinct']: 'estamos dando, metafísicamente, en lo íntimo de nuestro ser sensible, corporeidad palpitante al polvo real de esta asamblea que ahora resucitamos en efigies' ['we are giving, metaphysically, in the intimate depth of our sentient being, palpitating corporeality to the real dust of this gathering which we now resuscitate as effigies'].[37] The viewer transforms a relic into expressive actuality, clothing it with an incorruptible body '[dando] plasticidad a la ceniza de sus despojos y modelando, en vivo relieve estatuario ... antecedentes y fundamentos de nuestra mexicanidad' ['giving form to the ashes of their remains and moulding in vivid sculptural relief ... the antecedents and foundations of our Mexican identity'] – clothing it with the veil of knowledge.[38] But the viewer (rather than the passive beholder) undergoes a form of transubstantiation which inverts the relation of ontological density between him or herself and the sacralised photographs. The photographic effigies communicate their dependent alterity, their embodied mist: '... estamos ya, un poco desmaterializados, en la aptitud quimérica de salvar el resquicio de una frontera ideal. Y pasamos sutilmente, como pasa el fantasma por el muro, a la asamblea de nuestros antepasados' ['... we are already becoming a little immaterial, with the fantastic disposition to cross the threshold of an ideal frontier. And we pass subtly, like the ghost through a wall, to join the assembly of our ancestors'].[39] The viewer becomes the supporting ground of the image, the invisible premise of its visibility: if we gaze at the portraits 'en su inmovilidad, trémulas esculturas' ['in their immobility, wavering sculptures'] we are subsumed in semi-transparent correspondence with 'un mundo de donde venimos' ['a world from whence we came']. The 'resquicio' that opens through the photograph – alluding to a crack, a trace, a remnant, but also a glimmer and opportunity – beatifies the critical hour of death.

Before continuing to get embroiled in analysing the particular manifestations of *sábanas*, *rebozos*, *huipiles* and *lienzos de Verónica* and their multiple slippages and associations, let us revisit an admonitory parable casually included in the margins of Walter Benjamin's unpublished writings: 'Truth is the death of intention. This, indeed, is just what could be meant by the story of the veiled image of Sais, the unveiling of which was fatal for anyone who thought to learn the truth thereby'.[40] This philosophical parable could be said to alert us to the fallacious status of the photograph as an *hallazgo* [find], instantaneous aperçu or documentary happening, with a capacity to produce knowledge through its visual reproductions, as well as to a quasi-mystical notion that intentionality – the perceptual *búsqueda* [search] – cannot yield what it seeks because 'truth' is an unlooked for elsewhere that avails itself randomly not to cognition but to a receptive consciousness. This chapter does not promise to effect the unveiling of the veil in Mexican photography but rather to enter imaginatively into a transaction with its locales and displays so as to gauge the character of its continued fascination. The subject lends itself to a kind of interpretative torsion, a spiral turning against the platitudinous exhibition of identities. The material has been organised into three sections suggested by titles and phrases related to the photographic images: *El rebozo nacional* [*The National Shawl*], *La ley de la sábana* [*The Law of the Sheet*] and *Huipil de tapar* [*Head Covering*].

Following in Fernández Ledesma's gothicky footsteps, let us first consider two photographs, by his close friend and collaborator Manuel Álvarez Bravo, as virtual thresholds to the blurring of categories which marks the entry to the ambiguities of the veiled, draped and enveloped: *Caja de visiones* [*Box of Visions*] (1938) and *La abuela, nuestra abuela*

(1945).[41] Manuel Álvarez Bravo's interest in drapery of every sort has remained so constant and distinctive in a career that has spanned almost a century that in his 1990s work the variations on a theme became almost a parodic signature.[42] In *Caja de visiones*, a woman, her face peering incompletely lit from the shadows, holds a dark cloak stretched over her head (figure 7.9). The eyes are barely perceptible, veiled by shadow. The disembodied head overhangs a wooden box as in a phantasmagoric trick in a freak show or a macabre skull protruding from an ossuary case – a mystificatory box of tricks or holy relics. But the patterned stars bring to mind a celestial mantle and the semi-shrouded visage evokes the subtle imprint of a sudarium or the native *ayate* or *maguey*-fibre cloak on which the Virgin of Guadalupe impressed her image. The verticalised splitting of space into two levels is reminiscent of a device used in visionary painting to dramatise the confluence of the real and the imagined, the interior and the exterior. The divine would manifest itself in the upper level, drawing the mystic gaze upwards. In the photograph, the semi-covert visage hovers over the borderland of hidden significances of half-waking experience – the dangerous domain of the fantastic and the supernatural. The lower half of the surface of the box covered in peeling paint and paper decorations of fairground shows has three stereoscopic viewfinders fitted in a line. In Mexico, roving village photographers often showcased their trade at fairgrounds along with other carnival

Figure 7.9 Manuel Álvarez Bravo, *Caja de visiones* (1930s). © Center for Creative Photography, The University of Arizona, Tucson.

marvels and entertainments. The slightly tilted perspective and dramatic foreshortening gives prominence to the tripartite set of peep holes. In order to peer through them and to frame the photograph one would probably have had to crouch or kneel roughly at about the level of the invisible body's *regazo* [lap]. The stereoscopic masks seem to have sockets fixed onto blanks: boarded up windows blinding ocular penetration. Should our curiosity be tempted and we assume the requisite posture, we would be fitted with the dark, so to speak, an extinction of the world before the opening of what mystics might have termed, following Paul the apostle, 'the soul's perception', a blinding such as the ocular transgressions of surrealism might recommend in their cultivation of the profane. Ocular conceits and optical humour were staple surrealist gags of which Álvarez Bravo had produced his own suggestive variation in the *Parábola óptica* (1931). *Caja de visiones* expands the play on reversed significances and topsy-turvy inversions at the expense of positivism and, perhaps, injunctions against voyeurism.

By contrast, there is nothing cryptic in the analogy being made between the 'caja de visiones' and the camera itself. Simply consider the design of the 'little black box': the nineteenth-century's tripod-mounted wooden box, Fox Talbot's small box-like 'mouse-trap' camera and the Eastman Brownie Box camera (introduced in 1900 as the cheapest and easiest to use) marked the apprenticeship of such photographers as Cartier-Bresson, Manuel Álvarez Bravo's friend and co-exhibitor in Bellas Artes in 1935. In the 1930s Álvarez Bravo himself used the single-lens Graflex camera with 'its inimitable shape of cubic box with bellows extension and four-sided hood on top' in the hand or on tripod.[43] In 1934 he consigned his formal and poetic interest in the history of photography to a magazine article for *Revista de Revistas*, which discussed its origins and compared its early inventors to practitioners of the occult – akin to the alchemist's light experiments with lenses and chemicals. He taught photography at the Art Academy of San Carlos for several years in the 1930s. Throughout his life he was to engage his interest in the originary and archival dimension of photography by amassing a distinguished collection encompassing the reproductive medium's earliest technologies and materials.[44]

For Manuel Álvarez Bravo the camera also included its cinematographic counterpart. In 1934 he produced his only known full-length film, *Tehuántepec*, focusing on the southern region's matriarchal Zapotec Indian culture. This was a region which had been favoured by hunters of spectacular autochthony in the Mexican arts. The Tehuana woman, in particular, became a paragon of native seduction, mystery and cultural fecundity.[45] The celebrated costume of the Tehuana included a nimbus-like *huipil grande*, a white head-dress of lace resembling an inverted petticoat. He went on to work professionally as a cinematographer and as a stills photographer in the Mexican film industry in the 1940s.

What contributes to *Caja de visiones*'s subtle gendering of photography and its titillating choreography of semi-concealments is the half-hidden identity of the woman-effigy posing as part of the composite 'found' structure. In the same period that this image was constructed and shot Álvarez Bravo was photographing female mannequins in stalls and shop windows and absorbing the cubistic and collage distortions of Picasso, which were an acknowledged point of reference in the photographer's multimedia formation. For the marvellous 'mujer-caja' ['woman-box'], this 'ser compuesto and contrapuesto' ['composite and contrasting being'] is none other than the photographer Lola Álvarez Bravo, his then wife, darkroom assistant and mother to his son, also called Manuel. The notion of Lola as genetrix and embodied camera, as the historical receptacle of photography itself, its tutelary guardian and passage, conveyed by the image's allusions to sacred procreation and profane reproduction, may be less far-fetched than it may at first seem. After an early flirtation with pictorialism Álvarez Bravo embraced the associative promiscuities afforded by the ill-defined and incongruously juxtaposed. In later interviews he upheld this preference for plurality and fluidity of interpretation of an unstable, and only seemingly fixed, photographed subject. Influential cinematographers such as John Alton adopted the notion of *The Human Camera* in his writing, transposing figuratively the mechanical and its operations onto human anatomy, referring to the 'photo department latent in every human being'.[46] In *Caja de visiones*, the black box becomes an antenatal chamber.

Luis Buñuel (1900–83), whom Manuel Álvarez Bravo was to befriend in the 1940s and name as his master when it came to coining visual impurities, turned the concept of the female body as a divinely designed machine (termed *fabrica* in sixteenth-century anatomical illustration) into a different lifting of nature's veil from that imagined by the romantics.[47] He construed a different parting of lips from the theatrical drawing of curtains in the form of dissected flaps of skin executed by baroque medical effigies, with the circumference of the world replicated in an exposed female abdomen.[48] Buñuel blended and turned the culpable glimpses of disclosed flesh and the castigation of the avid eye in *Un chien andalou*, *L'age d'or* and his Mexican films (*Los olvidados*, *Abismos de pasión*, *Él*) into a startling *invención* in *Viridiana* – the actress Lola Gaos's sacrilegious photographing of the re-enacted tableau of the Last Supper. In this scene the black box's secret aperture is revealed between women's thighs as the uproarious beggar-woman,

Enedina, takes a simulated snapshot by drawing up her skirt to peel back the eyelid of her sex.[49] The screenplay is worth citing:

> *Poca* (addressing all of them): Enedina's going to take a picture. So we'll have a souvenir.
>
> *Don Amalio*: Where's the camera?
>
> *Enedina* (laughing cagily): It's a present from my parents. … Enedina sweeps her very ample skirt up to her face. The photograph is taken. She chokes with laughter behind her skirt.[50]

A portrait of Lola the photographer taken after her separation from Manuel Álvarez Bravo by her close friend the younger artist Juan Soriano reprised key elements of her ex-husband's ambivalent tribute to her.

In *Retrato de Lola Álvarez Bravo con Juan Soriano niño* [*Portrait of Lola Álvarez Bravo with Juan Soriano as a Child*] (1944) Lola is depicted leaning pensively over a box covered with a mantle whose pleated hanging resembles the curtains of a stage.[51] Soriano casts her as a full-bodied muse, surrogate mother and agent of her own commemoration through a 'desdoblamiento': a frontal Lola figured in the background and, in the foreground, a free-floating Lola, seen from behind, shawl partially covering her head, focusing her camera and directing it at herself posed with the box which screens the bottom half of her body and across which the curtains are drawn. Soriano's portrait, in which he emphasises his own dependent and humble position in terms of artistic seniority, visualises the implied production of a photographic self-portrait by Lola herself as an act of autogenesis and self-sufficiency arguably absent in her allegorised investiture in Manuel Álvarez Bravo's famous image. In the photographic self-portrait of Lola and Juan Soriano in turn-of-the-century costume (*c.*1945), the photographer stands in voluminous skirt and feathered hat holding the artist's hands, who sits dressed in boyish short-trousers and a cap. Both are smiling with Lola staring archly at the camera.[52]

Turning to the second point of entry, Manuel Álvarez Bravo's *La abuela, nuestra abuela* (1945), the womb-like camera box has morphed into an ancestral cave with pre-Hispanic overtones (figure 7.10). We behold a figure clad in white kneeling on the ground, with a darkened recess for a face beneath a canopy-like raised shawl, or is it a winding-sheet? For the limbless shape is construed as a living shrine, an originary bundle of in-drawn folds (those invisible grandmotherly wrinkles captured on cloth) – a symbolic gateway to the underlay of what is known because it cannot be seen, beyond the deceiving plenitude of appearance.

Figure 7.10 Manuel Álvarez Bravo, *La abuela, nuestra abuela* (1945). Familia Álvarez Bravo y Urbajtel.

El rebozo nacional

En el campo, en los alrededores de las ciudades y a veces hasta en las calles, se advierten mujeres completamente ocultas tras su rebozo. Esconden frente, nariz y boca y sólo se ven los puros ojos, como entre las mujeres árabes.[53]

[In the country, in the environs of cities and sometimes even in the streets, women are seen completely hidden behind their shawl. They hide forehead, nose and mouth, and only the eyes themselves are visible, as is the custom among Arab women.]

Because the *rebozo* occupies an unassailable place in the pantheon and pathos of Mexican national costume it is unsurprising to find it in modern photographs – draped over twisting nude bodies, shielding the muffled masses of the unwashed, enveloping anonymous *malinches*, cloaking sacred statues, framing native beauty, or shaping human *capillas* [chapels]. In pursuit of fastidious simplifications in the 1920s, Edward Weston had the period's most represented Indian model, Luz Jiménez from Milpa Alta, kneeling naked on the proverbial *petate* – the semiotic marker of a cross-grained culture.[54] She forms a pyramidal shape thanks to the enveloping *rebozo*, an article of clothing that inspired more than a few 'Homenajes al rebozo' in the arts (e.g. Jean Charlot, Diego Rivera, José Clemente Orozco, Manuel Rodríguez Lozano, Antonio Ruiz, David Alfaro Siqueiros, Frida Kahlo). The petrean quality of her pose, its foundational shape, is prescient of Luz Jiménez's representation in civic monuments to *La raza* [*The Race*] and Mexican national history (by Ignacio Asúnsolo, Carlos Bracho and Luis Ortiz Monasterio).

When shorn or strewn like detritus the *rebozo* attests to the precarious thereness of the humble, the quotidian invisibility of the very dark-skinned. So in Manuel Álvarez Bravo's *La tierra misma* [*The Earth Itself*] (1930s) (figure 7.11), a young Indian woman shot against an *adobe* wall, her fugitive gaze off-centre, becomes the telluric ground herself through

Figure 7.11 Manuel Álvarez Bravo, *La tierra misma* (1930). Familia Álvarez Bravo y Urbajtel.

an equivalence whose grain is partially revealed by the all-enwrapping *rebozo* gaping open at the breasts.[55] In his equally plangent, *La tercera caída* [*The Third Fall*] (1934), a collapsed body, on an interminable Viacrucis, covered in the ever-extendible *rebozo*, sleeps the sleep of the 'vencidos' [the vanquished], perhaps doubly subordinated by the overbearing perspective of the shot.[56] In Lola Álvarez Bravo's *El duelo* [*The Mourning*] (*c*.1940s), three figures in a crowd of craning onlookers have drawn the *rebozo* across their faces to exclude the peering intrusion of the photographer, although the photographer's appended title seems to co-opt the gesture into the traditional theatre of mourning.[57] In Tina Modotti's angled, deep perspective on the superficially textured variety of a gathering of women pilgrims seen from behind, the huddled generic forms make individual identity expendable in favour of the unity of communal piety.[58] Away from the archaic and arcane, Luis Márquez (1899–1978) opted for a mannered folklore, which aspired to choreograph a Mexicanist sublime for urban consumption with a nude studio model adopting aesthetic poses using the *rebozo* as her only prop.[59] The contagion of neo-*costumbrista* preciosity extended to the garment's cinematic consecration, especially through the cinematography of Gabriel Figueroa. In the overdetermined costume of the nationalist screen, the now glamorous *rebozo* often provided the contours for the allure of authentic femininity. A still from Roberto Gavaldón's *El rebozo de Soledad* [*Soledad's Shawl*] (1952), shot and lit by Figueroa, suffuses Stella Inda in an unearthly light, while the *rebozo* lends her profile the lapidary definition of an elegant stone idol.[60]

These collected photographic images clearly intersect with popular paeans to the *rebozo* in song and poetry from the period which point to this visualised garment's stitching of the sacred and the profane, the material and the impalpable. But the *rebozo*'s deflective as well as defining characteristics have also been ruminated. For instance, in Julio Guerrero's classic *De la génesis del crimen en México* [*The Origin of Crime in Mexico*] (1901), in which the proletarian *rebozo*'s equivocal uses and delinquent associations are described. Its collusive presence, and capacious folds, aid the evasion of policing vigilance. In this sociological study, Guerrero cites the Porfirian *costumbrista* writer, José T. Cuéllar, on the subject of the garment's potential for concealments, deceptions and obstructions of every sort, making its very definition a slippery undertaking:

El rebozo es un chal escurridizo y cuya docilidad confianzuda le da el aspecto de usado desde antes de venderse. Debajo del rebozo se oculta la cabeza desgreñada ... oculta a las líneas del talle, obliga al espectador a prescindir de todo examen; no es una pieza que viste, sino una funda que impide que se vea.[61]

[The *rebozo* is a slippery shawl whose docile familiarity lends it the appearance of having been worn before it is actually sold. Beneath the rebozo hides the unkempt head … it conceals the outline of the figure, it obliges the spectator to desist from all examination; it is not an article which clothes but rather a cover which impedes vision.]

After the Revolution the *rebozo* undergoes a rehabilitation and the salutary properties of the ordinary *rebozo* are celebrated in a kind of patriotic delirium. In the ranchero song 'El rebozo de mi madre' ['My Mother's Shawl'] (1948) it becomes a holy relic: the phases of an honest woman's life are calibrated in the folds of the garment which she inhabits until death turns it into a shroud. It is evoked as an organic part of the maternal body which is also a hearth and carries with it the measure that foreshadows the conclusion of her life:

Madrecita chula, guardo tu rebozo
como santo cariño …
Tu rebozo madre, me sirvió de cuna
se inició en tus hombros, como en un trigal,
con el me cubriste del sol a la luna,
El era mi cielo y era mi jacal …
El fue tu mortaja, madrecita mía;
la muerte en la noche del rancho llegó;
te arropó en su sombra, miró tu agonía
y el viejo rebozo también te lloró.[62]
[My darling Mother, I cherish your shawl
like a saintly affection …
Your shawl, Mother, acted as my cradle
began on your shoulders like in a field of wheat,
with it you covered me from the sun to the moon,
It was my sky and my hut …
It became your shroud, my dearest Mother;
death arrived during the ranch night;
it wrapped you in its shadow, watched your agony
and the old shawl also mourned you.]

In Gregorio de Gante's 'Piropos al rebozo' ['Flattering Comments on the Shawl'] (1944), published in the magazine of the Union of Charros, the author's masculinist gallantry raises the tone from the familial tribute to a resounding national hymn which turns sentiment into pomp:

Porque en tí se han mecido
los sueños infantiles de mi raza,
cuando como en un nido

trémulo de ternuras y de gozo,
la mujer de mi pueblo
a su vástago envuelve en el rebozo.
…
porque pasas por ferias y mercados,
rebozo mandadero,
queriendo atesorar el mundo entero.
…
Rebozo que eres cuna para el niño,
cabezal para el sueño, celosía
para el amor, dogal para el cariño,
venda para el herido, banderola,
mortaja y vida y llanto y alegría;
rebozo nacional, tu sombra sola
cubre a la patria mía.[63]
[Because in you have rocked
the childhood dreams of my race,
when as in a nest
trembling with caresses and joy,
the woman of my people
envelops her offspring in her shawl.
…
because you pass through fairs and markets,
demanding shawl,
wanting to hoard the whole world.
…
Shawl that is a cradle for the child,
pillow for sleep, lattice
for courting, halter for love,
bandage for the wounded, pennant,
shroud and life and tears and joy;
national shawl, your shadow alone
covers my homeland.]

Away from the populism of amateur poetasters, we find in 'Tenías un rebozo de seda' ['You had a shawl of silk'] the refined eroticism of the 'silk rebozo' being woven into Ramón López Velarde's poetic equivalent of furtive glances:

¿Guardas, flor del terruño aquel rebozo
de maleza y de nieve,
en cuya seda me dormí aspirando

la quinta esencia de tu espalda leve?[64]
[Have you saved, flower of the native ground that shawl
of wild undergrowth and snow,
in whose silk I slept inhaling
the quintessence of your delicate shoulder?]

La ley de la sábana

The unmade bed and its rumpled sheets has articulated a prurient interest in the absentee body, in its physical contact and imprint – from Dürer to Delacroix and beyond by way of the academic tradition of the draped nude.[65] In Mexico, closely observed sheets and the aura of their tacit or illicit encounters have motivated recent homages to the genre by such artists as Francisco Toledo and Carla Rippey.[66] Before them, soiled, serpentine or immaculate sheets provided the loci, backdrops and symbolic material of paintings by Orozco, Ruiz, Kahlo and Jesús Guerrero Galván.[67] In the eroticised Teatro de Revista of the 1920s and 1930s and in the art deco studio nudes of photographers such as Antonio Garduño and Martín Ortiz, the *sábana* operates as the profane counterpart to the *lienzo* and is again twinned with the female figure – but one who cloaks herself in disingenuous provocations which fetter and undo the impenitent gaze.[68] Anonymous stereoscopic photographs of erotic female nudes from late Porfirian Mexico, slyly furl and unfurl sheets over curves and between splayed limbs like unspiritual ectoplasmic emissions. The glass plates, measuring 6 x 13 cm, were placed under a viewer and held up to the light. By looking through the two eyepieces, similar to a pair of binoculars, the image was reproduced effectively in 3D: images such as that of a standing woman caught from behind, leaning on a bed, holding a sheet against her unglimpsable front while exposing her behind by raising the curtain of her hair; on the wall a print of her odalisque double wrapped in a sheet provides the missing frontal shot.[69]

The notion of the chastity and classical simplicity of the unsartorial sheet is glimpsed in Romualdo García's 1910 photograph *Mujer con ramo de flores* [*Woman with Bouquet of Flowers*] where it is poised precariously on the brink of indecent travesty.[70] A buxom matron cocooned expertly in a sheet impersonates a vestal virgin in the photographer's studio. In Salvador Quevedo y Zubieta's pulp fiction, *La ley de la sábana* (1935), sequel to the popular and aptly punning *Las ensabanadas* [*The Sheeted Women*] (or *empanadas* alluding to a stuffed pastry, with *empanar* a culinary term for coating), the cover boasts a balletic modernist nude outlined by an ovoid sheet on a theatrical plinth. The pose is artfully statuesque but the sheet is emblematic of the two novels' furtive sensationalism rather than the dignified neutrality of the drape: 'una pintura vigorosa de una familia que como un morbo hereditario va dejando en sus descendientes las costumbres licenciosas de la época' ['a vigorous painting of a family which like a hereditary pathalogical illness passes down to its descendants the licentious customs of the epoch'] – the *época* in question is Porfirian, and pre-Revolutionary. The opening epigraph of the book, a 'proverbio picaro' ['lewd saying'], verbalises the lubricious *guiño* of the cover: 'Cosa la madre, cosa la hija, cosa la sábana que las cobija' ['The mother's an object, so is the daughter, and so is the sheet that covers them'].[71]

This *picardía* [scurrilous comment] does summarise at least one of the modalities of the *sábana* in Mexican photography as well as convey some of its power as regards the objectification and plasticity of the female form in the visual arts. The visual scherzo of Manuel Álvarez Bravo's *Sábana caída* [*Fallen Sheet*] (1940) empties the textile form of bodily content in favour of hermeneutic play.[72] But there is an unsubtle connective tissue between this ascetic image and the choreography of sheets in his earlier series *Sábanas* (1933), in which Lola is again inveigled as a model and appears literally between the sheets hanging on parallel washing lines. In one of the shots she gracefully raises the edge of a dark veil over her profile while she stands between oceanic white sheets; Álvarez Bravo allegorised this gesture in the title, *El eclipse*.[73] In this image and in an untitled one[74] where, still between the sheets, she adopts the pose of a marine look-out searching the horizon, a hand shielding her eyes, arguably she is thoroughly *ensabanada*. In his late nudes, *Tentanciones en casa de Antonio* [*Temptations in Antonio's House*] (1970)[75] and *El trapo negro* [*The Black Cloth*] (1986)[76] with sheet and cloth creating a peep-show, nothing can rescue the material from the rhetoric of 'La ley de la sábana' and its flaccid aesthetic.[77] Despite first impressions, in the draped nude *Enotea* (n.d.)[78] Lola could be providing a derisory exposé and rotation of Gabriel Figueroa's sheeted Indian women standing monolithically looking out to sea in the film *La perla*,[79] directed by Emilio Fernández in 1945.[80] Shot in her studio, a nude model's body emerges uneuphemistically entire to stare down, lips pulled back over teeth, open mouth aligned with other orifices, her *ombligo* [belly button] and hirsute pubic triangle, wearing the shape of the *sábana* with challenging impudence. Effectively one-eyed, she reflects back the acquisitive desires of a female *polifemo* (or perhaps an 'ojosaura' ['eyesaurus'] adapting Frida Kahlo's term from her painted diary) with Lola Álvarez Bravo, photographer, beneath the pantomime black drape of her box.[81]

Lourdes Almeida's headless sheeted female nude kneaded into a rocky crevice, part of the series *Lo que el mar me dejó* [*What the Sea Left Me*]

(1988), wears its allegorical eloquence – its 'huellas desnudas' ['naked traces'] – like a badge of honour salvaged from the bric-à-brac of Mexican photographic modernism and a Western pictorial tradition which liked to personify liquid elements in the female form,[82] works such as Ingres's (1856) and Courbet's (1868) respective *The Source*[83] but also of the nineteenth-century Mexican academician Juan Cordero's *La bañista [The Bather]*.[84] Here a maiden in a tropical glade dips her toe in a pool, her body covered demurely by a white drape that ripples in anticipation of her immersion.

Kati Horna's assemblage, *Fetiche I (Oda a la necrofilia)* (1962), sets the scene for innumerable acts of devotional allusion to photographic scenographies and props past – in a side-swipe at the arcana of effect that exploit the mortuary drama of empty sheets – the false sentiment of photographic melancholy whose solemnity is a sham (figure 7.12).[85] The clutched or mangled sheet provides a gestural resource so heavy with mute expression that it can never be wrung dry. After all, countless *dolorosas* [mourning women] and *duelos* [wakes] elevate the tone of national photographic spectacle (as previously in the pictorial narratives of revolutionary struggle). See, for instance, Graciela Iturbide's *Chiapas* (1975) with its austere framing of three grieving women, part of an unspecified Pietà.[86] It offers an uncanny rehearsal of Eugene Smith's hyperbole and staging of feeling in his celebrated photo-essay for *Life* magazine, 'Spanish Village: It Lives in Ancient Poverty and Faith', of 1950.[87] One of the most reproduced images, manipulated in the darkroom to heighten the contrasts between inky black and cadaverous white, shows grieving women, heads covered, in semi-shadow at a wake. The light wafts from the dead man's visage as if it must infallibly infect the female mourners with its dubious halo.

Huipil de tapar

Huipil (del náhuatl: uipilli): vestido femenino de lienzos tejidos, cosidos sin mangas, especie de túnica, de uno a tres lienzos rectangulares. ...
Huipil de tapar: prenda femenina usada para tapar la cabeza.[88]
[*Huipil* (from the Nahuatl: uipilli): feminine dress of woven cloths, stitched without sleeves, a kind of tunic, made up of one to three rectangular cloths ...
Huipil de tapar: feminine garment used to cover the head.]

Looking at the woven fabrics and textiles, a paler shade of white, of Mariana Yampolsky's veiled, wrapped or sheathed figures – her rural and

Figure 7.12 © Kati Horna, *Fetiche I (Oda a la necrofilia)* (1962).

proletarian celebrants, pilgrims, ordinary *transeúntes* [passers-by] – is to look through a pane of shaved alabaster. Her work reclaims the opacity and impenetrable secrecy of 'the over there'. Often the form of layered and folded textiles supplants or overcomes the supporting figure: the garment is unavailing – it wears the wearer or vapourises like a white shadow in the frame. See, for instance, the incandescent crumpled figure of *Primera comunión* [*First Communion*] (1992).[89] In her photographs, draped and folded cloth can offer a kind of rigorous abstraction, a consummate avoidance of the subject. An abundance of cloth extends its traceless bodies across Yampolsky's work, nesting the Indian predilection for a white ground into the symbolism of Catholic worship and its pristine folds, filigrees and tunics. Sensitive to the popular accusation of spirit-catcher and voyeur, Yampolsky has often recorded the barriers to vision and undermined facile visuality. An amateur collector of Mexican textiles (like Luis Márquez before her), her wanderings have tended to concentrate on the terrain of the subtlest cotton weave and maguey thread in Mexico State, Puebla, Veracruz, Oaxaca. The materials of *mestizo* and Indian manufacture, and especially their varied density of weave, have often filtered her focal declensions, fashioning the poetic tactility of textures so typical of her handling of vernacular elements. Let us turn finally to an image which sheds a glimpse of Yampolsky the photographer.

The title of the well-known photograph *Huipil de tapar* (*c*.1970s) (figure 7.13) borrows the actual term for a regional variant of the pre-Hispanic garment and poeticises it visually. The triangular white head covering blows backwards as an Indian woman wearing an *enredo*-shift

Figure 7.13 Mariana Yampolsky, *Huipil de tapar* (n.d.), Pinotepa Nacional, Oaxaca. Courtesy of © FCMY.

walks away from the camera carrying her shadow before her. Her *tonalli* or shadowy soul – unensnared apparition – walks before her.[90] A sliver of shadow lying obliquely on the ground implicates the photographer and acts like the tenuous purchase of a supplicant on the most heartfelt votive plea. One of the photographer's fondest unrealised projects was to publish a book on death and its figurations in Mexico. Mariana Yampolsky had snapped and gathered material since her beginnings as a photographer. One is prompted to wonder, after her recent death, whether that invisible book, the one she never published, was perhaps dimly transcribed in the floating *lienzos* of her photographs, those recurrent textile torsions, and their language of binding and blinding absence. For the cotton cloth in its guise as *lienzo*, served as a 'lieux de mémoire' ['place of memory'] for both pre-conversion indigenous genealogy and the seventeenth-century narrative of localised Catholic revelation.[91] The membranous or veil-fine signifying cloth of pagan and Christian memorialisation conflated place with sight. In Yampolsky's photographs *huipiles* and other indigenous *indumentaria* [clothing] wear a fibred cultural history and its pre-conquest geography on textile in layers of deracinated referents, allusive but now inarticulate.

A way of discerning Yampolsky's perspicacious retention of evasion, omission and reticence in her photographs of indigenous individuals and communities, through what I have termed the 'torsions of the veil', is to compare her work with that of her one-time mentor, Lola Álvarez Bravo. Unlike Lola, Yampolsky seemed to recognise that strategies of disappearance in the performative domain of the veil and other coverings can be affirmative and defensive manipulations in relation to ethnocentric classifications, hegemonic cultural nationalism and, perhaps most significantly, the domain of photographic visuality itself. A celebrated photograph taken by Lola Álvarez Bravo (1946) of a funeral procession in the Indian village of Yalalag, Oaxaca stands back to let slightly out-of-focus veiled forms file past in a downward, flowing curve of white garments – veils and *huipiles*. It requires only a further slight adjustment, a degree of focal slur, on the part of the viewer to experience fully the white blur of pious humility. The feet of these multiples of the 'Indian pilgrim' are roughly outlined in shadow, accentuating the illusion of a host of levitating figures floating between the worldly and the otherworldly. Their evanescent shadow-prints help to reinscribe the atemporal portentousness of Indian culture as spectacle and national aphorism.

In Yampolsky's images of Mazahua and Nahua women which I have arranged together to better range over the remarkable density and complexity of folds and layers of the partially or wholly veiled figures and half-glimpsed, muffled or missing physiognomies, Mexican photography's fabric of vision is full of threads, webs and meshes knotted and overlayed, subtly cultivating its elisions rather than its demonstrations – casting the materials of ethnographic exhibition into the uncertain space of the always-to-be-revealed and always-questionable singularity of the shot – and its subjects (figures 14 and 15). It may well be that Yampolsky's focal attraction for hand-made or hand-stitched cloth speaks of her effort to include an active and productive principle to offset the insidious pacification of the directed shot and the spectacle of difference to which Indian culture has been notoriously subject. The productive agency of such manufacture – its fashions and wearability – personalises gestures and costume to the point of indecipherability. In other words, Yampolsky's images seem to resist the codification of costume – cloth is deregulated and even eccentric – even though she is attentive to the social rituals in which it is present. It is my contention that Yampolsky's images are not so much dignifying the imprint of labour, as in the 1920s close-up framing of pre-industrial vernacular materials, as they are cutting down to size the social status of photographic practice, its industrial processes and totalising proclivities. In the last decade the adaptive ingenuity of motley and broken-backed refashionings occupied the increasingly urban ranginess of her material.[92] Manufacture and the manufactured prised her away from the fabrications of the auteurist darkroom, which she renounced early in her career. Looking at her detailed obliquity, as in *Falda huichola* [*Huichol Indian Skirt*] (1993), with its hem of cross-stitched graffiti stick figures and toy vehicle, one might conclude that 'En el detalle está el chiste: pero cada detalle es también un chiste, una trampa de la fe' ['The devil is in the detail: but each detail is also a joke, a trick of faith'].

Coda: En que el/la fotográfo/a procura desmentir que el suyo:
es un afán caduco y bien mirado,
es cadáver, es polvo, es sombra,
es nada. (from Sor Juana Inés de la Cruz)[93]

[Coda: In which the photographer tries to refute that his/her:
exertions are decrepit and seen clearly,
no more than a corpse, dust, shadow,
nothingness.]

Flor Garduño's intriguing coffee-table catalogue of studio female nudes and still lifes of fruits and flowers redeployed to a remarkable degree the symbolic accoutrements of the archive of Mexican and Mexicana photographic and pictorial props, with considerable attention being paid to the veil, drape and *rebozo* and to their clinging, unlacerated permeability.[94] Allegories of the fecund seasons, allusions to germinating

Figure 7.14 Mariana Yampolsky, *Danza de las pastoras* (1989). Courtesy of © FCMY.

Figure 7.15 Mariana Yampolsky, *Peregrinos* (n.d.). Courtesy of © FCMY.

seed, antenatal pods, botanical phalluses, verdant protrusions, pot-bellied clay vessels, gothic familiars (felines, crows), sharp-nosed and serpentine fish conjure the terrain of a telluric Venus, the tutelary mythopoetic icon cited in the book. Nudes become the personifications of fruits and plants, as in *La nopala* [*The Cactus Woman*] (1998), in what constitutes a signature mutation by a photographer enchanted by the medium's potential for myth-making and mysticficatory refashionings. Female bodies and organic forms are arranged to maximise the symbiotic relationship between the implied subject and the all-too-apparent order of things.

Perhaps equally noteworthy in Garduño's book of highly polished production values is the degree of seemingly unquestioning citation of a Mexicanist aesthetic of limpid contrasts, spot-lit textures and elegant poses which borrows effects from both pictorialism and modernism. It is debatable to what extent the disturbing 'torsions of the veil' (the ironising and interrogating of demonstrable identities which we have encountered in some of the analogue photographers surveyed in this study) is toned down or silenced altogether by the occasionally emotive vacuity of stilled gesture, gratifying symmetries and contrived gendered symbolism. In the surreal *Aparición* (1998), a seemingly headless torso, face and shoulders shrouded in a blanking black veil emerge from the fish-mouth opening of a rice paper armature of a skirt. In the self-evidently entitled *La del velo* [*The Woman of the Veil*] (1997), we encounter a full-frontal nude figure posing behind a semi-transparent veil which she holds obediently above her with outstretched arms. In the studied elegance of *Gabriela* (1999), we have a nude torso with profiled head and shoulders draped and framed by a *rebozo*-like covering. In *Carla* (1998), the frontal view of the torso is overlayed by the flower and leaf patterns picked out through the lace veil that the model holds in a cruciform stretch before her. In *Terciopelo negro* [*Black Velvet*] (1999), we are presented with a back view of a darkly pigmented reclining nude, curves gilded by light, the head and torso receding into quasi-invisibility beneath a brackish, looping drape. Of the eight exercises on the draped and veiled female nude (and self-aware manipulations are indicated by the recurrent grid motif sectioning some of the images) two stray into the terrain of the metaphysical and supernatural, with not a few lingering glances at the archive of tried and tested photographic *artimañas* [snares] past. In *Rose* (1998), the most evocative composition in the context of the present study, a visage doubly veiled by shadow and a semi-translucent patterned scarf hovers precariously against the dark, eyes staring confidently at the lens, the mouth's shapely pout emphasised by the clinging veil. An inverted painted cameo portrait appears like a visionary imprint on the forehead with its mystic eyes up-ending the world. In *Magdalena* (1999), the model in full transparent body veil holds our gaze vigilantly, rigidly backed into a votive colonial canvas representing the virgin and child which has been turned on its side so that the heads and torsos of the figures protrude in a vertical line behind the penitential nude.

In contrast to the directed, markedly finished fantasies of Garduño, the photojournalist Francisco Mata Rosas (b. 1958), with his defence of documentary photography as an 'acción del pensamiento'[95] alert to its own paradoxes and ambiguities, re-encountered and sought to renegotiate the hermeneutics of the *Velo de la Verónica* – a totemic artefact of Mexican photography – in his recent book on popular celebrations.[96] Already in the mid-1990s, the mixed-media artist Mónica Castillo (b. 1961) revisited the iconicity of the sudarium as a parable of the material trace in the representational arts.[97] In *Autorretrato mimético* [*Mimetic Self-portrait*] (1996), a work of assimilative provocation, she pressed her own etherealised visage on a gauze-like veil, tresses of hair radiating through the cotton fabric, the semi-transparent cloth pinned up as in Zurbarán, producing a 'spontaneous' self-portrait and sacrosanct relic.[98] Perhaps more suggestively still, the deftly handled work effects the uncanny surfacing of the subordinated, supporting figure of Saint Veronica herself projecting through the dependent alterity of the represented other. In this meditative construction, the mystical *trompe-l'œil* is exposed and reinstated as in the most acute applications of Mexican photography, where revelation is always party to an affirmative and self-critical concealment.

Notes

1. D. and D. Cordry, *Mexican Indian Costumes* (Austin/London, 1968), 50.
2. D.F. Rubín de la Borbolla, 'Supervivencia y fomento de las artes populares indígenas de América', *América Indígena*, 19 (1959), 5–42 (26).
3. W. Benjamin, *Selected Writings*, ed. M. Bullock and M.W. Jennings (Cambridge, MA/London, 1996), I: 276–7.
4. J.A. Rodríguez, 'Una nueva memoria', *Cuartoscuro*, 33 (1998), 16.
5. Ibid., 18–19.
6. Reproduced in Yampolsky, *Imagen*, 113.
7. Kismaric, *Manuel Álvarez Bravo*, 104.
8. N. Bryson, *Looking at the Overlooked: Four Essays on Still Life Painting* (London, 1990), 31.
9. Ibid., 30.
10. A. Morales (ed.), *El Gran Lente: José Antonio Bustamante Martínez* (Mexico City, 1992), 74–5.
11. For examples of the Veil of St Veronica (and 'El Divino Rostro') in popular votive art, see C.M. Lovell and E. Netto Calil Zarur (eds), *Art and Faith in Mexico: The Ninenteenth-Century Retablo Tradition* (Albuquerque, 2001), 128–31. For a seventeenth-century Mexican original, see A. López de Herrera's *El Divino Rostro* in the collection of the Museo Nacional de Arte.

12. For a discussion of the problem of representing theophany in visionary painting, see V.I. Stoichita, *Visionary Experience in the Golden Age of Spanish Art* (London, 1995) 30.
13. H. Fox Talbot, *Some Account of Photogenic Drawing or the process by which Natural Objects may be made to delineate themselves without the aid of the Artist's Pencil* (London, 1839), 5.
14. *After Death – What?*, tr. W.S. Kennedy (London, 1909), 306.
15. *Der Kampf Um Die Materialisations-Phänomene* (Munich, 1914) 98.
16. Reproduced in J.A. Rodríguez (ed.), *Bernice Kolko: fotógrafa* (Mexico City, 1996), n.p.n.
17. Reproduced in Y. Andrade, *Los velos transparentes, las transparencias veladas*, (Villahermosa, 1988), 42, with an essay by C. Monsiváis. It is interesting to note that the Vatican under Pope John Paul II demoted Saint Veronica from the official list of authenticated figures but this has not affected her popularity in Mexican Holy Week pageants. See e.g. the photographic reportage by Alejandra Platt with several images of the sudarium carried in procession, including *Cuatro niñas representan a las tres Marías y a La Verónica*: 'Semana Santa en Tecoripa, Sonora', *México Desconocido*, 290 (2001), 10–17 (15).
18. Reproduced in Iturbide, *Sueños*, 64. For a detailed discussion of this photograph, see Ch. 6. For the significance of the Guadalupana in photography, see the discussion of Lola Álvarez Bravo's *La Patrona* in Ch. 5.
19. García, *México*, 11.
20. A. Bartra, 'Ver para descreer', *Luna Córnea*, 13 (1997), 72. Mora's photograph *Cadáver de Emiliano Zapata* was the centre of a montage of death masks of the revolutionary general, first published in *El Demócrata*, 10 April 1922.
21. Reproduced in A. Gómez de Tuddo and C. Zarebsk, *México inédito* (Mexico City, 1999), 46.
22. Reproduced in Méndez and Yampolsky, *Lo efímero*, II: 523. The ethnographic content of this work was compiled by the editors, with photographs by Manuel Álvarez Bravo and Mariana Yampolsky.
23. For Teresa de Avila's first complete vision of Christ resurrected, see Stoichita, *Visionary Experience*, 45.
24. For a discussion of Meyer's critique of analogue photography and nationalism in Mexico, see Ch. 6.
25. Reproduced in Meyer, *Espejo*, 54, 18, 19 respectively, with an essay by Carlos Monsiváis.
26. A. de los Reyes, *Cine y sociedad en México, 1896–1930* (Mexico City, 1993), 2: 80, with period photographs.
27. E.A. Maser (ed.), *Cesare Ripa – Baroque and Rococo Pictorial Imagery: The 1758–60 Hertel Edition of Ripa's 'Iconologia' with 200 Engraved Illustrations*, (New York, 1971), n.p.n. See also S. Sebastian, 'Los libros de emblemas: Uso y difusión en Iberoamérica', in J. Cuadriello (ed.), *Juegos de ingenio y agudeza: la pintura emblemática en la Nueva España* (Mexico City, 1994) 56–82.
28. F. Frankel and G.M. Whitesides, *On the Surface of Things: Images of the Extraordinary in Science* (San Francisco, 1997), 13.
29. On the relationship between spectators and representations of sacred narrative, see B. Merback, *The Thief, the Cross and the Wheel: Pain and the Spectacle of Punishment in Medieval and Renaissance Europe* (London, 1999), 45–48.

30. For the illustration of the statue of Lucina from Vicenzo Cartari's *Imagini de gli dei delli antichi* (1626), see Elkins, *Pictures of the Body*, 57.
31. Reproduced in Yampolsky, *La raíz y el camino*, with an essay by Elena Poniatowska, 16.
32. Reproduced in Kismaric, *Manuel Álvarez Bravo*, 127.
33. For a discussion of reflexivity, see Ch. 5.
34. Reproduced in Andrade, *Los velos transparentes*, 37.
35. R. Doniz, *Casa Santa* (Mexico City, 1986), 35, 43, with an essay by A. Alatorre.
36. E. Fernández Ledesma, *La gracia de los retratos antiguos* (Mexico City, 1950).
37. Ibid., 19–21.
38. Ibid., 20.
39. Ibid., 25–6.
40. Benjamin, *Selected Writings*, 272–5.
41. Kismaric, *Manuel Álvarez Bravo*, 124, 163.
42. See M. Álvarez Bravo, *Variaciones (1995–1997)* (Mexico City, 1997).
43. N. Rosenblum, *A World History of Photography* (New York, 1989), 443.
44. This collection is reproduced in V. Blasco, L. García-Noriega y Nieto, C. Pantoja et al. (eds), *Luz y tiempo: La colección fotográfica formada por Manuel Álvarez Bravo para la Fundación Cultural Televisa*, 3 vols. (Mexico City, 1995); now housed in Casa Lamm, see <www.coleccionxalvarezbravo.org.mx/>.
45. On this subject, see e.g. A.B. Cuéllar, cited in R. Pérez Montfort, 'Notas sobre el estereotipo de la Tehuana', *Acervos: Boletín de los Archivos y Bibliotecas de Oaxaca*, 19 (2000), 45–52, first published in *El Universal*, 8 June 1924: 'si hay en México regiones donde surjan instintivas maravillosas visiones de la gracia primitiva como griegas concepciones, es aquella faja ardiente que separa los dos mares como abrazo omnipotente donde reina la Tehuana con sus bailes y cantares' ['if there are regions in Mexico where emerge instinctive marvellous visions with the primitive grace of Greek conceptions, it is that burning strip which separates the two seas like an omnipotent embrace, where the Tehuana reigns with her dances and songs']. Both pictorialist and modernist artists and photographers celebrated the region and its culture through the emblematic curiosity of its Indian women: e.g. the photographers (excluding the Álvarez Bravos) C.B. Waite, Hugo Brehme, Lorenzo Becerril, Sotero Constantino Jiménez, Edward Weston, Tina Modotti and Luis Márquez; and the artists Saturnino Herrán, Adolfo Best Maugard, Roberto Montenegro, Diego Rivera, Miguel Covarrubias, and Frida Kahlo.
46. J. Alton, *Painting with Light* (Berkeley/Los Angeles, 1995), 187–90.
47. See e.g. George Rommey's *Nature Unveiling Herself to the Infant Shakespeare* (1786) in A. Hollander, *Fabric of Vision: Dress and Drapery in Painting*, (London, 2002), 113, and A. Vesalius's *De humani corporis fabrica librorum epitome* (1542).
48. See e.g. Giovan-Battista Manfredini's painted terracotta figure *Female Bust with Open Abdomen* (1773–6) in Kemp and Wallace, *Spectacular Bodies*, 66.
49. For the still of the scene, see J. Pierre, 'Buñuel gótico, prerrafaelista y surrealista', in J.J. Vázquez (ed.), *Luis Buñuel: El ojo de la libertad* (Madrid, 2000), 105–25 (107).
50. N. Fry, (ed. and tr.), *Luis Buñuel: Three Screenplays – Viridiana, The Exterminating Angel, Simon of the Desert* (New York, 1969), 91–2.
51. S. Pitol, *Juan Soriano: El perpetuo rebelde* (Mexico, 1993), 30.
52. Ibid., 19.

53. From August Genin, *Notes sur le Méxique*, 1908–10, in C. Barros and M. Buenrostro (eds), *Las once y serenooo!: Tipos mexicanos, siglo XIX* (Mexico City, 1994), 66.
54. B. Garduño Pulido, A. Híjar, J. Villanueva Hernández et al., *Luz Jiménez: Símbolo de un pueblo milenario, 1897–1965* (Mexico City, 2000), 94.
55. Kismaric, *Manuel Álvarez Bravo*, 65.
56. Ibid., 83.
57. Debroise, *Lola Álvarez Bravo*, plate 35.
58. P. Albers and K. Cordero-Reiman, *Tina Modotti: The Mexican Renaissance*, Paris, 2000), 74–5.
59. *Alquimia*, 10 (2000), cover.
60. Bonfil and Monsiváis, *A través del espejo*, 149.
61. J. Guerrero, *La génesis del crimen en México* (Mexico City, 1996), 136–7.
62. *Artes de México*, 142 (1971), 34.
63. G. de Gante, 'Piropos al rebozo', *Artes de México*, 142 (1971), 47,
64. R. López Velarde, *Obras*, ed. J.L. Martínez (Mexico City, 1979), 84–5.
65. See e.g. P. le Chanu, *Il drapeggio: Taccuino di disegni* (Paris, 2002).
66. See e.g. *Drawing after Dürer's Pillow* (1999) from Toledo's series of graphic works on the motif of the bed, in D. Ades, C. Lampert, C. Monsiváis et al., *Francisco Toledo* (London, 2000), 143. For Rippey's lesbian 'boudoir scene' *El sueño de la razón* [*The Sleep of Reason*] (1991), which reinterprets the voyeuristic fin-de-siècle *deshabillé*, see Barrios Lara et al., *El cuerpo aludido*, 103.
67. See e.g. Orozco's female nude *Espejo* [*Mirror*] (1930), Ruiz's *El sueño de la Malinche* [*The Dream of Malinche*] (1939), Kahlo's *Mi nacimiento* [*My Birth*] (1931), and Guerrero Galván's *La sábana blanca* [*The White Sheet*] (1940).
68. P. Dueñas, *Las divas en el Teatro de Revista mexicano* (Mexico City, 1994).
69. A. Vargas, *La Casa de Cita: Mexican Photographs from the Belle Époque* (London, 1986), 72.
70. Barrios Lara et al., *El cuerpo aludido*, 129.
71. S. Quevedo y Zubieta, *La ley de la sábana* (Mexico City,1935), cover. The final chapter is suggestively entitled 'De cómo la sábana conyugal se transformó en sudario' 'Of how the conjugal sheet became a shroud'.
72. Kismaric, *Manuel Álvarez Bravo*, 128.
73. *Ibid.*, 91.
74. M. Álvarez Bravo , *303 Photographies, 1920–1986* (Paris, 1986), plate 50.
75. Kismaric, *Manuel Álvarez Bravo*, 212.
76. Álvarez Bravo, *Photographs*, 37, with an essay by F. Kaufman.
77. For a selection of Álvarez Bravo's nudes from the 1930s to the 1990s, see M. Álvarez Bravo, *Nudes: The Blue House* (New York, 2002).
78. Blanco et al., *Lola Álvarez Bravo*, 147.
79. For the still, see J. Tuñón, *Los rostros de un mito: Personajes femeninos en las películas de Emilio 'Indio' Fernández* (Mexico City, 2000), 121.
80. For Lola's interest in playing with the sublimated eroticism of the martyred or suffering body of Christian iconography, see e.g. her female nude studies for *Tríptico de los martirios*, reproduced in Blanco et al., *Lola Álvarez Bravo*, 140–2.
81. Lola's friends Frida Kahlo and Guillermo Meza both coined images of a cyclopean monster in the 1940s. The former invented 'El horrendo ojosauro

primitivo', the latter a voracious beast, *Polifemo* (pen and ink, 1940) and *Polifemo* (oil on canvas, 1944).

82. *Mujer x mujer*, n.p.n., with an essay by E. Poniatowska.
83. S. Faunce, 'Courbet: Feminist in Spite of Himself', in A. Bond (ed.), *Body* (Sidney, 1997), 104.
84. E. García Barragán, 'Juan Cordero: el primer muralista y su siglo', *Saber Ver*, 41 (1998), 12–69 (68).
85. A.L. Anza and C. González, 'Una vida onírica en obra y amigos', *Cuartoscuro*, 50 (2001), 27–41 (37).
86. Iturbide, *Images*, 106–7.
87. J.T. Hill and G. Mora (eds), *W. Eugene Smith: Photographs, 1934–1975* (New York, 1998), 127.
88. C. Mapelli Mozzi, J. Vexler, I. Weitlaner Johnson et al., *El textil mexicano* (Mexico City, 1986), 44.
89. M. Yampolsky, *The Edge of Time* (Austin, Texas, 1998), plate 31, with texts by E. Poniatowska, S. Berler and F. Reyes Palma.
90. On the indigenous term *tonalli* and the physicality of the soul in pre-Hispanic beliefs, see J.L.M. Furst, *The Natural History of the Soul in Ancient Mexico* (New Haven, 1995).
91. See R.L. Kagan, *Urban Images of the Hispanic World, 1493–1793* (New Haven, 2000), 115: 'The *lienzos* were painted cloths upon which individual communities throughout New Spain recorded genealogical and geographical information pertinent to their history ... they were apparently once ubiquitous, integral to each community's definition of itself'.
92. See e.g. Yampolsky's humorous *Antz* (1997), where a woman street-seller sits embroidering a cloth with traditional flower designs flanked by mass-produced towels with Disney motifs hung out on a line like so many *lienzos* or cinema screens and wearing a white T-shirt imprinted with a Disney-inspired caricature of a bunny: M. Yampolsky, 'Lo efímero y lo eterno', *Tierra Adentro*, 108–9 (2001), n.p.n.
93. A.S. Trueblood (tr.), *A Sor Juana Anthology* (Cambridge, MA/London, 1988), 94.
94. F. Garduño, *Inner Light – Still Lifes and Nudes* (New York, 2002).
95. For Mata Rosas's lecture 'Fotografía documental paradoja de la realidad' at the Centro de la Imagen in 1995, see <http://zonezero.com/magazine/articles/mata/matatextsp.html>.
96. See F. Mata Rosas, *México Tenochtitlán* (Mexico City, 2005).
97. See also Paula Santiago's *Huipil* (1997), made of rice paper, blood and knitted hair in a glass box, in O. Debroise, S. Navarrete and P. Schneider, *Frida Kahlo, Diego Rivera and 20th-Century Mexican Art: The Jacques and Natasha Gelman Collection* (San Diego, 2000), 140. For Castillo's self-portraits, see L.-M. Lozano (ed.), *Mónica Castillo, (1993–2004)* (Mexico City, 2004).
98. A. Noreña, 'Mujeres en la avanzada escultórica', *Tierra Adentro*, 108–9 (2001), n.p.n.

Chapter 8

Relics and Disjecta in Modernism and Post-Modernism:

A Comparative Study of Archaeology in Contemporary Photography and Multimedia Art

My work is always a fragmented place; it's a place that basically is filled with *tepalcates*, these little pieces of clay that can be found everywhere and that cannot be reconstructed. I inhabit a space that is an archaeological site – it informs my reality.[1]

La loza suave de Guadalajara fué muy usada en tiempos coloniales, sobre todo para contener agua potable y los artefactos sin vidriar de esta pasta, que era porosa, blanquizca, rojiza y negra, se denominan *búcaros*. En el siglo XVII, tanto en México como en España se hizo de moda entre las señoras coleccionar estos búcaros, y muchas de ellas, atraídas por el agradable olor que despedía esta cerámica, dieron en romper pequeños fragmentos y comerlos'.[2]

[The soft china of Guadalajara was widely used in colonial times, especially to contain drinking water and the unglazed artefacts of this material, which was porous, off-white, russet and black, are termed *búcaros*. In the seventeenth century in Mexico as well as Spain it became fashionable amongst ladies to collect these receptacles, and many of them, attracted by the pleasant odour which emanated from this ceramic, were given to breaking off small pieces and eating them.]

These same characteristics of pre-Spanish Mexican art we can find later in colonial art and in folk art, although, of course, modified by the importation of European ideals. In the exhibition being held in this museum, the observant public will note that Mexican art is not just a name given to art which happens to come from one part of the world, but that there is a unity, an inspiration, a style which is truly Mexican.[3]

Perhaps the topos of the fragment, with its neo-classical provenance, is after all the legacy bestowed on modernism by the Mexican Revolution, with its iconoclastic demolition of the 'old' order, its eviscerated landscapes of battle littered with body parts, its aesthetic and social carnage. Relics and disjecta, conflating the material and the corporeal, offer a poetic of decomposition and expulsion; an archaeology of the broken, the maimed and the partially visible held together by faith in the decipherability of the manipulated object and the forensic trace. Run the images of the ruined and truncated in a newsreel montage of anatomical excision from photography and painting: from 1913 Agustín Casasola's shots of incinerated corpses in the streets of the capital (the *Decena trágica*) [*The Tragic Ten Days*][4] – the stench of the still fuming remains forcing onlookers to use their hands as protective masks;[5] from 1914 Francisco Goitia's Zacatecan mortuary landscapes with the skeletelised remains of the lynched or his portrait of the gape-mouthed, decomposing head of a *soldadera* [female soldier], curdled paint oozing her features;[6] from 1919 Zapata's blood-spattered profile emerging from a tilted coffin in Agustín Casasola's memento mori;[7] from 1926 or 1927 Tina Modotti's close-up shots of labourers' calloused and caked feet and hands, accorded the poignant monumentality of petrified formations, geological friezes and broken archaic statuary; from 1927–8 any one of the postcard gallery of executed and mutilated *cristero*[8] 'martyrs', flanked or supported by the surviving members of their family, any one of these staged or even collaged photographs operating as forensic trace, personal relic and visual indictment.[9] From *c*.1926 there is Modotti's photograph of José Clemente Orozco's panel *The Destruction of the Old Order*: two monumental *sarape*-clad figures confront the ascending jagged mound of cubistic facets from which toppled classical columns protrude;[10] from the 1930s Agustín Jiménez's optically cropped, abstracted or magnified studies of industrial objects, natural produce, handicrafts and human bodies subject to perspectival distortion or elision;[11] from 1934 Manuel Álvarez Bravo's photograph *Obrero en huelga, asesinado* [*Assassinated Striking Worker*], the black blood and gore expelled from the shattered cranium, painting his jaw, shading down in the shape of an arterial tree on the dusty ground, unimpeded to the edge of the picture frame, the very grain of the soil made tactile in the higher resolution filter of blood,[12] or from the same period his study of a shock of human hair on a tiled floor or of a ruined jamb or collapsing threshold (figures 8.1 and 8.2).[13] In his work *ruina* encompasses archaeological and corporeal remains.[14] From the 1930s and 1940s anatomical disjecta and archaeological finds intersect in Frida Kahlo's detail of a rubbish bin disgorging its undigested matter in the painting *Mi vestido cuelga ahí* [*My Dress Hangs There*] (1933), while in her self-portrait, *La columna rota* [*The Broken Column*] (1944), a visual pun arrests the process of corporeal disintegration and dispersal which it prefigures in the cracking architectural support. Human relics and commodities combined, shorn tendrils of hair, lie scattered like pressed botanical specimens on the ground in Kahlo's *Autorretrato con pelo cortado* [*Self-portrait with Shorn Hair*] (1940). In *Sin esperanza* [*Without Hope*] (1945), partly consumed organic matter emanates like a viscous speech bubble or volcanic explosion from the mouth of a prostrate figure.[15] In Kahlo's surfaces brittle cracks and craquelure marks in expanding webs recur as painted motifs interlaced with the costume and travesties of visible identity. Frequently subterranean cross-sections divide the picture plane, foregrounding ancestral as well as organic accretions.

Archaeological artefacts, pre-Hispanic, colonial, folkloric and industrial paraphernalia, surface to *interrogate* identity in Kahlo,

Figure 8.1 Manuel Álvarez Bravo, *Hair on a Tile* (1930s). J. Paul Getty Museum, Los Angeles.

Modotti, Manuel Álvarez Bravo (and to assert it in Saturnino Herrán and Diego Rivera).[16] Dislodged and restored masks, pots, bones, necklaces, clay and stone gods, reed mats, eroded and mutilated walls, temple fragments are exposed to view as if from a nation-wide excavation and burial site. Found objects, ready-mades, composites, heirlooms, syncretic or pagan amulets and relics, are settled and posed in a figurative art of cumulative detail, uncertain as to whether its curious display described that 'Suave Patria' ['The Gentle Homeland'], which, in 1921, Ramón López Velarde made palpable through ordinary things and vernacular materials: 'Tu barro suena a plata, y en tu puño su sonora miseria es alcancía' ['Your clay sounds like silver, and in your grasp its resonant poverty is a child's treasure trove'].[17] In the period's paintings and photographs, such totemic objects are often reproduced not *in situ* but extracted and installed, recontextualised yet ahistorical, as in those abstract cameras of the private collector. In a lighter vein, devoid of portentous associations, pre-Hispanic salvage inspires an archaeological chic which glamourises as well as unwittingly parodies the ancestry-fixated Mexicanist aesthetic of the 1930s and the 1940s in publicity posters, pin-up calendars and other kinds of commercial imagery. Recently excavated Zapotec tombs (in Oaxaca) yield up clay statues which provide synthetic originary touchstones for prurient art-deco

Figure 8.2 Manuel Álvarez Bravo, *Ruin A* (1930s). J. Paul Getty Museum, Los Angeles.

female portraits and nudes, as in the highly coloured graphics of Armando Drechsler (figure 8.3), while museum classics, such as the enraptured statue of the Aztec God of flowers, dance and song, are redeployed as provocative props for collectible native bodies supported, flanked or crowned by 'primitive' artefacts.[18] Neo-Aztec or neo-Maya art-deco architecture sculpts metropolitan and parochial skylines, finding official patronage since the erection of *El Pabellón de México* [*The Mexican Pavillion*], designed by Manuel Amabilis for the Ibero-American Exhibition of Seville of 1929.[19]

Although not all fragmentation need imply damage, deterioration or reification, through my exhibition reel of stills, the broken, maimed, dislocated and severed run together into a visual lament on the transitory and corrosive nature of man's passage. Divulging as well as expelling or decomposing, ruptured surfaces and infringed boundaries offer an archaeological dramaturgy of discovery and reclamation marked by destruction and loss. Strewn with the fractured or infracted props and accoutrements, the bits and pieces of a dematerialised material world, these discrete representations seem to capture a vein of ruminative disenchantment and valediction. The centre apparently will not hold – nor should it – and it takes the prescience of a classical scholar like Alfonso Reyes to voice the melancholy elegy to disintegration of the post-Revolutionary decades in *Palinodia del polvo* [*A Palinode* or *A Recantation on Dust*] (1940):

> esta disgregación diminuta de todo lo que existe. Microscopía de las cosas, camino de la nada; aniquilamiento sin gloria; desmoronamiento de inercias; 'entropía'; venganza y venganza del polvo, lo más bajo del mundo ... Porvenir menguado! Polvo y sopor! No te engañes, gente que funda en subsuelo blando, donde las casas se hunden, se cuartean los muros y se descascan las fachadas.[20]

> [This minute disintegration of everything that exists. Microscopy of things, route of nothingness; annihilation without glory; downfall of inertias; 'entropy'; vengeance and more vengeance of dust, the basest thing in the world ... Diminished future! Dust and torpor! Do not deceive yourselves, people who build on soft subsoil, where houses sink, walls crack and facades peel.]

This highly edited anthology of visual fragments helps, I would argue, to underline the inescapable and knowing banality of archaeological tropes in contemporary photography and mixed-media installations that enact an exploration of the already explored, a recovery of the already found, a rearrangement of the already reconstructed. For the making of copies, representations and re-creations forms an integral part of the recuperation, construction and valorisation of antiquity since the Renaissance. The reproductive arts have registered, shaped and

Figure 8.3 Armando Drechsler, *Untitled* (c.1930s), art deco colour glamour poster incorporating funerary urn.

reconfigured the rediscovered sculptural or domestic object, cannibalising and appropriating the evidence of anterior cultures. Amongst contemporary Mexican artists, Silvia Gruner (b. 1959) for one has explored through performative embodiments the notions of reclaiming, ingesting and reincorporating associated with the ritual of communion with the pre-Hispanic *Patrimonio cultural* [*Cultural Heritage*]. In one of the photographs from *De las formas ancestrales o uno comiéndose su propia cola* [*Of Ancestral Forms or One Eating One's own Tail*] (1991), a serpentine braid of hair coiled around the artist's own neck (there are echoes here of Kahlo's own strangulating filiations with nature and culture through the torsions of neck ribbons) conflates a feminine memento, conquest trophy or penitential offering with a sacrosanct relic, to play on the reflexive cannibalising and conceptual circularity of transactions with an embodied, fetishised past (figure 8.4). In a second still, a labial infraction seen in close-up turns the phallocentric severed coil into a recyclable human relic ripe for sacramental ingestion (figure 8.5).[21]

Since before the eighteenth century in Mexico, 'archaeological' practice – its products, scenarios and documentation – have offered mastery of the myths of origin and autochthony. A ground yielding what had been overwritten by colonial rule, lapidary inscriptions pointing to a forgotten cultural literacy, served to emblematise the claims to

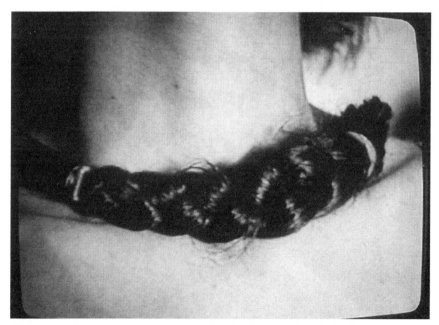

Figure 8.4 © Silvia Gruner, strangulating braid, colour still, from *De las formas ancestrales o uno comiéndose su propia cola* (1991). Courtesy of Silvia Gruner.

sovereignty and singularity of post-colonial regimes through the longevity of pre-conquest matrices. If in the nineteenth century the aesthetic exemplarity of such remains was problematic, the twentieth century completed the museological harvesting by ascribing beauty as well as essence to the pre-Hispanic, while edging, through ethnography and anthropology, towards the sacralisation of domestic implements and what might be termed the 'antiquing' of contemporary material culture.[22] A pre-Revolutionary photograph of an artisan in his workshop manufacturing replicas of pre-Hispanic figurines, from a series recording indigenous trades, is a salutary reminder of state promotion of archaeologically inspired collectibles before the epoch-making excavations of the 1930s,[23] especially when taken together with photographs of the dictator Porfirio Díaz, standing in front of the celebrated Aztec Calendar Stone in the National Museum (in 1905), or an engraved Maya stone plaque from Palenque in a precocious Eisensteinian superimposition of effigies.[24] Mexican photographers since Manuel Álvarez Bravo have used the medium's material status as producer of simulacra to replicate the pathos of the Indian artisan mimicking an ancestral object, without thereby purchasing or apprehending its essence. It could be argued that photography has a natural affinity with the archaeological fragment, as it too makes a virtue of the incomplete. It came as a belated realisation that the archaeological fragment, far from containing a diminished immanence, may point to a greater plenitude

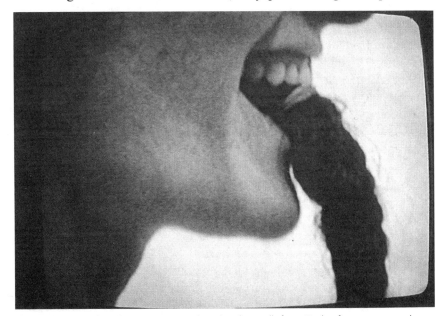

Figure 8.5 © Silvia Gruner, ingesting braid, colour still, from *De las formas ancestrales o uno comiéndose su propia cola* (1991). Courtesy of Silvia Gruner.

through its invocation of the imagination: the more ruined or partial, the more it inscribes – the unseen aggrandises the magnitude of the missing.[25] The focal attention in photography and painting lavished on ruptured surfaces from which contents emerge or are glimpsed, or matter is cross-sectioned, along with that on layers inscribed by traces or signs, brings to light conceits of ontological depth prompted by the spectacle of archaeological prospecting and salvage.

The productivity of fissures and cracks became singularly compelling in spectacular geological terms during the classic period of cultural nationalism with the emergence, in 1943, of an active volcano, the Paricutín, in a farmer's field. Dr Atl and Diego Rivera, amongst others, depicted the convulsive expression of subterranean forces and the generation of a new, mineral landscape.[26] If such fields had often turned up the clay heads and figurines of pre-Hispanic fertility rites, reinforcing the perception that only a fine membrane divided the present from the past, encapsulated in the 'Idolos tras los altares' ['Idols Behind Altars'] cliché,[27] the archaeologically inert would now be readily transposed through geological simile into a dormant but active substratum of tremendous recreative power. From the 1920s, the intermingling of the artistic avant-garde with archaeologists and connoisseurs, including visits to sites and recording commissions, propitiated the funnelling of amateur collecting and investigation into the visual arts. Diego Rivera, Miguel Covarrubias (1904–1957), Roberto Montenegro, Rufino Tamayo and Manuel Álvarez Bravo were all avid collectors of pre-Hispanic artefacts. Much of what they acquired was looted or casually unearthed and a considerable volume ingeniously faked. Covarrubias, a practised excavator, celebrated the revelatory power of 'dirt archaelogy', even as Álvarez Bravo set his lens on a sepulchral scavenging of mounds and interments in his photographs.[28] Disturbing refuse and remains, such archaeology peeled back compacted cultural deposits, unfurling significant marginalia. Visual artists followed in the infractions of the itinerant pot-hunter, unearthing a partially hidden and overwritten pre-contact Indian history: 'Practically the whole of the American continent is a vast archaelogical site … Throughout the centuries layer after layer of remains left by successive peoples … covered one another … everywhere the peasant's plows unearth broken pottery, clay figurines and sometimes … caches of gold objects'.[29]

Jorge Enciso articulated the period's collective homage to the earthenware fragment, to its heroic longevity, and to the residual potency of popular artefacts. In his influential study of ancient Mesoamerican seals, he provided a timely metaphor for the resurfacing and contemporaneity of pre-Hispanic manufacture and design. The symbolic marks incised in clay, and the possessive sign afforded by its imprint, could be revived and retraced through a process of frottage which made the latent symmetry grainily visible.

> De todos los vestigios de las antiguas culturas indígenas de México ninguno había atraído tanto mi curiosidad como esos pequeños objetos de barro cocido, llamados generalmente, sellos o pintaderas ... Encontré que retirando un papel delgado sobre el ornato y repasando el lápiz horizontalmente se obtenía una fiel reproducción; ... sólo quedaba entintar la huella obtenida.[30]

> [Of all the vestiges of the ancient cultures of Mexico, nothing had so attracted my curiosity as those small objects of baked clay, known generally as seals or stamps ... I discovered that by drawing a thin paper over the ornamentation and going over it horizontally with a pencil one obtained a faithful reproduction ... all that remained to be done was to ink the mark thus obtained.]

Enciso's finished rubbings delineated the past into the present as if in a cultural continuum. Photography (and the graphic arts) effected a similar revivalist rubbing. Full-page photographic illustrations of pre-Hispanic sculpture, ceramic art and lapidary pieces appeared in avant-garde cultural magazines in the 1920s, 1930s and 1940s, lit dramatically in studio so that the black background enhanced their grained plasticity. See, for instance, the display of archaic solemnity in the modernist *Forma* and *Artes Plásticas*. The aestheticising of the treatment of such objects with illumination effects borrowed from cinematography replicated the emergence from darkness into light of the buried ancestral artefact, which retained the mystery of its dim origins.

Manuel Álvarez Bravo's own poetic experiments with natural light, for instance, were conducted while he was engaged in the customary practice of producing reproductions of contemporary paintings and murals, along with archaeological and ethnographic items, for cultural publications.[31] The modernist habit of transposing old and new characterises his more personal ironies. In the 1940s Álvarez Bravo posed his American wife Doris Heyden (then a photographer who was raised in New Jersey, worked in New York and later turned to archaeology) alongside one of his trophy pieces from Western Mexico, subtly juxtaposing her profile and modish hairstyle with that of a stylised pre-Hispanic female effigy raised on a pedestal above her (figure 8.6).[32] Only rather belatedly has the importance of the genre of the still life and reproduction of fine art and archaeology for the development of his compositional style and visual metaphors begun to be recognised.[33] The place of classical statuary, other inanimate objects and architectural detail in the early history of photography is well known. It is the contention of this study that an archival density and melancholy or ironic reflexivity surrounds the creative photographs with/of archaeological motifs by Mexican modernists, such as Manuel Álvarez Bravo, and that contemporary Mexican photographers and multimedia artists, such as Silvia Gruner, Gerardo Suter (b. 1957), Pablo Ortiz Monasterio (b. 1952) and the collective *SEMEFO* (from *Servicio Médico Forense*), do not so much demystify canonical representations as reinvest in the metaphorical potential of archaeology – to resist official memory and collective amnesia.[34] The breakage of antiquity may foreshadow the ruins of modernity, but it also serves to substantiate the productivity of foundational myths.

Figure 8.6 Manuel Álvarez Bravo, *Portrait of Doris Heyden and Statue* (1940s). Private collection.

The publicising of excavations such as those conducted in the ruined city of Monte Albán by Alfonso Caso between 1931 and 1938, with their fabulous yield of subterranean gold treasure, certainly offered material for nationalist and anti-imperialist rhetoric; but the survival of such antiquities, disjointed and challenging to read, also invited aesthetic as well scholarly reconstruction.[35] Unearthing the past through invasive practices lent itself to telluric poetry which paid tribute to the way in which Mesoamerican languages commonly mark geographical and physical location with terms, 'locatives', derived from body parts – a corporeal semiotic of place and essence.[36] Alfonso Caso's own account of the momentous discovery and the making of the underground entry into the concealed chambers, 'la rendición final' ['the final surrender'] as he dubbed it, illustrates a kind of *mise en scène*, mined by photographers and mixedmedia artists such as Suter and Gruner in the post-nationalist, supposedly incredulous and sardonic 1990s:

La Montaña sagrada estaba al fin dispuesta a entregarse. Pero cómo se entrega una civilización que ha permanecido sepultada durante siglos? Pues se entrega lo mismo que una difícil mujer, o una plaza fuerte, después de un asedio prolongado ... mi primera impresión al entrar fue la de hallarse ante una inmensa riqueza. La luz de la lámpara hacía brillar las cuentas de oro y de cristal de roca, las perlas, los jades y las placas de turquesa desprendidas de sus antiguos mosaicos. En el centro destacaba una vasija cubierta de polvo. Acerqué la lámpara, iluminándola por dentro y la vasija cobró transparencia; estaba hecha de alabastro, el mármol mexicano llamado *tecali* ... Del polvo sobresalían ricos brazaletes y una corona con su pluma trabajadas en una fina lámina de oro. Las piedras grandes y chicas, desprendidas de la bóveda, habían lastimado la corona y, lo que era más sensible, destruyeron un cráneo revestido de turquesas.[37]

[The sacred mountain was at last ready to succumb. But how does a civilisation that has remained buried for centuries surrender itself? Well it yields like a difficult woman, or a fortress, after a prolonged siege ... On entering my first impression was that of finding myself before immense wealth. The light of the lamp made the gold and rock crystal beads, the pearls, jades and turquoise pieces dislodged from their ancient mosaics shine. In the centre a vessel covered in dust stood out. I brought the lamp closer, lighting it from inside, and the vessel became transparent; it was made of alabaster, the Mexican marble called *tecali* ... From the dust protruded rich bracelets and a crown with its feather worked in a fine sheet of gold. The small and large stones that had fallen from the domed ceiling, had damaged the crown and, what was more important, had destroyed a skull covered in turquoise.]

The photographic and videographic restagings of such discursively 'pregnant' scenarios and props in the work of Gruner and Suter tend not to pay parodic homage as in comparable extractions of autochthonous *médula* [marrow] in neo-Mexicanist figurative art of the 1980s (such as the works of Dulce María Nuñéz, Javier de la Garza, Elena Climent and Julio Galán), or as in the essentialist iconography of Chicano militancy. Instead of the contour-sealed ironic plagiarisms of the 'bad copy', we encounter fragmentariness devised as *catalizadora* [as a catalyst], every aspect of the broken inviting but not prescribing an imaginary reconstruction.[38] That is to say, that the most disassembled of Gruner and Suter's installations (for instance, as in the former's *Fetiches domésticos* [*Domestic Fetishes*] and the *Collares* [*Necklaces*] series), while seemingly unpicking the myths of archaeological epistemology and its ultra-nationalist associations, solicit a positive, re-creative response.[39] The cultural fetish is reborn in works which seek to calibrate the falsehoods of memory while aiding the production of further foundational fictions. Gruner's use of scrap and detritus to manufacture antiquities and revisit ancient sites has predictably led to her being cast in the role of the divinatory arranger of the scattered mosaic of contemporary Mexican culture: 'como una arqueóloga interesada en los frisos, las molduras, las huellas de otro tiempo' ['like an archaeologist interested in the friezes, mouldings and traces of another era']. Her work calls to mind 'una arqueología humana' ['a human archaeology'] or 'una especie de arqueología ... estética' ['a kind of archaeological aesthetic'].[40] Yet her declared interest in *tepalcates* or sherds of earthenware is predicated on the connotative potential of the fragment and the generative power of the incomplete, the unfinished ending of the remain – not on the fragment as a piece of a puzzling, hidden order. Her humorous response to such redemptive expectations of art (and national politics after the political blood-letting in the PRI?) is *Reparar* [*To Repair*] (1999), part of a multimedia project which took an oblique look at the City's chaotic infrastructure through the interaction between peripheral spaces, pedestrians and traffic, and which was later included in her 2000 exhibition *Circuito interior* [*Internal Circuit*].[41]

Gruner's work (figure 8.7) consists of an assemblage in grid format of twenty, uniformly sized monochromatic colour photographs of closely observed cracks in pavements – tears in the urban fabric which have been ineffectually sealed and stitched together by Sellotape.[42] The images resemble aerial shots of urban settlements connected by fractured transport arteries; or, more topically still, the doodled markings of seismic shocks. Curiously, the replicative aspects of the medium are directed as much to evidencing previous uses of such formats as to capturing the actual signs of disintegration. In the experimental 1970s the use of series, sequences and grids often signalled conceptual ideas about the equivocal nature of the image, but also of the artist-photographer. Gruner may well be disclosing and overwriting the material history of experimental practice in photography, incompletely assimilated in her own execution, as well as pointing to the unbridgeable gap between the object and image which requires a leap of faith or imagination. The

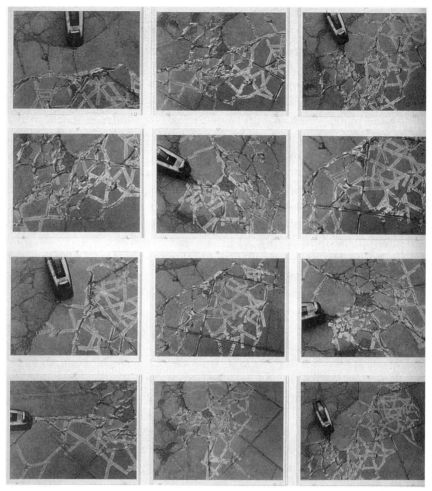

Figure 8.7 © Silvia Gruner, *Reparar* (1999), colour photographs, detail. Courtesy of Silvia Gruner.

adhesive properties of the supposedly transparent tape do not conceal its clumsy attempts at 'repair' and uncovered cracks remain, unsightly scars, outside those sections which have been covered. The photographs effectively resurface the traces of rupture without correcting, restoring or making right. The apparently orderly arrangement of adjacent but untouching frames does not offer a complete overall view in which the disparate coheres. The dividing spaces are made visible, not collaged over, so to speak, and the disposition suggests an illusory temporal contiguity and spatial alignment. So what might resemble a montage of shots stilled into its constitutive parts actually asserts the irreducibility of the fragment. The partial, intermittent presence of the tape dispenser, shot from different angles, brings to mind the mucous trajectory of a snail, a creature synonymous with futility from that still-life repertory of transitory and fugitive particulars so beloved of Álvarez Bravo, as in his classic *Calabaza y caracol* [Pumpkin and Snail] (1928) and the less familiar *Woman with Broken Glass* (1938–9).[43] Her assertion that in *Circuito interior* 'planteo la erosión física y espiritual de la persona' ['I'm addressing the physical and spiritual erosion of the person'] points, on the one hand, to an affinity with archaeology's dependence on the empirical vestige, the material trace, and, on the other – and what is perhaps more interesting as regards post-modern attitudes to the subject – her conjuring of human presence through the apparently impersonal site or material.[44] As an archaeologist Caso seems intent on restoring the grandeur of a humanist vision of the world when, in 1938, he writes of his unearthings and reconstuctions in Monte Albán: 'Behold a whole Mountain transformed by the hand of man!'.[45] Gruner, in contrast, may be disabused but the centrality her work accords to revisualising the artefact, the trace, the memento, the fetish, the vestige, temporally inscribed surfaces, speaks not so much of irreparable identities but of transcendent acts of individual experience. It is no coincidence that the manipulation of image-making in photography (the use of distorting lenses, or setting and action created and directed, scratching of negatives and so on) served to assert the non-mechanical aspects of the medium by emphasising the passage and manoeuvres of the individual imagination. Gruner is in some way impersonating through her work the past of photography as a replicative, experimental medium and rehistoricising its modernity. Equally, the startling tangibility achieved by Suter through the exacting contrasts, calibrated textures and heightened resolution of black-and-white prints and colour transparencies may be a testament to the significations of handled materials.

The five photographs that make up Gruner's *Grieta* [*Crack*] (1999–2000) (figure 8.8) stitch together visually discrete physiognomic

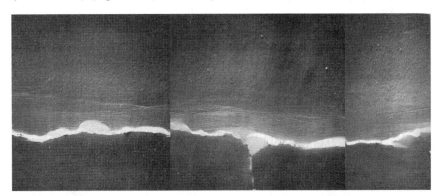

Figure 8.8 © Silvia Gruner, *Grieta* (1999–2000), colour photographs, detail. Courtesy of Silvia Gruner.

shots of sections of wall, the surface divided by an uneven crevice stretching across the frames.[46] Like individual building stones, the joins between them show subtly through the gradations of light and shadow, but the cracks do not always meet to create a continuous if jagged frontier across the shots. The work plays on a rhythm of *desencuentros* [disjunctions]. In some of the panels, the cracks ramify or create holes which strain the integrity of the piece. Lit from below, the crack resembles a lightning-tear in the negative, allowing the obliterated space behind to be glimpsed. The visual remains do not evidence identity but effects. Recourse to speculative similes gesture towards the unseen, presumed source, which perhaps is always necessarily elsewhere. Looking requires a reconstruction. The title serves as a prompt. It could be an archaeological or geological cross-section, a horizontal slice from a trench. Or stone panels in an underground chamber. Or a study of a crumbled edifice's supporting structure. And the forms of our cultural carrousel come to light in this exercise of uncertain affinities. Perhaps the technical procedure itself, using the chromogenic system, reinforces the layered image's symbolic charge, alluding to an invisible but immanent producer of visual fact. Colour images are created during the processing system, and in one of the methods the chemicals that will form the dyes are included in each layer of the emulsion and activated during processing.

Suter's increasingly mixed-media projects, moving from the monumental still photography of *Códices* (1991), his fanciful re-enactments of pre-Hispanic cosmovision through its surviving pre- and post-contact record, to an eclectic mix of analogical with video installations and objects in the mid-1990s, through *Cantos rituales* (1994) and the oneiric ecology of *Anáhuac* (1995), offer interesting examples of the reconversion of the metaphorical density of archaeological detritus – a reconversion which, despite its desecratory impulse, seems to retain an uneasy allegiance to the visual conceits of *desengaño* featured in photography and art from 1920s to 1940s, a period conventionally assumed to represent hegemonic cultural nationalism in the arts. It might be argued that Suter's embodied texts have something of the lapidary epigraph in their relation to Mexican discourses on identity. Essayist Julio Torri's defence of marginal inscriptions in 1917, a writing of interplay and allusion which makes a virtue of obliquity, points out the kind of creative misreadings elicited by Suter's *puestas en escena* [stagings]:

El épigrafe se refiere pocas veces de manera clara y directa al texto que exorna; se justifica pues por la necesidad de expresar relaciones sutiles de las cosas. Es una liberación espiritual dentro de la fealdad y pobreza de las formas literarias oficiales.[47]

[The epigraph seldom refers clearly and directly to the text it embellishes; it justifies itself through the need to express the subtle relations of things. It offers a spiritual liberation within the ugliness and poverty of official literary forms.]

Álvarez Bravo captured the sense behind his own little-studied archaeological restagings of the 1940s, in which he used his wife Doris Heyden as a model in simulated burials and sacrifices,[48] with an aphorism to which Suter's work could bear witness: 'Qué dejaré en pos de mí en esta tierra ...?, como decían los prehispánicos' [What will I leave behind on this earth ...?, as the pre-Hispanics used to say'].[49] Suter readily acknowledges his persistent 'apego a este mundo primigenio' ['attachment for this primeval word'], which introduces an autobiographical fixation in much of his manipulated work. Pre-Columbian sculpture and Indian codices provide a platform for a process of visual assimilation and personal 'recodification': 'Ese es, digamos, mi punto de partida, mi pretexto. Lo que hago es recodificar. Hago mi propio código con base en esa simbología' ['That is, let us say, my starting point, my pretext. What I do is to recodify. I make my own code based on that system of symbols'].[50]

In *Retorno al templo imaginario* [*Return to the Imaginary Temple*], from Suter's ironic reworking of nineteenth-century ethnographic albums, *El archivo fotográfico del profesor Retus* (1985), monolithic stone pillars loom portentously against a stormy sky (figure 8.9).[51] The pockmarked stone surface is lit in such a way as to emphasise the tactile scarring of the weathered stone. The photographed tear which splits the structure excavates a double aperture – onto the construction of ancestry through emblematic objects and on photography's own consecration of the trace as truth. The column is sliced as a physical support to a fractured

Figure 8.9 © Gerardo Suter, *Retorno al templo imaginario*, from *El archivo fotográfico del profesor Retus* (1985). Courtesy of Gerardo Suter.

temple, but also in the sense of exposing the physical support of image-making.

The 1996 installation *De los títulos primordiales* [*Of Primordial Bonds*] includes a black-and-white video projection of hands encrusted with mud pressing into kneaded earth onto the stained, peeling ceiling of a colonial building, the Convent of Tepoztlán (figure 8.10).[52] The remains of a sixteenth-century wall painting pattern, the cracked and grainy surface and the momentarily stilled image, adheres transparently so that a kind of transliteration appears to take place between the caked hands and the physical support. The image resembles a number of iconic compositions of Mexican artisans' hands by foreign photographers in the 1920s and 1930s, most particularly by two Americans: Anton Bruehl's *Hands of a Potter* (1933) (figure 8.11) and Edward Weston's *Hand of the Potter Amado Galván*, a photograph which was reproduced in the 1929 ethnographic essay *Idols Behind Altars*.[53] The symmetry in the dates of Weston's image (taken in 1926) and Suter's installation in one of the most celebrated colonial enclosures may be purely fortuitous, but the visual citation to the syncretic emblems thrown up by the discourses of identity in the 1920s and 1930s, which his layering projection duplicates, does suggest Suter's fascination with Mexican photography's own archaeology

Figure 8.10 © Gerardo Suter, *De los títulos primordiales* (1996), Convento de Tepoztlán, installation view, black-and-white video projection. Courtesy of Gerardo Suter.

of fragments. His interest in the photographic techniques deployed to reproduce images, in the potential for symbolic contiguity between subject and process, reminds us that such techniques and materials have their own poetic currency in the history of writing about Mexican photography. For instance, the gelatin silver print process which Suter used in *El archivo* and *Códices*, projects which explored cultural history as palimpsest and inscribed body, entails through emulsion the notion of 'coating' and through 'gelatin' the extraction of protein from animal tissue. In a 1939 article on Manuel Álvarez Bravo, the poet and critic

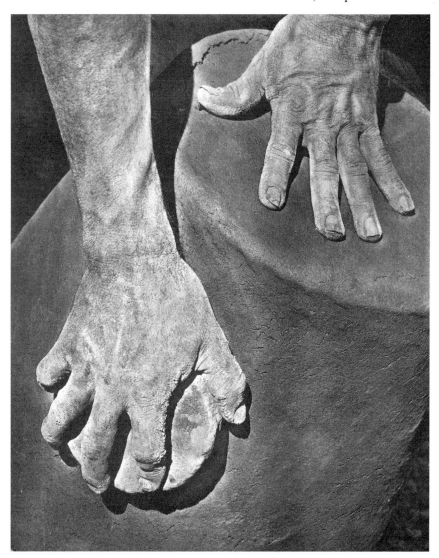

Figure 8.11 Anton Bruehl, *Hands of a Potter,* from *Photographs of Mexico* (1933), callotype. Private collection.

Luis Cardoza y Aragón praised photography's capacity to strip the world clean so that it may be 'rediscovered'. The photographs which prompted such musings, and which were reproduced in the article, included one of Álvarez Bravo's *ruinas* – that of a gaping threshold. For Cardoza y Aragón, things are 'reborn' photographically like Lazarus from corruption and death:

> The magic of the silver-bromide canvas, strips the objects of the dust of routines freeing them of purely conventional hindrances. Then, as if born from the light, things appear gloriously naked – like virgins never before having been seen by the eyes of man.[54]

In contrast, there is little that is 'virginal' in Gruner's multimedia reflections on the status of relics in a commodity-dominated post-nationalist culture. Hers is a world of overexposure, not of epiphanies. She tracks the sordid afterlife of objects and materials which have been made sacrosanct in the fabrication of national identity. The obligatory encounter with the past through its archaeological monuments marked the initiation of many a modernist into the arcana of national essence, as Álvarez Bravo's daughter reminds us: 'cada vez que atravesábamos un pueblo, o que nos aproximábamos a un sitio arqueológico, detenerse a mirar la iglesia o la pirámide era una especie de ley inamovible, me atrevería a decir sagrada' ['every time we crossed a village, or approached an archaeological site, stopping to look at the church or the pyramid was a kind of inescapable rule, I would venture to say, a sacred law.'].[55] In his photography Álvarez Bravo was, to a surprising extent, a devotee of the signatures of the real. In the 1940s he undertook to photograph the surviving painted walls of pre-Hispanic, colonial and nineteenth-century Mexico, before graffiti, institutional neglect and climatic damage erased their language of material signs.[56] And although Gruner revisits a well-worn discursive terrain and situates her works in historically inscribed spaces such as convents in Mexico and Guatemala, her approach is the obverse of rhapsodic contemplation. Nor, despite her reworking of Catholic iconography (such as rosary beads) and ritual, does she worship at the unpolluted shrine of origin. What she does share with the modernists as collectors and shrine builders is her acquisitive perspicacity for the language of things – for that personal treasure-trove of bits and pieces. Rubbing shoulders with distinctive rubbish seems to be an obsession she shares with Álvarez Bravo, the stern 'father of Mexican photography', who died in 2002 in his hundredth year. According to one of his daughters:

> … mi padre conserva toda clase de objetos curiosos, así sean envolturas de artículos de tocador, pilas usadas, figuritas de barro, pedazos de pruebas, espinas de pescado, huesos de res, y otros igualmente inusitados.[57]

[... my father keeps all kinds of curious things, be they wrappings of toiletries, used batteries, clay figurines, pieces of contact papers, fish scales, cattle bones, and other equally unusual things.]

In Gruner's provocative fourteen-minute video *In situ* (1995), a gaping mouth holds, as if in a niche, the clay head of a pre-Hispanic fertility fetish, seemingly one of many famously excavated from burial sites in Tlatilco, Mexico from 1947 to 1949 (figure 8.12). According to Miguel Covarrubias's original report on the excavations in progress (figure 8.13), the deposits of sacred artefacts had been extensively sacked by local makers of brick who recycled the relics in order to produce 'new' building materials.[58] Covarrubias was in charge of the dig through which archaeological salvage entered the pictorial domain of the Mexican avant-garde and its visual redeployment of 'impregnated' artefacts. Gruner's title refers to a find situated in its original place while in practice relocating archaeological debris and its originary markings in an indeterminate personal, rather than institutional, space. It is not clear whether the figurine has been inserted, as a ritual object in a burial might be, or surfaced from within, as if produced naturally; whether the female body is a vessel or a source. In the filmed performance, the tongue licks the archaeological artefact as if it were a morsel and its secretions penetrate the porous material as if initiating the process of disintegration and rebirth. Gruner reintroduces the cannibalistic practices which came to signify the inalienable otherness of pre-Hispanic cultures (and, in a

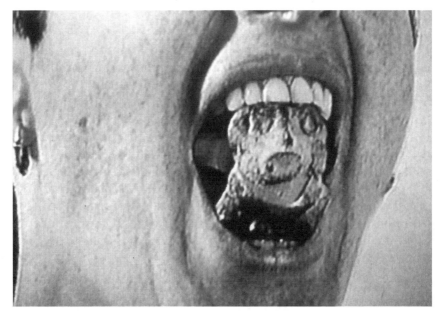

Figure 8.12 © Silvia Gruner, *In situ* (1995), colour video. Courtesy of Silvia Gruner.

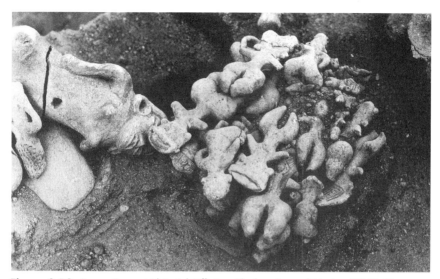

Figure 8.13 Anon., Excavated Burial Offering, Tlatilco, State of Mexico (1947–9). FINAH.

reflexive allusion to her own family history, the anti-Semitic demonising of Jews as child eaters?). She ransacks the telluric myths of pre-Hispanic religion, humorously impersonating an indigenous ancestry, to which she has no native blood line, in order to magnify the gendered conceits of nationalist archaeology. The evocation of anthropophagous acts provides an inroad, as it were, into the elemental activity of aesthetic and cultural appropriation, assimilation, destruction and reincorporation.

Open mouths figure prominently in Mesoamerican votive art: whether it be jaguar-mouthed Olmec heads; toothy smiling figurines from Veracruz; Xochipilli the Aztec god of flowers, dance and song in slack-mouthed intoxication; or the fertility god, Xipe-Tótec ('our flayed lord'), wearing the flayed skin of a victim as a mask with a hole for its mouth (figure 8.14). Terrestrial orifices such as caves were venerated as sites of origin, represented as wombs or mouths, and as passageways to the underworld.[59] Dental mutilation for aesthetic and religious purposes and the use of human teeth as beads in ornamental and ritual necklaces are well-documented examples of the manner in which the physical body and its parts was subject to symbolic transactions and manipulations. The rather theatrical illustration, based on a Zapotec funerary urn, that Covarrubias designed in 1951 for the cover of a dry-as-dust archaeological study on the ancient art of dental mutilations (figure 8.15), gives a measure of the prurient fascination exerted on the scientific imagination by the gaping mouths of pre-Columbian art and human remains.[60] Interest in the pre-Hispanic mask, its genres and ritual uses, predates and informs the focus on bucal openings.[61]

Figure 8.14 Anon., *Aztec Mask of Xipe-Tótec*, 'The flayed one' (basalt stone). British Museum.

In pre-Hispanic culture, the vagina dentata was associated with the rite of passage of death: the corpse was devoured by *Tlaltecuhtli, Señor de la tierra*, who was represented as an enormous mouth with sharp fangs. Once the individual had been consumed, he was expelled as if delivered from the womb: 'De ahí que a Tlaltecuhtli se le represente en posición de parto. Es la vagina dentada que toma a la persona para parirla nuevamente' ['That is why Tlaltecuhtli is represented as if about to give birth. It is the vagina dentata that takes the human being to give birth to him once more'].[62] Similarly, the terrifyingly fanged Coatlicue ('serpent skirt'), the fertility goddess who generated birth through human sacrifice, encapsulated the creative cycle through severance and disintegration. The orifice, in archaeological terms the opening to a repository of meaning, then marks an entry and an exit, the destructive assimilation of identity and its regeneration. On the one hand, Gruner plays with the sacramental investure of archaeological artefacts into the material of a fetishised

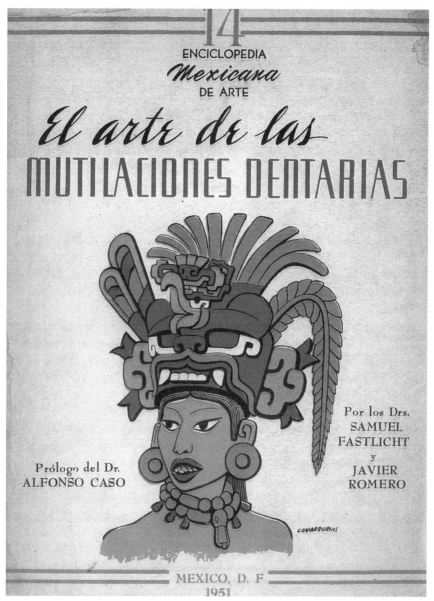

Figure 8.15 Miguel Covarrubias, colour cover illustration for *El arte de las mutilaciones dentarias* (1951). Private collection.

national identity; on the other, she challenges commonplace incarnations in art of the pre-Hispanic matrix as passive and inert inscription. In this work as in others by Gruner, most notably in her northern border installation *La mitad del camino* [*Middle of the Road*] (1994), there is an obligatory reference to Frida Kahlo's thematising of parturition. Gruner revisits Kahlo's painting *Mi nacimiento* [*My Birth*] (1932), in which an archaeological relic had undergone comparable appropriations and transformations to those effected by her additive and subtractive activities reusing the historical repertoire. In this representation of stalled autogenesis, the head of a corpse protrudes from the vaginal opening of a shrouded woman whose muffled torso is reminiscent of the classical representation of the goddess of childbirth, Lucina, sheathed in full-body veil. Kahlo's painting gives rise to a locus of visual syncretism as the eye line converges on the perforated aperture. The tracery of stains on the sudarium-like white sheet on the bed, tilted forward to add dramatic projection to the splayed figure, invests Kahlo's concern with crossed blood lines with a sacralising dimension akin to the veracity accorded to the physiognomic traces on the Veil of the Veronica or the soiled garment of forensic exhibits. Kahlo's commemorative reconstruction subsumes the Aztec sculpture of Tlazolteotl, the Aztec goddess of childbirth and filth (figure 8.16), that partly inspired it, in one of the most unusual interpretations of the still life in modern Mexican art. What is inert and truncated in Kahlo (the painting portrays a stillbirth) is visually animate and unstilled, although broken, in Gruner. It may well be that of the two uses of the statue of Tlazolteotl (*c.*1300–1521), Gruner's is the most 'authentic' translation of its original symbolic associations. Miguel Covarrubias had confirmed the piece's compelling singularity in his illustrated study *Indian Art of Mexico and Central America* (1957).[63] Since about 1947, the applite sculpture has formed part of the Dumbarton Oaks Research Library and Collections in Washington DC.[64] The sculpture's international celebrity as a museum exhibit is attested to by the stellar role a papier-mâché copy played in *Lost Magic Kingdoms and Six Paper Moons from Nahuatl* held in 1985 at the Museum of Mankind in London. The ethnographic exhibition was curated by the influential British sculptor Eduardo Paolozzi, who made the replica of Tlazolteotl himself.[65] In her principal aspect, the goddess is associated with birth and regeneration, but a no less important related facet has her linked with the purification of physical contamination, curing disease and the sexual maladies which afflicted the penitent willing to confess their trans-gressions and misdeeds to her. She would devour this culpable filth, cleansing the mortified and propitiating their rebirth. Ingestion and parturition mark her as a recyclatory as well as generative repository.

In Gruner's *La mitad del camino* (figure 8.17), 111 plaster figurines stage a rudimentary multiple replication of the Aztec sculpture with each piece straining and squatting on a separate metal stool suspended halfway along the infamously iconic *barda de acero* [iron fence] marking the porous frontier between Tijuana and San Diego. This geopolitically inscribed space, operating as a threshold productive of illicit transactions and elided identities, is made doubly fetishistic by Gruner's idolatrous

Figure 8.16 Anon., *Aztec Sculpture of Tlazolteotl*. Dumbarton Oaks Research Library and Collections.

superimposition. The *barda* is criss-crossed with stencilled messages and slogans, encrypted with anonymous signatures and daubings, serving both as a site of pilgrimage, a shrine to popular aspirations, and as a monument to the fallen, to truncated journeys and the bleeding out of personal identities in the passage of the *indocumentados* to an uncertain elsewhere. The originary deity's primal orifice becomes a troubling passageway linking expulsion to creation, and severance to recirculation. Tlazolteotl squats on the border as a mnemonic guardian, a fearful apparition synonymous with telluric allegiances disturbed by the flow of covert migrations away from the autochthonous source. Her anguished expression and the torsion of her body allude to the violent rupture and torment of new birth – appropriately enough when one considers her as the tutelary custodian of voluntary and involuntary displacements and disengagements undertaken by the Mexican populace in search of better prospects or even the Utopia of a 'new life'. An encounter with her presages a transgressive transition on the very edge of nationalist cartography. She literally embodies the confines of the matrix, the customary allegorisation of the birthplace through feminised cyphers. Intriguingly, the replicas of Tlazolteotl face inwards towards the Mexican hinterland, as if caught giving birth mid-way during a peregrination from North to South. Gruner may well be playing with the mythology of origin predicated on foundational migration of the Mexica from the North, away from the legendary Aztlán of Chicano militancy.

Part of this ludic revision entails Mexicanising the narrative of pioneering settlement and exclusivity of U.S. nationalist romance with its ever extendable Western frontier. Gruner devises a carnal or incarnated semantics which exploits the ambiguities of the word turned flesh, sifting the discursive textualities of the border shaped into material litter. If there is a paradigm for her exploration of cultural deposits, it would be a

Figure 8.17 © Silvia Gruner, *La mitad del camino* (1994), plaster figures, border fence between Tijuana and San Diego (in colour). Courtesy of Silvia Gruner.

midden rather than an archive. In *Autorretrato de pie en la frontera entre México y los Estados Unidos* [*Self-portrait on the Border between Mexico and the U.S.*] (1932), Kahlo had famously depicted herself on the contested line between Mexico and the U.S.A., flanked by a number of totemic archaeological objects including a pre-Hispanic fertility clay figure with her vulva prominently incised. Kahlo had traversed the actual and metaphorical frontier, negotiating in the process her own precarious sense of cultural integrity accentuated by the trauma of an aborted pregnancy in industrial Detroit (see *Hospital Henry Ford* (1932)). Gruner had herself 'crossed over', spending her formative years as an artist in the U.S.A; on returning to Mexico in 1989, her early work, using photography and video, explored and cultivated the cultural, aesthetic and political ambiguities of her liminal position. More so than Kahlo (whose father was from a Hungarian Jewish family settled in Baden-Baden), Gruner's German-Jewish ancestry problematised her identity vis-à-vis essentialist definitions of national and cultural identity.[66] Take, for instance, the *libro-objeto* [book-object] entitled *Destierro* [*Exile*], part of the larger installation project on the theme at the Centro Cultural Arte Contemporáneo (1992–3). It is made up of a sequence of black-and-white photographic stills of a body, wrapped like a morsel (as in a taco) or a corpse in a large *petate*, bound at each end by rope. Human remains were often wrapped in a *petate* in some pre-Columbian burial rites, as excavations in the north of Mexico by Walter W. Taylor and others in the late 1940s and 1950s revealed through the photographic record of finds. Gruner's images are reproduced sequentially in a slim book.[67] The traditional *petate*-mat's cross-grained mesh provided the supporting ground of innumerable paintings and photographs, evidencing the aesthetic of *mestizo* singularity in the 1920s to the 1940s. For example, Frances Toor's classic *Mexican Popular Arts* (1939), which emerged in response to what it described as the 'great wave of nationalism [that] swept the country and all the Mexican arts acquired a new dignity in the eyes of Mexicans', used photographs by Manuel and Lola Álvarez Bravo and Luis Márquez of vernacular textiles, basketry and natural weaves, including the latter's *The Petate Man*.[68] Gruner's choice of wrapping material is not incidental for it carries bound up with it a veritable bundle of Mexicanist associations which have underpinned the visual language of the canonical modern Escuela Mexicana. The native paper strip, which in the form of a roll was one of the kinds of indigenous painted books that pre-Cortesian and early post-conquest scribes produced, offers Gruner a subtle metaphor of the complex cultural transcriptions which marked competing originary mythologies in the colonial period. Gruner's own reintroduction to her homeland from long sojourns in Israel and the

U.S.A. is fraught with smuggled influences, artistic estrangement and interrogation.[69] The concentric folding, resembling a spiral, carries connotations of temporal genesis, but also of labyrinthine circularity, regardless of the specificities of the written narrative or annal recorded on its surfaces. Gruner's enveloped female body is simultaneously made inherent and contained, circumscribed within a vernacular textile, and entrapped by the essentialist embrace which defines it. The textual object (the book in which the photographic reproductions are interleaved) attempts to arrest the inescapable *transitoriedad* [transience] of the body through its pagination, while dramatising the conceptual displacement that fixes the female body in a perpetual relation of exile from the subjective self.

The trope of a membranous wrap, sheathing and semi-permeable, seems to play a recurrent role in the corporeal re-enactments of pre-Hispanic propitiatory rituals and artefacts through which Suter and Gruner play with the evidence and the omissions of a composite colonial archive of traces, transcriptions and recordings (codices, screenfolds, books of paper and skin, *lienzo* maps). Their ambivalent allusiveness when citing, parodying or reformulating archaeological and antiquarian imagery or matter acknowledges the existence of a potent precedent in Mexican modernism. Xipe-Tótec was photographer Manuel Álvarez Bravo's patron deity, wearing the shed skin of sacrificial victims just as the adhesive black-and-white snapshot impersonated the surface appearance of its photogenic subject. He referred to his nude studies of women, seen through, behind or enveloped in drapery, as his Xipe nudes.[70] And it is the mask of the transformative and predatory Xipe that he has his model-wife assume (or is it, impersonate?) as a facial rictus in his archaising still-life burials in which she lies prostrate, sampling the kiss of death of the lens, prefiguring herself as memento mori and timeless icon (figures 8.18 and 8.19). She becomes subject to the sacrificial rituals of photography, as imagined by Álvarez Bravo.[71] The transposition of archaeological installations or excavations into the space of the private collector is effected over his wife's body. There is a suggestive resemblance between Manuel Álvarez Bravo's necrophilic photographs and one of the pre-Hispanic clay heads from the state of Nayarit (figure 8.20), which he owned (and exhibited in 1946), with its gaping mouth and nose-ring, as well as with the generic masks of Xipe unearthed by his friend Caso and others with the flayed god's distinguishing 'nariguera' ['nose plug'] (figure 8.21).[72] Caso had speculated that one of the burial masks of Xipe found in Monte Albán represented gendered skin – that of a woman with tell-tale facial ornamentation.[73] If we turn to the contemporary anthropologist Alfredo López Austin, we can better locate the referential

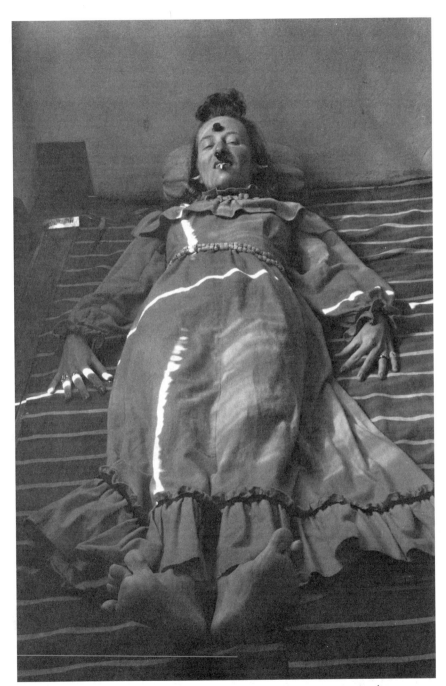

Figure 8.18 Manuel Álvarez Bravo, *A la mañana siguiente* (1945). Familia Álvarez Bravo y Urbajtel.

Figure 8.19 Manuel Álvarez Bravo, *Retrato desagradable* (1943). Familia Álvarez Bravo y Urbajtel.

suture of Álvarez Bravo's reworkings of archaeological finds. He helps
describe the function of the supine body in relation to the evocation of
Xipe in creative photography: 'Los *Xipeme*, eran muertos para obtener de
ellos la piel, indispensable par que otros hombres se vistiesen con ella y
recibiesen así, transitoriamente, al dios Xipe-Tótec' ['The *Xipeme* were
killed for their skin which was indispensable so that other men could
clothe themselves with it and thereby temporarily receive the god Xipe-
Tótec'].[74] Suter's splicings are comparatively less freighted. He opts for
sheets of Sellophane over transfixed bodies and the bucal mask of Xipe in
primordial relief glaring from the numinous shadows, speaking of
innumerable and indistinguishable appropriations and unpeelings (figure
8.22).[75]

Figure 8.20 Manuel Álvarez Bravo, *Pre-Hispanic Head from Western Mexico* (1946)
(from the photographer's private collection). Private collection.

In Suter and Gruner, bodily detritus alongside the remains of manufactured goods test a performative archaeology in which culture and nature interpenetrate in the display of material presence and its inferred significations. Both artists consciously cite and then scramble the diagrammatic design of museological display and its visual pedagogy. By turning to the description of one of the central halls of the Mexican National Museum of Anthropology by the well-known archaeologist Román Piña-Chán, we discover the narrative potency of excavated artefacts, the careful arrangement of material signs and the dramatic articulation of the language of salvaged objects. He relates the trajectory of the spectator in the space devoted to an evocation of the civilisation of the city of Teotihuacán, which lay abandoned at the time of the Aztec empire. The tableaux date the evolution of this ancient culture through the differing styles of its pottery vessels – a sort of earthenware short-

Figure 8.21 Anon., *Small gold mask of Xipe-Tótec*, one of 'The Treasures of Monte Albán', Oaxaca, excavated by Alfonso Caso. Museo Regional de Oaxaca.

hand. The chronological specifity is embedded as it were in the clay object or its remnant. This calibrating of time synonymous with the handling of such archaeological salvage has an almost talismanic allure for contemporary artists in Mexico, exercised as they are by post-national fluidity and relativism. Piña-Chán's explicatory text regulates a certain kind of instructive visuality, which Suter and Gruner simulate or travesty in invitations to overlook their own disabused syncretic mystifications:

Figure 8.22 © Gerardo Suter, *Xipe-Tótec* (1991), from the *Códices series*. Courtesy of Gerardo Suter.

Displays of archaeological objects, together with drawings, photographs, models, etc., serve to illustrate various cultural traits which were common to all pre-Hispanic peoples ... A model of the valley taking in the ceremonial centre, puts the visitor in the picture and explains the ecological condition of the site. He then passes on to a set of show-cases containing Teotihuacán pottery, which has been the means of establishing the various stages of its culture. First come examples of Teot. I-A or late Tzacualli, characterised by vessels shaped like flower vases, dishes with button supports ... The Teot.II or Miccaotli phase is represented by jars, bowls, and cups with button supports; a number of amphorae with handles.76

The list of indexical bits and pieces is lengthy. The emblematic inventory prepares the way for the diffusionist ethnographic showcases representing post-contact permutations and pre-Hispanic survivals through a range of displayed artefacts:

Customs and beliefs that have survived from pre-Hispanic times are also exemplified ... A display of feathers, votive dishes, necklaces, sacred arrows, crosses and other objects, staffs of office and various musical instruments enable the visitor to appreciate how certain human beliefs endured, while others underwent transformation or fused. To fill in the background there are numerous sketches and photographs.77

These institutional reference points, familiar to all Mexican schoolchildren inducted into the arcana of national essence, provide the subsumed framework for installations such as *Fetiches domésticos* (1992), Gruner's mock-*costumbrista* installation of an 'interior pueblerino' ['village interior'] in Itzamatitlan, Morelos (figure 8.23).78

Figure 8.23 © Silvia Gruner, *Fetiches domésticos* (1992), installation. Courtesy of Silvia Gruner.

The spectator strays before a pointedly symmetrical display of ordinary pots hanging from nails against a pockmarked adobe wall: helping to fill in the gaps, as in archaeologist Piña-Chán's tableaux, a faded studio photograph portrays the presumed absentee inhabitants. The discursive charge of the display evokes the metonymic strategies employed by photographers Luis Márquez and Hugo Brehme for publications such as *Mexican Folkways* in the 1930s – the golden age of Mexicanist visuality. The former captured *A Bit of Wall Space in a Humble Mexican Kitchen*, while the latter focused on *Indian Sandals*.[79] The invasive populism which accompanied the folkloric impulse in the arts culminated in proprietorial interior design by the governing elite, who, inspired by Dr Atl's groundbreaking exhibition of Mexican popular art in 1920–21 (sponsored by the Ministry of Commerce, Industry and Labour), installed domestic versions of the museum display: 'Since then it has become quite the mode among the well-to-do Mexican families, especially those connected with the government, to have a Mexican Room decorated with Indian handcrafts'.[80] Included in Gruner's illusionistic counterfeit is an inscrutable clay figurine of a hybrid quadruped, posed in space to enhance its portentous singularity, with an up-turned clay pot resembling a helmet for a head. It resembles a mutant version of a traditional earthenware toy, such as the *alcancía* [money box] in the shape of an animal, celebrated by artists such as María Izquierdo and Frida Kahlo in their still lifes in the 1920s, 1930s and 1940s, by photographers Tina Modotti and Edward Weston, and by illustrators-ethnographers such as Gabriel Fernández Ledesma.[81] It is a composite 'found object', an imitation of those disturbing familiars groomed by surrealism: one of that menagerie of counterfeit simulacra based on a modernist fallacy, which purported to exhibit the mundane turned aesthetic by the intervention of serendipity or the random workings of the unconscious. In Gruner's *camera*, its contrived mystery is included for scale to help measure the full extent of the display's deceptive naturalism and its roots in the gestures of both realism and anti-realism in figurative media. The untraceable provenance and purpose of the clay, adobe and plaster figurine encrusted with horse hair tempts us into the primitivist conjectures to which popular or pre-modern culture is often subjected. Gruner is intent on disturbing habitual literacy with the unobtrusive discordance of her contrived 'time capsule'.

Gruner's promiscuous dealings with the pre-Hispanic and its modern reinterpretations is nowhere more comically apparent than in her series of nine photographs (from an installation of sixteen prints), *Don't fuck with the past, you might get pregnant* (1995) (figure 8.24), which transgress the boundaries of archaeological detachment to finger and copulate with fertility idols on the screen.[82] Each shot consists of a represented gesture and a procedural manipulation which she termed 'mis pornografías'.[83] The exhibitionist violations infringe the boundaries of empirical and museographic decorum to perpetrate promiscuous interpenetrations with effigies inscribed with the discourse of origins.[84]

In Suter the earthenware fragment, stone pediment and geological stratum, the premises of so much archaeological essentialism, are treated as building material or wrapping annointed with telluric significance in fantastic reconstructions, which point to the Utopian impulse behind the re-erection of broken ancient sites (as in the notorious case of the partial reinvention of the Maya city of Palenque). Materials of authenticity, *barro* [clay] and *adobe*, pigments derived from or mixed with the earth, volcanic and quarried stone, frayed *petates*, are incorporated in the photographic composition or their textured, weathered surfaces simulated on human skin. Suter's human models ossify or disintegrate beneath a body casket of lava, leaving an imprint of dissolution or nothing but a vaporous trace. Others impersonate the hieratic stone effigies of tutelary Aztec gods, such as Coatlicue, Tlaloc and Xipe-Tótec, as well as their textual representations from codices in a gloaming masquerade.[85] He uses archetypal

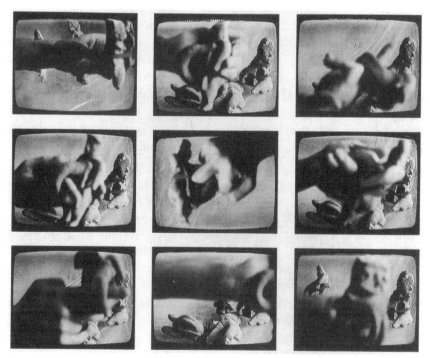

Figure 8.24 © Silvia Gruner, *Don't fuck with the past, you might get pregnant* (1995), colour photographs. Courtesy of Silvia Gruner.

archaeological relics from tombs and temple enclosures, transferring some of the qualities of the broken and used, the stucco pediment or stone frieze, onto bodies 'asumidos como ruinas de un mito' ['conceived as the ruins of a myth'],[86] and their representations in nation-building discourses. He imitates in his restagings the anachronistic liberties and miscastings which typify the commonplaces of such narratives, with ritually 'prepared' bodies and customised sacred objects, and the theatricality of gesture and symbol. He manufactures false replicas of pre-Columbian artefacts – actual things – which are then deployed in front of analogue or video camera to 'historicise' them visually. Perhaps there is something here which recalls Joan Fontcuberta's witty analogy between straight photographic endeavour and the 'elaborada teatralización' ['elaborate staging'] of taxidermy: 'taxidermista y fotógrafo comparten una tarea destinada a la duración y la posteridad' ['the taxidermist and the photographer share a task whose objective is permanence and posterity'].[87] Suter's partial re-enactments transform the obsolescence of flesh into a ruin of duplicitous perpetuity. Through large-scale black-and-white images on semi-transparent banner-length acetate sheets, *Anáhuac: radiografía de un valle* (1995) (which includes two videos), plays with aprocryphal journeys (relating to the founding of México-Tenochtitlán), exploring foundational myths based on itinerancy, catastrophe and existential *desencanto* [disenchantment], through spliced and displaced bodies or 'cuerpos-territorios', in Osvaldo Sánchez's felicitous phrase.[88] Moving literally away from the hieratic fixity of pre-Columbian monuments, the supporting material's moving transparency conjures a phantasmagoria of clinical and topographical effects, the delicate inscriptions of which speak of ephemerality. Suter's resistance to a contextual space in his close-up photographic compositions, added to the often diffuse or indeterminate light source, situates them in the penumbral locales of the imaginary and the internal. One of the still lifes from this complex series shows a lingam-shaped glass bell, of the kind familiar to naturalist exhibits, the polished transparency of which covers a small mound of sedimented earth, dust, ashes or sand, and could be said to contain a representative specimen of the vanitas image.[89] According to Suter, 'La existencia del tiempo tiene presencia, las cenizas, la tierra y la textura de éstas implica lo terreno, algo que fue antes de ser cenizas' ['The existence of time has a presence, the ashes, the soil and their textures point to the earthbound, to something that was before the ashes'].[90] But Suter's bell-jar, despite his interest in conservation, is unlike the photograph of a Mexican Revolutionary relic, such as the one by P. Zavala showing a jar of formaldehyde containing the severed hand of General Obregón; for its metaphotographic symbolism points to the medium's own self-referential ghostly signatures rather than to historical corroborations, and the absent whole invites not Alfonso Reyes's 'venganza del polvo' ['vengeance of dust'], but the creative possibilities afforded by the incompletely visible. One is encouraged to conclude that perhaps nothing returns conclusively to dust – not because it is remembered fully but because it is half-remembered.

Notes

1. Silvia Gruner, 1994, cited in T. Ziff (ed.), *Distant Relations* (Santa Monica, CA, 1996), 115, originally in English.
2. M. Romero de Terreros, *Las artes industriales en la Nueva España* (Mexico City, 1923), 153.
3. A. Caso (Director of the National Institute of Anthropology and History), 'Pre-Spanish Art', in A. Caso, R. Montenegro, M. Toussaint et al., *Twenty Centuries of Mexican Art* (New York, 1940), 23–30 (23). This was a groundbreaking exhibition, sponsored by the Mexican and U.S. governments, which consolidated the status of Mexican art in avant-garde circles following the influential touring exhibition, *Mexican Arts*, organised by The American Federation of Arts and curated by René d'Harnoncourt of 1930–1. The advisory committee of the earlier exhibition included Diego Rivera, Dr Atl, Jorge Enciso, Roberto Montenegro and others. Both events expressed forms of cultural essentialism with a comparativist slant which aimed to redefine the character of the difference between Mexico and the U.S.A.; see the catalogue, R. d'Harnoncourt, *Mexican Arts* (New York, 1930).
4. This title refers to the period of crisis from 9 to 19 February 1913, during which Francisco Madero's presidency was threatened by a failed military coup. The artillery duel between loyalist and rebel forces in the capital killed many innocent civilians whose bodies were left to rot in the streets. General Victoriano Huerta, commander of the loyalist troops, assumed the presidency himself. He placed Madero and his vice-president under arrest. Both prisoners were shot and killed 'while trying to escape'.
5. Reproduced in P. Ortiz Monasterio (ed.), *Jefes, héroes y caudillos: Fondo Casasola* (Mexico City, 1986), 36. The Fondo Culhuacan of the Fototeca Nacional del I.N.A.H holds two other shots: one of an incinerated corpse in Nuevo México street (no. 451421), and the other a close-up of the body of a soldier who had been burned alive (no. 423773).
6. Reproduced in B. de la Fuente, J.A. Manrique, O. Paz et al., *Mexico: Splendors of Thirty Centuries* (New York, 1990), 562, 565, 567.
7. Reproduced in Bartra, 'Ver para descreer', 72–85 (74).
8. The bloody uprising known as the Cristero Rebellion opposed the radical anti-clerical and agrarian reforms of the Calles regime between 1926 and 1929. Many of the ordinary rebel soldiers were peasants of Indian extraction who believed they were engaged in a religious war in which their salvation was at stake. Their Catholic slogan was 'Long Live Christ the King!'. Widely circulated and reproduced photographs of executions and of the bodies of executed rebels served to create a gallery of *cristero* martyrs.

9. For *cristero* mortuary photography and the iconography of martyrdom, see J. Meyer, *La cristiada: Grandeza mexicana* (Mexico City, 1997), 26, 31, 33, 44–5.

10. See A. Reed, *José Clemente Orozco* (New York, 1932) for photographs of frescoes by José María Lupercio, Tina Modotti and Edward Weston. The shot of the panel from the cycle of the National Preparatory School is usually attributed to Modotti.

11. Many of his studies were published in *Revista de Revistas*. For a representative selection, see Albiñana, 'Agustín Jiménez', 102–37.

12. The image appeared (printed horizontally) in the large format entitled *Mártir proletario*, which was part of a portfolio of Álvarez Bravo's work; see 'Fotografías', *Artes Plásticas*, 1 (1939), n.p.n. The year 1939 was important for the dissemination of his photography at home and abroad. In March his work was exhibited in a Parisian gallery under the auspices of André Breton and serious articles followed in the Mexican press. This image (along with ten by Álvarez Bravo) headed the opening page of Breton's essay in the special issue of *Minotaure* devoted to Mexican art and culture.

13. For *Hair on Tile* (1930s) and *Ruin A* (1930s), see R. Tejada (ed.), *Manuel Álvarez Bravo: Photographs from The J. Paul Getty Museum* (Los Angeles, 2001), 25, 71. He started photographing archaeological ruins in his formative years; see *Ruina en Mitla, Oaxaca* (1926).

14. See Álvarez Bravo, *303 Photographies*, plate 31.

15. The reverse of the painting carries the following inscription: 'A mi no me queda ya ni la menor esperanza … todo se mueve al compás de lo que encierra la panza' ['There is no hope left for me … everything moves at the rhythm of my belly'].

16. See e.g. Herrán's series of allegorical murals (commissioned for the National Theatre in 1914) *Nuestros Dioses* [*Our Gods*] (1918), which fuses pre-Hispanic with Christian symbolism. The preparatory sketch for the unfinished panel *Coatlicue transformada* depicts the celebrated monumental Aztec statue of the bloodthirsty fertility goddess undergoing a Christianising transposition as the form of the crucified saviour is delineated on the stone.

17. R. López Velarde, *La suave patria* (Mexico City, 1944), 9, with woodcuts by Julio Prieto.

18. See A. Caso, 'Los hallazgos de Monte Albán', *Mexican Folkways*, 7 (1932), 114–28. For commercial images, see J. Heimann (ed.), *Mexicana: Vintage Mexican Graphics* (Köln/London, 2002), n.p.n.

19. See M. Amabilis, *El Pabellón de México en la Exposición Ibero-Americana de Sevilla* (Mexico City, 1929), 25: 'El Proyecto del Pabellón de México responde [al] próposito … de demostrar que nuestro Arte Arcaico Nacional, puede solucionar los modernos problemas de edificación, sin perder ninguna de sus características, adaptándose a todas las estructuras y a todas las necesidades de nuestro confort moderno' ['The Mexican Pavilion Project is a response to the need … to demonstrate that our Ancient National Art can solve the modern problems of construction, without losing any of its characteristics, adapting itself to all structures and all of the requirements of our modern life style'].

20. J.L. Martínez (ed.), *El ensayo mexicano moderno* (Mexico City, 1971; repr. 1984), I: 293–8 (294).

21. Both colour photographs are reproduced in S. Gruner, *Reliquias-collares* (Mexico City, 1998), 21, 46.

22. For mid-nineteenth-century archaeology and its uses, see E.I. Estrada de Gerlero, 'La litografía y el Museo Nacional como armas del nacionalismo', in E. Acevedo, J. Cuadriello, F. Ramírez et al. (eds), *Los pinceles de la historia: De la patria criolla a la nación mexicana, 1750–1860* (Mexico City, 2000), 152–69.

23. The image *Artesano esculpe reproducciones prehispánicas* (*c.*1900) is held in the Fondo Culhuacan of the Fototeca Nacional del I.N.A.H., no. 351024. For a contemporary example by Antonio Vizcaíno, see C. Aguilera and P. Martínez Peñaloza, *México: genio que perdura* (Mexico City, 1988), fig. 104, of an artisan in his worshop: 'La olmeca es, probablemente, la cultura madre de Mesoamérica, se proyectó en el tiempo y en el espacio. Lapidario de Iguala, Guerrero, que elabora en piedra dura una máscara de estilo olmeca' ['The Olmec, probably the mother culture of Mesoamerica, projected itself in time and space. Here we see a stonemason from Iguala, Guerrero, carving in hard stone a mask in the Olmec style'].

24. The two anonymous photographs are reproduced in R. Casanova, 'Memoria y registro fotográfico en el Museo Nacional', *Alquimia*, 12 (2001), 7–16 (13, 16).

25. See L. Barkan, *Unearthing the Past: Archaeology and Aesthetics in the Making of Renaissance Culture* (New Haven/London, 1999), 124.

26. See.g. *El volcán Paricutín en erupción* (1943), one of several paintings which Gerardo Murillo ('Dr Atl') devoted to the subject.

27. See A. Brenner, *Idols Behind Altars* (New York, 1929). The American journalist, anthropologist, and art critic wrote her personal account of the historical development of Mexican culture, from pre-Hispanic to the present day, for a foreign readership. Brenner's vision was informed by her first-hand experience of Mexico in childhood (born in Aguascalientes) and in the 1920s where she moved among the elite of artists and intellectuals in Mexico City. Her presentation underlined the prevalence of ancient beliefs and traced its expression in syncretic practices in the contemporary context. She commissioned Tina Modotti and Edward Weston to provide photographic illustrations for her book.

28. Humble graves or mounds of earth and shrines are recurrent subjects. The grain of the soil or deposit is accorded space and focal resolution in these compositions. See e.g. *El espíritu de las personas* [*The Human Spirit*] (1927), *Tumba reciente* [*Recent Tomb*] (1933), *Tumba florecida* [*Flowering Tomb*] (1937), *Sepulcro traspasado* [*Pierced Sepulchre*] (1933), *El día seis conejo* [*Day Six Rabbit*] (1940).

29. M. Covarrubias, *The Eagle, the Jaguar, and the Serpent: Indian Art of the Americas* (New York, 1954), 4–5.

30. J. Enciso, *Sellos del antiguo México* (Mexico City, 1947). Manuel Álvarez Bravo was one of the editors of the series of large-format books produced by the prestigious Fondo Editorial de la Plástica Mexicana.

31. For an example of his unwavering interest in photographing archaeological exhibits, see M. León-Portilla and D. Sodi (eds), *Flor y canto del arte prehispánico de México* (Mexico City, 1964), with photographs by Álvarez Bravo, assisted by Pablo Méndez and Marco Octavio Peralta.

32. This unpublished photograph is reproduced in B. Barba de Piña Chán and M. Rodríguez-Shadow (eds), *Chalchihuite: Homenaje a Doris Heyden* (Mexico City, 1999). Along with Álvarez Bravo's other portrait studies of his wife are

photographs taken of her with friends Kahlo and Rivera. Photographs by Álvarez Bravo and Heyden started appearing in the same issues of the important avant-garde magazine *Dyn*, founded by W. Paalen (ed.): 3 (1942), n.p.n., and 6 (1944), n.p.n. The entry to 'New Contributors' (3 [1942], 46) reads: 'Doris Heydn, American photographer, born in East Orange, New Jersey, 1915. Went to Mexico as a reporter. Works with Manuel Álvarez Bravo since 1941'.

33. In 1949 Álvarez Bravo joined the expedition organised by the Instituto Nacional de Bellas Artes to the ruined Mayan city of Bonampak and published his photographs of the ancient murals and studies of contemporary Lacandon Indians; see C.R. Margain, 'Los mayas ayer y hoy: Bonampak', *México en el Arte*, 9 (1950), 36–54.

34. Although a consideration of Ortiz Monasterio's work and SEMEFO is beyond the scope of this chapter, the following projects are clearly relevant: Monasterio's photographic series *Bosquejos para una arqueología europea* [*Sketches towards a European Archaeology*], included as part of *Idolatrías: Proyectos para esculturas monumentales* [*Idolatries: Plans for Monumental Sculptures*] (Mexico City, 1997); and SEMEFO's installation *Mineralización estéril* (1997), in which the ashes of unidentified bodies from the municipal morgue (usually used for medical experiments, after which they are cremated and dumped as organic rubbish), were exhibited in an ostentatious glass bier; and *Memoria fosilizada* (1999), a piece which consisted of a cement block into which the collective had 'entombed' or 'interred' the personal effects found on the bodies of 247 victims of violent crimes.

35. The photograph of *Tumba 59* (*c.*1930) from the Monte Albán site is part of the Fondo Culhuacán, no. 368429, reproduced in I. Palacio Flores, *Tumba 59*, *Alquimia*, 9 (2000), 27.

36. See J. Monaghan, 'The Text in the Body, the Body in the Text: the Embodied Sign in Mixtec Writing', in E. Hill Boone and W.D. Mignolo (eds), *Writing Without Words: Alternative Literacies in Mesoamerica and the Andes* (Durham and London, 1994), 87–101 (95–6).

37. F. Benítez, 'La Tumba 7 Monte Albán', *Arqueología Mexicana*, 3 (1993), 26–34 (30–2). The author also consulted Heyden's personal copies of Caso's celebrated *El tesoro de Monte Albán* (Mexico City, 1969) and (with Ignacio Bernal), *Urnas de Oaxaca* (Mexico City, 1952). Photographic illustrations of numerous gold and clay masks of Xipe-Tótec found in tombs are particularly relevant for Álvarez Bravo's archaeological restagings with his wife as model.

38. For a discussion of the different relation to the pre-Columbian past manifested by Chicano and Mexican artists, see V.M. Fields and V. Zamudio-Taylor (eds), *The Road to Aztlan: Art from a Mythic Homeland* (Los Angeles, 2001), 38–77 (68). For a definition and critique of 'Neomexicanismo', see O. Sánchez, '¿Fuera de juego?', in *Mexico Now/México ahora: Point of Departure/Punto de partida* (Columbus, Ohio, 1997), 21–35, and 'El cuerpo de la nación: El neomexicanismo: La pulsión homosexual y la desnacionalización', *Curare*, 17 (2001), 136–46.

39. See A.M. Longi's interview with the artist, 'Busco Identidad Individual: Silvia Gruner', *Excelsior*, 29 February 2000, 5: '… [la obra] funciona como una especie de catalizador, para que cada quien se sumerja libremente en sus propios

pensamientos, en relación a lo que a través de ella vea dentro de sí' ['… (the work) operates like a kind of catalyst so that each person can immerse himself freely in his own thoughts'].

40. See B. Ruiz, 'Instala Silvia Gruner una "tragedia griega"', 1997; Yazmín Juandiego citing curator Magalí Arriola, '"Recorren" el interior de Silvia Gruner', *Reforma*, 1 March 2000, 4 ('Se quiere mostrar las construcciones emocionales, la arqueología humana que Gruner se plantea a sí misma. Su trabajo es una especie de interiorización del mundo circundante, es decir, ingiere todo lo que sucede y la manera en la que lo digiere se muestra en la obra' ['It attempts to show the emotional constructions, the human archaeology that Gruner interrogates. Her work is a kind of internalisation of the surrounding world, that is to say, she consumes everything that happens and the manner in which she digests it appears in the work']); K. Cordero Reiman, '*La expulsión del paraíso*: Instalación de Silvia Gruner', *Curare*, 2 (1993), 2 (originally published as part of *La Jornada*): 'el trabajo de Gruner se sitúa como una especie de arqueología o estructuralismo estético … rompiendo una lógica científica o lineal en favor de significados traslapados y simultáneos' ['Gruner's work operates like a kind of archaeology or a structuralist aesthetic … breaking with a scientific or linear logic in favour of overlapping and simultaneous meanings'].

41. The exhibition was held at the Museo de Arte Carrillo Gil, from 1 March to 28 May 2000. See the exhibition's catalogue, S. Gruner, *Circuito interior* (Mexico City, 2000), with an essay by Magalí Arriola.

42. For a two-page reproduction, see O. Sánchez, *Arte contemporáneo de México en el Museo Carrillo Gil* (Mexico City, 2000), 170–1.

43. See Kismaric, *Manuel Álvarez Bravo*, 46; Tejada, *Manuel Álvarez Bravo*, plate 30.

44. See Juandiego, '"Recorren" el interior de Silvia Gruner', *Reforma*, 1 March 2000, 4.

45. A. Caso, 'Monte Alban: An Archeological Zone of World-wide Renown', *Mexican Art and Life*, 4 (1938), n.p.n., which includes a photograph of the interior of tomb no. 103 before its exploration and also of the god Xipe-Tótec unearthed in the same cache.

46. Reproduced in Gruner, *Circuito interior*, 44–5.

47. J. Torri, *Ensayos y poemas*, 2nd edn (Mexico City, 1937), 27–8.

48. See *A la mañana siguiente* (1945) and *Retrato desagradable* (1943) (reproduced).

49. See 'Aforismos' collected by Teresa del Conde in M. Álvarez Bravo, *Mucho sol* (Mexico City, 1989), 94.

50. See P. Gola, 'Escenarios rituales: Coversación con Gerardo Suter', *Luna Córnea*, 2 (1993), 26–35 (34).

51. Reproduced in Suter, *Labyrinth*, fig. 7; also in Sánchez, *Arte contemporáneo*, 94–5.

52. For a reproduction as a still, see O. Debroise, 'Gerardo Suter: Primary Machines', in Suter, *Labyrinth*, 22–33 (31).

53. See A. Bruehl, *Photographs of Mexico* (New York, 1933), plate 15; Edward Weston's *Hand of Amado Galván* (1926), frontispiece to Brenner (1929).

54. L. Cardoza y Aragón, 'Light and Shadow: Manuel Álvarez Bravo photographer', *Mexican Art and Life*, 6 (1939), n.p.n.

55. See A. Álvarez Urbajtel, 'Mi padre fotógrafo', in M. Álvarez Bravo, *Por puro placer: 40 fotografías en platino* (Mexico City, 1992), n.p.n.

56. See his copious illustrations in E. Edwards, *Painted Walls of Mexico from Prehistoric Times until Today* (Austin, 1966).

57. See Álvarez Urbajtel, 'Mi padre fotógrafo', n.p.n.

58. For a period photograph of the burial find and an excerpt from the *Informe sintético provisional de las exploraciones arqueológicas en Tlatilco, Estado de México*, see M. del Carmen Solanes Carraro and E. Vela Ramírez, 'Imágenes históricas de la arqueología en México, siglo xx', *Arqueología Mexicana*, 1 (2001), 62.

59. Chicomoztoc, the place of the Seven Caves, was considered the mythological homeland of the Chichimecs, the predecessors of the northwestern Mexicas whose migration culminated in the Aztec dominions. It is represented as a literal birthplace, its caves serving as a womb or a mouth.

60. See S. Fastlicht and J. Romero, *El arte de las mutilaciones dentarias* (Mexico City, 1951), with a prologue by Alfonso Caso: ('Al juzgar las mutilaciones dentarias de nuestros aborígenes, no debemos … considerarlas como un rasgo de incultura, sino como característica de otra cultura' ['When judging the dental mutilations of our aborigines, we must not … consider them as signs of ignorance, but as characteristics of another kind of culture'], p. 4).

61. See e.g. R. Montenegro and X. Villaurrutia, *Máscaras mexicanas* (Mexico City, 1926) and A. Caso, 'El uso de las máscaras entre los antiguos mexicanos', *Mexican Folkways*, 5 (1929), 111–13.

62. See E. Matos Moctezuma, 'Los rostros de la muerte', *Arqueología Mexicana*, 6 (2000), 12–17 (14–15).

63. (New York, 1957), 327.

64. It is interesting to note that Nickolas Muray, whose colour photographs of Frida Kahlo are well known, produced three illustrations of Tlazolteotl (two in black-and-white, and one in colour, using a deep blue background for contrast), along with many other reproductions of objects: W. Foshag, S.K. Lothrop, J. Mahler et al., *Pre-Columbian Art: the Robert Woods Bliss Collection*, 2nd edn (London, 1959), xxxvi–xxxvii.

65. See A. Locke, 'Exhibitions and Collectors of Pre-Hispanic Mexican Artefacts in Britain', in E. Matos Moctezuma and F. Solís Olguín (eds), *Aztecs* (London, 2003), 80–91 (85).

66. In 1945 Gruner's grandmother and mother were rescued from the Ravensbruck concentration camp by the Swedish Red Cross. They arrived in Mexico in 1946.

67. See Gruner's own comments in the book cum catalogue: '*Destierro* es un libro-objeto en el cual se describe fotográficamente un juego ritualizado que transgrede lo cotidiano. La condición de "destierro" radica en la conciencia del cuerpo, y su transitoriedad' ['*Exile* is a book-object in which a ritualised game that infringes the everyday is described photographically. The exilic condition derives from an awareness of the body and its transience'].

68. See F. Toor, *Mexican Popular Arts* (Mexico City, 1939), 10 (text) and 42 (image).

69. Gruner studied at the Betzalel Academy of Art and Design in Jerusalem and at the Massachusetts College of Art in Boston.

70. See Kaufman, 'An Essay of Memories', 4–13: 'One of the figures that has fascinated me most from pre-Hispanic mythology is Xipe-Tótec, the god of seedtime and planting. Vegetation dries up and dies in the winter and then comes the spring and the earth is covered with new skin. That is why Xipe-Tótec is also

known as *El Descarnado* – "The Flayed One"' (p. 5); 'The idea came to me of how people shed an artificial skin – and then put it on again. I have made various photographs exploring this idea, Xipe nudes not holding their skin, but their clothing in their hands' (p. 11).

71. During the Tlacaxipehualiztli festival associated with the worship of Xipe-Tótec, held before the rainy season, captives or slaves were sacrificed. The bodies were then flayed and priests wore the skin for twenty days.

72. Photographs of his private collection of pre-Hispanic figures were included in P. Kirchnoff, D.F. Rubin de la Borbolla and S. Toscano, *Arte Precolombino del Occidente de México* (Mexico City, 1946), with the head in plate 25.

73. Caso, *El tesoro de Monte Albán*, 98.

74. A. López Austin, *Cuerpo humano e ideología: Las concepciones de los antiguos nahuas*, 2nd edn (Mexico City, 1984), 435. Suter cites López Austin's book as a source of inspiration.

75. For Suter's *Xipe-Tótec*, see Ferrer, *Shadow*, 98. For a standing female nude sheathed in a transparent cocoon, see G. Suter, *Anáhuac: radiografías de un valle* (Mexico City, 1995).

76. I. Bernal, F. Cámara-Barbachano, R. Piña-Chán et al., *The Mexican National Museum of Anthropology* (London, 1968), 21, 49.

77. *Ibid.*, 176.

78. Photographs of this installation are reproduced in Gruner, *Reliquias-collares*, 28–9, and in Barrios Lara et al., *El cuerpo aludido*, 177.

79. See E.A. Jewel, 'Exposiciones de la Galería Moderna', *Mexican Folkways*, 1 (1930), 48–51 (50), and E. Clewes Parsons, 'La Institución de la Mayordomía', *Mexican Folkways*, 2 (1930), 72–78 (77), respectively.

80. See Toor, *Mexican Popular Arts*, 10.

81. See e.g. G. Fernández Ledesma, 'El sentimiento estético de los juguetes mexicanos', *Forma*, 1 (1926), 32–3; also E. Weston, 'Fotos de juguetes mexicanos', *Forma*, 7 (1928), 16–17.

82. Photographically reproduced in Gruner, *Reliquias-collares*, 11–13, 49, and Ziff (ed.), *Distant Relations*, 116.

83. C. Medina, 'La prohibición como incitación', in Gruner, *Reliquias-collares*, 6–37 (11).

84. Gruner explains her desecratory humour when faced with the commercialisation of Mexican identity in an interview with Malú Huacuja del Toro, 'Saber usar cualquier tecnología es saber integrarla a la expresión personal', *El Financiero*, 26 November 1996, 68: '… tengo un video … que se llama *In situ*, donde una figura prehispánica hace cochinada y media con la boca. El otro día fui a la embajada francesa, donde pasaban videos de turismo mexicano, y me entraron unas ganas terribles de tener ese video ahí puesto' ['… I have a video … which is called *In situ*, where a pre-Hispanic figure performs lewd acts with a mouth. The other day I went to the French embassy, where they were showing Mexican tourist videos, and I felt an irresistible urge to screen my video'].

85. See Suter's gelatin silver prints *Inscripción* (1989) and, from the series *Códices*, *Tlaloc* (1991) and *Coatlicue* (1991), reproduced in Suter, *Labyrinth*, figs. 21–3.

86. Critic Osvaldo Sánchez cited by M.E. Matadamas, 'Gerardo Suter: Fotografía y dolor: Una exposición para rememorar Aztlán', *El Universal*, 6 December 1995, 2.

87. See his commentary on *Águila disecada para muestra del escudo nacional* (1916), a photograph from the Fondo Casasola, in J. Fontcuberta, 'El cielo y la claridad, la tierra y las tinieblas', *Alquimia*, 9 (2000), 32–3.
88. See Sánchez's essay 'Incierta cartografía – Uncertain Cartography', in G. Suter, *Cartografía* (Mexico City, 1996).
89. The image is reproduced in Suter, *Anáhuac*, 19, with an essay by O. Sánchez, ('Cuerpos de Aztlán: Cartografía de un reino', 3–7).
90. M. Vacio, 'Cantos rituales: la obra más reciente de Gerardo Suter en la galería OMR', *El Financiero*, 30 April 1994, 40.

Bibliography

Acevedo, E. (ed.) *Hacia otra historia del arte en México: La fabricación del arte nacional a debate (1920–1950)*. Mexico City: CURARE and CNCA, 2002.

——— 'Los hombres del lápiz y la pluma: la prensa oposicionista de 1869 a 1877', in Acevedo and Ramírez, *La fabricación del estado*, 2003, 90–109.

Acevedo, E., and F. Ramírez, (eds) *Testimonios artísticos de un episodio fugaz, (1864–1867)*. Mexico City: MNA and INBA, 1995.

———, and F. Ramírez, (eds) *La fabricación del estado, 1864–1910*. Mexico City: MNA, 2003.

Acevedo, E., J. Cuadriello, and F. Ramírez (eds) *Los pinceles de la historia: De la patria criolla a la nación mexicana, 1750–1860*. Mexico City: MNA, 2000.

Acevedo, E., D.R. McClelland, M. Schneider Enríquez et al. *México: Una visión de su paisaje/A Landscape Revisited*. New York: Smithsonian Institution, Instituto Cultural Mexicano and Universe Publishing, 1994.

Ades, D., C. Lampert, C. Monsiváis et al. *Francisco Toledo*, London and Madrid, Whitechapel Art Gallery, Museo Nacional de Arte Reina Sofía and Turner Libros, 2000.

Agostoni, S. 'Región abdominal', *ZoneZero*. <http://zonezero.com/...folios/experimental/agostoni/1en.html>

Agrasánchez, R. Jr., (ed.) *Carteles de la época de oro del cine mexicano/Poster Art from the Golden Age of Mexican Cinema*. Mexico City: Universidad de Guadalajara and IMCINE, 1997.

Agüeros, V. *Escritores mexicanos contemporáneos*. Mexico City: I. Escalante, 1880.

Aguilera, C., and P. Martínez Peñaloza. *México: genio que perdura*. Mexico City: San Ángel Ediciones, 1988.

Aguirre Beltrán, G., A. Caso, A. Salas Ortega et al. *Los centros coordinadores indigenistas (edición conmemorativa en ocasión del XXV Congreso Internacional de Americanistas)*. Mexico City: INI, 1962, with photographs by Nacho López.

Albers, P. *Shadows, Fire, Snow: The Life of Tina Modotti*. Berkeley: California University Press, 2002.

Albers, P., and K. Cordero-Reiman. *Tina Modotti: The Mexican Renaissance*. Paris: Jean-Michel Place, 2000.

Albiñana, S. 'Agustín Jiménez', in Albiñana and Fernández, *Mexicana*, 1998, 102–37.

Albiñana, S., and H. Fernández (eds) *Mexicana: Fotografía moderna en México, 1923–1940*. Valencia: IVAM Centre Julio González and Generalitat Valenciana, 1998.

Alpers, S. 'The Studio, the Laboratory and the Vexations of Art', in Galison and Jones, *Picturing Science*, 1998, 403–17.

Alquimia, 4 (1998).

Alquimia, 10 (2000).

Altamirano, I.M. *Revistas literarias de México (1821–1867)*. Mexico City: T.F. Neve, 1868.

——— *La Navidad en las montañas*. Mexico City: Ignacio Escalante, 1871.

——— *Paisajes y leyendas, tradiciones y costumbres de México*. Mexico City: Imprenta Española, 1884.

——— *Obras completas*, ed. C. Sierra Casasus and J. Sotelo Inclán. Mexico City: SEP, 1986, vol. I.

——— *Obras completas*, ed. J.J. Blanco. Mexico City: SEP, 1986, vol. V.

——— *Obras completas*, ed. S. Reyes Nevares. Mexico City: SEP, 1987, vol. VI.

——— *Obras completas*, ed. C. Monsiváis. Mexico City: SEP, 1987, vol. VII.

—— *Obras completas*, ed. J.L. Martínez. Mexico City: SEP, 1988, vols. XII–XIII.

Alton, J. *Painting with Light*. Berkeley and Los Angeles: California University Press, 1995.

Alvarado Lang, C. 'La necesidad de conjugar todas las artes plásticas con un sentido integral', *Espacios*, 1 (January 1949), n.p.n.

Álvarez Bravo, M. 'Fotografías de Manuel Álvarez Bravo', *Contemporáneos: Revista Mexicana de Cultura*, 33 (1931), 136–9.

—— 'Cine', *Artes Plásticas*, 1 (1939), n.p.n.

—— 'Fotografías', *Artes Plásticas*, 1 (1939), n.p.n.

—— *303 Photographies, 1920–1986*. Paris: Musée d'Art Moderne, 1986.

—— *Mucho sol*. Mexico City: FCE, 1989.

—— *Por puro placer: 40 fotografías en platino*. Mexico City: Galería Juan Martín, 1992.

—— *Photographs and Memories*. New York: Aperture, 1997.

—— *Variaciones (1995–1997)*. Mexico City: Centro de la Imagen and CNCA, 1997.

—— *Nudes: The Blue House*. New York: Distributed Art Publishers, 2002.

Álvarez-Buylla Roces, E., and M. Lavín (eds) *Formas de vida: plantas mexicanas vistas por M. Yampolsky*. Mexico City: FCMY, INE and SEMARNAT, 2003.

Álvarez Lima, J.A., G. Estrada, D. de la Torre et al. *México en la obra de Jean Charlot*. Mexico City: CNCA and UNAM, 1994.

Álvarez Urbajtel, A. 'Mi padre fotógrafo', in Álvarez Bravo, *Por puro placer*, 1992, n.p.n.

Amabilis, M. *El Pabellón de México en la Exposición Ibero-Americana de Sevilla*. Mexico City: Talleres Gráficos de la Nación, 1929.

Anda Alanís, E.X. de. *Art Déco: un país nacionalista, un México cosmopolita*. Mexico City: INBA, 1997.

Andrade, Y. *Los velos transparentes, las transparencias veladas*. Villahermosa, Gobierno del Estado de Tabasco, 1988.

—— *Pasión mexicana*. Mexico City: Casa de las Imágenes, CONACULTA and FONCA, 2002.

Anza, A.L., and C. González. 'Una vida onírica en obra y amigos', *Cuartoscuro*, 50 (2001), 27–41.

Aragón Leiva, A. (tr.) 'Sergio Eisenstein: montaje', in Durán, *Antología*, 1973, 294–304.

Arias, J. de D. 'El cajero', in Herrera Castañeda, *Los mexicanos pintados*, 1986, I: 77–86.

Armstrong, C. *Scenes in a Library: Reading the Photograph in the Book, 1843–1875*. Cambridge, MA: MIT Press, 1998.

Arnal, A., and P. Massé. 'Nacho López: cronista en blanco y negro', *Luna Córnea*, 8 (1995), 32–9.

Arteaga, A., O. Sánchez, and R. Stearns. *Mexico Now/México Ahora: Point of Departure/Punto de Partida [arte contemporáneo en México]*. Columbus, OH, The Arts' Council Riffe Gallery, 1997.

Artes de México, 49 (2000).

Ayala Blanco, J. *La aventura del cine mexicano en la época de oro y después*. Mexico City: Grijalbo, 1993.

Bablot, A., and R. Masson. 'Prospecto', *El Daguerreotipo: revista enciclopédica y universal*, 1 (1850), n.p.n.

Bali, J., and V.H. Valencia. 'Acervos fotográficos: imágenes de la historia, historia de la fotografía', *México en el Tiempo*, 2 (1994), 45–8.

Ballent, A. 'El arte de saber vivir: modernización del habitar doméstico y cambio urbano, 1940–1970', in García Canclini, *Cultura y comunicación*, 1998, I: 65–131.

Baranda, J. *Obras*. Mexico City: V. Agüeros, 1900.

Barba de Piña Chán, B., and M. Rodríguez-Shadow (eds) *Chalchihuite: Homenaje a Doris Heyden*. Mexico City: INAH, 1999.

Barkan, L. *Unearthing the Past: Archaeology and Aesthetics in the Making of Renaissance Culture*. New Haven and London: Yale University Press, 1999.

Barrios Lara, J.L. 'Cuerpo fragmentado', in Barrios Lara et al. (eds), *El cuerpo aludido*, 1998, 172–81.

Barrios Lara, J.L., I.M. Benítez Dueñas, K. Cordero Reiman et al. *El cuerpo aludido: anatomías y construcciones, México, siglos XVI–XX*. Mexico City: MNA, CONACULTA and INBA, 1998.

Barros, C., and M. Buenrostro (eds) *Las once y serenooo!: Tipos mexicanos, siglo XIX*. Mexico City: CNCA, Lotería Nacional and FCE, 1994.

Barros, C., and C. Sierra. *Ignacio Manuel Altamirano: iconografía*. Mexico City: CNCA, FCE and Estado de Guerrero, 1993.

Barthes, R. *Image, Music, Text*, tr. S. Heath. London: Fontana, 1977.

Bartra, A. 'Ver para descreer', *Luna Córnea*, 13 (1997), 72–85.

Bartra, A., A. Moreno Toscano and E. Ramírez Castañeda. *De fotógrafos y de indios*. Mexico City: Ediciones Tecolote, 2000.

Batchen, G. 'Phantasm: Digital Imaging and the Death of Photography', in Haworth-Booth, *Metamorphoses*, 1994, 46–51.

—— *Forget Me Not: Photography and Remembrance*. Amsterdam and New York: Van Gogh Museum, Princeton, 2004.

Batis, H. *Índices de 'El Renacimiento'*. Mexico City: UNAM, 1963.

—— (ed.) *El Renacimiento: periódico literario*. Mexico City: F. Díaz de León & Santiago White, 1869, repr. UNAM, 1979.

Benítez, F. 'La Tumba 7 Monte Albán', *Arqueología Mexicana*, 3 (1993), 26–34.

Benjamin, W. *One Way Street and Other Writings*, ed. and trs. E. Jephcott and K. Shorter. London: NLB, 1979.

—— *Selected Writings*, ed. M. Bullock and M.W. Jennings. Cambridge, MA and London: Harvard University Press, 1996, vol. I.

Bermúdez, M.T., P. Gonzalbo, D. Tanck de Estrada et al. *Historia de la lectura en México*, 2nd edn. Mexico City: El Colegio de México, 1997.

Bernal, I., F. Cámara-Barbachano, R. Piña-Chán et al. *The Mexican National Museum of Anthropology*. London: Thames & Hudson, 1968.

'Bibliografía: América poética', *El Álbum Mexicano*, 1 (1849), 614–15.

Billeter, E., C. Fuentes, M. Glantz et al. *México: Juan Rulfo fotógrafo*, Barcelona: Lunwerg, 2001.

Blanco, J.J., M. Fernández Perera, L. Zapata et al. *Lola Álvarez Bravo: Recuento fotográfico*. Mexico City: Editorial Penélope, 1982.

Blasco, V., L. García-Noriega y Nieto, C. Pantoja et al. (eds) *Luz y tiempo: La colección fotográfica formada por Manuel Álvarez Bravo para la Fundación Cultural Televisa*, 3 vols. Mexico City: Centro Cultural Arte Contemporáneo and Fundación Cultural Televisa, 1995.

Blühm, A. (ed.) *The Colour of Sculpture, 1840–1910*. Amsterdam, Van Gogh Museum, 1996.

Boils, G. 'Arquitectura y producción del espacio social', in Loyola, *Entre la guerra y la estabilidad política*, 1990, 321–38.

Bond, A. (ed.) *Body*. Sidney: The Art Gallery of New South Wales, 1997.

Bonfil, C., and C. Monsiváis. *A través del espejo: el cine mexicano y su público*. Mexico City: Instituto Mexicano de Cinematografía and Ediciones El Milagro, 1994.

Bonpland, A., and A. von Humboldt. *Personal Narrative of Travels to the Equinoctial Regions of America during the Years 1799–1804*, ed. and tr. T. Ross. London and New York: G. Routledge & Sons, 1851, vol. I.

Braun, B. *Pre-Columbian Art and the Post-Columbian World: Ancient American Sources of Modern Art*. New York: Harry N. Abrams, 1993.

Brenner, A. *Idols Behind Altars*. New York: Payson & Clark, 1929.

Bruehl, A. *Photographs of Mexico*. New York: Delphic Studios, 1933.

Bryson, N. *Looking at the Overlooked: Four Essays on Still Life Painting*. London: Reaktion, 1990.

Burian, E.R. (ed.) *Modernity and the Architecture of Mexico*. Austin: Texas University Press, 1997.

Calderón de la Barca, Mme. *Life in Mexico: During a Residence of Two Years in the Country (1839–1841)*. London: Century, 1987.

Calderón, F. *Obras poéticas de Fernando Calderón*, ed. I. Cumplido. Mexico City: I. Cumplido, 1844.

Camarillo, J. 'Autorretrato', *ZoneZero*. <http://zonezero.com/... olios/experimental/camarillo/ 1en.html>

Canales, C. *Romualdo García: Un fotógrafo, una ciudad, una época*. Guanajuato: Gobierno del Estado, INAH, SEP and Museo Regional de la Alhóndiga de Granaditas, 1990.

Cardoza y Aragón, L. 'Light and Shadow: Manuel Álvarez Bravo Photographer', *Mexican Art and Life*, 6 (1939), n.p.n.

—— *La pintura mexicana contemporánea*. Mexico City: UNAM, 1953.

—— *Pintura contemporánea de México*. Mexico City: Era, 1991.

Cardoza y Aragón, L., A. Rodriguez and J. Vasconcelos. *Diego Rivera: Los murales en la Secretaría de Educación Pública*. Mexico City: SEP, 1986.

Carmen Solanes Carraro, M. del and E. Vela Ramírez, 'Imágenes históricas de la arqueología en México, siglo xx', *Arqueología Mexicana*, 7 (2001), 62.

Carrillo Trueba, C., and J. Lépez Vela. *Nacho López: los rumbos del tiempo*. Mexico City: INI, INAH and Gobierno del Estado de Hidalgo, 1997.

Casanova, R. 'Memoria y registro fotográfico en el Museo Nacional', *Alquimia*, 12 (2001), 7–16.

Casanova, R., and O. Debroise. *Sobre la superficie bruñida de un espejo: Fotógrafos del siglo XIX*. Mexico City: FCE, 1989.

Caso, A. 'El uso de las máscaras entre los antiguos mexicanos', *Mexican Folkways*, 5 (1929), 111–13.

—— 'Los hallazgos de Monte Albán', *Mexican Folkways*, 7 (1932), 114–28.

—— 'Monte Alban: An Archeological Zone of World-wide Renown', *Mexican Art and Life*, 4 (1938), n.p.n.

—— 'Pre-Spanish Art', in Caso et al., *Twenty Centuries*, 1940, 23–30.

—— *El tesoro de Monte Albán*. Mexico City: INAH and SEP, 1969.

Caso, A., and I. Bernal. *Urnas de Oaxaca*. Mexico City: INAH and SEP, 1952.

Caso, A., R. Montenegro, M. Toussaint et al. *Twenty Centuries of Mexican Art*. New York: Museum of Modern Art, 1940.

Castellanos, A. 'Espacio y espejo', in Castellanos et al., *La ciudad de los viajeros*, 43–55.

—— 'Nacho López: los rituales de la modernidad', *Alquimia*, 2 (1998), 7–11.

—— (ed.) *Memoria fotográfica de México*. Madrid, Ayuntamiento de Madrid and Centro Cultural de la Villa, 1998.

Castellanos, A., and M. García. 'Encuentros con el fotógrafo Manuel Álvarez Bravo', *Kalías: Revista de Arte*, 15–16 (1996), 122–30.

Castellanos, A., N. García Canclini and A. Rosas Mantecón. *La ciudad de los viajeros: Travesías e imaginarios urbanos: México, 1940–2000*. Mexico City: UAM and Grijalbo, 1996.

Castellanos, A., J. Mraz, L. Ortiz Monasterio et al. *Foto Hnos Mayo*. Valencia: IVAM Centre Julio González and Generalitat Valenciana, 1992.

Castellanos, A., L. Kaplan, P. Meyer et al. *The Real and the True: The Digital Photography of Pedro Meyer*. Berkeley: New Riders, 2006.

Castellanos, A., E. Poniatowska, F. Reyes Palma et al. *Homenaje Nacional a M. Yampolsky*. Mexico City: CONACULTA, INBA, INAH and FCMY, 2002.

Castelló Yturbide, T. 'Cajitas de entretenimientos', *México en el Tiempo: Revista de Historia y Conservación*, 13 (1996), 66–71.

Castro, C. *México y sus alrededores. Colección de monumentos, trajes y paisajes dibujados al natural y litografiados*. Mexico City: Decaen Editor, 1855–6.

'Catecismos y manuales', *El Mosaico Mexicano*, 4 (1840), 169–73.

Catherwood, F. *Views of Ancient Monuments in Central America, Chiapas and Yucatán*. London: F. Catherwood, 1844.

Cevallos, F.J. (ed.) *Sor Juana Inés: Antología poética*. Salamanca: Colegio de España, 1989.

Chanu, P. le. *Il drapeggio: Taccuino di disegni*. Paris: Bibliothèque de l'Image, 2002.

Charlot, J. *The Mexican Mural Renaissance, 1920–1925*. New Haven and London: Yale University Press, 1963.

—— *An Artist on Art: Collected Essays of Jean Charlot*, 2 vols. Honolulu: Hawaii University Press, 1972.

Cherry P., and W.B. Jordan. *Spanish Still Life from Velázquez to Goya*. London: National Gallery, 1995.

Clewes Parsons, E. 'La Institución de la Mayordomía', *Mexican Folkways*, 2 (1930), 72–8.

Cohen, L. 'Naturaleza muerta', *ZoneZero*. <http://zonezero.com/... ciones/fotografos/cohen/default.html>

—— *Obra reciente*. Mexico City: Galería OMR, 1997.

Composiciones leidas en la velada literaria que consagró El Liceo Hidalgo a la memoria de Sor Juana Inés de La Cruz. Mexico City: Imp. de *El Porvenir*, 1874.

Cooper, T., and P. Hill. *Dialogue with Photography*, Stockport: Dewi Lewis, 1998.

Cordero Reiman, K. '*La expulsión del paraíso*: Instalación de Silvia Gruner', 2 *Curare*, 1993, 2.

—— 'Síntomas culturales: cuerpos del siglo XX en México', in Barrios Lara et al., *El cuerpo aludido*, 1998, 89–109.

—— 'La invención del arte popular y la construcción de la cultura visual moderna en México', in Acevedo, *Hacia otra historia*, 2002, 67–90.

Cordova, C.A., *Agustín Jiménez y la vanguardia fotográfica mexicana*. Mexico City: Editorial RM, 2005.

Cordry, D., and D. *Mexican Indian Costumes*. Austin and London: Texas University Press, 1968.

Cortés Juárez, E. *El grabado contemporáneo*. Mexico City: Ediciones Mexicanas, 1951.

Covarrubias, J.E. (ed.) *Alejandro de Humboldt en México*. Mexico City: INAH, 1997.

Covarrubias, M. *The Eagle, the Jaguar, and the Serpent: Indian Art of the Americas*. New York: Alfred A. Knopf, 1954.

—— *Indian Art of Mexico and Central America*. New York: Alfred A. Knopf, 1957.

Cuadriello, J. (ed.) *Juegos de ingenio y agudeza: la pintura emblemática en la Nueva España*. Mexico City: MNA, Ediciones del Equilibrista and Turner Libros, 1994.

Cuevas, J.L., E. Krauze, R. Tovar y de Teresa et al. *Pintura Mexicana 1950–1980: homenaje a Fernando Gamboa*. Mexico City: 1993.

Cumplido, I. 'A nuestros lectores', *El Mosaico Mexicano*, 2 (1837), 477–8.

—— 'La carcel de la Acordada en México: modelos para una reforma', *El Mosaico Mexicano*, 5 (1841), 145–53.

—— (ed.) 'Introducción', *El Museo Mexicano*, 1 (1843), n.p.n.

—— (ed.) 'Introducción', *La Ilustración Mexicana*, 4 (1854), 1.

Cumplido, I., and I.R. Gondra (eds) 'Advertencia preliminar', *El Mosaico Mexicano*, 2 (1837), 3–5.

'Curiosa relacion de todos los que se han publicado en Mérida, desde que se estableció la libertad de prensa', *Registro Yucateco*, 1 (1845), 233–7.

Debroise, O. *Fuga mexicana: un recorrido por la fotografía en México*. Mexico City: CNCA, 1994.

—— *Lola Álvarez Bravo: In Her Own Light*. Tucson: Arizona University Press, 1994.

—— 'Gerardo Suter: Primary Machines', in Suter, *Labyrinth*, 1999, 22–33.

—— (ed.) *Laura Cohen: albercas*. Mexico City: CNCA and Círculo de Arte, 2005.

Debroise, O., S. Navarrete and P. Schneider. *Frida Kahlo, Diego Rivera and 20th-Century Mexican Art: The Jacques and Natasha Gelman Collection*. San Diego: Museum of Contemporary Art, 2000.

Debroise, O., J.D. Oles and M.C. Ramírez. *David Alfaro Siqueiros: Portrait of a Decade, 1930–1940*. Mexico City: MNA and INBA, 1997.

Dehesa, G. (ed.) *México indio: Testimonios en blanco y negro*. Mexico City: InverMex, 1994.

Delpar, H. *The Enormous Vogue of Things Mexican: Cultural Relations between the United States and Mexico, 1920–1935*. Tuscaloosa and London: Alabama University Press, 1992.

Diener, P. 'El perfil del artista viajero en el siglos XIX', in Trabulse, *Viajeros europeos*, 1996, 63–85.

Diez de Bonilla, F. 'Arqueologia Mexicana', *El Liceo Mexicano*, 1 (1844), 145.

'Diferencias de la especie humana calculadas sobre la linea facial', *El Mosaico Mexicano*, 3 (1840), 449–55.

Doniz, R. *Casa Santa*. Mexico City: FCE, 1986.

Doremus, A.T. *Culture, Politics and National Identity in Mexican Literature and Film, 1929–1952*. New York: Peter Lang, 2001.

Downs, L., R. Eder, I. Rodríguez-Prampolini et al. *Diego Rivera: A Retrospective*. New York and London: Founders Society Detroit Institute of Arts and Hayward Gallery, 1986.

Doy, G. *Drapery: Classicism and Barbarism in Visual Culture*. London and New York: I.B. Tauris, 2002.

Duarte, C. (ed.) *Camaristas: Fotógrafos mayas de Chiapas*. Mexico City: Centro de la Imagen, CIESAS and Casa de las Imágenes, 1998.

Dueñas, P. *Las divas en el Teatro de Revista mexicano*. Mexico City: Asociación Mexicana de Estudios Fonográficos, 1994.

Durán, M. (ed.) *Antología de la Revista Contemporáneos*. Mexico City: FCE, 1973.

Edwards, E. *Painted Walls of Mexico from Prehistoric Times until Today*. Austin: Texas University Press, 1966.

—— (ed.) *Anthropology and Photography, 1860–1910*. New Haven and London: Yale University Press, 1992.

'El daguerrotipo en el harem', *El Mosaico Mexicano*, 4 (1840), 145.

El Gabinete de Lectura: periódico literario, político, artístico, de industria y de teatros, o miscelánea instructiva de variedades y costumbres de ambos mundos y en particular de la República Mexicana, Introduction, 1 (1845), 1–2.

'El rebozo de mi madre', *Artes de México*, 142 (1971), 34.

Elkins, J. *The Poetics of Perspective*. Ithaca and London: Cornell University Press, 1994.

—— *Pictures of the Body: Pain and Metamorphosis*. Stanford: Stanford University Press, 1999.

Enciso, J. *Sellos del antiguo México*. Mexico City: Fondo Editorial de la Plástica Mexicana, 1947.

Enríquez Fuentes, E. 'Altamirano, nuestro contemporáneo: entrevista con Nicole Giron', *Tierra Adentro*, 82 (1996), 41–7.

Estrada de Gerlero, E.I. 'La litografía y el Museo Nacional como armas del nacionalismo', in

Acevedo et al., *Los pinceles de la historia*, 2000, 152–69.

Falcón, R. *Las rasgaduras de la descolonización: españoles y mexicanos a mediados del siglo XIX.* Mexico City: El Colegio de México, 1996.

Fane, D. (ed.) *Converging Cultures: Art and Identity in Spanish America.* New York: Harry N. Abrams, 1996.

Farago, C. (ed.) *Reframing the Renaissance: Visual Culture in Europe and Latin America, 1450–1650.* New Haven: Yale University Press, 1995.

Fastlicht S., and J. Romero. *El arte de las mutilaciones dentarias.* Mexico City: Ediciones Mexicanas, 1951.

Faunce, S. 'Courbet: Feminist in Spite of Himself', in Bond, *Body*, 1997, 95–108.

Favrot Peterson, J. *The Paradise Garden Murals of Malinalco: Utopia and Empire in Sixteenth-Century Mexico.* Austin: Texas University Press, 1993.

Fernández, H. (ed.) *Fotografía pública/Photography in Print, 1919–1939.* Madrid: Museo Nacional Centro de Arte Reina Sofia and Aldeasa, 1999.

Fernández, J. *Orozco: Forma e idea*, 2nd edn. Mexico City: Porrua, 1975.

Fernández Ledesma, E. *La gracia de los retratos antiguos.* Mexico City: Ediciones Mexicanas, 1950.

Fernández Ledesma, G. 'El sentimiento estético de los juguetes mexicanos', *Forma*, 1 (1926), 32–3.

Ferrer, E. *A Shadow Born of Earth: New Photography in Mexico.* New York: American Federation of Arts and Universe Publishing, 1993.

—— (ed.) *The True Poetry: The Art of María Izquierdo.* New York: Americas Society Art Gallery and Arizona University Press, 1997.

Fields, V.M., and V. Zamudio-Taylor (eds) *The Road to Aztlan: Art from a Mythic Homeland.* Los Angeles: Los Angeles County Museum of Art, 2001.

50 años TGP: Taller de Gráfica Popular, 1937–1987. Mexico City: Museo Palacio de Bellas Artes, Museo Nacional de la Estampa and Galeria Jose Maria Velasco, 1987.

Figarella, M. *Edward Weston y Tina Modotti en México: su inserción dentro de las estrategias estéticas del arte posrevolucionario.* Mexico City: UNAM and IIE, 2002.

Figueroa, G. 'Untitled', in Rodríguez Prampolini, *Leopoldo Méndez*, 1981, 39–44.

—— 'Un pueblo despojado de color', *Artes de México*, 10 (1990), 47–8.

Flores, E. 'Los hombres infames', *Luna Córnea*, 13 (1997), 55–63.

Flores Olea, V. *Eros en el espacio virtual. ZoneZero.* <http://zonezero.com/exposiciones/fotografos/vfo/default2.html>

Florescano, E. *Etnia, estado y nación: ensayo sobre las identidades colectivas en México.* Mexico City: Aguilar, 1997.

Folgarait, L. *Mural Painting and Social Revolution in Mexico, 1920–1940.* Cambridge: Cambridge University Press, 1998.

Fontcuberta, J. *El beso de Judas: fotografía y verdad.* Barcelona: Gustavo Gili, 2000.

—— 'El cielo y la claridad, la tierra y las tinieblas', *Alquimia*, 9 (2000), 32–3.

Fontcuberta, J., P. Gasparini, P. Meyer et al. *V Coloquio latinoamericano de fotografía.* Mexico City: Centro de la Imagen and CNCA, 1996.

Foshag, W., S.K. Lothrop, J. Mahler et al. *Pre-Columbian Art: the Robert Woods Bliss Collection*, 2nd edn. London: Phaidon, 1959.

Fotoseptiembre. Mexico City: Centro de la Imagen, 1996.

Fox Talbot, H. *Some Account of Photogenic Drawing or the process by which Natural Objects may be made to delineate themselves without the aid of the Artist's Pencil.* London: R & J.E. Taylor, 1839.

Frankel, F., and G.M. Whitesides. *On the Surface of Things: Images of the Extraordinary in Science.* San Francisco: Chronicle Books, 1997.

'Frenologia', *El Mosaico Mexicano*, 1 (1837), 485–7.

Frías y Soto, H. 'El alacenero', in Herrera Castañeda, *Los mexicanos pintados*, 1986, I: 113–17.

—— 'El pulquero', in Herrera Castañeda, *Los mexicanos pintados*, 1986, I: 25–32.

—— 'La chiera', in Herrera Castañeda, *Los mexicanos pintados*, 1986, I: 15–22.

Fry, N. (ed. and tr.) *Luis Buñuel: Three Screenplays – Viridiana, The Exterminating Angel, Simon of the Desert*. New York: Orion, 1969.

Fuente, B. de la, J.A. Manrique, O. Paz et al. *Mexico: Splendors of Thirty Centuries*. New York: Metropolitan Museum of Art and Bulfinch, 1990.

Fulgueira, M.A. *Cuadernos de la Cineteca Nacional: Testimonios para la historia del cine mexicano*. Mexico City: Secretaría de Gobernación, 1976, vol. III.

Furst, J.L.M. *The Natural History of the Soul in Ancient Mexico*. New Haven: Yale University Press, 1995.

Galison, P., and C.A. Jones (eds) *Picturing Science: Producing Art*. London and New York: Routledge, 1998.

Gamio, M. *Forjando patria, pro-nacionalismo* [1916]. Mexico City: Editorial Porrua, 1960.

Ganado Kim, E. (ed.) *Las transgresiones del cuerpo: arte contemporáneo de México*. Mexico City: CNCA, INBA and MACG, 1997.

Gante, G. de. 'Piropos al rebozo', *Artes de México*, 142 (1971), 47.

García Barragán, E. 'Juan Cordero: el primer muralista y su siglo', *Saber Ver*, 41 (1998), 12–69.

—— (ed.) *Saturnino Herrán: Jornadas de homenaje*. Mexico City: UNAM, 1989.

García Canclini, N. (ed.) *Cultura y comunicación en la ciudad de México*, 2 vols. Mexico City: UAM and Grijalbo, 1998, vol. I.

García Riera, E. *Emilio Fernández (1904–1986)*. Guadalajara: Universidad de Guadalajara and Cineteca Nacional de Mexico, 1987.

—— *México visto por el cine extranjero: 1894–1940*. Mexico City: Ediciones Era, 1987.

—— *Historia documental del cine mexicano*. Mexico City: Universidad de Guadalajara, Istituto Mexicano de Cinematografía, CNCA and Gobierno de Jalisco, 1993, vol. VII.

—— *Breve historia del cine mexicano: primer siglo, 1897–1997*. Mexico City: CONAC-ULTA, IMCINE, Ediciones Mapa and Universidad de Guadalajara, 1998.

García Torres, V. 'Introduccion', *Panorama de las Señoritas: Periódico Pintoresco, Científico y Literario*, 1 (1842), 1–2.

García, H. *México sin retoque*. Mexico City: UNAM, 1987.

—— *Camera oscura*. Mexico City: Gobierno del Estado de Veracruz, 1992.

Garduño, F. *Inner Light – Still Lifes and Nudes*. New York: Bulfinch and Little, Brown & Co., 2002.

Garduño Pulido, B., L. González Matute, S. Morales Mora et al. *Misiones culturales: Los años utópicos, 1920–1938*. Mexico City: CONACULTA, INBA and Museo Casa Estudio D. Rivera & F. Kahlo, 1999.

Garduño Pulido, B., A. Híjar, J. Villanueva Hernández et al. *Luz Jiménez: Símbolo de un pueblo milenario, 1897–1965*. Mexico City: CNCA and Museo Estudio Diego Rivera, Mexic-Arte Museum, 2000.

Garza, M. *Foto-Escultura: A Mexican Photographic Tradition*. Albuquerque: University of New Mexico Art Museum, 1998.

Georgel, C. 'The Museum as Metaphor in Nineteenth-Century France', in Rogoff and Sherman, *Museum Culture*, 1994, 113–21.

Giménez Cacho, M. 'Juan Rulfo, fotógrafo', *Luna Córnea*, 6 (1995), 50–5.

Glantz, M. (ed.) *Del Fistol a la Linterna: Homenaje a José Tomás de Cuéllar*. Mexico City: UNAM, 1997.

Goded, M. *Tierra negra: fotografías de la costa chica en Guerrero y Oaxaca, México*. Mexico City: CNCA and Luzbel, 1994.

Gola, P. 'Escenarios rituales: Coversación con Gerardo Suter', *Luna Córnea*, 2 (1993), 26–35.

Goldman, S.M. *Contemporary Mexican Painting in a Time of Change*. Albuquerque: New Mexico University Press, 1995.

Gómez de la Cortina, J.J. 'Esposicion sumaria: del sistema frenológico del doctor Gall por José Ramon Pacheco', *Revista Mexicana*, 1 (1835), 383.

——— 'Necesidad de la critica en las ciencias', *Revista Mexicana*, 1 (1835), 21–3.

——— 'Prólogo', *Revista Mexicana*, 1 (1835), 3–9.

Gómez de Tuddo, A., and Zarebsk, C. *México inédito*. Mexico City: Basilisco Editores, AGN, CONACULTA and INBA, 1999.

Gondra, I.R. (ed.) 'Introducción', *El Mosaico Mexicano*, 1 (1836), 3–4.

——— 'Antigüedades mexicanas', *El Mosaico Mexicano*, 2 (1837), 281–4.

——— 'Antigüedades mexicanas: Extracto del viaje...', *El Mosaico Mexicano*, 2 (1837), 330–4.

——— 'Campeche visto desde el mar', *El Mosaico Mexicano*, 2 (1837), 101–4.

González Cruz Manjarrez, M. *Tina Modotti y el muralismo mexicano*. Mexico City: IIE-UNAM, 1999.

González Matute, L. (ed.) *¡30-30! contra la Academia de Pintura? (1928)*. Mexico City: INBA and Centro Nacional de Investigación, 1993.

González Obregón, L. *Breve noticia de los novelistas mexicanos en el siglo XIX*. Mexico City: O.R. Spindola, 1889.

González Peña, C. *Historia de la literatura mexicana. Desde los orígenes hasta nuestros días*. Mexico City: Cultura and SEP, 1928.

——— 'México en la pantalla (1917)', in Miquel, *Los exaltados*, 1992, 65–6.

Good, C., and J.V. Waldron (eds) *The Effects of the Nation: Mexican Art in an Age of Globalization*. Philadelphia: Temple University Press, 2001.

Green, J. 'Pedro Meyer's Documentary Fictions', in Haworth-Booth, *Metamorphoses*, 1994, 32–7.

Grimberg, S. (ed.) *Lola Álvarez Bravo: The Frida Kahlo Photographs*. Dallas: Society of Friends of Mexican Culture, 1991.

Gruening, E. *Mexico and its Heritage*. London: Stanley Paul, 1928.

Gruner, S. *Reliquias-collares*. Mexico City: Centro de la Imagen, FONCA and CNCA, 1998.

——— *Circuito interior*. Mexico City: MACG, CONACULTA and INBA, 2000.

Gualdi, P. *Monumentos de Méjico tomados del natural y litografiados por Pedro Gualdi, pintor de perspectiva*. Mexico City: Massé y Decaen, 1841.

Guerrero, J. *La génesis del crimen en México*. Mexico City: CNCA, 1996.

Hale, C.A. *The Transformation of Liberalism in Late Ninenteenth-Century Mexico*. Princeton: Princeton University Press, 1989.

Harnoncourt, R. d'. *Mexican Arts*. New York: The American Federation of Arts, 1930.

Haus, A. *Moholy-Nagy: Photographs and Photograms*. London: Thames & Hudson, 1980.

Haworth-Booth, M. (ed.) *Metamorphoses: Photography in the Electronic Age*. New York: Aperture Foundation, 1994.

Hazlitt, W. 'On the Picturesque and Ideal: A Fragment', in Howe, *The Complete Works*, 1931, VIII: 317.

Heimann J. (ed.) *Mexicana: Vintage Mexican Graphics*. Cologne and London: Taschen, 2002.

Helm, M. 'The School of Mexico City', in *Modern Mexican Painters*, 1941, 10–15.

Henares Cuellar, I., F. Ramírez, R. Velásquez Martínez del Campo et al. *El espejo simbolista: Europa y México, 1870–1920*. Mexico City: MNA, UNAM, CONACULTA and INBA, 2004.

Hermosa, J. *Manual de geografía y estadística de la República Mexicana*. Paris: Librería de Rosa y Bouret, 1857, repr. Mexico City: Instituto Mora, 1991.

Hernández Monroy, R. 'Ignacio Manuel Altamirano, crítico literario', in Rueda de la Serna, *Historiografía de la literatura mexicana*, 1996, 89–106.

Herrera Castañeda, M. (ed.) *Los mexicanos pintados por sí mismos*, 2 vols. Mexico City: 1853–5, repr. Querétaro: Ediciones del Goberno del Estado, 1986.

Hill Boone, E., and W.D. Mignolo (eds) *Writing without Words: Alternative Literacies in Mesoamerica and the Andes*. Durham, NC and London: Duke University Press, 1994.

Hill, J.T., and G. Mora (eds) *W. Eugene Smith: Photographs, 1934–1975*. New York: Harry N. Abrams, 1998.

Hollander, A. *Fabric of Vision: Dress and Drapery in Painting*. London: National Gallery and Yale University Press, 2002.

Honour, H. *Romanticism*. London: Penguin, 1981, repr. 1991.

Hooks, M. *Tina Modotti: Photographer and Revolutionary*. London: HarperCollins, 1993.

Hopkinson, A. (ed.) *Desires and Disguises: Five Latin American Photographers*. London and New York: Serpent's Tail, 1992.

Howe, P.P. (ed.) *The Complete Works of William Hazlitt*. London and Toronto: J.M. Dent & Sons, 1931, vol. VIII.

Humboldt, A. von. *Essai politique sur le royaume de la Nouvelle-Espagne*. Paris: Schoell, 1808.

—— *Vues de cordillères et monuments des peuples indigenes de l'Amérique*. Paris: Schoell, 1810.

—— *Atlas géographique et physique du royaume de la Nouvelle Espagne*. Paris: Schoell, 1811.

Humphrey, R. *Walter Scott: Waverley*. Cambridge: Cambridge University Press, 1993.

Hyde, R. *Panoramania!: The Art and Entertainment of the 'All-Embracing' View*. London: Trefoil Publications and Barbican Art Gallery, 1988.

Isaac, A. *Conversaciones con Gabriel Figueroa*. Guadalajara: Universidad de Guadalajara, Universidad de Colima and Centro de Investigación y Enseñanza Cinematográficas, 1993.

Iturbide, G. *Sueños de papel*. Mexico City: FCE, 1988.

—— *Juchitán de las mujeres*. Mexico City: Ediciones Toledo, 1989.

—— *En el nombre del padre*. Mexico City: Ediciones Toledo, 1993.

—— *Images of the Spirit*. New York: Aperture, 1996.

—— *Travel Notebook*. Mexico City: Carrillo Gil Museum, 1999.

Iturriaga, J.N. *Litografía y grabado en el México del XIX*. Mexico City: Telmex, 1994, I: 128.

Jakobson, R. 'Aspects linguistiques de la traduction', in Ruwet, *Essais de linguistique générale*, 1963, 78–86.

Jewel, E.A. 'Exposiciones de la Galería Moderna', *Mexican Folkways*, 1 (1930), 48–51.

Jiménez Codinach, G. 'Casimiro Castro y sus alredededores, 1826–1889', in Codinach et al., *Casimiro Castro*, 1996, 27–49.

Jiménez Codinach, G., C. Monsiváis, R. Pérez Escamilla et al. *Casimiro Castro y su taller*. Mexico City: Banamex, 1996.

Jiménez Rueda, J. *Historia de la literatura mexicana*. Mexico City: Polis, 1928.

—— *Letras mexicanas en el siglo XIX*. Mexico City: FCE, 1944.

Johnson, G.A. (ed.) *Sculpture and Photography: Envisioning the Third Dimension*. Cambridge: Cambridge University Press, 1998.

Jordanova, L., and D. Petherbridge. *The Quick and the Dead: Artists and Anatomy*. London: The South Bank Centre, 1997.

José Guadalupe Posada: Ilustrador de la vida mexicana. Mexico City: Fondo Editorial de la

Plástica Mexicana, 1963; repr. 1982.

Kagan, R.L. *Urban Images of the Hispanic World, 1493–1793.* New Haven: Yale University Press, 2000.

Katzew, I. (ed.) *New World Orders: Casta Painting and Colonial Latin America.* New York: American Society Art Gallery, 1996.

Kaufman, F. 'An Essay of Memories', in Álvarez Bravo, *Photographs and Memories*, 1997, 4–13.

Keller, J., *El Taller de Gráfica Popular: Block Prints and Lithographs by Artists of the TGP from the Archer M. Huntington Art Gallery.* Austin: Archer M. Huntington Gallery, 1985.

Kemp, M., and M. Wallace. *Spectacular Bodies: The Art and Science of the Human Body from Leonardo to Now.* London: Hayward Gallery and California University Press, 2000.

Kirchnoff, P., D.F. Rubin de la Borbolla, S. Toscano et al. *Arte Precolombino del Occidente de México.* Mexico City: SEP, 1946.

Kismaric, S. (ed.) *Manuel Álvarez Bravo.* New York: The Museum of Modern Art and Harry Abrams, 1997.

—— (ed.) *Héctor García.* Mexico City: Turner, Equilibrista and CONACULTA, 2004.

Klor de Alva, J.J. 'Mestizaje from New Spain to Aztlán: On the Control and Classification of Collective Identities', in Katzew, *New World Orders*, 1996, 58–71.

'La nariz o manera de conocer por su figura las inclinaciones de las personas', *El Mosaico Mexicano*, 3 (1840), 180–2.

'La patria', *El Liceo Mexicano*, 2 (1844), 231.

Labastida, J. 'Humboldt y la antropología en México', in Covarrubias, *Alejandro de Humboldt*, 1997, 135–51.

Lafragua, J.M. 'Caracter y objeto de la literatura', in Rueda de la Serna, *La misión del escritor*, 1996, 69–77.

Lafragua, J.M., and M. Orozco y Berra. *La Ciudad de México.* Mexico City: Editorial Porrúa, 1987.

Lavin, I. (ed.) *Erwin Panofsky: Three Essays on Style.* Cambridge, MA: MIT Press, 1995.

Lenz, H. *Historia del papel en México y cosas relacionadas (1525–1950).* Mexico City: Miguel Angel Porrúa, 1990.

León-Portilla, M. 'Manuel Gamio y el indigenismo', in García Barragán, *Saturnino Herrán*, 1989, 107–20.

León-Portilla, M., and D. Sodi (eds) *Flor y canto del arte prehispánico de México.* Mexico City: Fondo Editorial de la Plástica Mexicana, 1964.

'Literatura del siglo diez y nueve', *El Ateneo Mexicano*, 1 (1844), 161–3.

Locke, A. 'Exhibitions and Collectors of Pre-Hispanic Mexican Artefacts in Britain', in Matos Moctezuma and Solís Olguín, *Aztecs*, 2003, 80–91.

Lombroso, C. *After Death—What?*, tr. W.S. Kennedy. London: T. Fisher Unwin, 1909.

López, C. 'Nacho López: un artista multidisciplinario', *Generación*, 9 (1996), 10–12.

López, N. *Los Pueblos de la Bruma y el Sol.* Mexico City: INI-FONAPAS, 1981.

—— *Antología de fetiches.* Xalapa, Veracruz: Galeria del Estado IVEC [Instituto Veracruzano de Cultura], 1996.

—— 'Fotopoemáticos', *Generación*, 9 (1996), 16–18.

—— 'Mi punto de partida', *Generación*, 9 (1996), 13.

—— *Los rumbos del tiempo*, ed. J. Lépez Vela. Mexico City: INI, INAH and Gobierno del Estado de Hidalgo, 1997.

López Argoutia, L. 'México en la lente de Gabriel Figueroa: Entrevista', *Vice-Versa*, 5 (1993), 32–7.

López Austin, A. *Cuerpo humano e ideología: Las concepciones de los antiguos nahuas*, 2nd edn. Mexico City: UNAM, 1984.

López Velarde, R. *La suave patria*. Mexico City: Imprenta Universitaria, 1944.

—— *Obras*, ed. J.L. Martínez. Mexico City: FCE, 1979.

Lovell, C.M., and E. Netto Calil Zarur (eds) *Art and Faith in Mexico: The Nineteenth-Century Retablo Tradition*. Albuquerque: New Mexico Press, 2001.

Lowe, S.M. (ed.) *Tina Modotti: Photographs*. New York: Harry N. Abrams and Philadelphia Museum of Art, 1995.

Loya, A. 'En tiempos de Cantolla', *México en el Tiempo*, 19 (1997), 27–33.

Loyola, R. (ed.) *Entre la guerra y la estabilidad política: el México de los 40*. Mexico City: CNCA and Grijalbo, 1990.

Lozano, L.-M. (ed.) *Del Istmo y sus mujeres: Tehuanas en al arte mexicano*. Mexico City: CNCA, INBA and MNA, 1992.

—— (ed.) *Arte moderno de México, 1900–1950*. Mexico City: Antiguo Colegio de San Ildefonso, 2000.

—— (ed.) *José Chávez Morado: En memoria*. Mexico City: MAM, 2004.

—— (ed.) *Mónica Castillo, (1993–2004)*. Mexico City: CNCA, INBA and MAM, 2004.

Luna Arroyo, A. *Juan O'Gorman: Autobiografía, antología, juicios críticos y documentación exhaustiva de su obra*. Mexico City: Cuadernos Populares de Pintura Moderna, 1973.

Macklin, J. (ed.) *Convivium: Festschrift for Ronald Cueto*. Leeds: Leeds Iberian Papers, 1997.

Magdaleno, M. 'Dos cabezas indias', *El Libro y el Pueblo*, (January 1934), 1–12.

Manthorne, C.E. *Tropical Renaissance: North American Artists Exploring Latin America, 1839–1879*. Washington and London: Smithsonian Institution, 1989.

Mapelli Mozzi, C., J. Vexler, I. Weitlaner Johnson et al. *El textil mexicano*. Mexico City: Museo Rufino Tamayo, 1986.

Margain, C.R. 'Los mayas ayer y hoy: Bonampak', *México en el Arte*, 9 (1950), 36–54.

Martínez, J.L. (ed.) *El ensayo mexicano moderno*. Mexico City: FCE, 1971; repr. 1984, vol. I.

Maser, E.A. (ed.) *Cesare Ripa – Baroque and Rococo Pictorial Imagery: The 1758–60 Hertel Edition of Ripa's 'Iconologia' with 200 Engraved Illustrations*. New York: Dover, 1971.

Massé Zendejas, P. 'Tarjetas de visitas mexicanas: retratos de Cruces y Campa', *Luna Córnea*, 3 (1993), 49–53.

—— *Simulacro y elegancia en tarjetas de visita: fotografías de Cruces y Campa*. Mexico City: INAH, 1998.

Mata Rosas, F. *México Tenochtitlán*. Mexico City: Era, CONACULTA, FONCA and Casa de las Imagenes, 2005.

—— 'Fotografía documental paradoja de la realidad', *ZoneZero*. <http://zonezero.com/magazine/articles/mata/matatextsp.html>

Mata Rosas, F., and E. Martínez Ulloa. *Litorales*. Mexico City: Centro de la Imagen, CONACULTA and FONCA, 2000.

Matabuena Peláez, T. *Algunos usos y conceptos de la fotografía durante el Porfiriato*. Mexico City: Universidad Iberoamericana, 1991.

Matos Moctezuma, E. 'Los rostros de la muerte', *Arqueología Mexicana*, 6 (2000), 12–17.

Matos Moctezuma, E., and F. Solís Olguín (eds) *Aztecs*. London: Royal Academy, 2003.

Mayer, L. 'Humboldt y sus aportaciones al desarrollo de la geografía y la estadística en México', in Covarrubias, *Alejandro de Humboldt*, 1997, 43–53.

Medina, C. 'La prohibición como incitación', in Gruner, *Reliquias-collares*, 1998, 6–37.

Méndez, L. *En nombre de Cristo … han asesinado a más de 200 maestros*. Mexico City: TGP, Centro Productor de Artes Plásticas del Departamento de Bellas Artes and SEP, 1939.

Méndez, L., and M. Yampolsky (eds) *Lo efímero y lo eterno del arte popular mexicano*, 2 vols. Mexico City: Fondo de la Plástica Mexicana, 1971.

Merback, M.B. *The Thief, the Cross and the Wheel: Pain and the Spectacle of Punishment in*

Medieval and Renaissance Europe. London: Reaktion, 1999.

Mexican Folkways, 4 (1928).

Meyer, J. *La cristiada: Grandeza mexicana.* Mexico City: Clío, 1997.

Meyer, P. *Espejo de espinas.* Mexico City: FCE, 1986.

—— 'Inside the USA', in Ziff, *Between Worlds*, 1990, 46–57.

—— *I Photograph to Remember*, CD-ROM: CDAC014900, Windows/Macintosh, Voyager, 1991.

—— *Truths and Fictions: A Journey from Documentary to Digital Photography.* New York: Aperture Foundation, 1995; PC Windows CD-ROM, Voyager, 1995.

—— (ed.) 'Hacia una redefinición de la fotografía documental', *ZoneZero*, Editorial 22 (April 2000). <http://zonezero.com/editorial/editorial.html>

—— (ed.) 'Sobre la cuerda floja', *ZoneZero*, Editorial 25 (July 2000). <http://zonezero.com/editorial/editorial.html>

—— (ed.) 'Fotografía tradicional vs. fotografía digital', *ZoneZero*, Editorial 28 (March 2001). <http://zonezero.com/editorial/editorial.html>

Miquel, Á. (ed.) *Los exaltados: Ántología de escritos sobre cine en periódicos y revistas de la ciudad de México (1896–1929).* Guadalajara, Mexico: Universidad de Guadalajara, 1992.

Modern Mexican Painters: A Loan Exhibition of Their Works Organized by The Institute of Modern Art. Boston: The Institute of Modern Art, 1941.

Modotti, T. 'Sobre la fotografía/On Photography', *Mexican Folkways*, 4 (1929), 196–8.

—— 'Frescoes of José Clemente Orozco in the National Preparatory School' (photographs), *Mexican Folkways*, 4 (1928), 194–9.

—— 'Frescoes of José Clemente Orozco in the National Preparatory School' (photographs), *Contemporáneos*, 8 (1929), 24–31.

Moholy-Nagy, L. *Painting, Photography, Film*, tr. J. Seligman. London: Lund Humphries, 1969.

Molina, J.A. 'Entre el objeto y el concepto: la buena fama de la fotografía construida', *Tierra Adentro*, 102 (2000), 58–63.

Monaghan, J. 'The Text in the Body, the Body in the Text: the Embodied Sign in Mixtec Writing', in Hill, Boone and Mignolo, *Writing Without Words*, 1994, 87–101.

Monroy Nasr, R. *Historia para ver: Enrique Díaz, fotorreportero.* Mexico City: UNAM, IIE, CNCQA and INAH, 2003.

Monsiváis, C. 'Prologue', in Morales, *El Gallo Pitagórico*, 1987, xxii.

—— 'Sociedad y cultura', in Loyola, *Entre la guerra y la estabilidad política*, 1990, 259–80.

—— '"Así nos gustaría ser en el caso de que no fuéramos así": los estudios fotográficos', *Luna Córnea*, 3 (1993), 54–61.

—— 'Before the Flood: Nacho López and Hector García', *Aperture*, 153 (1998), 40–2.

—— 'La toma del poder desde las imágenes (el socialismo y el arte en México)', in Pérez Escamilla, *Estética socialista en México*, 2003, 23–31.

—— (ed.) *Foto Estudio Jiménez: Sotero Constantino, fotógrafo de Juchitán.* Mexico City: Era and H. Ayuntamiento Popular de Juchitán, 1984.

Monsiváis, C., and F. Reyes Palma. *Mariana Yampolsky: Ritos y regocijos.* Mexico City: Lunwerg and FCMY, 2005.

Monsiváis, C., L. Ortíz Monasterio, J. Souza et al. *Foto Hnos. Mayo.* Valencia: IVAM Centre Julio Gonzalez and Generalitat Valenciana, 1992.

Montellano, F. *C.B. Waite, Fotógrafo: Una mirada diversa sobre el México de principios del siglo XX.* Mexico City: Grijalbo and CNCA, 1994.

Montenegro, R., and X. Villaurrutia. *Máscaras mexicanas.* Mexico City: Talleres Gráficos de la Nación, 1926.

Mora, C.J. *Mexican Cinema: Reflections of a Society 1896–1988*. Los Angeles and London: California University Press, 1989.

Morales, A. (ed.) *El Gran Lente: José Antonio Bustamante Martínez*. Mexico City: INAH, SEP and Jilguero, 1992.

Morales, E.C. (ed.) *Homenaje nacional a José Agustín Arrieta, (1803–1874)*. Mexico City: MNA, 1994.

Morales, J.B. *El Gallo Pitagórico*. Mexico City: Ignacio Cumplido, 1845; facsimile edn, Guanajuato, Mexico: Gobierno del Estado de Guanajuato, 1987.

Moreno Cora, S. *La crítica literaria en México*. Orizaba: T.A. Dehesa, 1907.

Mraz, J. *La mirada inquieta: nuevo fotoperiodismo mexicano: 1976–1996*. Mexico City: Centro de la Imagen, CNCA and Universidad Autónoma de Puebla, 1996.

—— *Nacho López y el fotoperiodismo mexicano en los años cincuenta*. Mexico City: CONACULTA, INAH and Océano, 1999.

Muestra de fotografía latinoamericana. Mexico City: CNCA and Centro de la Imagen, 1996.

Mujer x mujer: 22 fotógrafas. Mexico City: CNCA and INBA, Museo de San Carlos, 1989.

Naggar C., and F. Ritchin (eds) *Mexico through Foreign Eyes, 1850–1990*. New York and London: W.W. Norton, 1993.

Nebel, K. *Viaje pintoresco y arqueológico sobre la parte más interesante de la República Mexicana, en los años transcurridos desde 1829 hasta 1834*. Paris and Mexico City: Impr. de Renouard, 1839.

Noelle Merles, L. 'The Architecture and Urbanism of Mario Pani: Creativity and Compromise', in Burian, *Modernity and the Architecture of Mexico*, 1997, 177–89.

Noreña, A. 'Mujeres en la avanzada escultórica', *Tierra·Adentro*, 108–9 (2001), n.p.n.

Novelo, V. (ed.) *Artesanos, artesanías y arte popular de México*. Mexico City: INI, Universidad de Colima, Agualarga and CNCA, 1996.

Novo, S. 'El arte de la fotografía', *Contemporáneos*, 33 (1931), 165–72.

O'Gorman, E. 'Reflexiones sobre la distribución urbana colonial de la Ciudad de México', in *Pasado y presente*, 1993, 12–29.

O'Reilly et al. (eds) 'Introducción', *Registro Yucateco*, 1, 1845, 3–8.

Octava bienal de fotografía. Mexico City: Centro de la Imagen, 1997.

Olavarría y Ferrari, E. de. *El arte literario en México: noticias biograficas y críticas de sus más notables escritores*. Madrid: Espinosa y Bautista, 1878.

Oles, J. 'México en veintitantas tomas: la obra mexicana de Paul Strand y Anton Bruehl', *Luna Córnea*, 1 (1992–3), 73–8.

—— *South of the Border: Mexico in the American Imagination*. Washington and London: Smithsonian Institution Press, 1993.

—— 'Ensayos en el estudio/Tested in the Studio', in Cohen, *Obra*, 1997, 3–7.

Orellana, M. de. *La mirada circular: el cine norteamericano de la Revolución mexicana, 1911–1917*. Mexico City: Joaquín Mortiz and Planeta, 1991.

—— 'Palabras sobre imágenes: entrevista con Gabriel Figueroa', *Artes de México*, 2 (1992), 37–53.

Orozco, J.C. *Autobiografía*. Mexico City: SEP and Era, 1971.

Orozco y Berra, F. 'Influencia de los periódicos en México', *La Ilustración Mexicana*, 3 (1852), 35–7.

Ortíz Gaitan, J. *Entre dos mundos: los murales de Roberto Montenegro*. Mexico City: IIE, 1994.

Ortiz Monasterio, J. 'Los primos del norte', *Luna Córnea*, 13 (1997), 64–71.

Ortiz Monasterio, P. (ed.) *Jefes, héroes y caudillos: Fondo Casasola*. Mexico City: FCE, 1986.

—— *Idolatrías: Proyectos para esculturas monumentales*. Mexico City: MAM, 1997.

——— (ed.) *India – México: Vientos paralelos: Graciela Iturbide, Raghu Rai, Sebastião Salgado*. Mexico City: Antiguo Palacio de San Ildefonso, 2002.

——— (ed.) *Mirada y memoria: Archivo fotográfico Casasola, México 1900–1940*. Mexico City: CNCA, INAH and Turner, 2002.

Paalen, W. (ed.) *Dyn*, 3 (1942), n.p.n.

——— *Dyn*, 6 (1944), n.p.n.

Pacheco, C. *La luz de México: entrevistas con pintores y fotógrafos*. Mexico City: FCE, 1995.

Palacio Flores, I. 'Tumba 59', *Alquimia*, 9 (2000), 27.

Panofsky, E. 'Style and Medium in the Motion Pictures' (1937/1947), in Lavin, *Erwin Panofsky*, 1995, 93–125.

Paranaguá, R.A. (ed.) *Mexican Cinema*. London: British Film Institute, 1995.

Parcero, T. 'Cartografías. <http://zonezero.com/...iones/fotografos/tatiana/default.html>

——— 'Interior Cartography/Cartografía interior', *Southward Art: Latin American Art Review*, 2 (2001), 116–29.

Pasado y presente del Centro Histórico. Mexico City: Banamex, 1993.

Patterson, C., and M.S. Peden. *Out of the Volcano: Portraits of Contemporary Mexican Artists*. Washington and London: Smithsonian, 1991.

Payno, M. 'Instrumentos de optica', *El Mosaico Mexicano*, 5 (1841), 243–5.

——— 'Prologue', in Calderón, *Obras poéticas*, 1844, xiii.

——— *Los bandidos de Río Frío*, ed. A. Castro Leal. Mexico City: Editorial Porrúa, 1986.

——— *Obras completas*, ed. B. Rosen Jélomer. Mexico City: CNCA, 1996, vol. I.

Payno, M., and G. Prieto. 'Conclusión', *Revista Científica y Literaria de Méjico*, 2 (1846), 380.

Paz, O. *Essays on Mexican Art*, tr. H. Lane. New York: Harcourt Brace, 1993.

Pérez Escamilla, R. (ed.) *Estética socialista en México, siglo XX*. Mexico City: MACG, CNCA and INBA, 2003.

Pérez Montfort, R. 'Notas sobre el estereotipo de la Tehuana', *Acervos: Boletín de los Archivos y Bibliotecas de Oaxaca*, 19 (2000), 45–52.

Pesado, J.J. (ed.) *Poesías de Manuel Carpio*. Mexico City: M. Murguia, 1849.

Pick, D. *Faces of Degeneration: a European Disorder, c.1848–1918*. Cambridge: Cambridge University Press, 1989.

Pierre, J. 'Buñuel gótico, prerrafaelista y surrealista', in Vázquez, *Luis Buñuel*, 2000, 105–25.

Pimentel, F. *Dos obras*, ed. E. Semo. Mexico City: CNCA, 1995.

Pinney, C. 'The Parallel Histories of Anthropology and Photography', in Edwards, *Anthropology*, 1992, 74–95.

Pitol, S. *Juan Soriano: El perpetuo rebelde*. Mexico City: Era and CNCA, 1993.

Platt, A. 'Semana Santa en Tecoripa, Sonora', *México Desconocido*, 290 (2001), 10–17.

Poniatowska, E. 'Preface', in Yampolsky, *La raíz y el camino*, 1985, 5–10.

——— *Luz y luna, las lunitas*. Mexico City: Era, 1994.

——— *Mariana Yampolsky y la buganvillia*. Barcelona: Plaza y Janés, 2001.

——— *Las mil y una... (la herida de Paulina)*. Barcelona: Plaza y Janés, 2001, with photographs by Mariana Yampolsky.

Prescott, W.H. *History of the Conquest of Mexico*. New York: Harper & Brothers, 1843; *Historia de la conquista de México*, tr. V. García Torres. Mexico City: I. Cumplido, 1844–46.

Prieto, G. 'Literatura nacional: cuadros de costumbres', *Revista Científica y Literaria de Méjico*, 1 (1845), 27–9.

——— 'Ojeada a varios lugares de la república: un paseo a Cuernavaca', *Revista Científica y Literaria de Méjico*, 1 (1845), 85–8.

——— *Memorias de mis tiempos*. Paris and Mexico City: Librería de Bouret, 1906; Mexico

City: Editorial Porrúa, 1985.

—— *Obras completas*, ed. B. Rosen Jélomer. Mexico City: CNCA, 1993, vol. II.

—— *Obras completas*, ed. B. Rosen Jélomer. Mexico City: CNCA, 1993, vol. V.

—— *Obras completas*, ed. B. Rosen Jélomer. Mexico City: CNCA, 1994, vol. X.

Prignitz, H. *El Taller de Gráfica Popular en México (1937–1977)*, tr. E. Siefer. Mexico City: INBA, 1992.

Quevedo y Zubieta, S. *La ley de la sábana*. Mexico City: Botas, 1935.

R.M.E. 'Obras de Tina Modotti', *Forma: Revista de Artes Plásticas* 4 (1927), 30–3.

Ramírez, F. 'El simbolismo en México', in Henares Cuellar et al., *El espejo simbolista*, 2004, 29–59.

Ramírez, M.C. 'The Masses Are the Matrix: Theory and Practice of the Cinematographic Mural in Siqueiros', in Debroise, Oles and Ramírez, *David Alfaro Siqueiros*, 1997, 68–95.

Ray, M. 'Rayografías de Man Ray', *Contemporáneos*, 13 (1929), 257–61.

Reed, A. *José Clemente Orozco*. New York: Delphic Studios, 1932.

Revilla, D. 'Escenas de campo', *Revista Científica y Literaria de Méjico*, 1 (1845), 248.

Revueltas, J. 'Lugar del cine en el arte', *Anthropos*, 1 (1947), 2–10.

—— *Obras completas*, ed. E. García Riera. Mexico City: Era, 1981; repr. 1991, vol. XXII.

Reyes Nevares, B. *Trece directores del cine mexicano*. Mexico City: SEP, 1974.

Reyes Palma, F. (ed.) *Memoria del tiempo: 150 años de fotografía en México*. Mexico City: CNCA and INBA, 1989.

Reyes Palma, F., and N. Schnaith (eds) *Mariana Yampolsky*. Salamanca: Universidad de Salamanca, 1995.

Reyes, A. de los. *Los orígenes del cine en México (1896–1900)*. Mexico City: FCE, 1984.

—— *Cine y sociedad en México, 1896–1930*. Mexico City: UNAM, 1993, vol. II.

Richter, S. *The Art of the Daguerreotype*. London: Viking, 1989.

Riley, J., and A. Rowley (eds) *Tina Modotti: Photographs*. New York: Robert Miller Gallery, 1997.

Rivera, D. 'Edward Weston and Tina Modotti', *Mexican Folkways*, 2 (1926), 16–28.

Rivera, J.M. 'El cómico de la legua', in Herrera Castañeda, *Los mexicanos pintados*, 1986, I: 55–66.

—— 'La china', in Herrera Castañeda, *Los mexicanos pintados*, 1986, I: 121–31.

—— 'La costurera', in Herrera Castañeda, *Los mexicanos pintados*, 1986, I: 69–75.

Robb, G. *Balzac: A Biography*. London: Papermac, 1995.

Robinson, D. *The Lantern Image: Iconography of the Magic Lantern, 1420–1880*. London: The Lantern Society and the author, 1993.

Rochfort, D. *Mexican Muralists: Orozco, Rivera, Siqueiros*. London: Laurence King, 1993.

Rodríguez, A. (ed.) *José Guadalupe Posada: 150 años*. Mexico City: La Mano Press, 2003.

Rodríguez, G. 'Miradas sin rendición', *Luna Córnea*, 13 (1997), 25–31.

Rodríguez, J.A. 'La gramática constructiva de Agustín Jiménez', *Luna Córnea*, 2 (1993), 72–9.

—— 'Una nueva memoria', *Cuartoscuro*, 33 (1998), 2–26.

—— 'Fotografía mexicana de hoy', *Tierra Adentro*, 105 (2000), 35–48.

—— 'Nuevos paisajes, nuevas proyecciones de deseos', *Tierra Adentro*, 105 (2000), 62–8.

—— (ed.) *Bernice Kolko: fotógrafa*. Mexico City: Ediciones del Equilibrista, 1996.

Rodríguez Prampolini, I. (ed.) *Leopoldo Méndez: Artista de un pueblo en lucha*. Mexico City: UNAM and Centro de Estudios Económicos y Sociales del Tercer Mundo, 1981.

Rogoff, I., and Sherman, D.J. (eds) *Museum Culture: Histories, Discourses, Spectacles*. Minneapolis: Minnesota University Press, 1994.

Romero de Terreros, M. *Las artes industriales en la Nueva España*. Mexico City: Librería de

Pedro Robredo, 1923.

Romero, E. *Fisiologia del gusto de Brillat Savarin*. Mexico City: Juan R. Navaro, 1842.

Roqué, M.I., and A. Sánchez (eds) *La ciudad de Juan Rulfo: Textos y fotografías de Juan Rulfo*. Mexico City: CNCA and INBA, 1996.

Rosenblum, N. *A World History of Photography*. New York: Abbeville Press, 1989.

Rubín de la Borbolla, D.F. 'Supervivencia y fomento de las artes populares indígenas de América', *América Indígena*, 19 (1959), 5–42.

Rubín de la Borbolla, S. 'Las artes populares en el siglo XIX', in Sáenz González, *Arte Popular Mexicano*, 1996, 69–75.

Rueda de la Serna, J. (ed.) *Historiografía de la literatura mexicana: ensayos y comentarios*. Mexico City: UNAM, 1996.

—— (ed.) *La misión del escritor: ensayos mexicanos del siglo XIX*. Mexico City: UNAM, 1996.

Ruiz, B. 'El laboratorio terminó: entrevista con Pedro Meyer', *Tierra Adentro*, 105 (2000), 69–72.

Ruwet, N. (ed. and tr.) *Essais de linguistique générale*. Paris: Éditions de Minuit, 1963.

Ruy-Sánchez, A. 'El fundamentalismo fantástico del arte joven de México', *Universidad de México: Revista de la Universidad Nacional Autónoma de México*, 508 (1993), 24–8.

Sáenz González, O. (ed.) *Arte Popular Mexicano: Cinco Siglos*. Mexico City: Antiguo Colegio de San Ildefonso, 1996.

Sánchez Lacy, A.R. 'Homenaje o exageración', *Artes de México*, 28 (1995), 22–5.

Sánchez Mármol, M. *Las letras patrias*. Mexico City: J. Ballesca, 1902.

Sánchez, O. '¿Fuera de juego?', in *Mexico Now/México ahora*, 1997, 21–35.

—— *Arte contemporáneo de México en el Museo Carrillo Gil*. Mexico City: INBA and Landucci Editores, 2000.

—— 'El cuerpo de la nación: el neomexicanismo: la pulsión homosexual y la desnacional-ización', *Curare*, 17 (2001), 136–46.

Santacilia P. *Del movimiento literario en México*. Mexico City: Imprenta del Gobierno del Palacio, 1868.

Sántiz Gómez, M. *Creencias (de nuestros antepasados)*. Mexico City: Centro de la Imagen, CIESAS and Casa de las Imágenes, 1998.

Schneider, L.M. (ed.) *El estridentismo: un gesto irreversible*. Mexico City: INBA, Museo Nacional de la Estampa and CNCA, 1998.

Schrenck-Notzing, Baron von. *Der Kampf Um Die Materialisations-Phänomene*. Munich: Verlag Von Ernst Reinhardt, 1914.

Sebastian, S. 'Los libros de emblemas: Uso y difusión en Iberoamérica', in Cuadriello, *Juegos de ingenio y agudeza*, 1994, 56–82.

Segre, E. 'Cultural Nationalism and Buñuel in Mexico, 1946–1955', in Macklin, *Convivium*, 1997, 265–97.

—— '*El Iris: periódico crítico y literario* (1826): Republican Exiles and Autochthony in Post-Independence Mexico', *Bulletin of Hispanic Studies*, 74 (1997), 331–50.

Sheridan, G. *México en 1932: La polémica nacionalista*. Mexico City: Ediciones Sin Nombre, CONACULTA and CNCA, 2004.

Sinkin, R.N. *The Mexican Reform, 1855–1876: A Study in Liberal Nation-building*. Austin: Texas University Press, 1979.

Siqueiros, D.A. *No hay más ruta que la nuestra*. Mexico City: SEP, 1945.

—— 'La función de la fotografía' [1945], in Tibol, *Textos de David Alfaro Siqueiros*, 1998, 70–6 (74).

Snyder, J. 'Nineteenth-Century Photography of Sculpture and the Rhetoric of Substitution', in Johnson, *Sculpture and Photography*, 1998, 21–34.

Staples, A. 'La lectura y los lectores en los primeros años de vida independiente', in Bermúdez et al., *Historia de la lectura*, 1997, 94–126.

Stephens, J.L. *Incidents of Travel in Central America, Chiapas and Yucatán*. New York: Harper & Brothers, 1841.

——— *Incidents of Travel in Yucatán*. New York: Harper & Brothers, 1843.

Stoichita, V.I. *Visionary Experience in the Golden Age of Spanish Art*. London: Reaktion, 1995.

Street, B. 'British Popular Anthropology: Exhibiting and Photographing the Other', in Edwards, *Anthropology and Photography*, 1992, 122–31.

Suter, G. *Anáhuac: radiografías de un valle*. Mexico City: Centro de la Imagen, 1995.

——— *Cartografía*. Mexico City: FNCA, 1996.

——— *Circulaciones*. Puebla, Mexico: Museo Amparo, 1999.

——— *Labyrinth of Memory*. New York: The Americas Society Art Gallery, 1999.

——— 'Una forma de memoria', *Alquimia*, 9 (2000), 38.

Tablada, J.J. 'La abeja de la crítica y la "tiple-jazz" (1927)', in Miquel, *Los exaltados*, 1992, 53.

Taibo I, P.I. *El Indio Fernández: el cine por mis pistolas*. Mexico City: Joaquín Mortiz and Planeta, 1986.

Tejada, R. (ed.) *Manuel Álvarez Bravo: Photographs from The J. Paul Getty Museum*. Los Angeles: The J. Paul Getty Museum, 2001.

Tenorio-Trillo, M. *Mexico at the World's Fairs: Crafting a Modern Nation*. Berkeley, Los Angeles and London: California University Press, 1996.

Tibol, R. *Gráficas y neográficas en México*. Mexico City: UNAM and SEP, 1987.

——— *Frida Kahlo: An Open Life*, tr. E. Randall. Albuquerque: New Mexico University Press, 1993.

——— (ed.) *Die Schrift. Mexikanische Fotografen 13x10*. Frankfurt: Fotografie Forum Frankfurt and CNCA, 1992.

——— (ed.) *Textos de David Alfaro Siqueiros*. Mexico City: FCE, 1998.

Toor, F. 'Exposición de fotografías de Tina Modotti', *Mexican Folkways*, 5 (1929), 192–5.

——— *Mexican Popular Arts*. Mexico City: Frances Toor Studios, 1939.

Tornel, J.M. 'Noticias sobre las poesias aztecas', *El Mosaico Mexicano*, 5 (1841), 143–4.

Torri, J. *Ensayos y poemas*, 2nd edn. Mexico City: Ediciones Porrúa, 1937.

Trabulse, E. *José María Velasco: un paisaje de la ciencia en México*. Toluca, Mexico: Instituto Mexiquense de Cultura, 1992.

——— *Historia de la ciencia en México*. Mexico City: FCE, 1997.

——— (ed.) *Viajeros europeos del siglo XIX en México*. Mexico City: Banamex, 1996.

Trueblood, A.S. (tr.) *A Sor Juana Anthology*. Cambridge, MA and London: Harvard University Press, 1988.

Tuñón, J. 'Emilio Fernández: A Look behind the Bars', in Paranaguá, *Mexican Cinema*, 1995, 184.

——— 'La ciudad actriz: la imagen urbana en el cine mexicano (1940–1955)', in Castellanos et al., *La ciudad de los viajeros*, 1996, 48.

——— *Los rostros de un mito: Personajes femeninos en las películas de Emilio 'Indio' Fernández*. Mexico City: CONACULTA and IMCINE, 2000.

Turner, J.K. *Barbarous Mexico: An Indictment of a Cruel and Corrupt System*. London and New York: Cassell, 1911.

Tytler, G. *Physiognomy in the European Novel: Faces and Fortunes*. Princeton: Princeton University Press, 1982.

Umberger, E. 'The *Monarchía Indiana* in Seventeenth-Century New Spain', in Fane, *Converging Cultures*, 1996, 46–58.

Vargas, A. *La Casa de Cita: Mexican Photographs from the Belle Époque*. London: Quartet, 1986.

Vasconcelos, J. *Indologia* (excerpts), in V. Magdaleno (ed.), 'El problema del Indio', *Universidad: Mensual de Cultura Popular*, 7 (August 1936) 1–5 (5).

Vázquez, J.J. (ed.) *Luis Buñuel: El ojo de la libertad*. Madrid: Residencia de Estudiantes, 2000.

Vega Alfaro, E. de la. 'Origins, Development and Crisis of the Sound Cinema (1929–64)', in Paranaguá, *Mexican Cinema*, 1995, 84.

―― *Del muro a la pantalla: S.M. Eisenstein y el arte pictórico mexicano*. Mexico City: Instituto Mexiquense de Cultura, IMCINE and Universidad de Guadalajara, 1997.

Velada literaria en honor de Ignacio M. Altamirano. Mexico City: Secretaría de Fomento, 1889.

Warner Marien, M. *Photography and Its Critics: A Cultural History, 1839–1900*. Cambridge: Cambridge University Press, 1997.

Wechsler, J. *A Human Comedy: Physiognomy and Caricature in 19th-Century Paris*. London: Thames & Hudson, 1982.

Weston, E. 'Fotos de juguetes mexicanos', *Forma*, 7 (1928), 16–17.

Widdifield, S.G. *The Embodiment of the National in Late Ninenteenth-Century Mexican Painting*. Tucson: Arizona University Press, 1996.

Wilcox, S. 'El panorama de Leicester Square', in Trabulse, *Viajeros europeos*, 1996, 127–35.

Yampolsky, M. *La casa en la tierra*. Mexico City: INI and Fonapas, 1981.

―― *La casa que canta*. Mexico City: SEP, 1982.

―― *La raíz y el camino*. Mexico City: FCE, 1985.

―― *Haciendas poblanas*. Mexico City: Universidad Iberoamericana, 1992.

―― *Mazahua*, Toluca. Mexico, Gobierno del Estado, 1993.

―― *The Traditional Architecture of Mexico*. London: Thames & Hudson, 1993.

―― *The Edge of Time*. Austin: Texas University Press, 1998.

―― *Imagen – memoria*, ed. F. Reyes Palma. Mexico City: CONACULTA, FONCA and Centro de la Imagen, 1999.

―― *Casas de tierra*. Mexico City: TURMEX, 2000.

―― 'Lo efímero y lo eterno', *Tierra Adentro*, 108–9 (2001), n.p.n.

Yarrington, A. 'Under the Spell of Madame Tussaud: Aspects of "High" and "Low" in 19th-century Polychromed Sculpture', in Blühm, *Colour of Sculpture*, 83–92.

Zarco, F. 'Estado de la literatura en México', *La Ilustración Mexicana*, 3 (1852), 5–8.

―― *Castillos en el aire y otros textos mordaces*. Tlahuapan, Puebla: Premia, 1984.

Ziff, T. (ed.) *Between Worlds: Contemporary Mexican Photography*. London: Bellew, 1990.

―― (ed.) *Distant Relations*. Santa Monica, CA: Smart Art Press, 1996.

Zurian, C. *Fermín Revueltas: Constructor de espacios*. Mexico City: CONACULTA, INBA and Museo Mural Diego Rivera, 2002.

Suggested Further Reading

Aguilar Ochoa, A. *La fotografía durante el imperio de Maximiliano*. Mexico City: UNAM, 2001.

Billeter, E. *Canto a la realidad: Fotografía latinomericana, 1860–1993*. Barcelona: Lunwerg, 1993.

Cordero Reiman, 'Corporeal Identities in Mexican Art: Modern and Post-modern Strategies', in Good and Waldron (eds), *Effects of the Nation*, 2001, 53–72.

Curiel, G., F. Ramírez, A. Rubial and A. Velázquez. *Pintura y vida cotidiana en México, 1650–1950*. Mexico City: Banamex and CONACULTA, 1999.

Fernández, J. *Arte moderno y contemporáneo de México*, 2 vols. Mexico City: UNAM, 2001.

Garduño, F. *Witnesses of Time*. London: Thames & Hudson, 1992.

Gruzinski, S. *La pensée métisse*. Paris: Arthème Fayard, 1999.

Heinzelman, K. (ed.) *The Covarrubias Circle: Nickolas Muray's Collection of Twentieth-Century Mexican Art*. Austin: Texas University Press, 2004.

Iturbide, G. *Graciela Iturbide*. London: Phaidon, 2001.

Miquel, A., J. Nieto Sotelo and J.A. Rodríguez. *La linterna mágica en México*. Cuernavaca: Universidad Autónoma del Estado de Morelos and Ediciones Sin Nombre, 2003.

Rosenblum, N. *A History of Women Photographers*. New York: Abbeville Press, 1994.

Newspapers Cited

El Demócrata, 10 April 1922.
El Financiero, 26 November 1996.
El Financiero, 30 April 1994.
El Informador, 4 September 1925.
El Libro y el Pueblo, January 1934.
El Museo Popular, 15 January 1840.
El Nacional, 12 December 1933.
El Nacional, 30 August 1938.
El Universal, 6 December 1995.
El Universal, 8 June 1924.
Excelsior, 29 February 2000.
Mañana, 18 November 1950.
Reforma, 1 March 2000.
Revista de Revistas, 18 September 1932.
Siempre!, 19 June 1954.
Unomásuno, 4 December 1984.

INDEX